COSMOS IN THE A

How did the ancient Greeks and Romans conceptualise order? This book answers that question by analysing the formative concept of *kosmos* ('order', 'arrangement', 'ornament') in ancient literature, philosophy, science, art and religion. This concept encouraged the Greeks and Romans to develop theories to explain core aspects of human life, including nature, beauty, society, politics, the individual and what lies beyond human experience. Hence, Greek *kosmos*, and its Latin correlate *mundus*, are subjects of profound reflection by a wide range of important ancient figures, including philosophers (Parmenides, Empedocles, the Pythagoreans, Democritus, Plato, Aristotle, the Stoics, Lucretius, Cicero, Seneca, Plotinus), poets and playwrights (Sophocles, Euripides, Aristophanes, Plautus, Marcus Argentarius, Nonnus), intellectuals (Gorgias, Protagoras, Varro) and religious exegetes (Philo, the Gospel writers, Paul). By revealing *kosmos* in its many ancient manifestations, this book asks us to rethink our own sense of 'order' and to reflect on our place within a broader cosmic history.

PHILLIP SIDNEY HORKY is Associate Professor of Ancient Philosophy at Durham University. In addition to his monograph *Plato and Pythagoreanism* (2013; paperback, with corrections, 2016), he has published articles and book chapters on topics in ancient philosophy ranging from metaphysics and cosmology to political theory and ethics. While continuing his research on Pythagoreanism in the Hellenistic and Post-Hellenistic worlds (in *Pythagorean Philosophy, 250 BCE–200 CE: An Introduction and Collection of Sources in Translation*, forthcoming with Cambridge University Press), he is also writing a monograph on pre-Aristotelian theories of language and ontology, provisionally titled *Prelude to the Categories*.

COSMOS IN THE ANCIENT WORLD

EDITED BY

PHILLIP SIDNEY HORKY

University of Durham

CAMBRIDGE
UNIVERSITY PRESS

CAMBRIDGE
UNIVERSITY PRESS

University Printing House, Cambridge CB2 8BS, United Kingdom

One Liberty Plaza, 20th Floor, New York, NY 10006, USA

477 Williamstown Road, Port Melbourne, VIC 3207, Australia

314-321, 3rd Floor, Plot 3, Splendor Forum, Jasola District Centre, New Delhi - 110025, India

103 Penang Road, #05-06/07, Visioncrest Commercial, Singapore 238467

Cambridge University Press is part of the University of Cambridge.

It furthers the University's mission by disseminating knowledge in the pursuit of
education, learning and research at the highest international levels of excellence.

www.cambridge.org
Information on this title: www.cambridge.org/9781108438223
DOI: 10.1017/9781108529082

First published 2019
First paperback edition 2022

A catalogue record for this publication is available from the British Library

Library of Congress Cataloging in Publication data
NAMES: Horky, Phillip Sidney, editor.
TITLE: Cosmos in the ancient world / edited by Phillip Sidney Horky,
University of Durham.
DESCRIPTION: New York : Cambridge University Press, 2019. | Includes bibliographical
references and index.
IDENTIFIERS: LCCN 2018056586 | ISBN 9781108423649 (alk. paper)
SUBJECTS: LCSH: Cosmology, Ancient.
CLASSIFICATION: LCC BD495 .C676 2019 | DDC 113.093–dc23
LC record available at https://lccn.loc.gov/2018056586

ISBN 978-1-108-42364-9 Hardback
ISBN 978-1-108-43822-3 Paperback

Roberto, magistro meo.

Qui strepitus circa comitum! Quantum instar
in ipso!
Sed nox atra caput tristi circumvolat umbra.
Virgil, *Aeneid* 6.865–6

Mundus est universitas rerum, in quo omnia sunt et extra quem nihil, qui graece dicitur κόσμος.

Lucius Ampelius, *Liber Memorialis* 1.1
(third century CE?)

That as the greater world is called Cosmus, from the beauty thereof the inequality of the Centre thereof contributing much to the beauty and delightsomenesse of it: so in this Map or little world of beauty in the face, the inequality affords the prospect and delight.

John Bulwer, *Anthropometamorphosis:
man transform'd* (1653: 242)

Contents

Contributors

CAROL ATACK is Postdoctoral Research Associate on the Anachronism and Antiquity project in the Faculty of Classics, University of Oxford, and Junior Research Fellow at St Hugh's College. Her research focuses on developments in fourth-century BCE Greek political thought and on the political culture of Athenian democracy and its contemporary reception. She is currently writing a monograph on temporality in Platonic dialogue and argument and editing a volume on democracy in antiquity.

GEORGE BOYS-STONES is Professor of Ancient Philosophy at Durham University. His publications include *Platonist Philosophy 80 BC to AD 250: An Introduction and Collection of Sources in Translation* (Cambridge University Press, 2018).

LUC BRISSON is Director of Research (Emeritus) at the National Centre for Scientific Research (Paris [Villejuif], France; UMR 8230 Centre Jean Pépin). He is known for his works on both Plato and Plotinus, including bibliographies, translations and commentaries. He has also published numerous works on the history of philosophy and religion in antiquity.

RENAUD GAGNÉ is Reader in Ancient Greek Literature and Religion at the University of Cambridge and Fellow of Pembroke College. His research focuses on religious representations in early Greek literature.

ROBERT GERMANY was Associate Professor of Classics at Haverford College. His research focused on Greek and Roman literature, with special emphasis on poetics and meta-theatre in Roman comedy. In 2016, he published *Mimetic Contagion: Art and Artifice in Terence's Eunuchus*. At the time of his death in March 2017, he was writing his second monograph, *The Unity of Time: Temporal Mimesis in Ancient and Modern Theater.*

PHILLIP SIDNEY HORKY is Associate Professor of Ancient Philosophy at Durham University. He works widely in ancient philosophy. Subsequent to his first monograph, *Plato and Pythagoreanism* (2013), he is writing a source book on *Pythagorean Philosophy: 250 BCE–200 CE* (Cambridge, forthcoming) and a monograph on the philosophy of language prior to Aristotle, tentatively titled *Prelude to the Categories.*

MONTE RANSOME JOHNSON is Associate Professor of Philosophy at the University of California, San Diego, and Director of the UC San Diego Program in Classical Studies. He is the author of *Aristotle on Teleology* (2005) and of articles on Democritus, Lucretius and Aristotle, including Aristotle's lost work, the *Protrepticus* (*Exhortation to Philosophy*).

ARNAUD MACÉ is Professor of History of Philosophy at the University of Franche-Comté. His research primarily focuses on the history of natural and political thought in ancient Greece, from Homer to Plato. Recent publications in English include 'Two Forms of the Common in Ancient Greece', *Annales* 69.3 (2014), 441–69, and 'Nature from the Greeks: Empirical Philology and the Ontological Turn in Historical Anthropology', in P. Charbonnier, G. Salmon and P. Skafish (eds.), *Comparative Metaphysics: Ontology after Anthropology* (2016), 201–20.

PAULIINA REMES is Professor of Theoretical Philosophy (with specialisation in the history of philosophy) at Uppsala University. She has written, among other things, on soul, self, agency and action in ancient philosophy. Her new research projects focus on self-governance and autonomy and rationalist conceptions of self-knowledge as well as norms that guide good philosophical conversation according to the Platonists. She is the author of *Plotinus on Self: The Philosophy of the 'We'* (Cambridge, 2007) and *Neoplatonism* (2008) and the editor, together with Svetla Slaveva-Griffin, of *The Routledge Handbook of Neoplatonism* (2014).

GILLES SAURON is Professor of Roman Archaeology at Sorbonne University. He is author of numerous books and papers on Roman art. His research is mainly based on comparing ancient sources, iconographic tradition and surviving ancient monuments. He focuses on architectural semantics, ornamental symbolism and the connection of forms and meanings between public and private decorations in ancient Rome.

MALCOLM SCHOFIELD is Emeritus Professor of Ancient Philosophy at the University of Cambridge and a fellow of St John's College. He is co-author with G. S. Kirk and J. E. Raven of the second edition of *The Presocratic Philosophers* (Cambridge, 1983). His most recent book is an English edition (with Tom Griffith) of *Plato's Laws* (Cambridge, 2016).

W. H. SHEARIN is Associate Professor of Classics at the University of Miami. His research focuses on the intersection of philosophy and literature in antiquity, especially during the Roman period. He is author of a book on Lucretius, *The Language of Atoms* (2015), and is currently writing on a range of topics, including human and animal intelligence in Roman philosophical and legal discourse as well as the Epicurean roots of Nietzschean epistemology.

VICTORIA WOHL is Professor at the University of Toronto. She studies the literature and culture of democratic Athens. Her publications include *Love among the Ruins: the Erotics of Democracy in Classical Athens* (2002), *Law's Cosmos: Juridical Discourse in Athenian Forensic Oratory* (Cambridge, 2010), *Euripides and the Politics of Form* (2015) and (as editor) *Probabilities, Hypotheticals, and Counterfactuals in Ancient Greek Thought* (Cambridge, 2014).

Acknowledgements

Contributions to this volume are the product of a research seminar undertaken in the Department of Classics and Ancient History at Durham University from September 2012 to September 2013, under the auspices of the Centre for the Study of the Ancient Mediterranean and Near East, and culminating in a conference titled 'Ancient Cosmos: Concord among Worlds', on 20–22 September 2013. Participants in the research project over that productive year included Ahmed Alwishah, Carol Atack, Nicolò Benzi, Gábor Betegh, George Boys-Stones, Luc Brisson, Sarah Broadie, David Creese, Jackie Feke, Robert Germany, Phillip Horky, Donald Lavigne, Arnaud Macé, Grant Nelsestuen, Helen van Noorden, Pauliina Remes, Christopher Rowe, Malcolm Schofield, Gilles Sauron, Will Shearin, Edmund Thomas and Marijn Visscher. Papers commissioned for the volume specifically are those by Carol Atack, Renaud Gagné, Monte Ransome Johnson, Victoria Wohl, and the second chapter by Phillip Horky. It was during the Durham sessions of 2013 that the seeds of this volume were sown, but the contributions recorded here are only a shadow of the rich and, in many cases, surprising results of dialogue that continued throughout the year and beyond. In addition to the topics treated here, we glimpsed flashes of cosmic chaos reflected in the literary characters of Thersites and Silenus; sought to unravel the cosmological theory of Socrates' enigmatic teacher in Athens, Archelaus; moved to the plectral harmonies that fascinated Ptolemy and inspired his take on cosmic first principles; observed in our collective mind's eye the harmonic proportions upon which monumental ancient buildings in South Italy were founded; advanced upon the Greek philosopher Xenophon's and the Roman polymath Varro's correlative theories of agronomy and cosmonomy; and imagined the flood of divine essence that, for the Islamic philosopher Avicenna, constituted the universe itself and guaranteed its identity and knowability. Such topics express the range that was covered in the research seminar and indicate many avenues for further research on *kosmos* in the ancient and medieval worlds that remain, at this point, only partially disclosed.[1]

The editor would like to acknowledge the manifold support of his colleagues in Durham – notably Richard Beniston, Nicolò Benzi (now University College London), George Boys-Stones, James Corke-Webster (now King's College London), Helen Foxhall-Forbes, Johannes Haubold (now Princeton), Jane MacNaughton, Christopher Rowe, Amy Russell, Corinne Saunders and Edmund Thomas. Beyond the Bailey, special thanks go to those who contributed to the final shape of the work and to the editor's own individual contributions to it: Monte Ransome Johnson, John Esposito (who helped out with Systems Theory), Richard Mizelle, Grant Nelsestuen, Don Rutherford, Stefan Vranka, Victoria Wohl (who kindly accepted the invitation to write an afterword) and the two anonymous readers for Cambridge University Press. Thanks to those involved in the production process, and especially to Michael Sharp, who provided encouragement at many stages of this book's development.

This volume was initially conceived in Durham in early 2014; revised and further developed at the National Humanities Center in the Research Triangle, North Carolina, in late 2016; and completed in Durham in early 2018. For the academic year 2016–17, the editor was supported by a residential fellowship from the Rockefeller Foundation (at the NHC), a grant from the Wellcome Foundation (for the Life of Breath project, hosted by Durham's Centre for Medical Humanities) and institutional leave granted by the Faculty of Arts and Humanities at Durham University. The editor received excellent support from the staff at the NHC, especially the librarians Brooke Andrade, Sarah Harris and Joe Milillo, and expert administration from Lois Whittington and Robert D. Newman, the NHC's Director. Lest anyone think musical harmony be separated from the words recorded here, the soundtrack for the editing and arrangement of this work included American Football, Art Blakey, Benny Goodman, Bon Iver, Eunoia, Grimes, Hum, Mastodon, S. Carey, the Shins and Sufjan Stevens. Specially reserved for preparing the indexes was John Coltrane. The cover art, *Floating Skies* by Etnik (2016), reflects the significance of cosmic expression in today's urban art scene; the editor kindly thanks the artist for the opportunity to use this sublime image of the world taking shape.

As always, the editor's greatest thanks go to Eliana, daughter of the sun, who provides life and love without pause or limit. For the Pythagoreans,

---

[1] The contribution on Archelaus has been published as Betegh 2016, and a version of the piece on Xenophon and Varro has been published as Nelsestuen 2017.

there is a fire in the heart of the *kosmos*; for him, it was, is and always will be her.

Just as this volume was approved for publication, one of its contributors, Robert Germany, passed away at the untimely age of forty-two years. Robert was a perpetual source of intellectual generation, expanding the boundaries of ideas into new shapes, with colours and hues that flickered with every passing word. He thought much on life, love, fate and the passage of time; on God, family, friends and strangers. His was a gaze fixed incessantly on the heavens. This volume is dedicated to his enduring memory.

> Et cum tempus advenerit, quo se mundus renovaturus extinguat, viribus ista se caedent et sidera sideribus incurrent et omni flagrente materia uno igni quicquid nunc ex dispositio lucet ardebit. Nos quoque felices animae et aeterna sortitae, cum deo visum erit iterum ista moliri, labentibus cunctis et ipsae parva ruinae ingentis accessio in antiqua elementa vertemur. (Seneca, *To Marcia, On Consolation* 26.6–7)

An Historical Note on Κόσμος – Terminology

The title and topic of the first chapter notwithstanding, the reader might wish to know when ancient Greek κόσμος was translated *into English* – in the notion of the 'cosmos'. This presents an opportunity to reflect upon the life of this concept in the English-speaking world. The word κόσμος is anglicised for the first time in Middle English in a twelfth-century poem called *The Ormulum*, composed by a monk named Orm (or Orrm) and dedicated to biblical exegesis.[1] There, in a commentary on the Gospel of John 3:16 (in the vulgate translation into Latin, *Sic Deus dilexit mundum, et filium suum unigenitum daret*),[2] we read,

> & forr þatt manness sawle iss her
> Wel þurrh þe werelld tacnedd,
> Forr baþe fallenn inntill an
> Affterr Grickisshe spæche,
> Forr werelld iss nemmnedd Cossmós,
> Swa summ þe Grickess kiþenn,
> Forr þatt itt iss wurrþlike shridd
> Wiþþ sunne & mone & sterrness,
> Onn heffness whel all ummbetrin,
> Þurrh Godd tatt swillc itt wrohhte.   (*Ormulum*, 17,555–64)

Reconstruction of the poem's contents is challenging, even for medievalists, but we can infer from the previous lines that the account here deals with the body and soul of man, both of which 'fallenn intill an' (fall into one). Orm explains that the 'werelld' (world) is called 'Cossmós' in the Greek language by 'summ Grickess' (certain Greeks), and he provides a description of the firmament as 'wurrþlike shridd / Wiþþ sunne & mone & sterrness' (richly arrayed with sun, moon and stars) like a 'whel

---

[1] Holt (1878). On the reception of the Greek concept κόσμος in English prior to 1850, also see Algeo 1998: 65. I thank Corinne Saunders and Helen Foxhall-Forbes for guidance with this text.
[2] The original Greek text reads οὕτως γὰρ ἠγάπησεν ὁ θεὸς τὸν κόσμον, ὥστε τὸν υἱὸν τὸν μονογενῆ ἔδωκεν …

all ummbetrin' (wheel all round). The author of the *Ormulum* apparently knew that *mundus* was the Latin term for Greek κόσμος, and Greek 'Cossmós' is taken to refer to English 'werelld' for the first time, although a lack of evidence showing similar adoptions from roughly 1200 to 1650 CE would be thought to indicate that Orm's coinage, as remarkable as it is, did not take hold.[3]

The term κόσμος once again makes its way into the English language in the seventeenth century, when it is transliterated from ancient Greek into English via a Latinisation to 'Cosmus'. This occurs in John Bulwer's *Anthropometamorphosis: Man Transform'd; or the Artificiall Changeling* (first edition 1650; second edition 1653; third edition 1654), a curious work that blends medical observations, especially the physiognomy of the face, with cultural anthropology:[4]

> That as the greater world is called Cosmus, from the beauty thereof the inequality of the Centre thereof contributing much to the beauty and delightsomenesse of it: so in this Map or little world of beauty in the face, the inequality affords the prospect and delight. (Bulwer 1653: 242)

Bulwer expressly employs an argument by analogy: just as the asymmetry of the Cosmus is indicative of its beauty, so too the minor imperfections of the human face afford pleasure and joy. As interesting as these texts are, neither Orm's appeal to the Cossmós nor Bulwer's employment of Cosmus would have any traceable lasting effect on the English language.

Quite by the way, the transliteration of κόσμος most commonly recognised today, as 'cosmos', was popularised through two English translations of Alexander von Humboldt's influential five-volume work *Kosmos: Entwurf einer physischen Weltbeschreibung* (vol. 1 published in German in 1845). The first translation of this work into English, in 1845, by A. Prichard, and published by Hippolyte Baillière Publisher in London, was superseded by the authoritative version published in 1849 by Henry G. Bohn in London and translated by E. C. Otté. Both versions of Humboldt's compendium of natural philosophy anglicised *kosmos* to 'cosmos', effectively creating the expression of a concept that would have a lasting legacy in the English-speaking world. With the Greek notion of

[3] Orm refers to 'Cossmós' twice (at lines 17,559 and 17,592) and even, in relation to this, to the 'Mycrocossmós', the human being, which, as Orm explains, 'þatt nemmnedd iss / Affterr Ennglisshe spæche / Þe little werelld' (ll. 17,593–7).

[4] Bulwer, a physician and author of five works that dealt with subjects like hand gesturing among the deaf, non-verbal facial communication and comparative cultural anthropology, is comparatively poorly studied.

the κόσμος, Humboldt found the concept he needed for his unique systematic contribution to the history of natural science:

> By uniting, under one point of view, both the phenomena of our own globe and those presented in the regions of space, we embrace the limits of the science of the *Cosmos*,[5] and convert the physical history of the globe into the physical history of the universe; the one term being modelled upon that of the other. The science of the Cosmos is not, however, to be regarded as a mere encyclopaedic aggregation of the most important and general results that have been collected together from special branches of knowledge ... In the work before us, partial facts will be considered only in relation to the whole. The higher the point of view the greater the necessity for a systematic mode of treating the subject in language at once animated and picturesque. (Humboldt 1849: 36, trans. Otté)

Humboldt, who is to be considered responsible for the modern conceptualisation and terminology of 'cosmos', constructed his own theory of nature in reference to ancient philosophers, and especially to the Pythagorean Philolaus of Croton (DK 44), by building upon philological work done especially by August Boeckh in his 1819 edition of Philolaus' fragments.[6] In a representatively eclectic footnote, Humboldt traced the history of the trio of concepts indicated by Greek κόσμος – Latin *mundus*, German *Welt* – back to Homer and worked through the evidence from Plutarch, Aristotle, the pseudo-Aristotelian *On the Kosmos*, Ennius, Cicero, Greek inscriptions in the Roman Empire and Hesychius.[7] The notion of 'cosmos' remained present in the popular imagination from Humboldt forward, but it was significantly re-popularised with the 1978–79 television documentary *Carl Sagan's Cosmos*, co-produced by the PBS affiliate KCET in Los Angeles and the BBC in the United Kingdom – where the editor of this volume first encountered this concept. It has remained a formative notion for his entire life. Hence, this volume is titled *Cosmos in the Ancient World* – a nod to Humboldt's and Sagan's inspiration for conceptualising systems of order in the universe, but also to the first appearance of this word in English, as Cossmós, in Orm's elegant twelfth-century commentary on the verses of the Gospel of John.

For the purposes of consistency, this volume employs a strict transliteration, rather than a Latinisation, of κόσμος and words related to *kosmos* (e.g. *kosmoi, kosmioi, diakosmos, diakosmêsis*). This also follows for all Greek terms when they are transliterated (e.g. *koinônia*), although in the case of

---

[5] Italics original.   [6] Boeckh 1819.   [7] Humboldt 1849: 51–3.

proper names, this volume employs the Latinised form (e.g. Empedocles of Agrigentum rather than Empedoklês of Akragas). It regularly refers to what in English is commonly understood to be 'the cosmos' with 'the *kosmos*', as differentiated from the more general conceptualisation of order or arrangement implied by the simple term '*kosmos*'.

Abbreviations

This volume standardly employs abbreviations for ancient texts from the *Oxford Classical Dictionary*, 4th edn (2012). The citations of ancient texts in the Index Locorum at the end of the book are translated into English. Diels-Kranz's edition of the Presocratic fragments is cited according to the standard convention of using 'A' for biography, titles of works and testimonies; 'B' for fragments; and 'C' for imitation by later authors. In the process of preparing the manuscript, the impressive new nine-volume Loeb Classical Library edition of *Early Greek Philosophy*, edited and translated by André Laks and Glenn W. Most, appeared in publication, but it arrived too late to be consulted by the authors included in this volume.

The following list of abbreviations refers to standard collections of ancient materials (fragmentary, epigraphical, numismatic, papyrological, etc.) and other resource works.

Amato	Amato, E. (ed. and trans.) 2010. *Favorinos d'Arles: Oeuvres, Tome III, Fragments*. Paris: Les Belles Lettres.
Cardauns	Cardauns, B. (ed.) 1976. *M. Terentius Varro, Antiquitates Rerum Divinarum*, 3 vols. Mainz: Akademie der Wissenschaften und der Literatur Mainz Geistes- und Sozialwissenschaftliche Klasse.
Cèbe	Cèbe, J.-P. (ed.) 1972–99. *Varron: Satires Ménippées*, 13 vols. Rome: Publications de l'École Française de Rome.
DHR	Dareste, R., Haussoullier, B., and Reinach, T. (eds.) 1891–1904. *Recueil des inscriptions juridiques grecques*, 2 series. Paris: Ernest Leroux.
DK	Diels, H. and Kranz, W. (eds.) 1960. *Die Fragmente der Vorsokratiker*, 6th edn., 3 vols. Berlin: Weidmann.
FGrH	Jacoby, F. (ed.) 1923–. *Die Fragmente der griechischen Historiker*, 18 vols. Berlin: Weidmann.

Düring	Düring, I. (ed.) 1960. *Aristotle's* Protrepticus. Götheburg: Acta Universitatis Gothoburgensis.
G.-M.	Goldberg, S. and Manuwald, G. (trans.) 2018. *Ennius, Fragmentary Republican Latin, Volume II: Ennius, Dramatic Fragments, Minor Works*, Loeb Classical Library 537. Cambridge, MA: Harvard University Press.
IC	Guarducci, M. (ed.) 1935–50. *Inscriptiones Creticae*, 4 vols. Rome.
IGR	Cagnat, R., et al. (eds.) 1906–. *Inscriptiones Graecae ad res Romanas Pertinentes*. Paris: Ernest Leroux.
FHS&G	Fortenbaugh, W. W., Huby, P. M., Sharples, R. W. and Gutas, D. (eds.) 1993. *Theophrastus of Eresus: Sources for His Life, Writings, Thought and Influence*. Parts 1 and 2. Leiden: Brill.
Fortenbaugh and Schütrumpf	Fortenbaugh, W. W. and Schütrumpf, E. (eds.) 2000. *Demetrius of Phalerum: Text, Translation and Discussion*. New Brunswick, NJ: Transaction Publishers.
G.-P.	Gow, A. S. F. and Page, D. L. (eds.) 1968. *The Greek Anthology: the Garland of Philip and Some Contemporary Epigrams*, 3 vols. Cambridge: Cambridge University Press.
IP	Isnardi Parente, M. (ed. and trans.) 1980. *Speusippo: Frammenti*. Naples: Bibliopolis.
IP²	Isnardi Parente, M. and Dorandi, T. (eds. and trans.) 2012. *Senocrate e Ermodoro: Testimonianze e Frammenti*. Pisa: Scuola Normale Superiore.
Jocelyn	Jocelyn, H. D. (ed.) 1969. *The Tragedies of Ennius*. Cambridge: Cambridge University Press.
LfgrE	Thesaurus Linguae Graecae 1955–. *Lexicon des früh griechischen Epos*, 25 vols. Berlin: Vandenhoeck & Ruprecht.
K.-A.	Kassel, R. and Austin, C. (eds.) 1998–. *Poetae Comici Graeci*, 8 vols. Berlin: Walter de Gruyter.
Kidd	Edelstein, L. and Kidd, I. G. (eds. and trans.) 1972–88. *Posidonius*, 3 vols. Cambridge: Cambridge University Press.
Koerner	Koerner, R. (ed.) 1993. *Inschriftliche Gesetzestexte der frühen griechischen Polis*. Cologne: Böhlau-Verlag.

Lasserre	Lasserre, F. 1966. *Die Fragmente des Eudoxos von Knidos.* Berlin: Walter de Gruyter.
L&S	Long, A. A. and Sedley, D. (eds. and trans.) 1987. *The Hellenistic Philosophers*, 2 vols. Cambridge: Cambridge University Press.
LSJ	Liddell, H. G., Scott, R., and Jones, H. S. 1996. *A Greek-English Lexicon*, 9th edn. Oxford: Oxford University Press.
Merkelbach and West	Merkelbach, R., and West M. L. (eds.) 1967. *Fragmenta Hesiodea.* Oxford: Oxford University Press.
Mirhady	Fortenbaugh, W. W., Schütrumpf, E., and Mirhady, D. C. (eds. and trans.) 2001. *Dicaearchus of Messana: The Sources, Text and Translation.* New Brunswick, NJ: Transaction Publishers.
NRSV	Coogan, M. D. (trans.) 2007. *The New Oxford Annotated Bible*, Augmented 3rd edn., New Revised Standard Version. Oxford: Oxford University Press.
OLD	Glare, P. G. W. 1968. *Oxford Latin Dictionary.* Oxford: Oxford University Press.
P. Derv.	Kouremenos, T., Parássoglou, G. M., and Tsantsanoglou, K. (eds. and trans.) 2006. *The Derveni Papyrus.* Florence: Olschki.
Radt	Radt, S. (ed.) 1977. *Tragicorum Graecorum Fragmenta*, vol. 4, *Sophocles.* Göttingen: Vandenhoeck & Ruprecht.
Ribbeck	Ribbeck, O. (ed.) 1898. *Scaenicae Romanorum Poesis Fragmenta: Comicorum Romanorum praeter Plautum et Terentium Fragmenta*, 3rd edn, vol. 2. Leipzig: Teubner.
RO	Rhodes, P. J. and Osborne, R. (eds.) 2007. *Greek Historical Inscriptions, 404–323 BC*, Rev. edn. Oxford: Oxford University Press.
Rose[3]	Rose, V. (ed.) 1886. *Aristotelis Fragmenta.* Leipzig: Teubner.
Ross	Ross, W. D. (ed.) 1955. *Aristotelis Fragmenta Selecta.* Oxford: Oxford University Press.
RRC	Crawford, M. H. (ed.) 1974. *Roman Republican Coinage.* Cambridge: Cambridge University Press.
Schütrumpf	Schütrumpf, E. (ed. and trans.) 2008. *Heraclides of Pontus: Texts and Translation.* New Brunswick, NJ: Transaction Publishers.

SEG	Chaniotis, A., et al. (eds.) 1923–. *Supplementum epigraphicum Graecum.* Leiden: Brill.
Skutsch	Skutsch, O. (ed. and trans.) 1985. *The Annales of Ennius.* Oxford: Oxford University Press.
Soubiran	Soubiran, J. (ed. and trans.) 2002. *Cicéron: Aratea, Fragments Poétiques.* Paris: Les Belles Lettres.
SVF	von Arnim, H. (ed.) 1903–21. *Stoicorum Veterum Fragmenta,* 4 vols. Leipzig: Teubner.
Thesleff	Thesleff, H. (ed.) 1965. *The Pythagorean Texts of the Hellenistic Period.* Åbo: Åbo Akademi.
VA	von Herrmann, F.-W. (ed.) 2000. *M. Heidegger, Gesamtausgabe,* vol. 7, *7 Vorträge und Aufsätze: 1936–53.* Frankfurt am Main, Germany: Klostermann.
Wehrli	Wehrli, F. (ed.) 1967. *Die Schule des Aristoteles,* vol. 2, *Aristoxenos,* 2nd edn. Basel, Switzerland: Schwabe.
West	West, M. L. (ed.) 1989–92. *Iambi et elegi Graeci ante Alexandrum cantati,* 2 vols., rev. edn. Oxford: Oxford University Press.
Willetts	Willets, R. F. (ed.) 1967. *The Law Code of Gortyn.* Berlin: Walter de Gruyter.

Introduction

Phillip Sidney Horky

1 Preface

Self-reflection excites questions about our relationship to the world in which we live: is that world a priori ordered, or a chaos well arranged, or simply an indiscriminate chaos? If there is an observed order, is that order *merely* observed, or is it an image that obscures a more fundamental order, or *even* a disorder? If we do accept that there is a concept of 'order' at play, what is that order made up of? Does it have constituents, or perhaps properties that are unique to it? Assuming that we exist in some ordered world that we can describe, how do we set out to define it? Where, and how, do we draw its boundaries, either conceptual or physical? Is the ordered world one, or many? If many, are there ordered worlds within an ordered world, or even ordered world*s*, or are there separately existing ordered worlds? Does this order repeat? If so, what unifies it in such a way that it can be observed as persisting? Are we human beings 'ordered' in a way similar to the world around us? And if there *is* order at various levels of reality (psychological, social, natural), what is ultimately responsible for such an order?

These are not novel questions: they are just as relevant today as they were in the ancient world, from the Delphic Oracle's enigmatic injunction to know and explain oneself, to St Augustine's search for human meaning within the world of change.[1] Modern scholars who work on 'systems theory' and 'systems philosophy' ask similar questions to these in the pursuit of a holistic understanding of the many parts of a 'system' and the ways in which they come to relate to one another.[2] According to Alexander Laszlo and Stanley Krippner, a 'system' is most generally understood to be a 'complex of interacting components together with the relationships among them that permit the identification of a boundary-maintaining entity or process'.[3] For some

---

[1] For Augustine's response to Platonic, Aristotelian and Plotinian cosmology, see Nightingale 2010: Chapter 2.
[2] See e.g. Capra and Luisi 2014, Rosen 1991, Laszlo 1972, and Von Bertalanffy 1968.
[3] Laszlo and Krippner 1998.

scholars working in this idiom, such 'systems' can be proper to individual disciplines and areas of scientific enquiry, whereas a sort of 'supra-system' is assumed to obtain over and above particular disciplines: the investigation of this 'supra-system' is the project of formulating a 'general system theory', following the terminology of biologist and philosopher Ludwig von Bertalanffy.[4] So, while individual scientific pursuits might have special laws that we enquire after in the hunt for knowledge, and that condition the knowability of those sciences, there is a kind of isomorphism that obtains across the laws that govern particular sciences, which indicates the possibility of a universal system under which particular systems of knowledge fall.[5] For committed systems theorists, it is possible to discover, or at least to approximate, a general theory of systems which applies to all sciences, but most notably those that deal with the sphere of human action and experience.[6]

Recently, scholars seeking to find an ancient imprimatur for their notion of 'general system theory' turned to the ancient world, and in particular to Presocratic and Classical philosophy in Ancient Greece.[7] In particular, they noticed that a special concept that helped the ancient Greeks to explain the many inner workings of various spheres of life was established sometime in the mid to late sixth century BCE: *kosmos* (κόσμος). *Kosmos* was a term common from Homer a few centuries prior, where it was applied interestingly to the good arrangements of soldiers as well as to well-spoken words;[8] and it was also employed in political discourse from the Archaic period forward, to refer to administrators whose responsibilities

---

[4] See Von Bertalanffy (1968: xxi): 'There is systems philosophy, i.e. a reorientation of thought and worldview ensuing from the introduction of "system" as a new scientific paradigm (in contrast to the analytic, mechanistic, one-way causal paradigm of classical science). As every scientific theory of broader scope, general system theory has its "metascientific" or philosophical aspects.'

[5] Consider Wittgenstein's discussion of systems and their relationship to knowledge in *On Certainty* (§105): 'All testing, all confirmation and disconfirmation of a hypothesis takes place already within a system. And this system is not a more or less arbitrary and doubtful point of departure for all our arguments: no, it belongs to the essence of what we call an argument. The system is not so much the point of departure, as the element in which arguments have their life' (tr. by Paul and Anscombe).

[6] See e.g. Rosen's description of the relationship between 'formal' and 'natural' systems (1991: 44): 'The extraction of a formalism from a natural language has many of the properties of extracting a system from the ambience. Therefore, I shall henceforth refer to a formalism as a *formal system*; to distinguish formal systems from systems in the ambience or external world, I shall call the latter *natural systems*. The entire scientific enterprise, as I shall argue, is an attempt to capture natural systems within formal ones, or alternatively, to embody formal systems with external referents in such a way as to describe natural ones. That, indeed, is what is meant by a *theory*.' Italics original.

[7] See Capra and Luisi 2014: 1–6 and Rosen 1991: 5, where Pythagoras is credited with establishing the dualism between idealism and materialism, the basis for his own distinction between formal and natural systems.

[8] For the significance of *kosmos* to Homeric poetics, see Elmer 2013: 49–55. Consider the challenges offered by Parmenides to the Homeric notion of *kosmos*, discussed in the contributions by Macé (Chapter 2) and Schofield (Chapter 3).

must have included keeping some sort of order in the city-state. It had taken on new meanings that went far beyond, and perhaps in contra-distinction to, Homer's usage.[9] Still, the early usages hardly implied a 'general system', in the sense of the meta-system whose laws apply to diverse systems subordinate to it. Around the time that democracy was born in Athens, the kings expelled from Rome, and the Persian Empire established as a major world power, in the late sixth century BCE, some-thing had changed, and *kosmos* took on a significance beyond its traditional deployment in Greek culture. Amazingly, over the next millennium – a period which saw dramatic growth and expansion in philosophy, science, music, literature, art and performance across the Greco-Roman world – various figures involved in the production of human knowledge and art continued to investigate what sorts of 'order' could be fruitfully explained by appeal to *kosmos*. Whatever *kosmos* was taken to mean at various points throughout antiquity – at some fundamental level, it indicated an order that is somehow arranged through forces of opposition, equilibrium or measure – the word and its derivatives were employed in order to illustrate not only how the universe, in its myriad constituent parts, works, but also how it *should* work. That is, *kosmos*, as it was deployed by ancient thinkers for their understanding of the world that surrounded them, functioned both descriptively and normatively to structure knowledge of reality.

This double aspect of *kosmos*, which, as the following chapters in this volume will aim to demonstrate, persists throughout its history in Greco-Roman antiquity, reflects a similar binarism that one sometimes finds in investigation into *kosmos* and its usages: descriptive approaches to *kosmos* tend to pursue a unified notion, an absolute *kosmos*, or, if we are to go one step further, *the kosmos*; this is a powerful idea that, so far as we can tell, received its most memorable illustration in the philosopher Plato of Athens' (ca. 428/7–348/7 BCE) masterpiece *Timaeus*, probably the most influential cosmological text in the ancient world.[10] As Plato's authoritative interlocutor Timaeus of Epizephyrian Locri, who delivers Plato's most complete discussion of the universe and its nature, says:

> The entire heaven – whether *kosmos*, or indeed any other name that it would be most convenient to call it by, let it be called so by us – we must make an

[9] On which, see the contribution of Atack in Chapter 8 of this volume.

[10] The influence of *Timaeus* upon later philosophy and science is paramount: see, among others, Baltes 1976, Reydams-Schils 1999, the essays collected in Sharples and Sheppard 2003 and the essays collected in Mohr and Sattler 2010. Excellent recent comprehensive studies of the *Timaeus* itself include Johansen 2004 and Broadie 2012. *Timaeus* will appear in references throughout this volume, but given the ubiquity of its importance, there is no single chapter devoted to this work.

investigation concerning it, the sort of investigation that, it is granted, should be undertaken concerning everything at first, whether it has always existed, having no origin of generation, or whether it was generated, having originated from a certain beginning. It was generated. (Plato, *Timaeus* 28b2–7)

Hence, Plato's character Timaeus understands that the fundamental question we face in our investigation of the universe is whether it originated from a particular beginning, or has existed eternally. It was one of the most important questions in ancient philosophy. Within the dialogue, discussion of the *kosmos* leads to examinations of its many parts, and to the question of how its parts were brought together by the divine Demiurge and his ancillaries to form a complete living universe, subject to change over time, but nevertheless eternal after its initial generation. This discussion comes to inform Timaeus' description of the biological generation of the human being, bridging the macro- with the microcosm, as Plato sought to provide a unified image of anthropo-cosmic generation.[11]

In the same light, consider the Roman statesman and philosopher Cicero's (106–43 BCE) marvellous Dream of Scipio, which, like the Myth of Er in Plato's *Republic*, closed his dialogue of the same name. A young and ambitious Scipio Aemilianus gladly receives a vision of the universe, described by his grandfather Scipio Africanus, with the commitment to follow in his grandfather's footsteps and gain glory in Rome. His adoptive grandfather responds by comparing the body (*corpus*) with the *kosmos* (here using the Roman term for the same concept, *mundus*):[12]

> Keep at it; and know this: it is not you that is mortal, but your body. You are not what your physical shape reveals, but each person is his mind, not the body that a finger can point at. Know then that you are a god, as surely as a god is someone who is alert, who feels, who remembers, who looks ahead, who rules and guides and moves the body of which he is in command just as the leading god does for the world [*quam hunc mundum ille princeps deus*]. And just as the eternal god moves the world, which is partly mortal [*ut mundum ex quadam parte mortale ipse deus aeternus*], so too does the eternal soul move the fragile body.[13] (Cicero, *On the Republic*, 6.26)

Scipio Africanus' association of the animal body with the *kosmos* reveals Cicero's Platonic inheritance, but it is notable that Cicero's cosmology reveals a point of ambivalence among philosophers of the Post-Hellenistic

---

[11] The macro- and microcosm relation is drawn explicitly at the end of the dialogue (*Ti.* 89a–90d).

[12] See the first epigram to this book, from the incipit of Lucius Ampelius's *Liber Memorialis* (1.1): 'Mundus est universitas rerum, in quo omnia sunt et extra quem nihil, qui graece dicitur κόσμος'.

[13] Translation after Zetzel.

period, namely whether the *kosmos* was mortal or immortal – he claims, rather vaguely, that it possesses a 'certain mortal part'. Is this a way of accepting Plato's claim that the universe was generated? Is it a differentiation of the cosmic body from the cosmic soul (or 'World-Soul')? Or is it perhaps referring to the World-Soul's 'mortal' parts, which are the spirited and appetitive aspects? Despite the ambivalence on this point, Scipio goes on to make claims that run counter to Plato's position in the *Timaeus*, but reflect positions staked out elsewhere in his dialogues, such as in the *Phaedrus*:[14] consider the statement at *On the Republic* 6.28 that the soul is not generated (a claim expressly rejected by Timaeus at 34 c). As soon as Plato has solidified the analogy between the generation of the *kosmos* and the human in the *Timaeus*, he initiates a messy, if persistently potent, debate that fuelled speculation for at least a millennium, in both the Greek and Roman worlds.[15]

At the other end of the historical spectrum in antiquity, the problem of relating the eternal and the generated natures of the *kosmos* is taken up by the Neoplatonist philosopher Proclus (ca. 411–485 CE). It prompts him to seek to explain how the universe could persist in its various fluctuations to and from Being:

> Before his entire journey begins, Plato appropriately makes definitions regarding these terms, when he names the universe 'heaven' [οὐρανός] and '*kosmos*' [κόσμος] and states of 'the entire heaven' – to ensure that you do not think that he is only speaking about the divine body – 'let it be called "*kosmos*" by us or any other name' that it is 'pleased to be called' [*Ti.* 28b2–3]. It seems that he calls it 'heaven' on the grounds that it seems best to everyone, but '*kosmos*' on the grounds that [it seems best] for himself, for he says of the heaven, 'let it be called "*kosmos*" by us'. It is appropriate to apply the name '*kosmos*' because it is something crafted, even if it is also possible to call it by both [names], 'heaven' because it looks upon the things above [ὁρῶντα τὰ ἄνω] and contemplates the intelligible realm, and because it participates in the intellective essence; and '*kosmos*' because it is always filled and arranged [κοσμούμενον] apart from the beings that really exist; also 'heaven' as having reverted [to its source], '*kosmos*' as proceeding [from that source], for it is from there that it is generated, and reverts back, to Being. (Proclus, *Commentary on Plato's Timaeus* 2, pp. 272.26–273.10 Diehl)

Nearly nine centuries after Plato had laid the foundations for the debate concerning the *kosmos* and its nature, Proclus finds himself employing the philosophical and hermeneutic tools that had accumulated in the study of

---

[14] Cicero here is translating into Latin Plato's *Phaedrus* 245c–246a.

[15] For the early history of the debate, see Reydams-Schils 1999: Chapter 1.

Plato – from his earliest exegetes and critics in the Academy, such as Xenocrates and Aristotle, to those who would ultimately codify his philosophical views in a new system, such as Plotinus. His account gives us a place where we might draw the line in late antiquity concerning the assessment of Platonic cosmology. Proclus' lexical analysis of the term '*kosmos*' builds from Plato's account of the generation of the universe, but employs etymologisation from the term's function – the 'entire heaven' is called '*kosmos*' due to its being arranged (κοσμούμενον) apart from true beings, e.g. the Forms or the Demiurge. There is, of course, only one *kosmos* but it undergoes constant change despite its propensity for unity and existence.[16] In this way, because the *kosmos* is the paradigm of what changes but retains its identity, it functions as a heuristic model for the individual, the person who persists in growing older while remaining the same. By understanding the universe in its manifold generation, I better understand myself as a potentially well-ordered being.[17]

Normative discussions of *kosmos* in Greco-Roman antiquity sometimes focus on the multiplicity of the term, how there can be many well-ordered things, or how many participants in the larger *kosmos* can be 'arranged' so as to be *kosmioi*: the stars, planets, and other meteorologica;[18] city-states and their laws;[19] land and buildings;[20] speeches, poems, and other dramatic performances;[21] social practices and habits;[22] the souls and bodies of individual human beings;[23] and the basic elements of the universe.[24] Others reject, or scorn, the centrality of the notion of *kosmos* to questions of nature or theology.[25] *Kosmos* features quite a range of applications and goes far beyond the notion of the *kosmos*:[26] the sophist Gorgias of Leontini, who flourished in the mid-fifth century BCE, contributes something quite

---

[16] Compare with his predecessor Plotinus' presentation of the *kosmos*, discussed in Remes's contribution (Chapter 7).

[17] See especially the contributions of Brisson and Remes (Chapters 6 and 7).

[18] See Sauron's, Gagné's and Shearin's contributions to this volume (Chapters 11, 9 and 12).

[19] See the contributions of Atack and Brisson (Chapters 8 and 6).

[20] These are discussed in the contributions of Brisson, Germany and Sauron (Chapters 6, 10 and 11).

[21] See Macé's, Germany's and Gagné's contributions (Chapters 2, 10 and 9).

[22] See the contributions of Brisson and Boys-Stones (Chapters 6 and 5).

[23] These topics are treated in the contributions of Brisson, Boys-Stones and Remes (Chapters 6, 5 and 7).

[24] Discussed in Schofield's and both of Horky's contributions (Chapters 3, 1 and 13).

[25] See Johnson's discussion of Aristotle and Horky's discussion of early Christianity in this volume (Chapters 4 and 13).

[26] In analysing the *kosmos* of law and rhetoric in Classical Athens, Wohl (2010: 2) helpfully identifies the possible divergences between 'order' and 'adornment', showing that a preference for the former is implicit in many accounts of early Greek law.

remarkable to the history of the concept by assuming that a *kosmos* must be a *kosmos* of something; and that each *kosmos* of something is diverse, peculiar to that object. Or, put more philosophically, *kosmos* is fundamentally *relative*. The beauty of Gorgias' sentiment lies in in the pithiness of its expression:

> The *kosmos* of a polis is manpower, of a body beauty, of a soul wisdom, of an action virtue, of a speech truth, and the opposites of these make for *akosmia*. (Gorgias, *Encomium of Helen* 1)

Gorgias excites the possibilities for understanding *kosmos* by grounding it in its many relative applications; but implicit is the assumption that *kosmos* itself is a meta-system with universal application across many areas of human experience, including warfare, aesthetics, ethics and rhetoric. Indeed, Gorgias' conceptualisation, marked by differentiation of 'order' from 'disorder' by contrariety, was influential in antiquity: not only does Plato mark a nuanced, if slippery, notion of *kosmos* in his dialogue concerned with challenging the dominance of rhetoric in his dialogue *Gorgias*.[27] Plato's student Aristotle (384–322 BCE) adapts Gorgias' contra-distinction between '*kosmos*' (good arrangement) and '*akosmia*' (chaotic arrangement) in a fragment from one of his lost dialogues (perhaps *On Philosophy*; see Fr. 17 Rose³), which is used to point to the notion that a single first principle is one over many other principles:

> The first principle is either one or many. If there is one, we have the object of our investigation. If there are many, either they are ordered or disordered. If, on the one hand, they are disordered, their products are more disordered [than they are], and the *kosmos* is not a *kosmos* but an *akosmia*, and this is the thing that is contrary to nature, whereas what is in accordance with nature does not exist. But if, on the other hand, they are ordered, they were either ordered by themselves, or by some external cause. But if they were ordered by themselves, they have something in common that conjoins them, and this is the first principle.

Because this fragment was originally embedded in a dialogue, it is difficult to know whether it reflects Aristotle's alleged Platonic metaphysical inclinations, or whether it represents a summary of a Platonic 'one over many' argument that he sought to criticise elsewhere, including his fragmentary treatise *On Ideas*.[28] It is possible that it is meant to represent a 'Platonic'

[27] As discussed by Horky in Chapter 1 and Boys-Stones in Chapter 5.
[28] The standard work on Aristotle's criticisms of Plato's 'One Over Many' arguments is Fine 1993. See Johnson's discussion of this fragment in the larger context of Aristotle's criticisms of theories of the *kosmos* and *kosmoi* in Chapter 4.

view that would have been subject to dialectical challenge later on in the dialogue. Regardless, this passage supports the proposition that what is *kosmos* is, in some fundamental way, *in accordance with nature*; and what is its opposite is contrary to nature. In this way, the argument builds upon Gorgias's seemingly trifle speculations concerning the fundamental – we might even venture to say axiomatic – divergence between what is *kosmos*, and what is *akosmia*.

One of the most remarkable aspects of *kosmos* in its usage throughout antiquity is its applicability at the macro- or micro-levels. As we emphasised before, the Greeks seem to have understood *kosmos* extensively, and to have applied it in the case of all kinds of ordered beings, at all levels, from the inestimable expanses of space and time, to the imperceptible principles and elements of existence.[29] This appears to have obtained from early on in the life of the concept, and it is attested in two fragments of the Presocratic Heraclitus of Ephesus (fl. around 500 BCE) that concern themselves with *kosmos*:

> This *kosmos*, the same for all – neither did any god nor any human make it, but it eternally was, is, and will be: ever-living fire, being kindled in measures and being snuffed out in measures. (Heraclitus, DK 22 B 30)

> The most beautiful *kosmos* is a heap of sweepings at random. (Heraclitus, DK 22 B 124)

Like Gorgias, Heraclitus conceives of multiple species of *kosmos*. But Heraclitus' usage denies to *kosmos* what, in the writings of Aristotle and Plato, is a property genial to it: conceptual isomorphism in reference to the objects that take it on. In the first fragment, the *kosmos* under discussion, the one that is the 'same for all', is eternal but ungenerated, and subject to measure as it increases and decreases. One wonders, with Malcolm Schofield in his contribution to this book (Chapter 3), whether Heraclitus is referring to *the kosmos*, i.e. the world, as Heraclitus' ancient commentators took him to be doing[30] – yet it would be difficult to account for the deictic 'this' (τόνδε) in that circumstance, and, if we compare with other fragments, the sun is revealed to be the most likely referent of the specific *kosmos* under discussion.[31] On the other hand, in the second fragment, the *kosmos* described as 'most beautiful' is but a heap of dust,

---

[29] See especially Schofield's discussion in Chapter 3.   [30] E.g. Clem. Al. *Strom.* 5.105.
[31] See Plato's jocund criticisms of Heraclitus at *R.* 497e–498b along with DK 22 B 94 and P. Derv. Col. IV. For a good discussion of this issue, see Hülsz 2012.

collected at random.[32] It is hence an 'arrangement' of any sort that obtains in natural conditions. With Heraclitus, we are quite far from the position of, say, the fifth-century BCE Pythagorean Philolaus of Croton, who anticipated later philosophers, physicists, and systems theorists in believing that 'nature in the *kosmos*', as well as the 'whole *kosmos* and all things in it', were 'fitted together out of limiters and unlimiteds' (DK 44 B 1). For Heraclitus, even though it can indeed be considered at the macro- or microcosmic level, the arrangement implied in *kosmos* is not always the same for all the objects to which it is applied. Nevertheless, we could still see family resemblance between Aristotle's and Heraclitus' notions of *kosmos*: both are revealed in nature, and what this shared conceptualisation does is show how, throughout the ancient world, the peculiar way in which intellectuals formulated *kosmos* as a sort of good arrangement often has a knock-on effect on what they thought nature to be. And, indeed, one of the most important legacies of Presocratic philosophy was the identification of 'nature' as a fundamental object of scientific inquiry.

If Plato and Heraclitus are to be taken as roughly representative of two extreme points in the spectrum of meaning and usage for *kosmos*, we might further consider whether this notion is proprietary to Ancient Greece, or can be detected, with similar conceptual parameters, in other cultures of the ancient world. Of course, other ancient cultures had notions of an ordered universe. The Romans called this the *mundus*, and they distinguished between various sorts of *mundus* that they could, in their religious practices, observe and contemplate.[33] Some scholars have attempted to link these terms together through comparative linguistics, and although their arguments must remain tentative – nobody is actually sure exactly what the etymology of *kosmos* and related words is – there can be no doubt that the Roman and Greek notions are kindred.[34] There may be some shared semantics with Hebrew texts as well: according to Genesis 2:1, on the sixth day, Yahweh created the heaven and the earth, and צְבָאָם: (ṣə·ḇā·ʾām), a word that the Septuagint translates in the third/second centuries BCE into κόσμος, but whose semantics indicate the assembly or mass of an army (i.e. the 'host') – the translation represents a throwback to a usage found in Homer. Beyond the Greco-Roman and Jewish worlds,

---

[32] The consequences of this fragment will be discussed in Wohl's Afterword.

[33] See especially Germany's contribution (Chapter 10).

[34] Generally, see Puhvel 1976. Also see Alexander von Humboldt's (1849: 52–53) eccentric summary of the etymologies of Greek κόσμος and Latin *mundus*, which he traced back to, respectively, Sanskrit *sud*, or 'to purify' (e.g. in Greek καθαρμός), and Sanskrit *mand*, or 'to shine'. The *Etymologicum Magnum* (532.12–13 Sylburg) derives κόσμος from κάζω and καίνυμαι, or 'I excel'.

there are some interesting comparisons with other cultures, but no strictly equivalent concepts: the Egyptians posited *Maat* as the moral ideal of order and righteousness, as did the Babylonians *Kittu* and *Misharu*,[35] and the Zoroastrians *Aša*.[36] These conceptual ideals are perhaps closer to the notion of 'justice' or 'righteous order' than to *kosmos*: they refer to cosmic order as essentially just, something that was likely emphasised by Anaximander, but we must remember that justice, in the sense of equilibrium, need not be an *essential* attribute of *kosmos* (consider Gorgias' description earlier in the Introduction).[37] Moreover, from the period in which *kosmos*, conceived of as good arrangement, becomes the *kosmos*, the links to mathematics, and especially to technical harmonics, are uniquely attested in the Greco-Roman traditions.[38] Indeed, one might think that the concepts of *Maat, Kittu, Misharu,* and *Aša* are closer in meaning to early Greek Δίκη or θέμις.[39] A complete comparison of notions of 'order' or 'system' in these cultures is beyond the scope of this volume, but it would surely lead to promising results in the history of thought.[40] One might expect that it would highlight the strangeness of the Greek concept of *kosmos* in the relief of these other moral and existential ideals, which persist across ancient cultures regardless of linguistic family origin.

This book aims, among other things, to present thirteen diverse contributions to our understanding of *kosmos* as a formative concept that has had impressive effects upon Western thinking. It is one of many core notions bequeathed by the Greco-Roman traditions to us today. Individual chapters vary in their treatment of this concept, ranging from historical-philological assessments, philosophical investigations, analyses of literary expression and evaluations of its practical application in ancient societies. The scholars who have generously contributed their papers were encouraged to embrace the many possibilities afforded by *kosmos* and *mundus*, broadly from Homer in the eighth century BCE through Nonnus in the fourth/fifth centuries CE; each contribution is interdisciplinary, selecting as relevant the topics its pursues with a close attention to the ancient evidentiary bases available to us. The reader will encounter

---

[35] For a useful summary of *Maat*'s attributes and scholarship relating to this topic, see Karenga 2004: 5–11.

[36] For the latter as a cosmological principle, see Horky 2009: 55–60 and West 2010: 12–13.

[37] Anaximander DK 12 B 1. See Burkert 2008: 68–69.   [38] See Horky's contribution in Chapter 1.

[39] Burkert (2008: 69 n. 29) notes that Parmenides' notion of the alternation of day and night is based on justice (DK 28 B 1.11–15); but this need not refer to *kosmos* itself, a term that Parmenides found problematic (see Schofield and Macé's contributions in Chapters 2 and 3).

[40] An excellent recent collection of papers on comparative approaches to cosmology and cosmogony is Derron 2015.

literary texts from the Greek and Roman canons, including poetry of various sorts (epic, lyric, and didactic/philosophical); prose texts (historical, philosophical, rhetorical, religious, and satirical); and dramatic texts (comedic and tragic). Several contributions will examine evidence from material culture, including inscriptions, architecture and civic design. The reader will note a propensity in the contents of the volume towards philosophical texts that focus on cosmology: this is chiefly a consequence of the evidentiary base that conditions our understanding of *kosmos* in the ancient world, although the reader will also find manifestly non-philosophical expressions of *kosmos*. Indeed, what makes this a book about *kosmos* in the ancient world, and not simply about ancient *cosmology*, is this broader and more inclusive sense of the term.[41] Contributors have been encouraged to consider the chapters of other authors in composing their own, and one effect of this has been the weaving of a web of thematic connections that persists across the book. Whether this network of ideas obtains its proper measure, as does Heraclitus' sun, or assumes the character of a random whirl of stuffs, as Heraclitus' heap of sweepings, it is hoped that by seeing the ancient *kosmos* in its many manifestations, the reader will be stimulated to further engagement with the topic, and might even find some value in the contributions the ancient Greeks and Romans made to the universal study of 'order' – a study which has its most fundamental analogue in the study of ourselves.

2 Summary of the Contents of the Volume

Cosmos in the Ancient World is structured progressively based on topical clusters: general notions of *kosmos* and their relations especially to cosmology (Horky's Chapter 1, followed by those of Macé, Schofield and Johnson, Chapters 2, 3 and 4, respectively); *kosmos* as applied to the individual (the contributions of Boys-Stones, Brisson and Remes, Chapters 5, 6 and 7, respectively); *kosmos* and society (the chapters of Atack, Gagné, Germany and Sauron, Chapters 8, 9, 10 and 11); and *kosmos* and what lies beyond (Shearin's Chapter 12 and Horky's Chapter 13). The volume is closed by an Afterword by Victoria Wohl, with reflections upon its contributions and suggestions about how to take the concept of *kosmos* further. Attempts to bring chapters into dialogue with one another have led to their relative proximity, although the reader is encouraged to see thematic continuity across the volume as a whole. Generally, although

---

[41] Again, for cosmology, see especially the volume edited by Derron 2015.

the design is topical, contributions tend to progress diachronically, from the late sixth and early fifth centuries BCE to the second and third centuries CE under the Roman Empire – although the volume will range as far forward as the fifth century CE (e.g. in the contribution of Gagné) and it may circle back to Archaic Greece from time to time (e.g. in the chapters of Remes and Atack). The reader may note implicit symmetries within the arrangement of contributions – this is a book on *kosmos*, after all.

The volume begins with the early history of the development of the term *kosmos* and related terms in early Greek philosophy, especially by reference to natural science, from the Presocratics to Plato and Aristotle. In Chapter 1, 'When Did *Kosmos* Become the *Kosmos?*', **Phillip Sidney Horky** asks the fundamental question: when did *kosmos* come to mean 'world-order'? Horky ventures a new answer by examining later evidence often underutilised or dismissed by scholars. Two late doxographical accounts in which Pythagoras is said to be first to call the heavens *kosmos* (in the anonymous *Life of Pythagoras* and the fragments of Favorinus) exhibit heurematographical tendencies that place their claims in a dialectic with the early Peripatetics about the first discoverers of the mathematical structure of the universe. Likewise, Xenophon and Plato refer to 'wise men' who nominate *kosmos* as the object of scientific inquiry into nature as a whole and the cosmic 'communion' (*koinônia*) between all living beings, respectively. Again, later testimonies help in identifying the anonymous 'wise men' by associating them with the Pythagoreans and, especially, Empedocles. As Horky argues, not only is Empedocles the earliest surviving source to use *kosmos* to refer to a harmonic 'world-order' and to illustrate cosmic 'communities' between oppositional pairs, but also his cosmology realises the mutual correspondence of these aspects in the cycle of love and strife. Thus, if later figures posited Pythagoras as the first to refer to the universal 'world-order' as the *kosmos*, they did so because they believed Empedocles to have been a Pythagorean natural scientist, whose combined focus on cosmology and ethics exemplified a distinctively Pythagorean approach to philosophy.

In Chapter 2, 'Ordering the Universe in Speech: *Kosmos* and *Diakosmos* in Parmenides' Poem', **Arnaud Macé** seeks to advance beyond the traditional dilemma about Parmenides' cosmology that arises out of the fragmentary nature of our evidence. If Parmenides holds that any inquiry into physics is impossible, then how could a consistent cosmology even be found in the poem? As he suggests, its inconsistency would be the best proof of its being false. Recent scholarship, however, has sought to construct a consistent cosmology in the second part of the poem, usually referred to as the *Doxa* ('Opinion') and often concludes that there must therefore be some truth that can be obtained from it. Macé posits a third way, in which he constructs a nuanced theory of cosmic order in Parmenides' *Doxa*, but also argues that there are clear signs that it is Parmenides himself who encourages us to reject the cosmic order as an illusion – a deceitful *kosmos*, as the Goddess puts it. Macé attempts to show that the study of Parmenides' use of the terms *kosmos* and *diakosmos* stages his critique of Homer, whose texts help the reader to reconstruct the missing steps of the *Doxa*. Parmenides transposes the Homeric vocabulary of dividing and ordering troops to the field of cosmology in order to illustrate how the words of men are hasty in their attempts to arrange a beautiful representation of the universe. The shaping and ordering of the universe is, for Parmenides, but an arrangement of words, assigned the power to construct a world in and of themselves that leads mortals astray.

Malcolm Schofield's contribution in Chapter 3, '*Diakosmêsis*', bridges the contributions to the study of Pythagoras, Empedocles and Parmenides in Chapters 1 and 2 with subsequent chapters on Plato and Aristotle by examining the Atomists' cosmic models. Schofield begins by noting that while deployment of the notion of *kosmos* has been much discussed in the scholarship on Presocratic philosophy, *diakosmos* and *diakosmêsis* have been almost entirely neglected. He argues that in describing the business of articulating 'mortal belief' as *diakosmos*, Parmenides bequeathed to his successors among the Presocratics a question – intended as deflationary – about the main agenda for physics and physical explanation: how is the universe arranged? As Schofield suggests, Parmenides is responsible for coining a concept designed to articulate it, an argument that extends the results of Macé's contribution. According to Schofield, *diakosmos* was a concept Parmenides' successors, especially the Atomists Democritus and Leucippus, were determined to reinforce, but only at the price of contestation between believers in a single world produced by design and proponents of infinite undesigned worlds. Finally, for Schofield, in Aristotle, *diakosmêsis* is reinvested with a hint of the deflationary.

It is in **Monte Ransome Johnson**'s contribution in Chapter 4, 'Aristotle on *Kosmos* and *Kosmoi*', that we see the emergence of a wide-ranging criticism of the simple natural *kosmos*-theories advanced by Plato and his predecessors, as discussed by Horky, Macé and Schofield. As Johnson argues, while the concept of *kosmos* was central to Aristotle's predecessors and even his successors, it does not play the leading role in Aristotle's physics that it does in (say) Atomistic, Pythagorean, Platonic or Stoic physics. Aristotle may be interpreted as a transitional figure in the development of cosmology, since, as Johnson argues, his natural science prioritises other concepts over the notion of 'order', beginning with nature itself, the forms of natural bodies, and the causal factors of change and, specifically, motion. Despite the interpretation of some ancient commentators, the work *On the Heaven* does not have as its scope the entire *kosmos*; and the spurious work *On the Kosmos*, attributed to Aristotle, is the product of a Hellenistic Peripatetic trying to fill in an evident gap in Aristotle's physics: no work explicitly dedicated to the topic of *kosmos* itself. In the fragments of Aristotle's dialogue *On Philosophy* and the esoteric treatises, Aristotle primarily utilises the concept of *kosmos* in the context of refuting his predecessors' views about the generation (or creation, non-eternality) of the world, and about the plurality of worlds (*kosmoi*). For Aristotle, physical principles, which are explanatorily prior to cosmological ones, determine that the universe (*to pan*) and *kosmos* are identical; there can only be one *kosmos* and heaven (*ouranos*); and the singular *kosmos* cannot be generated or destroyed. Thus, his predecessors' theories about how *kosmoi* are created (*kosmopoieia*) and ordered (*diakosmêsis*) are rendered moot, because they do not start off from the proper physical principles, which necessitate a single eternal spherical *kosmos* with only internal structure and order. Johnson's chapter dovetails with Schofield's in seeing Aristotle as presenting a deflationary view of *diakosmêsis*. Despite this, so Johnson argues, Aristotle actually makes use of something like a plurality-of-worlds view in his own meteorological theory, which requires a strict demarcation of 'the *kosmos* around the earth' and 'the *kosmos* around the upper motion' (i.e. the heaven), worlds understood to consist of different kinds of matter and to operate according to different physical principles of motion. This can either be seen as evidence of an earlier stage in Aristotle's regimentation of natural scientific concepts, or as an adaptation of his principles to the specialised field of meteorology. Hence, for Johnson, Aristotle's employment of the concept of *kosmos* is primarily instrumental and epexegetical, and the evidence for his contributions to natural cosmology has been overemphasised by scholars, both ancient and modern.

   The volume shifts from the broader discussion of the macrocosm of the universe to the microcosms of the city and the individual that are 'well ordered' (*kosmios*) with the chapter of **George Boys-Stones**. In Chapter 5, 'Order and Orderliness: The Myth of "Inner Beauty" in Plato', Boys-Stones argues that Plato effectively pre-empts the Stoics in defining virtuous action as conformity with cosmic order. Boys-Stones notes first that scholarship has been beguiled by Alcibiades' striking analysis of Socrates in the *Symposium* as someone ugly to look at but beautiful within, and misled into thinking that Plato defines virtue as 'inner beauty', something private which only accidentally manifests itself in public benefit. As he argues, as a closer examination of Diotima's account of the lover's ascent towards beauty in the same dialogue shows, the distinction that actually interests Plato is that between the body and its activity – not the body and the soul as such. And by referencing this activity to cosmic order (as he does most clearly in *Gorgias* 507e–508a, a passage discussed extensively by Horky in Chapter 1), Plato guarantees essentially that virtue is not only publicly manifest, but of essential benefit to others as well as self – a sentiment that found expression in Plato's *Laws* as well, as Brisson contends in the next chapter. Hence, as Boys-Stones argues, the manifestation of virtue in the person who is *kosmios* is of the utmost importance to Plato's moral philosophy.

Chapter 6 sees **Luc Brisson** investigating the other main Platonic political text in which *kosmos* looms large: *Laws*. In 'Polis as *Kosmos* in Plato's *Laws*', Brisson argues that the *Laws* are more than a legislative code, and more than a work of political philosophy. In effect, they call for the realisation of a project towards which Plato's work converges, i.e. to account for the whole of reality: individual, city and world. This discourse in which the law (*nomos*) consists derives its origin from the intellect, which represents what is most akin in the soul to the divine, because it is the principle of order (*kosmos*). This order, which is manifested in the celestial bodies, must be present in man's soul, in which the intellect has to rule over pleasures and pains. Thus, according to Brisson, an order will be assured by means of the law within the city, an order based on the contemplation of the regularity and permanence of the movements of the celestial bodies, which the citizens shall imitate, even in their movements around the territory. In the *Laws*, then, Plato brings the cosmology of the Presocratics, discussed extensively by Horky, Macé and Schofield at the beginning of this volume, to its (natural) conclusion. The city, which is to bring about the birth of the whole of virtue in all the human beings who constitute it, is organised by means of a legislation that takes the functioning of the world as its model. The opposition between *nomos* and *physis* therefore disappears, because the law becomes the expression of nature.

In Chapter 7, 'Relating to the World, Encountering the Other: Plotinus on Cosmic and Human Action', **Pauliina Remes**'s discussion of Plotinus' cosmic moral psychology takes ancient philosophers' endless fascination with Homer as a point of departure for his own philosophy of action. According to Remes, in Plotinian Neoplatonism the *kosmos* is the first ideal entity that human beings can emulate in their search for god-likeness.

Unlike higher hypostases, the *kosmos* is an embodied god, involved in temporality; in it, the intelligible structures already present themselves as unfolded spatially (or materially) and in time. Its life or peculiar mode of existence is thereby closer to that of embodied human existence than that of a pure, unembodied and eternal Intellect – not to speak of the altogether indivisible One beyond being. At the same time, the *kosmos* displays perfection, harmony and completeness. This kind of unified harmony and perfection are undeniably worthy of being ideals for human life and activity, and as such regulative of ideal selfhood. Remes's chapter aims to contextualise human action within the cosmic ideal, but to also show, importantly, the limits as such an ideal. Human action is characterised already by Plato as a complex relation of affecting and being affected: of a limited thing meeting other things external to it, and either effecting a change in the thing encountered or suffering an affecting in this encounter. In an understudied passage (3.3.5.40–46), Plotinus offers a brief but telling glimpse at the challenges of human moral life. By using the example of the Trojan War, Plotinus outlines different scenarios, that is, different kinds of encounters between virtuous and vicious people. Through unravelling the Homeric example and situating it in the above Platonic framework of affecting and being affected, so Remes concludes, the passage yields an interesting opening for a theory on practical action and morality by Plotinus.

Plotinus' profound reflections upon Homer encourage us to circle back to Archaic Greece, and to investigate the meanings of the civic theories and practices related to the Greek *kosmos* and its Roman counterpart, the *mundus*. Indeed, the subsequent chapters show how notions of order reverberated throughout the Greek and Roman political and domestic worlds, especially in reference to public and private civic performance. In Chapter 8, 'Tradition and Innovation in the *Kosmos*–Polis Analogy', **Carol Atack** notes that the idea that the organisation of human community somehow reflected the organisation of the *kosmos* as a whole was commonplace in both Archaic and Classical Greek political thought and practice. But, as Atack argues, the diversity of both Greek political arrangements and interpretations of myths of cosmic origin and change complicate the analogy. The association between human and cosmic order in the Archaic age is reflected in the political terminology of historical city-states, seen in the titles of officials from the *kosmoi* of Crete to the *kosmopolis* of Epizephyrian Locri. Aristotle, in noting the limited capacities of the Cretan *kosmoi* (*Pol.* 2.10.1272b1–11), identifies the Cretan constitution as proto-political, suggesting that the '*kosmos*–polis' analogy identifies a primitive, hierarchical form of polis society. Similarly, the order of Zeus, as related in Archaic cosmological texts such as Hesiod's *Theogony*, seems to reflect stratified hierarchical societies in which individuals occupy fixed positions. In fifth-century democratic Athens, however, dramatists explored the implications of cosmic political ordering in new ways: for example, *Prometheus Bound* inverts the *kosmos*–polis analogy by describing Zeus' rule as tyranny (*PV* 324–57), whereas Aristophanes constructed an Athenian everyman whose destructive legal powers resemble those of the thunder god himself (*Wasps* 619–30). In the fourth century BCE, however, Plato reasserts the importance of a hierarchical cosmic order for politics, in describing ideal (and less-than-ideal) cities such as Atlantis (in the *Critias*) and Magnesia (in the *Laws*), but with his own cosmology from the *Timaeus* replacing the traditional versions.

In Chapter 9, 'Cosmic Choruses: Metaphor and Performance', **Renaud Gagné** pursues a chronologically wide-ranging study of how the motion of the heavenly bodies was conceptualised through the idea of choral dance. This chapter compares various unrelated, self-reflexive usages of the astral chorus metaphor in three genres of poetry, and briefly considers how the specificities of one illuminate the others. Instead of a teleological narrative, a dialogue of commonalities and contrasts is sought in the juxtaposition of comparable case studies; hence, Gagné's approach reflects a more Heraclitean approach to the ordering of phenomena, as discussed earlier and in Victoria Wohl's Afterword. For Gagné, each case of astral chorus solicited develops the contours of the series, and the series gives greater relief to the unique 'texture' of each case. This is significant thematically: the striking image of the astral chorus was, among many other things, a powerful catalyst for reflecting upon *mimesis* in action. Indeed, a vision of the cosmic order is used in all three case texts to reflect on the boundaries of poetic representation. The first text is a short epigram from the Augustan poet Marcus Argentarius (*Anth. Pal.* 9.270 = G.-P. XXVI). The second passage is the long ecphrasis of Dionysus' shield in the *Dionysica* of Nonnus of Panopolis (25.380–572), composed sometime around the fifth century CE. The third text is another shield ecphrasis, that one from the first stasimon of Euripides' *Electra* (432–86), composed sometime around 420 BCE. The readings illustrate how a key figure of cosmic harmony was revisited time and again to ponder the limits of poetic representation. Projecting itself on the *kosmos*, the idea of the choral dance could also reflect the *kosmos* back on song itself.

In Chapter 10, 'All the World's a Stage: *Contemplatio Mundi* in Roman Theatre', **Robert Germany** investigates the significance that Roman augural practice, as a kindred practice to Greek θεωρία/*theôria*, held for Roman comedy and tragedy. Central to his arguments are notions of time and space that ultimately show the broad importance of Aristotelian concepts, as investigated in Johnson's chapter, to the broader Hellenistic world. Germany argues that augury-taking involved sitting in a terrestrial temple while gazing at a specially demarcated zone of sky or as it was sometimes called a 'whole-world' (*mundus*). This temporarily legible space in which the gods would direct the signifying flight of birds was more than a celestial backdrop; it was also itself a temple (*templum caeli*) and the technical term for this temple-gazing was *contemplatio*. As Germany argues, the institution of Roman theatre has not generally been associated with practices of auspication, but because of the emphatic insistence on the temporary stage, the conventional 'Unity of Time', and the probable placement of audience seating, there was a suggestive similarity between the Middle Republican audience's spectation at tragedies and comedies and traditional augural contemplation. Most tellingly, so Germany suggests, Plautus plays up this homology, fashioning his stage as a zone of auspication for the audience, while within the play-world the characters are caught trying to predict the future of their own fictional *mundus*. The structural echo between augural and theatrical contemplation outlives the Republican temporary stage in Seneca, where it has become a distinctively Roman mode of construing the intersection of the cosmic gaze and philosophical or spectatorial θεωρία/*theôria*.

The application of Greco-Roman notions of gazing upon the various worlds, both those of the heavens and those of the earth, to architectural design motivates **Gilles Sauron**'s contribution in Chapter 11, 'The Architectural Representation of the *Kosmos* from Varro to Hadrian'. Sauron expands upon insights in Gagné's and Germany's chapters, while at the same time paying close attention to the cosmology of Plato as discussed in the contributions of Brisson and Atack, in his investigation of cosmic representation as one of the leading themes of Roman architectural decoration. As Sauron notes, while cosmic representation in the public sphere is generally well discussed in the scholarship (e.g. at the Pantheon in Rome), this phenomenon is not often examined in private spaces, despite the fact that it was of especial importance to Roman elites. His chapter addresses this topic by investigating evidence related to architecture attested in written texts and in archaeological monuments themselves which are associated with aristocratic houses or imperial palaces. Two examples of cosmic private representation, two centuries apart, are especially noteworthy for Sauron's case: the aviary that Varro had built around 80 BCE inside his villa at Casinum, and the Teatro Marittimo that the Emperor Hadrian erected in his villa at Tivoli. Additionally, he considers possible cosmic structures in the arrangement of the cave at Sperlonga, which was part of Tiberius' Praetorium, and the *Cenatio Rotunda* of Nero's Domus Aurea, to which some recently discovered monuments on the Palatine Hill have been attributed. Finally, Sauron contextualises his analysis of trends detected in these monuments with Pompeian frescos of the so-called Second Style, which illustrate the *kosmos* through impressive allegories situated in fantastic architectural structures. In all these cases, the representations of the private sphere are arranged according to the particular point of view of the person who frequents the place; and the inspiration for these decorations and arrangements appears to have come from philosophers, especially Plato, and from Greek astronomers who fascinated the Roman elite, such as Aratus, whose *Phaenomena* was translated into Latin first by Cicero, and then by Germanicus.

The final chapters in *Cosmos in Ancient Philosophy* return our gaze to the heavens and beyond, the seat of the origins of philosophical investigation. In Chapter 12, '"The Deep-Sticking Boundary Stone": Cosmology, Sublimity and Knowledge in Lucretius' *De Rerum Natura* and Seneca's *Naturales Quaestiones*', **W. H. Shearin** considers the issue of contemplating the heavenly orders as discussed by Johnson, Germany and Sauron in their contributions – but through the distinctive eyes of an Epicurean or a Stoic. As Shearin notes, Atomists generally, and the Epicurean school specifically, offer an approach to cosmology that stands in stark contrast to the main lines of the earlier ancient philosophical tradition. Dismissing the divine mind as a structuring principle, Atomists instead explain the origins of the *kosmos* (and everything in it) from the bottom up, in contradistinction to Aristotle (as formulated by Johnson). Plant life, animal life, meteorological phenomena and natural disasters are all at root products of the chance interaction of atoms and void. On the one hand, such an approach, defined as it is in opposition to earlier tradition, grants cosmological study less inherent importance. As Shearin notes, observing the *kosmos* cannot yield any more basic insight into the structure of the universe than studying motes in a sunbeam. On the other hand, there is abundant evidence for Epicurean science and more specifically for Epicurean attempts to explain meteorological phenomena. Yet this science, as Shearin's chapter explores, is rooted first and foremost in Epicurean ethics and, for Lucretius, in the didactic aims of his poem. Its intent is not a deeper understanding of the world, but rather securing calm and assuaging the anxieties of the troubled mind. More specifically, Shearin explores the intersection of Lucretius' and Seneca's natural scientific investigations with the sublime, a powerful sentiment that marks and models the viewer's response to the *kosmos*. He contends that we find subtle differences in Lucretius' and Seneca's approaches to the sublime, differences that are rooted in larger philosophical disparities with regard to knowledge in Stoic and Epicurean science. The Stoic Seneca grants great value to knowledge per se, whereas the Epicurean Lucretius views knowledge as purely instrumental to the more important aim of psychic calm. In Seneca's hands, then, the sublime is rooted in the human approach to divine omniscience, while for Lucretius, the sublime is a consequence (and reminder) of the stark limits of human knowledge.

Chapter 13, **Phillip Sidney Horky**'s 'Cosmic Spiritualism among the Pythagoreans, Stoics, Jews and Early Christians', traces how the dualism of body and soul, cosmic and human, is bridged in philosophical and religious traditions through appeal to the notion of 'breath' (πνεῦμα). Horky pursues this project by way of a genealogy of pneumatic cosmology and anthropology, covering a wide range of sources, including the Pythagoreans of the fifth century BCE (in particular, Philolaus of Croton); the Stoics of the third and second centuries BCE (especially Posidonius); the Jews writing in Hellenistic Alexandria in the first century BCE (Philo); and the Christians of the first century CE (the gospel writers and Paul). Starting from the early Pythagoreans, 'breath' and 'breathing' function to draw analogies between cosmogony and anthropogony – a notion ultimately rejected by Plato in the *Timaeus* and Aristotle in his cosmological works, but taken up by the Posidonius (perhaps following the early Stoa) and expanded into a rich and challenging corporeal metaphysics. Similarly, the Post-Hellenistic philosopher and biblical exegete Philo of Alexandria, who was deeply influenced by both Platonist and Stoic physics, approaches the cosmogony and anthropogony described in Genesis (1:1–3 and 1:7) through Platonist-Stoic philosophy, in his attempt to provide a philosophically rigorous explanation for why Moses employed certain terms or phrases when writing his book of creation. Finally, the chapter sees a determined shift in the direction of rejecting pneumatic cosmology for a revised pneumatic anthropogony in the writings of the New Testament: by appeal to the 'Holy Spirit' or 'Holy Breath' (πνεῦμα ἅγιον), early Christians effectively adapted the Stoic metaphysics of 'breath', with its notions of divine intelligence and bonding, to the prophetic and ecclesiastical project of building a Christian community conceived of as the 'body of Christ'. Hence, according to Horky, the spiritual cosmogony of the Pythagoreans, Stoics, and Philo is effectively subordinated to the spiritual anthropogony that facilitates the construction of the Christian *kosmopolis*, only fully realised in the form of New Jerusalem, the 'bride' which, in tandem with the Holy Spirit, calls to the anointed. At the end of the Christian worldview, the *kosmos* of Greek philosophy is supplanted by the pneumatic *kosmopolis*.

In the Afterword, **Victoria Wohl** synopsises and synthesises the contributions of the preceding chapters. Approaching *kosmos* as a 'distribution of the sensible' (in Jacques Rancière's phrase), she traces the way *kosmos* operates to organise reality on the level of aesthetics, politics, ethics and epistemology and to integrate these various domains into a holistic vision. The Afterword also stresses, however, the provisionality and partiality of that cosmic whole and considers the alternative visions of reality it precludes, the disorderly order that Heraclitus characterised as 'the sweeping of random things scattered' and that James Joyce terms '*chaosmos*'.

CHAPTER I

When Did Kosmos *Become the* Kosmos?

Phillip Sidney Horky

When did *kosmos* come to mean 'the *kosmos*', in the sense of finite 'world' or 'world-order'? This question fascinated historians of philosophy both in antiquity and throughout the last century, from Walther Kranz in the early 1930s to Jaap Mansfeld in the early 1970s. During that period, it was treated by many eminent scholars, most of whom, it will be of no surprise, reached divergent conclusions. Charles Kahn, adapting arguments by Reinhardt, Kranz and Gigon, believed that Anaximander was the first person whom we know to have referred to multiple *kosmoi*, in the sense of sub-orders of the world; it is thereby understood that *kosmos* seems to offer some traction to Ionian science, despite the troubling fact that there is not a single surviving reference to *kosmos* meaning 'world-order' unambiguously among the fragments of the Ionian *physikoi* until Diogenes of Apollonia (fl. after 440 BCE).[1] Geoffrey Kirk argued that prior to Empedocles, Diogenes and possibly Philolaus of Croton, various senses of 'order' are implied in the use of the term *kosmos*, but only with these mid- to late fifth-century BCE figures does the sense of 'world-order' come to be dominant.[2] Jaap Mansfeld followed Kerschensteiner in rejecting the links to Anaximander, but he also excused himself from the debate concerning who first spoke of the world-order as a *kosmos*, suggesting without further argument that 'it may have been Pythagoras or one of his early followers'.[3] With the exception of two scholars, Carl Huffman and Aryeh Finkelberg, nobody to my knowledge since Mansfeld in the early 1970s has developed a detailed analysis of this fascinating question.[4] Huffman has cautiously

---

[1] Cf. Kahn 1960: 219–30.

[2] Cf. Kirk 1962: 311–16. On Parmenides, see Furley 1987: 49–60 and Arnaud Macé's contribution to this volume (Chapter 2).

[3] Mansfeld 1971: 42–45.

[4] See Finkelberg 1998 and Huffman 1993: 97–99; Graham (2006: 26) avers discussing this problem extensively, instead claiming 'it is a fact that from Anaximander on, philosophers were attempting to explain the *kosmos*, whether they had a word for the world or not'. In my opinion, this is a potentially

suggested that Heraclitus' use of the term 'seems to mark the transition' to the sense of 'ordered whole' but that it is with Empedocles that we get the meaning 'world', and with Philolaus the meaning becomes 'world-order';[5] alternatively, Finkelberg argues that the '*kosmos*'-fragments of Philolaus are likely to be a post-Platonic forgery, and that it is with the later Platonic dialogues, especially *Timaeus, Statesman* and *Philebus*, that the word *kosmos* first comes to mean 'world-order'.[6]

So at one end, we have Charles Kahn's influential argument – still accepted by some scholars today[7] – that it is with Anaximander, at the fountainhead of Milesian scientific inquiry sometime in the mid sixth century BCE, that we have the first use of the term *kosmos* to refer to a 'world-order', or, to be more precise, multiple 'world-orders' (*kosmoi*); and at the other end, we have Aryeh Finkelberg, who believes that such a distinction should be associated in the first with the dialogues Plato penned in his advanced age, in the 360s–50s BCE. Two hundred years of philosophical history separate these two possible termini. Clearly, then, a debate is still to be had. In this chapter, I would like to make my own contribution by focusing on an aspect of the question that has tended to fall by the wayside, generally speaking, namely the evidence to be found in the doxography concerning the term *kosmos* and its meanings. One might dismiss doxographical reports that relate to the topic of the origins of the concept of the *kosmos* on the grounds that they are simply 'late', or Platonising or coloured by Peripatetic or Stoic modes of classification. Such a dismissal of the doxography, in my opinion, would be born out of a hyper-scepticism concerning the reliability of the doxographical traditions or of a distrust of the programmatic intentions of the authors who sought to provide classifications of the ideas they found associated with major philosophers who came before.[8] Scholarship since the early 1990s has sought to obtain a more nuanced approach to the study of doxography, and the study of Aristotle and other early historians of philosophy and science within the Lyceum, such as Theophrastus, Eudemus and Aristoxenus, has seen significant advances in the past twenty years with the advent of new critical

---

confusing claim, especially given the fact that it does not differentiate between the '*kosmos*' and any other type of universal construct, whether finite or infinite (cf. Furley 1989: 2). Other scholars are less incautious: see, for example, Wright (2008: 413), who, in my view, correctly identifies the proper object of study and explanation among the earliest Milesians as 'all things' (πάντα), 'the all' (τὸ πᾶν) or 'the whole thing' (τὸ ὅλον). Also cf. Hussey 1995: 530–1.

[5] Huffman 1993: 97–98.   [6] Finkelberg 1998: 127–28 with n. 92.
[7] Including Schofield, in his contribution to this volume (Chapter 3).
[8] See, for example, Kerferd's review of Kerschensteiner's book (1964: 183).

editions, commentaries and discussions.[9] Moreover, especially within the past decade, the field has seen a similar growth in study of the relevant areas of Platonic philosophy and Pythagoreanism, with scholars seeking to revive the critical discussion of what to us seem to be relatively obscure figures whose imprint upon the traditions of Platonic and Pythagorean thought bears the signs of sophistication and intellectual value.[10] Given the state of the history of philosophy today, it would be uncharitable at best, and out of touch at worst, to consign later doxographical reports to the dusty shelves of mere antiquarianism.

Now the most decisive report from antiquity which expressly associates the first use of the term *kosmos* with some sort of order within the universe comes from the sceptic philosopher Favorinus of Arles, a rough contemporary of Plutarch who was also critiqued by Galen; hence his activities can be dated to the late first or early second century CE.[11] In a work titled *History of All Sorts*, he appears to have devoted at least one book (Book 8) to heurematography, that is, to the recording of 'first discoveries' in philosophy and science:[12]

> Favorinus says that he [sc. Pythagoras] (was the first) to employ definitions in the subject of mathematics; and Socrates and his disciples extended this, and afterwards Aristotle and the Stoics; moreover, he [sc. Pythagoras] was the first to call the heavens '*kosmos*' [τὸν οὐρανὸν πρῶτον ὀνομάσαι κόσμον], and the earth round; according to Theophrastus, however, it was Parmenides; and according to Zeno[13], it was Hesiod. (Favorinus Fragment 99 Amato = Diogenes Laertius 8.48)

This testimony has received very little commentary, and its content is almost universally rejected.[14] But I think it deserves a closer look. When scholars tend to cite this fragment of Favorinus, they unfortunately tend to leave out the first portion, which actually bridges the section of relevance for our study, namely the claim that Pythagoras 'was the first to call the heavens "*kosmos*"', with other useful information concerning Pythagoras' proposed intellectual activities. Pythagoras is there credited with being an

---

[9] See, inter alia, Mansfeld and Runia's three volumes devoted to Aëtiana (1997–2010) and Zhmud 2013 (for an alternative perspective).
[10] See Palmer 2014; Horky 2013; and Bonazzi, Lévy and Steel 2007.
[11] For Favorinus' Academic Scepticism, see Ioppolo 1993.   [12] Cf. Zhmud 2006: 176 n. 39.
[13] We do not know for sure who this Zeno is, but one possibility is Zeno of Citium.
[14] As it is, for example, by Macé in Chapter 2. One exception has been Kerferd (1964: 183). It is likely that the references at the end of Theophrastus and Zeno are focused on who was first to refer to the earth as round and not to the concerns over who first used *kosmos* to refer to 'heavens'. Favorinus appears to be arranging the positions dialectically.

innovator in the use of definitions in mathematics, followed interestingly by Socrates and the Socratics, and then Aristotle and the Stoics. So Favorinus' doxographical source, whoever it was, appears to have established a philosophical lineage from Pythagoras to the Stoics based on the use of definitions in mathematics; and somewhere (perhaps nearby in his source?), Favorinus found Pythagoras being credited with 'first discoverer' (*prôtos heuretês*) of the use of the term *kosmos* to refer to the heavens.[15] Are these two aspects connected? We have evidence from other works that Favorinus devoted some energy to the history of mathematics: he appears to have claimed that Plato was the discoverer of the method of analysis in mathematics and that he was an innovator in the development of mathematical terminology.[16]

With the focus on Pythagoras' innovations in mathematics and cosmology, Favorinus reflects what seem to have been commonplaces by, at the latest, the beginning of the second century CE, especially in doxographical accounts that show themselves to be under the influence of Stoic, Middle Platonist and Neo-Pythagorean conventions. It is also the case in other, roughly contemporary and earlier reports of Middle Platonists that testify to Pythagoras' innovations in mathematics and cosmology.[17] For example, there is the account from the anonymous *Life of Pythagoras*, likely composed in the first century BCE (perhaps by Eudorus of Alexandria, or someone in his philosophical circle there), which features explanation through etymologisation, a familiar trope from Stoic and later Neopythagorean philosophy: 'Pythagoras was the first to call the heavens "*kosmos*", because it is perfect and adorned with all the living beings [stars?] and the fineries [πρῶτος Πυθαγόρας τὸν οὐρανὸν κόσμον προσηγόρευσε διὰ τὸ τέλειον εἶναι καὶ πᾶσι κεκοσμῆσθαι τοῖς τε ζῴοις καὶ τοῖς καλοῖς]'.[18] Given the complexities that attend Hellenistic and Post-Hellenistic Pythagorean doxography, it is difficult to know with confidence what Favorinus' immediate sources might have been; but it is important to note that his information differs quite substantially from, for example, that employed by another sceptic

---

[15] On Favorinus' preservation of information that ultimately appears to trace back via Eratosthenes to Eudemus of Rhodes, see Zhmud 2006: 176 and 249.

[16] Diog. Laert. 3.24 = Favorinus Fr. 62 Amato. Favorinus also suggested that Anaximander had invented the gnomon and set it up in Sparta in order to indicate solstices and equinoxes. For discussion of the scientific plausibility of this statement, see Evans 1998: 56.

[17] Discoveries of the mathematical means in particular are attributed to Pythagoras by Nicomachus (*Ar.* 2.28), and it became a commonplace to associate the discovery of 'Pythagoras' theorem' with Pythagoras by the first century BCE (on which, see Zhmud 2012: 267).

[18] Anon. Phot. *Bibl.* Cod. 249.440a 27–29 = Thesleff p. 240.3–5.

(of a more distinctly Pyrrhonian variety), Sextus Empiricus, when he sought to describe 'Pythagorean' arithmetic.[19] The attribution of specific scientific discoveries in mathematics to Pythagoras, to be sure, antedates the Post-Hellenistic period, as it has its origins in the writings of Aristotle, the Early Peripatetics and the Early Academy in the fourth century BCE.[20] For example, Aristotle argued that the Pythagoreans were the first philosophers to employ crude definitions, followed by Socrates, who also employed definitions in ethics (Arist. *Metaph*. 1.5.987a13–27; cf. Arist. Fr. 203 Rose³);[21] and Aristotle more explicitly associated Pythagoras himself with definition (of some sort) as well as observation of the heavens as a θεωρὸς τῆς φύσεως in his lost, but very influential and well-distributed, dialogue *Protrepticus*.[22] Similarly, Aristotle's junior associate Aristoxenus claimed that Pythagoras invented weights and measures, identified the Evening and Morning Stars with Venus (Fr. 24 Wehrli) and advanced the subject of mathematics, which had originally been discovered by the Egyptian god Thoth (Fr. 23 Wehrli).[23] Aristotle's contemporary Heraclides of Pontus, who was in antiquity associated with both the Academy and the Lyceum, portrayed Pythagoras in a dialogue as the *prôtos heuretês* of the actual term *philosophy* (*philosophia*), which Heraclides himself also seems to have associated with an Aristotelian notion of theoretical or first philosophy;[24] Xenocrates, the second successor in the Academy to Plato who was a direct competitor of Aristotle, attributed the discovery of harmonic intervals to Pythagoras;[25] and Aëtius, whose chief source concerning first discoveries may have been Aristotle's successor Theophrastus, claimed that 'Pythagoras was the first to call the enclosure of totality [τὴν τῶν ὅλων περιοχὴν] "*kosmos*" because of its inherent arrangement'.[26]

---

[19] Sext. Emp. *Math*. 4.2. In the first century BCE, Alexander Polyhistor also claimed (*ap*. Diog. Laert. 8.25) that the four elements 'change and turn into each other completely, and what is generated from them is a *kosmos*, ensouled, intelligent, spherical, which holds the earth as its centre – the earth too being spherical and inhabited in the round'. This is a far cry from Favorinus' position. Ju (2013: 113–16) has suggested that Poseidonius might be the source behind Sextus' analysis of Pythagorean dogmatism, but see the hesitation of Brennan 2015.

[20] Generally, see Zhmud 2006: Chapter 6, although I do not agree with all of his conclusions.

[21] On Pythagorean definition, see Horky 2013: 29–30.

[22] Arist. *Protr*. B 16 and B 18 Düring. Cf. Horky 2013: 52. On the later history of *contemplatio mundi*, see especially Germany's contribution to this volume (Chapter 10).

[23] On this subject, see Horky 2013: 45–46 and Zhmud 2006: 224–27.

[24] Generally, see Dillon 2014: 257–60.   [25] Fr. 87 Isnardi Parente = Porph. *In Ptol. Harm*. 30.1.

[26] Aët. 2.1.1 (Diels, *Dox. Graec*. 327). Contrast the report of Achilles (ad loc.) which claims that Pythagoras 'referred to the universe as "*kosmos*" because of *diakosmêsis*; nobody prior to him did

In this way, then, the account of Favorinus concerning Pythagoras' innovations, especially in referring to the heavens as the *kosmos*, appears to be of a piece with earlier heurematographical accounts of Pythagoreanism from the middle of the fourth century BCE. Hence, we would be in danger of oversimplifying, and perhaps be simply mistaken, if we were to say of Favorinus' account that it has 'no historical value' whatsoever.[27] Of historical value to whom, and when? Favorinus is participating in a heurematographical tradition that associates 'discoveries' in mathematics and astronomy to Pythagoras which traces back at least to Aristotle and the Early Academy.[28] In fact, this raises the possibility that Favorinus' heurematographical account, like those accounts of the anonymous first-century BCE author of the *Life of Pythagoras* preserved by Photius and of Aëtius, is reacting (in some way – perhaps dialectically, as Sextus did) to earlier doxographical statements concerning the cosmological or ouranological use of the term *kosmos*.

We can only speculate about what the sophists, such as Hippias of Elis, said about Pythagoras or what role they played in the development of the doxography concerning cosmology. Both Xenophon and Plato, writing in the first half of the fourth century BCE, lay the groundwork for a later aporia over who, in particular, was first in using the term *kosmos* to refer to the ordered universe. The account of Xenophon explicitly pits Socratic philosophy against speculation in natural science and by appeal to the peculiarity of the latter's inquiry into the '*kosmos*':

> But no one ever heard or saw Socrates say or do anything profane or impious. For he didn't even discuss the nature of all things after the manner of most of the others, that is, by inquiring into how the '*kosmos*', as it is called by the professors, is, and by what laws each of the heavenly objects came into existence [περὶ τῆς τῶν πάντων φύσεως ᾗπερ τῶν ἄλλων οἱ πλεῖστοι διελέγετο, σκοπῶν ὅπως ὁ καλούμενος ὑπὸ τῶν σοφιστῶν κόσμος ἔφυ καὶ τίσιν ἀνάγκαις ἕκαστα γίγνεται τῶν οὐρανίων]; instead, he demonstrated how those who pondered such subjects were engaged in sheer folly. In the first place, he would inquire regarding them whether they really thought that they had sufficient enough knowledge of human affairs to proceed onto speculation concerning these topics, or whether they believed

---

this'. This interpretation can hardly be right, since *diakosmēsis* is not obviously relevant to early Pythagoreanism (see Schofield's contribution in this volume [Chapter 3]).

[27] Kahn 1960: 219 n. 1.

[28] Aristotle too (*Metaph.* 14.3.1091a13–26), in his discussion of Platonist and Pythagorean mathematics, explicitly associates Pythagorean 'making of the *kosmos*' (κοσμοποιία) with natural philosophy: '[the Pythagoreans] are making the world and intend to speak in terms of nature' (κοσμοποιοῦσι καὶ φυσικῶς βούλονται λέγειν). On Aristotle's view of Pythagorean κοσμοποιία, see Horky 2013: 80–82.

that they were doing their duty by ignoring human affairs and investigating divine ones. (Xenophon, *Memorabilia* 1.1.11–12)

Here, Xenophon contrasts the investigative activities of the 'professors' (οἱ σοφισταί), whose approach to natural science focuses on the way in which the '*kosmos*' came into existence and the laws in accordance with which the heavenly bodies were generated, with Socrates' ethics. Xenophon emphatically marks the term *kosmos* as 'called by' (καλούμενος) the professors, thus differentiating their investigative approach to cosmology from a *more general* (τῶν ἄλλων οἱ πλεῖστοι) investigative approach to the nature of the universe, or, as he puts it, 'the nature of all things' (ἡ τῶν πάντων φύσις). Xenophon himself does not explicitly tell us who these 'professors' are. Just after this passage (*Mem.* 1.1.14), Xenophon differentiates, from among those who investigate the nature of the universe, the monists, who believe that there is 'only one Being', that 'nothing is ever put into motion' and 'nothing is ever generated or corrupted', from pluralists, who ascribe to nature 'an infinity, the many', as well as the notions that 'all things are constantly in motion' and 'all things are generated and corrupted'. There is a clear differentiation being drawn between two types of philosopher who commit to diverse metaphysical positions, and the information appears to have had doxographical value.[29] The later explicit appearance of the name 'Anaxagoras' in the context of the sort of astronomy Socrates rejects (*Mem.* 4.7.6) might suggest the natural scientist from Clazomenae, and the obvious comparison with the famous passage of Plato's *Phaedo* (96a ff.) might also recommend Anaximenes, Alcmaeon and Diogenes of Apollonia, as well as Philolaus and Empedocles.[30] Indeed, as I've argued elsewhere, the mathematical Pythagoreans Philolaus and Empedocles are likely to be in Plato's crosshairs when he criticises those who engage in what Socrates calls περὶ φύσεως ἱστορία in the *Phaedo*.[31] Generally, then, we might admit a plethora of possible intellectuals, and it seems unlikely that Xenophon would be interested in the question we're interested in, namely who, precisely, these 'professors' are who commit to using the term *kosmos* and investigate the natural laws that brought it into existence.

---

[29] Palmer (2009: 532) sees a possible reference to Gorgias' dialectical activities (cf. DK 82 B 1; Arist. [*MXG*] 979a13–18). It is likely that the sophists, indeed, were the first doxographers (cf. Hippias DK 86 B 6).

[30] Cf. Huffman 1993: 318.

[31] Horky 2013: 175–76 and 194. On Socrates' rejection of this activity, see Mansfeld 1990: 64–65. It may be worth noting that the earliest testimony we have concerning the intellectual activities of Pythagoras, that of Heraclitus B 129, associates his *historia* with his peculiar brand of *sophia*, although precisely what this activity called *historia* constituted remains the subject of scholarly debate. See Horky 2013: 209–10 and Huffman 2008.

An article by Aryeh Finkelberg (1998) has provocatively argued that those 'professors' who speak about the *kosmos* are, specifically, Plato and his associates in the Academy. He bases this positive claim on several arguments. First, he argues that uses of the term *kosmos* to refer to 'world' or 'world-order' in Plato's dialogues occur only in the late works, *Timaeus, Statesman* and *Philebus*.[32] Earlier usages in *Gorgias* and *Phaedrus*, he contends, refer to 'heaven' rather than to a 'world' that is structured according to some rules or principles.[33] Second, he suggests that the *Memorabilia* 'cannot be earlier, or at least much earlier', than the *Timaeus*, which, in his estimation, was the first dialogue to use the term *kosmos* to mean 'world' or 'world-order' unambiguously.[34] Third, he notes – and I do think this is an important point – that Plato seems to highlight the terminological invention in the *Timaeus* (28b), through marked elaboration upon the more common word for 'heaven', οὐρανός, as well as in *Philebus* (29e), where Socrates speaks of 'that very thing which we call "*kosmos*"' (περὶ τοῦδε ὃν κόσμον λέγομεν).[35] Hence, so the argument goes, Plato exhibits propriety over the term and its particular usage.

Now Finkelberg's three arguments vary in terms of quality and all are problematic. The first argument is speculative and depends a lot on dating of the works of Plato, a notoriously difficult project. If, however, we accept the notion that the earlier dialogues (it's not at all self-evident that *Phaedrus* is earlier than *Timaeus* or *Statesman*, I should note) all assume that *kosmos* means 'heaven', then his first argument is weakened if, and when, we find an example that bucks the trend. The second is equally speculative, and more problematic, because it depends on the first argument: nobody, to my mind, has been able to prove that Xenophon's *Memorabilia* is earlier, later or contemporary with any dialogue of Plato; we simply cannot know. Finally, the argument that Plato shows proprietary usage over the term *kosmos* to refer to 'world-order' is worth testing by reference to one of Plato's 'early' dialogues (that much is agreed by most scholars), discussed extensively by many scholars both ancient and modern, in which Socrates expressly associates use of the term *kosmos* with 'wise' people *other* than himself:

> Yes, Callicles, the wise men claim that partnership [κοινωνία], friendship and orderliness, temperance and justice [φιλία καὶ κοσμιότης καὶ σωφροσύνη καὶ δικαιότης], hold together heaven and earth, and gods and men, and that is why they call the totality a '*kosmos*', my friend, and not

---

[32] Finkelberg 1998: 127. [33] Finkelberg 1998: 127. [34] Finkelberg 1998: 129.
[35] Finkelberg 1998: 127–30.

a 'un-*kosmos*', nor even 'intemperance' [καὶ τὸ ὅλον τοῦτο διὰ ταῦτα κόσμον καλοῦσιν, ὦ ἑταῖρε, οὐκ ἀκοσμίαν οὐδὲ ἀκολασίαν]. I believe that you don't pay attention to these facts, even though you're a wise man in these matters. You've failed to notice that the geometrical equality has great power among both gods and men, and you suppose that you ought to practice getting the greater share. That's because you neglect geometry. (Plato, *Gorgias* 507e6–508a8)

Two things leap out of this remarkable passage. First, it is pretty clear that Socrates is *not* avowing proprietary use of the term *kosmos* but rather is using it within a broader explanation of why 'partnership' (κοινωνία), which is glossed as 'friendship and orderliness, temperance and justice' (φιλία καὶ κοσμιότης καὶ σωφροσύνη καὶ δικαιότης), binds the representative aspects of the divine and the mortal, i.e. the divine and mortal regions (heaven and earth), and the divine and mortal occupants of those regions (gods and men).[36] Second, in order to explain to Callicles why he fails to understand what the 'wise men' say, namely that the right partnership between heaven and earth, gods and men, is a 'world-order' and not its opposite, Socrates appeals, perhaps surprisingly, to mathematics. Specifically, he refers to the 'geometrical equality' (ἡ ἰσότης ἡ γεωμετρική), which is said to hold powerful sway (μέγα δύναται)[37] over both gods and men; from this perspective, the geometric proportion is to be considered something like the means by which gods and men achieve the partnership (κοινωνία) they hold. The geometric proportion, as cited here, has been thought to be the equivalent to what the Athenian Stranger in Plato's *Laws* (757b–c) calls the 'judgment of Zeus' (Διὸς κρίσις), the proportion that 'distributes more to the greater and a smaller amount to the lesser' and is the principle of distributive justice in the fourth century BCE.[38]

---

[36] Finkelberg (1998: 126) misconstrues the Greek by claiming that the rendering of κόσμος as 'world' or 'world-order' raises some problems. First, κόσμος is contrasted with ἀκολασία, but 'world' can hardly be the opposite of 'intemperance'. To be sure, κόσμος is explicitly contrasted with ἀκοσμία, then elaborated (οὐδὲ) to refer to ἀκολασία by Socrates in the context of his discussion with Callicles, the determined adherent to *pleonexia*. This is unsurprising as a Socratic dialectical appropriation. The contrasting of opposite elements through κόσμος and ἀκοσμία is not an invention of Plato: it is attested in other contemporary philosophical contexts, before (e.g. Gorg. *Hel.* 1 and *Pal.* 30) and after Plato (e.g. Arist. Fr. 17 Rose³).

[37] Is this a jab at Gorgias, who claimed (*Hel.* 8–9) that he could prove that 'speech is a great dynast, who achieves the most divine effects by employing the smallest and most invisible body' (λόγος δυνάστης μέγας ἐστίν, ὃς σμικρωτάτῳ σώματι καὶ ἀφανεστάτῳ θειότατα ἔργα ἀποτελεῖ)? On the psychological power of Gorgias' *logos*, see Horky 2006: 375–79.

[38] Dodds 1959: 339, who cites Isocrates (*Areop.* 21) and Aristotle (*Eth. Nic.* 5.3.1131b13 and *Pol.* 5.1.1301b39). Burkert (1972: 78 n. 156) has argued, by contrast, that Plato must refer to something more general, something like the 'power of mathematics that governs the world' (citing ps-Aristotle's *Problemata* 16.9

To whom, then, is Socrates referring when he describes the saying of the 'wise men'? Many scholars have followed Dodds in assuming that the Pythagoreans are intended referents.[39] Dodds gained his insight from the Scholiast to Plato's *Gorgias* (Proclus?), who said of these 'wise men', 'he is speaking of wise Pythagoreans here, especially Empedocles, who declared that friendship unifies the sphere, and that it is the unifier [σοφοὺς ἐνταῦθα τοὺς Πυθαγορίους φησί, καὶ διαφερόντως τὸν Ἐμπεδοκλέα, φάσκοντα τὴν φιλίαν ἐνοῦν τὸν σφαῖρον, ἐνοποιὸν εἶναι]'.[40] I will turn to consider Empedocles below, but let us begin by examining the surviving fragments of the early Pythagoreans, in order to test Dodds's hypothesis. Carl Huffman has argued that Plato has Archytas of Tarentum in mind when he refers to the 'geometrical equality' (but also others), and Fragment 3 of Archytas holds special relevance to our discussion:[41]

> Once calculation was discovered, it put a stop to discord and increased concord. For there is no 'wanting more than one's share' [πλεονεξία τε γὰρ οὐκ ἔστι], and equality exists, once this [sc. calculation] has come into being. For by means of it [sc. calculation] we will seek reconciliation in our dealings with one another. Through this, then, the poor receive from the powerful, and the wealthy give to the needy, both in the confidence that they will have what is far on account of this [sc. calculation]. (Archytas of Tarentum DK 47 B 3 = Stobaeus 4.1.139, pp. 88.13–89.3 Hense)[42]

It is true that a loose relationship obtains between Plato's account and Archytas' B 3, but there are at least three problems with determining too strong an association. First, Archytas does not expressly refer to the entity which eradicates *pleonexia* and promotes concord among the various groups as the 'geometrical equality' but rather calls that entity 'calculation' (λογισμός), which might be thought *to produce* a type of equality but *is not itself* an equality. Second, Archytas does not in his political thought describe 'calculation' as bringing gods and men together, but instead he refers to the wealthy and the poor. Indeed, references to divinity are notably absent in Archytas' fragments, with the exception of one testimonium from Aristoxenus' *Life of Archytas* which might be thought to reflect

[= DK 47 A 23a] as comparandum). But see Huffman's reassessment of this testimonium, in which he ingeniously argues that the 'proportion of the equal' which is ascribed to Archytas must refer to the arithmetical proportion (Huffman 2005: 529–40).

[39] Dodds 1959: 338–39. See Finkelberg 1998: 126 n. 87.

[40] Schol. *ap. Grg.* 507e. Dodds also quotes Sextus Empiricus (*Math.* 9.127) and Iamblichus (*VP* 237) as evidence that κοινωνία was a key Pythagorean term.

[41] Huffman 2002: 268–69 and 2005: 210.

[42] I refer to Diels–Kranz numeration, but the reader should consult Huffman's authoritative 2005 edition of Archytas' fragments.

the ideas of Archytas in a debate against the 'voluptuary' Polyarchus (A 9), in which Archytas may have said that the law-givers of old deified Temperance (Σωφροσύνη), Self-Control ('Εγκράτεια) and Justice (Δίκη) and erected altars to them. Unfortunately, the content of that testimonium is in negative relief, since we are learning the voluptuary Polyarchus' arguments against Archytas' moral philosophy; in the absence of other direct testimony, Archytas' specific positive arguments for ethical modera- tion here remain undisclosed. Finally, and most importantly, the surviving fragments and testimonia of Archytas make no reference to *kosmos* at all; in fact, the only reference to Archytas' cosmology comes in a questionable testimonium from ps.-Plutarch's *On Music* (A 19 c), in which the author associates Archytas' cosmological theories of motion according to harmony not only with those of Pythagoras but also with those of Plato and 'the rest of the ancient philosophers'. This can hardly be accepted as reliable evidence for Archytas' cosmology.

Other natural scientists associated with early Pythagoreanism, such as Hippasus, Ecphantus and Alcmaeon, might recommend themselves as the referents for the 'wise men' in the account of Plato, but the scarcity of evidence makes it impossible to evaluate this proposition.[43] There is of course one exception, Philolaus of Croton (DK 44), who unques- tionably uses '*kosmos*' to refer to contraries arranged in an order in a number of fragments.[44] Philolaus is familiar to most scholars as the absent teacher of Simmias and Cebes in Plato's *Phaedo*. In the fragments of Philolaus, we see something more similar to the κοινωνία between oppositional described by Socrates in the *Gorgias*. In Fragments B 1 and 6, this '*kosmos*' is forged from the fitting together of the oppositional principles, the limiters and unlimiteds, which are understood to come into relation with one another through the supervenience of

---

[43] Hippasus is associated by various later authors with cosmological theorisation (DK 18 Frs. 1, 11), but this association cannot be traced back any earlier than the Early Academy (cf. Horky 2013: Chapter 2). Hippon is said by Hippolytus (*Haer.* 1.16 = DK 38 B 3) to have believed that fire, subsequent to its being generated by water, 'subdued' (κατανικῆσαι) water's power and constituted the κόσμος. Alcmaeon of Croton theorised about the divinity of the 'whole of heaven' (in Aristotle's words (*De an.* 1.2.405b1 = DK 35 A 12): τὸν οὐρανὸν ὅλον), but there is no specific reference to *kosmos* anywhere else in his fragments or testimonia. Again, according to Hippolytus (*Haer.* 1.15 = DK 51 Fr. 1), the later Pythagorean Ecphantus posited that the *kosmos* is the 'shape' of the divine power (τὸν κόσμον εἶναι ἰδέαν [θείας δυνάμεως]), which he referred to as 'mind and soul', and which generates spherical form. He was probably adapting Democritus' physics (e.g. DK 68 A 101 and 106). On Ecphantus, see Zhmud 2012: 107.

[44] The word *kosmos* occurs six times in the surviving fragments of Philolaus (twice in B 1, once in B 2, twice in B 6 and once in B 17). Finkelberg's rejection of the authenticity of Philolaus' fragments (1998: 128 n. 92) does nothing to address the specific arguments of Burkert or Huffman, whose claims he dismisses unreasonably.

harmony.[45] As Huffman has noted, *kosmos* in the fragments of Philolaus ranges in meaning from 'world' (B 1 and B 2), 'organised system' (B 1, B 2, and B 6) or simply 'order' (B 6), and to 'whole world' (B 17), if we accept B 17 fragment as authentic (and I have some doubts about this).[46] What is clearly missing in Philolaus' fragments, however, is the particular focus on the establishment of an actual *partnership* (κοινωνία) between the divine and the human aspects of the *kosmos*, which is explicit in Plato, and is implicit in the account of Xenophon.[47] Indeed, it is Socrates' extension of the notion of the *kosmos* to 'partnership' that is peculiar in Plato's account and warrants further analysis.

We will recall that Socrates raises the notion of the '*kosmos*' with Callicles in order to lay stress on the importance of the κοινωνία, a word that has significance not only for Plato's political philosophy, but also for his metaphysics.[48] The concept of 'community/communion' (κοινωνία) takes us back to Pythagoras and the Pythagoreans, once again. It is a key notion in Aristotle's criticisms of Pythagorean soul–body relationships in *On the Soul* (1.3.407b13-24 = DK 58 B 39), especially in their ill-expressed notion of how transmigration of the soul works.[49] Much later in the Pythagorean tradition, Iamblichus, who is probably deriving his

---

[45] I refer to Diels–Kranz numeration, but the reader should consult Huffman's 1993 edition of Philolaus' fragments. On the supervenience of harmony on the limiters and unlimiteds, see Horky 2013: 144–46.

[46] Huffman 1993: 97–98. As Huffman admits (1993: 215–19), several scholars (e.g. Mansfeld 1971: 62–63) have opted against authenticity for this fragment on various grounds, including the important fact that the diction is Ionic rather than Doric, and similarity to Plato's *Timaeus* (62c). I am doubtful that the two fragments preserved under the title *Bacchae* (B 17 and B 18, considered genuine by Huffman, and B 19, considered spurious by Huffman) are authentic.

[47] Xenophon claims that the 'professors' failed to understand the human aspects before rushing into discuss the divine ones in their inquiry into natural science. A similar charge is levelled against the Pythagoreans by Aristotle, whose focus on mathematical objects compels them to ignore empirical facts (*Metaph.* 1.5.985b23–986a21). See Horky 2013: 22–24. In B 6, Philolaus is clear about differentiating divine and human knowledge.

[48] A point often overlooked by some scholars who wish to see the 'political' as chief in Plato's mind here (e.g. Kerschensteiner 1962: 223–24 and Finkelberg 1998: 126 n. 87). The most explicit use of *koinein* and related words in metaphysics occurs in Plato's *Sophist*, when the Eleatic Stranger enumerates the 'greatest kinds' of the Forms (starting from 254b; also cf. Pl. *Soph.* 250b, 256b, 257a, etc.).

[49] Aristotle there says: 'A further absurdity occurs both in this argument and in the majority of arguments concerning the soul: for people attach the soul to a body and place it in a body, without specifying through what cause and how the body is so. And yet someone would think that this is necessary: for it is *through communion* (διὰ κοινωνίαν) that one acts and the other is acted upon, that one is moved and the other moves, but neither of these exists relative to the other in chance occurrences. But they only attempt to explain what sort of thing is the soul, whereas concerning the body that is to receive it, they do not specify anything further, as if it were to be possible, as in the Pythagorean myths, for any chance soul to be clothed in any chance body; for each [body] seems to have a peculiar form and shape.'

information from Nicomachus via Porphyry, describes the 'partnership' (μετοχή) that obtains between all living beings, with special reference to humans and non-human animals:

> And he [sc. Pythagoras] ordered law-givers of communities to abstain from living beings; for since they wished to act completely in justice, it was necessary, surely, not to injure kindred animals, since how could they persuade others to behave justly if they themselves be caught in the pursuit of a greater share [ἐπεὶ πῶς ἂν ἔπεισαν δίκαια πράττειν τοὺς ἄλλους αὐτοὶ ἁλισκόμενοι ἐν πλεονεξίᾳ]? The partnership among living beings is congenital [συγγενικὴ ἡ τῶν ζῴων μετοχή], since, through the communion of life and the same elements and the mixture arising from these [διὰ τὴν τῆς ζωῆς καὶ τῶν στοιχείων τῶν αὐτῶν κοινωνίαν καὶ τῆς ἀπὸ τούτων συνισταμένης συγκράσεως], they are yoked together with us by brotherhood [ὡσανεὶ ἀδελφότητι], as it were. (Iamblichus, *On the Pythagorean Life* 108)

We see the elements of Socrates' speech in the *Gorgias* being adapted to a debate concerning doing injustice towards other animals, in particular, with regard to sacrificing and eating them. Humans are considered 'kindred' to other animals (τῶν συγγενῶν ζῴων), and it is this kinship that provides the justification for not doing them harm.[50] The 'congenital partnership' (συγγενικὴ ἡ μετοχή) between all living beings, which arises out of the 'communion' (κοινωνία) of life and elements in the universal mixture (σύγκρασις), is elicited in order to show us that *pleonexia* is contrary to justice and just behaviour. The law-givers, if they are to act justly, must therefore abstain from eating other animals, which would constitute a type of *pleonexia* (a 'wanting beyond one's share'). We have seen above that Archytas explicitly criticises *pleonexia* and encourages unity within the polity by way of distribution according to what he calls 'calculation'; and it is possible that, in his debate with Polyarchus as preserved by Aristoxenus, he expressly discussed the positive benefits of the 'law-givers' to society, in particular, through deification of Temperance, Self-Control and Justice. But Archytas focused explicitly on the eradication of stasis within the polis, and among its constituents; there is no evidence that he was more broadly concerned with the 'cosmic' society that comprises, for example, divine and human, or living beings regardless of their status within the *scala naturae*.[51] Moreover, there is no evidence of Archytas

---

[50] Compare Porph. *VP* 19, probably following Dicaearchus (Fr. 41a Mirhady).

[51] This is all the more surprising, given Aristoxenus' explicit ascription to the Pythagoreans a definite axiological *scala naturae* in the *Pythagorean Precepts* (Frs. 33 and 34 Wehrli), with 'divine' (τὸ θεῖον) over and above all other things. See Horky 2013: 42–48.

recommending abstention from eating animals, or even of espousing theories of metempsychosis, as described by Aristotle. If Archytas was indeed a Pythagorean, and if he was developing his own philosophical approaches to the problems of equity and fairness, he seems not to have concerned himself with anything beyond the immediate political environment.[52] Iamblichus' information concerning the Pythagorean 'congenital partnership' of animals is suggestive, but it cannot be considered definitive for our study of the early usages of *kosmos*: since it is impossible from a historiographical perspective to evaluate the material concerning Pythagoras' purported discussion of κοινωνία, we might wish to press more on Plato's playful reference to the 'wise men's' co-implication of '*kosmos*' and 'partnership' – but with Iamblichus' information as a possible heuristic tool.

If we return for a moment to the Scholiast's gloss on the 'wise men' of *Gorgias* 507e–508a, however, we will see that the Scholiast's source (Proclus?) refers to the 'wise' Pythagoreans, and then goes on to describe Empedocles, 'who declared that friendship unifies the sphere, and that it is the unifier [σοφοὺς ἐνταῦθα τοὺς Πυθαγορίους φησί, καὶ διαφερόντως τὸν Ἐμπεδοκλέα, φάσκοντα τὴν φιλίαν ἑνοῦν τὸν σφαῖρον, ἑνοποιὸν εἶναι]'. The Scholiast's source seems to focus on the 'friendship' attribute (φιλία) of the 'community/communion' that he found in the text of Plato, which might explain why he was reminded of Empedocles at all. But, I think, this cannot be the whole story. Here, we need to consider another important, but often understudied part, of the doxography, this time from Sextus Empiricus:

> Well then, the followers of Pythagoras and Empedocles and the remaining lot of Italians declare not only that there is a community between us men and one another and with the gods, but also with the irrational animals [μὴ μόνον ἡμῖν πρὸς ἀλλήλους καὶ πρὸς τοὺς θεοὺς εἶναί τινα κοινωνίαν, ἀλλὰ καὶ πρὸς τὰ ἄλογα τῶν ζῴων]. For, they say, there is one *pneuma* which pervades the entire *kosmos*, in the manner of a soul, which also unifies us with them. This is why if we kill them and feed on their flesh, we will be committing an injustice and acting impiously, on the grounds that we are destroying our kin. Hence, too, these philosophers recommended abstinence from animal food, and they declared impious those people who 'reddened the altar of the blessed ones with warm blood'. And Empedocles somewhere says:
> Will you not desist from harsh-sounding bloodshed? Do you not see

---

[52] In this way, his political thought would be best compared with that of Solon, on which see Carol Atack's contribution in this volume.

That you are devouring one another in the heedlessness of your understanding?[53] (Sextus Empiricus, *Against the Mathematicians* 9.127)

We can see three of the elements found in the arguments attributed by Socrates to the 'wise men' in the *Gorgias* in this passage: the 'community' of gods and men, the unity of the '*kosmos*', and justice; and we also see the elements of the account of Iamblichus, namely the argument for the abstinence from animal food as a consequence of the sharing of kinship with irrational animals, an argument associated with Pythagoras in some form as early as Eudoxus of Cnidus.[54] There is the intrusion, if we can call it that, of what looks to be the Stoic *pneuma* (πνεῦμα) here, as well (perhaps standing in for something like *aether*). Now, typically, scholars have speculated that Sextus' source for his information on Pythagoreanism was Posidonius.[55] I have my doubts about this, especially given our evidence that neither Chrysippus nor Posidonius believed that justice extended from humans to other animals, on the grounds that other animals simply did not share of rationality.[56] And it is clear that the source isn't Alexander Polyhistor either, since he underscores the importance of all living beings, including the sun and stars, as well as gods and men, sharing in 'heat' (τὸ θερμόν) as a modality of *aether*.[57]

Still, the appearance of the extension of the πνεῦμα through all things looks Stoic, which would place the source of this testimony at the earliest in the late fourth century BCE, when Zeno of Citium apparently wrote a work on the Pythagoreans, of which nothing survives except a title (*Pythagorica*).[58] Indeed, the association of Pythagoreanism and '*kosmos*' in the terms discussed here points us to Zeno in particular. Zeno appears to have argued in the *Republic* that all individuals within the *kosmos* were unified under a common law (συννόμου νόμῳ κοινῷ),[59] and it is relatively common in the doxography to see that breath (πνεῦμα) is extended throughout all parts of the *kosmos* and holds

---

[53] DK 31 B 136.

[54] Eudoxus Fr. 325 Lasserre = Porph. *VP* 7. It is moreover one of the *acousmata*: 'abstain from animals' (Iambl. *Protr.* 21, p. 108.15 Pistelli).

[55] Generally, on this issue, see Brennan 2015.   [56] Cf. Posidonius Fr. 39 Kidd = Diog. Laert. 7.129.

[57] Diog. Laert. 8.26–28. Cf. Long 2013: 150–52, who also notes that Alexander's system of reproduction shares much with the account of Anonymous Londiniensis on Philolaus' embryology (DK 44 A 27). Note too that while Alexander Polyhistor does refer to a Pythagorean notion of human συγγένεια with the gods (Diog. Laert. 8.27), there is no discussion of non-human animals to be found there.

[58] SVF 1.41. I should note that the significance of 'breath' (πνεῦμα) to the Pythagorean cosmology is attested prior to Stoicism by Aristotle (*Phys.* 4.5.213b22–29; Fr. 201 Rose³ = DK 58 B 30). I discuss this extensively in Chapter 13.

[59] SVF 1.262.

them in place through relationships of tension.[60] But Zeno did not appear to hold that 'kinship' or 'participation' unified all creatures within the *kosmos*: others criticised Zeno for arguing that only the virtuous, and not the inferior, could obtain real friendship and were truly akin to one another.[61] Either Sextus preserves a Stoic doxographical record of the communal cosmology of the Pythagoreans and Empedocles that was dialectical – in which case it would be difficult to see what the Stoic source thought was *wrong* with the Pythagorean-Empedoclean account of the human–beast partnership[62] – or we will need to reconsider the apparent Stoicism of the Pythagoreanism/Empedocleanism described in this passage of Sextus.

One solution to our puzzle about Sextus' passage, I suggest, arises if we take our cue from both the Scholiast and from Sextus, and from the somewhat surprising reference in Iamblichus' account to the 'mixture arising out of these elements' (τῶν στοιχείων ... τῆς ἀπὸ τούτων ... συγκράσεως), and focus our attention on Empedocles. It is clear, first of all, that Empedocles was considered a natural philosopher by Aristotle, and one who is to be credited with philosophical innovations (especially in developing a nuanced approach to the efficient cause and proposing four elements, rather than one).[63] In particular, Aristotle indicates the extent to which Empedocles was concerned with describing the constitution of the *kosmos*, even referring to a portion of his work as the 'making-of-the-*kosmos*' (κοσμοποιία).[64] But he was concerned with ethics and proper moral conduct as well. In fact, he is the earliest Greek we know of who unquestionably rejected the eating of flesh – the evidence for Pythagoras before him is inconsistent, at best.[65] Empedocles also dedicated a surprising amount of his poem to illustrating the consequences of the fact that all animals breathe, as several of his fragments attest[66], and moreover he associated the aether with a part of the soul.[67] He also claimed of the divine (possibly the godhead Apollo?) that it 'is only a sacred and ineffable thought organ / <u>Darting through the entire</u> *kosmos* with swift thoughts' (ἀλλὰ φρὴν ἱερὴ καὶ

---

[60] See Long and Sedley 1987, vol. 1: 320–21.   [61] Diog. Laert. 7.32–33; *SVF* 3.631.

[62] For example, Cicero (*Rep.* 3.33) only understands law, as right reason, to be distributed throughout all peoples and cities rather than the entire *kosmos* (like the soul). He criticises those who adopt a notion of metempsychosis that would not see the transmigration of a rational soul into a beast as problematic (*Rep.* 4.1c).

[63] DK 31 A 22, A 37 and A 39. Cf. Kahn 2001: 18.

[64] Arist. *Phys.* 2.4.196a22–23 = DK 31 B 53. Aristotle also associates this with the activity of Mind in Anaxagoras (*Metaph.* 1.5.987a19).

[65] Cf. Burkert 1972: 180–82; Kahn 2001: 17–18; Riedweg 2005: 36–37.   [66] DK 31 B 100 and A 74.

[67] If Aristotle (*De an.* 1.2.404b8–15) has read him correctly (DK 31 B 109).

ἀθέσφατος ἔπλετο μοῦνον, / φροντίσι κόσμον ἅπαντα καταΐσσουσα θοῇσιν).[68] It is not hard to imagine the source of Sextus' passage attempting to Stoicize Empedocles' lines by assuming that he was actually referring to the *pneuma* when he spoke of the divine rational force in its modality as a thought organ (φρήν).[69] Moreover, Empedocles believed that the *kosmos* was unified, shaped like an egg,[70] and, most importantly, was constituted by friendship (φιλία), as we see in fragment B 26:

> And, in turn, they dominate as the cycle rolls around,
> And they dwindle and grow into one another in the turn of fate,
> For these things are the same, and running through one another
> They become men and the races of other beasts,
> And at one time **coming together by Love into one *kosmos***,
> And at another time again each being borne apart by Strife's enmity,
> Until, all of them grown together into one, the universe is subsumed.
> Thus insofar as they learned to grow as one from many,
> And they finish up many as the one again grows apart,
> In this respect they come to be and have no constant life;
> But insofar as they never cease from continually interchanging,
> In this respect they are always unchanged in a cycle.

> ἐν δὲ μέρει κρατέουσι περιπλομένοιο κύκλοιο,
> καὶ φθίνει εἰς ἄλληλα καὶ αὔξεται ἐν μέρει αἴσης.
> αὐτὰ γὰρ ἔστιν ταῦτά, δι'ἀλλήλων δὲ θέοντα
> γίγνοντ' ἄνθρωποί τε καὶ ἄλλων ἔθνεα θηρῶν,
> ἄλλοτε μὲν **φιλότητι συνερχόμεν' εἰς ἕνα κόσμον**,
> ἄλλοτε δ'αὖ δίχ' ἕκαστα φορούμενα νείκεος ἔχθει,
> εἰσόκεν ἐν συμφύντα τὸ πᾶν ὑπένερθε γένηται.
> οὕτως ᾗ μὲν ἓν ἐκ πλεόνων μεμάθηκε φύεσθαι,
> ἠδὲ πάλιν διαφύντος ἑνὸς πλέον' ἐκτελέθουσι,
> τῇ μὲν γίγνονταί τε καὶ οὔ σφίσιν ἔμπεδος αἰών·
> ᾗ δὲ τάδ' ἀλλάσσοντα διαμπερὲς οὐδαμὰ λήγει,
> ταύτῃ δ' αἰὲν ἔασιν ἀκίνητοι κατὰ κύκλον.   (Empedocles, DK 31 B 26)

What exactly Empedocles' *kosmos* is, and perhaps more importantly when and how it comes into existence, remains a topic of debate among scholars.[71] Yet there can be no doubt that when he mentions the *kosmos*,

---

[68] DK 31 B 134. On this passage, see Inwood 2002a: 68.

[69] Interestingly, this term is also used by Alexander Polyhistor in reference to the Pythagorean soul (Diog. Laert. 8.30).

[70] DK 31 A 50 and A 58.

[71] Aëtius (1.5.2 = DK 31 A 47) says that Empedocles believed that there was only one *kosmos*, but the *kosmos* is not identical with the universe; rather, it is said to be a small part of the universe, while the rest is inert matter.

Empedocles is speaking of a 'world' made up of many diverse objects, and given order in accordance with the cycles of fate, which impose alternation upon them.[72] And elsewhere (B 115), Empedocles is explicit not only in attributing a causal role to the 'oracle of necessity, ancient decrees of the gods, sealed with broad oaths' (ἀνάγκης χρῆμα, θεῶν ψήφισμα παλαιόν, / ἀίδιον, πλατέεσσι κατεσφρηγισμένον ὅρκοις) to growth, alteration and locomotion of the individual through the cycle of strife, but he also associates this process with the sins that accrue when one sacrifices improperly or swears false oaths.[73] Indeed, Plutarch's interesting description of the cycles of Strife and Love helps us to fill in the gaps left from an incomplete text of Empedocles' poem, and it also links Empedocles' cosmology to Plato's in the *Timaeus* by way of the critical importance of 'partnership' (κοινωνία). In mocking the Stoics' approach to cosmology, Plutarch elaborates a vision of the ἀκοσμία that obtains in Empedocles' cycle of Strife:

> Earth had no share of warmth, nor water any share of breath; none of the heavy things was up nor any of the light things down; but the principles of the universe were unblended, unloving, solitary, not desiring combination or communion with one another [μὴ προσιέμεναι σύγκρισιν ἑτέρου πρὸς ἕτερον μηδὲ κοινωνίαν]; fleeing and not admitting of blending or communion with one another, turning away and executing their separate and self-willed movements, they were in the condition which Plato [*Ti.* 53a–b] attributed to everything from which god is absent, i.e. in the condition of bodies when deserted by mind and soul. They were in that condition until by providence desire came into their nature [ἄχρι οὗ τὸ ἱμερτὸν ἧκεν ἐπὶ τὴν φύσιν ἐκ προνοίας] because of the presence of love and Aphrodite and Eros, as Empedocles, Parmenides, and Hesiod say, so that [the elements] by changing places and sharing their powers amongst each other, some being bound by the necessities of movement, some of rest, [all] being forced to give in and move from their natural state towards the better, they might create the harmony and communion of the universe [ἁρμονίαν καὶ κοινωνίαν ἀπεργάσηται τοῦ παντός]. (Plutarch, *Concerning the Face that Appears in the Orb of the Moon* 926e–927a; tr. after Inwood)

It is difficult, as always, to extract the genuine Presocratic substrate from the Middle Platonist dressings. Surely the appearance of providence is dialectical, and functions within the broader criticism of Stoic physics

---

[72] For a description of how Empedoclean alternation works, see Horky 2013: 179–81.

[73] A similar notion is exhibited by the Hippocratic author of *On the Nature of Man*, a text probably composed in the latter half of the fifth century BCE, where we see (*Nat. Hom.* 7) that all the elemental powers of the universe exist with one another according to 'necessity'.

and ethics.[74] Be that as it may, it is clear that Empedoclean cosmology and Pythagorean κοινωνία came to be so deeply intertwined that ancient historians of thought and doxographers found it difficult to separate the strands out; it may have been unnecessary, or even unfruitful, for them to do so. Empedocles' place within the history of Pythagoreanism was fixed sometime in the early Hellenistic period – in the writings of Neanthes of Cyzicus and Timaeus of Tauromenium, at the very latest (late fourth to mid third centuries BCE).[75] This is a *terminus ante quem*. But it is possible that such associations originated in the Socratic dialogues of Plato and Xenophon, through their typically elusive method of describing the positive contributions made to their own respective philosophies.

Now I would like to offer some concluding remarks. Our study has attempted to work backwards chronologically from the Hellenistic and Post-Hellenistic testimonies concerning the first discovery and usage of the term '*kosmos*' to refer to the 'world-order' to the Classical period, in order to sketch out a reception-history of the heurematographical tradition. Our analysis suggested that the most extensive account that makes Pythagoras the first person to refer to the heavens as the '*kosmos*', that of the sceptic philosopher and historian Favorinus of Arles, seems to represent the continuation of a tradition that associated Pythagoras with various discoveries and innovations in mathematics and cosmology in the mid fourth century BCE, both in the Academy and in the Lyceum. Consequently, we sought to examine whether sources prior to Aristotle, Aristoxenus and Theophrastus, as well as the Early Platonists, might also hint at similar associations. This led us to the puzzle of solving the identity of some anonymous 'professors' (οἱ σοφισταί) in Xenophon's *Memorabilia*, as well as some anonymous 'wise men' (οἱ σοφοί) in Plato's *Gorgias*, whose marked use of the term '*kosmos*' was associated with, respectively, natural science and its laws, and 'partnership' (κοινωνία) between the various divine and mortal aspects of the universe. The likeliest candidates to identify with these figures were Pythagoreans, in particular, Archytas of Tarentum, whose focus on mathematical proportions, especially 'calculation' (λογισμός), as a means to eradicate stasis within the community, parallels Socrates' description of the 'geometrical equality' in the *Gorgias*;

---

[74] As noted by Cherniss in his Loeb translation. Plutarch's *Amatorius* (756d–f) provides some guidance: there, Plutarch describes a similar cosmogony by reference to Empedocles' B 17.20–21, Parmenides B 13, and Hesiod's *Theogony* line 120. According to Aëtius (2.3.3 = DK 51 F 4), another later 'Pythagorean', Ecphantus of Syracuse, believed that the *kosmos* was 'constituted out of atoms, and that it is overseen by providence'.

[75] See Horky 2013: 116–18 and Schorn 2014: 307–9.

Philolaus of Croton, whose marked use of '*kosmos*' and cosmological theory of the harmonisation of oppositional limiters and unlimiteds reflected the basic tenor of Plato's account, while also retaining Xenophon's concern with astronomy and the generation of the heavens; and Empedocles of Agrigentum, who is directly associated with the 'wise men' of Plato's account by the Scholiast to Plato's *Gorgias,* and whose implication of the generation of the '*kosmos*' within the universe and the objects that constitute it through the influence of Love strikes closest to both accounts, while retaining the all-important association between 'partnership' and '*kosmos*' that distinguished Plato's version.

In the end, however, *none* of these figures can be directly paralleled with both the earliest dialectical accounts – that of Xenophon and that of Plato – of those clever people who used '*kosmos*' in a marked way to refer to the world-order. But this should not surprise us: neither Plato nor Xenophon wrote their dialogues primarily in order to entertain our curiosities about the history of philosophy; they sought to develop and promote their own philosophical agendas through their peculiar preservations of the memory of Socrates. No single piece of the evidence presented here can be considered the smoking gun that solves our question, 'when did '*kosmos*' become the *kosmos*?'; it is clear that the concept of '*kosmos*' came to mean 'world' or 'world-order' by, at the latest, the first few decades of the fifth century BCE.[76] But the evidence presented here does suggest that early Pythagoreans of the experimental sort, the 'exoterics' who were often considered 'outsiders' or 'scientific' Pythagoreans by later traditions, adopted the term *kosmos* and in order to explain the relationship that obtains between the recurrent modes of alteration and change within the observable universe and the balance that is meant to undergird systems of justice and fairness between the living participants of that universe. The indications from the later doxographical traditions, combined with the surviving fragments of the second- and third-generation 'Pythagoreans' themselves, all point in the same direction, back to the enigmatic and elusive Pythagoras of Samos. It's the usual problem with Pythagoras: no smoking gun, and all smoke and mirrors.

---

[76] Also see Malcolm Schofield's chapter (Chapter 3), where he argues that Heraclitus in DK 22 B 30 was attacking those who used κόσμος to refer to the 'world' or 'world-order'. I have raised some worries about which *specific* (τόνδε) κόσμος is being appealed to, however, in the Introduction.

CHAPTER 2

Ordering the Universe in Speech
Kosmos *and* Diakosmos *in Parmenides' Poem*

Arnaud Macé

We forget that calling the universe a '*kosmos*' once was a metaphorical act,[1] when someone applied to the heavens a word which had so far been used in different contexts. The Greek word κόσμος, the related verb κοσμέω, and the phrase κατὰ κόσμον are commonly found in Archaic Greek culture.[2] They refer to the process of getting various items to fit together, or to the result of such a process. This general idea was applied to many things: adorning a horse or oneself, preparing dinner, sorting out cattle, putting soldiers in order for battle, composing a fine song. But it was not originally applied to the universe. Both Plato and Aristotle tell us that wise men did at some point extend this view of order to the sum of all things (τὸ ὅλον). They did so because they found order in it,[3] because they 'put the whole of nature into order (τὴν ὅλην φύσιν διακοσμοῦσιν)'[4] – in a marching order, so to speak. We might wonder: what drove these people to conceive of the sum of all things in terms of poetic and military regularity? My hypothesis is that Parmenides, who chose to express himself in the verse, vocabulary, and images of Homer,[5] can be chiefly credited with making the categories of Archaic poetry available for cosmology, so that the universe could start to openly be described as another κόσμος that resulted from the process described by the verbs κοσμέω and διακοσμέω. Only such a daring move could have opened the way to call the universe simply a '*kosmos*', or even *the kosmos*.[6]

---

[1] This reflection opens Kerschensteiner 1962.

[2] Diller counted seventy-six occurrences of these various forms in Archaic poetry until the mid sixth century (Diller 1956: 48).

[3] See Plato, *Gorgias* 507e6–508a4: τὸ ὅλον τοῦτο ... κόσμον καλοῦσιν ... Both George Boys-Stones (Chapter 5) and Phillip Horky (Chapter 1) discuss this passage.

[4] See Arist. *Eth. Eud.* 8.1.1235a10.

[5] How much Parmenides is embedded in the realm of Archaic poetry, both epic and lyric, has been well explored over the last century (see e.g. Bowra 1937, Mansfeld 1964, Mourelatos 2008 and Coxon 2009).

[6] Against both Kranz and Kerschensteiner, I believe that later testimonies (including the one presented as a fragment of Anaximenes DK 13 B 2) of earlier thinkers using κόσμος to name the universe are

My further claim is that Parmenides is able to bring the universe into the list of items that a poet would call well-ordered precisely because he exposes and criticises the traditional epic relation of word to reality: a well-ordered song is one that tells the truth about what actually happened,[7] its order fitting the order of reality itself.[8] I would like to suggest that the way Parmenides weaves κόσμος and διάκοσμος together at the end of B 8 both exposes and denounces the claim that a combination of verses, a κόσμος ἐπέων, should be expected to turn into the disclosure of a διάκοσμος. Only this time the great ordering is not the catalogue of ships ready for battle, but the division of the great principles according to which the universe is organised by mortals. Parmenides exposes the delusion of a song claiming to disclose the organisation of the whole of reality, ordered like the armies of the Achaeans. Such an approach changes the way we look at the status of cosmology and cosmogony in Parmenides: we usually think it should either be true and consistent or false and inconsistent. Parmenides shows us how human words, projecting human practices and institutions on the universe, make it a very consistent order – and all the more deceitful because of its consistency.

2.1 κόσμος ἐπέων: The Deceitful Revelation of a διάκοσμος

2.1.1 *Singing in Order: An Implicit Claim to Truth?*

The words κόσμος and διάκοσμος are used in the same sequence of Parmenides' poem, at the end of fragment B 8. Κόσμος appears at verse 52,[9] when the Goddess invites her auditor to listen to her 'κόσμος ἐπέων'.

> Here I put an end, for you,[10] to the reliable discourse, and also
> to the thought embracing truth. From now on learn the opinions of mortals,
> listening to the arrangement of my words, a deceitful one.

probably anachronistic. For instance, according to Diogenes Laertius (8.48), Favorinus said that Pythagoras was 'the first to call the heaven "*kosmos*" and the earth round [τὸν οὐρανὸν πρῶτον ὀνομάσαι κόσμον καὶ τὴν γῆν στρογγύλην]', although Theophrastus claims it was Parmenides, and Zeno Hesiod. I suggest, instead, that it might have happened after Parmenides, and under his influence. See Horky's close examination of Favorinus in this volume, Chapter 1. The case Horky makes for identifying Empedocles and other Pythagorean 'outsiders' as the first to call the heavens '*kosmos*' is concordant with our own story.

[7] Diller 1956: 57.   [8] See Elmer 2010.
[9] The word appears first in the fragments in the κατὰ κόσμον phrase at B 4.3. We will return to this fragment at the very end of this chapter.
[10] See Palmer's argument in favour of Nehamas's conjecture for B 6 in the light of the echo between πρώτης γάρ σ' ἀφ' ὁδοῦ ταύτης διζήσιος <ἄρξω> (B 6.3), and σοι παύω here at B 8.50 (Palmer 2009: 67–68, without necessarily following his reading of τοι παύω at n. 49).

ἐν τῷ σοι παύω πιστὸν λόγον ἠδὲ νόημα
ἀμφὶς ἀληθείης· δόξας δ' ἀπὸ τοῦδε βροτείας
μάνθανε κόσμον ἐμῶν ἐπέων ἀπατηλὸν ἀκούων.

(Parmenides, DK 28 B 8.50–2)[11]

Why an 'arrangement' or 'composition' rather than an 'ornament of words'?[12] The fact that κόσμος ἐπέων can also be the object of the verb τεκταίνομαι[13] suggests it could refer to the result of an art of composition and construction similar to that of the carpenter working on wood.[14] Even the two Homeric occurrences where the meaning of 'ornament' really comes to mind chiefly describe elaborate compositions, either with regard to the whole arrangement, or to the detail that fits in the right place and completes the whole process.[15] Whether one is getting dinner ready, tidying up a mess, taking good care of a garden, ordering weapons and chariots, getting armies ready for battle, providing laws for a human community, or composing a song,[16] the same underlying general scheme comes with the use of κόσμος and κοσμέω: the idea of putting every piece where it belongs in a complex whole.[17] The use of the phrase κατὰ κόσμον is also explained in reference to the same notion of putting a set of things in

---

[11] I use the Greek text by H. Diels and W. Kranz, unless otherwise specified. Unless otherwise noted, translations from Greek are mine.

[12] This is Edmonds' translation of the same expression in Solon, Fr. 1.2 West (Edmonds 1931). We translate by 'words' and not 'verses' for two reasons. One is to give the art of composition a greater scope, encompassing the combination of words within each verse; the other is to keep the generality of an expression also used to describe prose writing (on this matter, see later in the chapter).

[13] Democritus (DK 68 B 21) says about Homer that he 'framed the composition of many words of all kinds' (ἐπέων κόσμον ἐτεκτήνατο παντοίων).

[14] One might think that the 'kosmos of the wooden horse' (ἵππου κόσμον ... δουρατέου) at Od. 8.492–99 refers to the construction of the horse (Diller 1956: 51; Kranz 1958: 10; Kerschensteiner 1962: 8–9); but it might rather mean the 'story' of the horse, in the sense of a composition of episodes (Latacz 1991a: 383–84), which is in any case still a process of putting elements together. There are eighteen occurrences of κόσμος in Homer, fourteen of them in the phrase κατὰ κόσμον, two with an instrumental dative case with a meaning very close to κατὰ κόσμον (Il. 12.225 and Od. 12.77). The three remaining occurrences, most important for our discussion, are at Il. 4.145, 14.187 and Od. 8.492.

[15] Diller (1956: 48–49) rightly emphasises how at Il. 14.187 the word κόσμος sums up the long list of preparations (bathing, clothing, accessories included) that Hera has just gone through, one after another: 'Then, when she had made all these arrangements around her body' (αὐτὰρ ἐπεὶ δὴ πάντα περὶ χροῒ θήκατο κόσμον). At Il. 4.145, a cheek-piece for horses is mentioned, from the king's treasure, described as 'both an ornament for the horse and a glory for the driver' (ἀμφότερον κόσμός θ' ἵππῳ ἐλατῆρί τε κῦδος). The piece represents the final part for preparation of the horse before it can go to battle and bring glory to its driver.

[16] For examples of all these, see the occurrences listed by Diller (1956: 51–54). For song composition, see especially the Homeric Hymn to Dionysus 59: γλυκερὴν κοσμῆσαι ἀοιδήν. For its political tenor, see Chapter 8 in this volume by Atack.

[17] Concerning the general idea of 'ordering' being prior to any more specific meaning, see Kerschensteiner 1962: 6–9. Diller (1956) has rightly pointed out the role of the parts in the shaping of a κόσμος: 'Ausstattung des Ganzen durch Ordnung der Teile', p. 51; 'Das κοσμεῖν als Einfügen des einzelnen in die Ordnung des Ganzen', p. 53.

order (internal order),[18] accomplishing a set of actions in their proper order (sequential order),[19] or doing the right thing within a context where this action is fitting (external order).[20] The idea that order comes from assigning each individual thing to the right place is reinforced by the synonymity of κατὰ κόσμον with κατὰ μοῖραν and κατ’ αἶσαν.[21]

Hence, the phrase κόσμος ἐπέων refers to the result of a careful arrangement of words, where each of them has found its right place in the greater composition. Such an arrangement might be found in prose as well as in verse,[22] because creating order is common to the rhapsode's sewing together of verses and to the orator going through the steps of his speech in the right order.[23] The Goddess, as she turns from her previous λόγος to the opinions of the mortals in B 8.50–52, mimics the announcement of human poets, such as Solon, as they prepare to deliver their poetic content:

> As a herald I come from lovely Salamis,
> and I have arranged a composition of words, a song instead of a speech.
>
> αὐτὸς κῆρυξ ἦλθον ἀφ’ ἱμερτῆς Σαλαμῖνος
> κόσμον ἐπ<έω>ν †ᾠδὴν ἀντ’ ἀγορῆς θέμενος. (Solon, Fragment 1.1–2 West)[24]

A few lines later in B 8, the Goddess reflects upon this transition and concurrently introduces the term διάκοσμος:

> This order, I am telling you, is fitting in every way,
> so that no conception of mortals could ever overtake you.
>
> τόν σοι ἐγὼ διάκοσμον ἐοικότα πάντα φατίζω,
> ὡς οὐ μή ποτέ τίς σε βροτῶν γνώμη παρελάσσῃ.
>
> (Parmenides, DK 28 B 8.60–1)

---

[18] E.g. weapons on three rows (*Il.* 10.472–73) and chariots in line (*Il.* 11.48 and 12.85). 'In good order' or 'in good shape' even could be implied at *Il.* 8.12: οὐ κατὰ κόσμον ἐλεύσεται Οὔλυμπον δέ. For a similar use of κατὰ κόσμον in Parmenides B 4, see the end of this chapter.

[19] Killing the animal and cutting it into parts, *Il.* 24.622; singing the fate of the Achaeans as it should be done, *Od.* 8.489. Contrariwise, the same things can be done recklessly, see *Il.* 2.213–14, 5.579, *Od.* 3.138.

[20] It is not fitting that Hector should strip Patrocles of his weapons (οὐ κατὰ κόσμον *Il.* 17.205–6); Euryale's words to Ulysses are inappropriate (*Od.* 8.179); Ulysses begging seems out of place to the rivals (*Od.* 20.181–82). Eumaeus objects to the stranger's speech because it is false, and it is unfitting because it is false (*Od.* 14.363).

[21] On the similar use of these phrases, see Kerschensteiner 1962: 5. See the careful comparison of the use of κατὰ κόσμον and κατὰ μοῖραν in Homer in Du Sablon 2014: 99–133.

[22] For prose, see Thuc. 3.67.6 (cf. Diller 1956: 57).

[23] See Patzer 1952: 323. For a more recent explanation of the rhapsode as weaver of songs, see Nagy 2002: 70–98.

[24] I am thankful to Johannes Haubold for drawing my attention to these verses.

There are striking resemblances with the opening verses of the sequence found at lines 50–61: the Goddess stresses the fact that the words she utters are directed to someone's particular attention (ἐν τῷ σοι παύω/τόν σοι ἐγώ); she refers to the mortals' δόξαι, as well as to the γνώμη of a mortal; and she finally has διάκοσμος echo κόσμος. The substantive noun διάκοσμος makes its first appearance here in what remains of Archaic Greek literature.[25] The verb διακοσμέω is used by Homer to describe the sorting out and arraying of troops, especially when separating and dividing is involved.[26] The catalogue of ships of *Iliad* book 2, which will later be labelled a διάκοσμος by the scholiasts, is the result of a great process of organisation undertaken by the Achaean kings.[27] The διάκοσμος of ships is the greatest attempt by the poet to prove he can describe a κόσμος as it really was, piece by piece.[28] The organisation of the song itself is not only a proof of internal order in Archaic poetry but also a condition for a song to speak the truth, the order in which things really happened. When Odysseus compliments Demodocus for singing the fate of the Achaeans κατὰ κόσμον, he explains that he has done so because the bard told 'the things they did, the things they underwent, all they suffered' (ὅσσ' ἔρξαν τ' ἔπαθόν τε καὶ ὅσσ' ἐμόγησαν Ἀχαιοί, 490); because Demodocus sings all the right elements, it appears as if he was personally present or heard it from someone who was.[29] The truthfulness of the song is exactly attested by the fact that a speaker is able to represent things seen and done in their right order – to describe the ornament on dresses and horses, the weapons in good order, and all the things carried out just as in fact they were carried out. When Odysseus invites him next to 'sing the story of the wooden horse' (ἵππου κόσμον ἄεισον / δουρατέου),[30] by calling it a κόσμος, he actually makes explicit what good and truthful songs are about: their narrative structure fits the structure of the reality they describe, unfolding each and every event as it actually happened. If oral poets love ornaments and details, it is not for the sole aim of making their songs longer by adding many details on each horse or garment, but because doing so is essential to

---

[25] For further discussion of διάκοσμος in Presocratic thought, with a focus on Democritus, see Chapter 3 of this volume by Schofield.

[26] Cf. Diller 1956: 52 and Macé and Therme 2013.

[27] This background of Parmenides' use of διάκοσμος has been well examined (Mourelatos 2008: 230; Gregory 2014: 180). For the scholiast's take on the catalogue, see Kerschensteiner 1962: 7 n. 2.

[28] Cf. Elmer 2010: 492–93.

[29] *Od.* 8.491: ὥς τέ που ἢ αὐτὸς παρεὼν ἢ ἄλλου ἀκούσας. As Diller puts it, 'κατὰ κόσμον heisst hier also geradezu "wahrheitsgemäss"' (Diller 1956: 57).

[30] *Od.* 8.492–99. I follow Latacz 1991a on the idea that Homer refers to the narrative structure of the story, which must be told in the right order.

their representation of the truth.[31] This all explains very well why Parmenides' Goddess would echo the announcement of her singing at lines 50–52 by a declaration that the content of her song is a great διάκοσμος, and a 'fitting' one – likely to be true *because* it is fitting.[32] Parmenides is simply exposing the conditions for truth in epic poetry – ordering words as a way to describe the order of actions and things. The most surprising feature of the use of the expression κόσμον ἐμῶν ἐπέων by the Goddess, then, is the very disappointing addition she makes, in which the composition of her verses will be ἀπατηλὸν, or deceitful.

2.1.2 *Only What Claims to Be True Can Be Deceitful*

There would be no such disappointment, nor yet any possibility of deceit, at the Goddess's words, if the announcement of a well-composed song did not ring in the ears of the auditor accustomed to epic poetry as a promise to deliver the truth. Such an auditor, however, would also be familiar with the idea from Hesiod that those who know what is true are also the ones who know what is false: the Muses, who know how to tell the truth whenever they like to, are those who also know to tell what is false as if it were true.[33] To the Archaic mind, to know the truth and to know what is not true are two sides of the same privilege. Parmenides' Goddess made it clear from the very beginning that her discourse would not be complete without having gone through what is true and what is not.[34]

> You must learn about all things,
> both the still heart of well persuasive truth
> and the opinions of mortals, in which there is no true conviction.

> χρεὼ δέ σε πάντα πυθέσθαι
> ἠμὲν ἀληθείης εὐπειθέος ἀτρεμὲς ἦτορ
> ἠδὲ βροτῶν δόξας, ταῖς οὐκ ἔνι πίστις ἀληθής.

(Parmenides, DK 20 B 1.28–30)

This announcement fits very well with our passage in B 8, where we can assume that the 'reliable discourse' (πιστὸν λόγον 8.50) is also the

---

[31] Cf. Elmer 2010.
[32] For a detailed study on this use of ἐοικότα see Bryan 2012: 58–113, also referred to by Schofield in Chapter 3.
[33] Hes. *Theog.* 27–28: ἴδμεν ψεύδεα πολλὰ λέγειν ἐτύμοισιν ὁμοῖα, / ἴδμεν δ' εὖτ' ἐθέλωμεν ἀληθέα γηρύσασθαι. For the Homeric use of ψεύδεα πολλὰ λέγων ἐτύμοισιν ὁμοῖα see *Od.* 19.203; also see Theognis l. 713 West.
[34] On the importance of going through both what is true and what is false in Eleatic logic, see Castelnérac 2014.

expression of a 'thought about truth' (νόημα ἀμφὶς ἀληθείης). In B 1, the way distinguished from persuasive truth is what is without 'true conviction' (πίστις ἀληθής 1.30), and it is only natural that what is truthful ('the heart of truth', ἀληθείης ... ἦτορ) should also be associated with ease of persuasion (εὐπειθέος), a quality of what is πιστός, trustworthy – both verbal adjectives being related to the verb πείθω.[35] It is therefore no surprise that the composition of verses announced by the Goddess as a way to convey the opinions of mortals is 'deceitful' (ἀπατηλός), a quality especially opposed to what is trustworthy.

Let us, however, notice that for the deceit to take place, some conviction has to be possible, albeit not a trustworthy one. We should not conclude that only the truth can convince, even when at B 2.4 the way of being (asserting the impossibility of non-being) is said to be 'a road of persuasion, because persuasion attends to truth' (πειθοῦς ἐστι κέλευθος, ἀληθείη γὰρ ὀπηδεῖ). For, in B 2, the Goddess is not obviously opposing the way of truth to the opinions of the mortals, but to the way of non-being (asserting the necessity of not-being), a 'path from which nothing can be learned' (παναπευθέα ἀταρπόν) (B 2.6). Significantly, the adjective ἀπευθής is formed on the verb πυνθάνομαι, used at the end of B 1 to refer to both the way of truth and the opinion of the mortals, about which the young man is supposed to learn. So, the opinions of mortals, even if they are not one of the two ways of inquiry there are to be conceived (εἰσι νοῆσαι), for they yield no necessity and mix what should not be mixed (mortals are 'tribes unable to decide (ἄκριτα φῦλα, B 6.7)'[36] between these two roads), still share with the way of truth the possibility that something can be learnt from them, however deceitful. An earlier verse of B 8 shows how it is possible for mortals to be convinced not only by truth, but also by what only appears to be true:

> They will be names,
> all the things that mortals have laid down, convinced that they are true:
> coming into being and passing away, being and not being,
> changing place and altering bright colours.

> τῷ πάντ' ὄνομ' ἔσται,
> ὅσσα βροτοὶ κατέθεντο πεποιθότες εἶναι ἀληθῆ,

---

[35] See Chantraine 1968–80: 868–69 (πείθομαι): πιστός as an ambivalent verbal adjective (that which can be trusted/one which places trust in someone/something), p. 868 (A.1), πειθός, verbal adjective, meaning 'persuasive', p. 869 (B.10).

[36] For this meaning of ἄκριτος see Hdt. 8.124.

γίγνεσθαί τε καὶ ὄλλυσθαι, εἶναί τε καὶ οὐχί,
καὶ τόπον ἀλλάσσειν διά τε χρόα φανὸν ἀμείβειν.

(Parmenides, DK 28 B 8.38–41)

Conviction that something is true can arise in reference to something that is not reliable: conviction is therefore not the necessary sign of possessing truth. To be deceived precisely supposes that one has made the mistake of taking something untrue for something true. Hence, humans persuade themselves that they possess the truth and that there are, in truth, many things being born and passing away, changing places and changing colours. We are told that the words humans use are 'words only'. As Vlastos has convincingly argued (Vlastos 2008), this does not entail absence of meaning or inconsistency. The Goddess has warned that these beliefs should be learned as well as the truth, and she never fails to repeat that opinions are what is believed (τὰ δοκοῦντα at B 1.31), and so they need to be acceptable (χρῆν δοκίμως εἶναι at B 1.32) and fitting (ἐοικότα at B 8.60). The arrangement of words provided by the Goddess will now display the type of order that human words, words of poets, usually display – a well-arranged composition of words claiming to fit the composition of reality, an attempt to display a world of things being born and disappearing again, changing places and colours. To add that all these things will be 'words only' is simply to deny their claim to fit reality, and not the order that this claim is based upon.

2.1.3 Human Words, Human Institutions

By inviting us to hear human words for what they are – *mere* human words – the Goddess opens a new world. The opinions these words express are thus obtained as the result of purely human convention, a dimension conveyed by the repeated use of the verb κατατίθημι (B 8.39 and 53; B 19.5), which indicates that what humans name is what they have 'laid down' and 'established'.[37] This key association of κατατίθημι and ὀνομάζειν will be repeated at various moments of the *Doxa* part of the poem, and especially at the point where the Goddess wants to explain what the opinions of mortals are about:

---

[37] The usual Archaic meaning of κατατίθημι without a preposition is to 'lay down', for instance a prize, see *Il.* 23.267 or, more specifically, 'dedicate' when gods are the dedicatees. On the idea of laying down as a way to create a common good, see the frequent use of κ. τι ἐς μέσον and the analysis by Gernet 1947.

For they laid down principles, in order to name two forms,
neither of which[38] was necessary, and that is where they have gone astray.

μορφὰς γὰρ κατέθεντο δύο γνώμας ὀνομάζειν,
τῶν μίαν οὐ χρεών ἐστιν, ἐν ᾧ πεπλανημένοι εἰσίν·

(Parmenides, DK 28 B 8.53–4)

Most translators read γνώμας as the complement of κατατίθημι, although
some choose μορφάς.[39] It has often been thought that the association of the
verb κατατίθημι with γνώμας should yield the meaning 'taking decisions'
or recording them. The independent use of both terms κατατίθημι (B 8.39
and 53; B 19.5) and γνώμη (B 8.53 and 61) in the poem does not plead in
favour of such an option,[40] nor does the only occurrence of such an
association (probably) before Parmenides, in Theognis:

Nay, every man should lay to heart this saying:
What hath most power for all is wealth.[41]

ἀλλὰ χρὴ πάντας γνώμην ταύτην καταθέσθαι
ὡς πλοῦτος πλείστην πᾶσιν ἔχει δύναμιν.   (Theognis ll. 717–18 West)

Even when it is used as a complement of κατατίθημι, γνώμη in the singular
does not combine strongly with the verb to produce an idiomatic sense: the
γνώμη here is simply one of the many items that can be 'laid down' and
'held on to'. If one thinks he predates Heraclitus, Aeschylus and
Parmenides, Theognis might have been the first to use this word, otherwise
absent in Homer and Hesiod.[42] In Theognis it has meanings both subjective (a capacity to reflect, as opposed to foolishness)[43] and objective: the
latter indicates what is the result of the same subjective reflection – notions,
conceptions, principles, sayings, exactly the type of things that one might
want to lay down and remember.[44] Such a γνώμη can be a proposition,
expressing a certain hierarchy of values. In this case, it indicates the superiority of being wealthy. Such principles therefore help to identify and
recognise characters and patterns of behaviour:

---

[38] There are several options on the meaning of τῶν μίαν; see a comprehensive exposition by Mansfeld
(1964: 123–31). I follow the τῶν μίαν οὐ = οὐδέτεραν reading (option b in Mansfeld, represented by
Reinhard, Kranz, Cornford, Verdenius and Deichgräber, among others; see n. 2 on p. 124).

[39] In favour of κατέθεντο μορφάς, see Bollack 2006: 209.

[40] Bollack mentions the echo of the previous use of κατατίθημι as a reason for not merging its meaning
with γνώμας in the present passage (Bollack 2006: 209). See further criticism against such
a construction, especially with the plural γνώμας instead of a singular, in Mourelatos 2008: 229.

[41] Translation by Edmonds 1931.   [42] I follow Snell 1924: 34–38.

[43] See the occurrences collected by Snell 1924: 34 n. 1.

[44] Verses 717–18 are quoted by Snell, n. 2, as precisely an example for this meaning (Snell 1924: 34).

Yet they deceive one another and mock each other,
having no idea of the principles of the bad or of the good.

ἀλλήλους δ᾽ ἀπατῶσιν ἐπ᾽ ἀλλήλοισι γελῶντες,
οὔτε κακῶν γνώμας εἰδότες οὔτ᾽ ἀγαθῶν.   (Theognis ll. 59–60 West)

Theognis describes the situation of a city in which values have been turned
upside down: the common people have become the new elite, and the good
men of yesterday are now dismissed. No one knows what it is to be good or
bad any more, what values are to be praised or blamed. The γνῶμαι have
become confused, impossible to differentiate, and consequently deception
reigns. Parmenides holds more radically that a fundamental deception
reigns among men even when their principles are well established.
Underneath their words, there are basic principles that humans have laid
down. The Goddess has made us adopt a new epistemic stance in the face
of human words. We are now no longer listening to what they pretend to
say about things out there: we are hearing human conventions at work in
this construction of reality. We are now ready to hear what social institutions of their own men project onto the sky. This is why the account of the
universe that will follow cannot be surpassed by any human, since we are
going to unfold a total projection of human basic principles on the
universe.

2.2 The Beautiful Order

2.2.1 *Separating Night and Fire*

The verb κοσμέω, with δια as prefix or as preposition, is used in Homer in
the context of marshalling troops as an equivalent of διακρίνω and κρίνω,
describing what war chiefs and herdsmen alike do, i.e. sort out their own
men and cattle when they are scattered among others.[45] So the διάκοσμος
of B 8.60 must really be understood in the light of the use of κρίνω at
B 8.53, itself an explanation of the distinction of the two shapes by the
mortals:

> They differentiated opposites according to their bodily appearance and set
> up signs
> independently one from another . . .

---

[45] See especially *Il.* 2.474–76 and the examination of the use of διακοσμέω, διακρίνω and κρίνω in
Homer by Macé and Therme 2013: 236–42.

τἀντία δ' ἐκρίναντο δέμας καὶ σήματ' ἔθεντο
χωρὶς ἀπ' ἀλλήλων . . .   (Parmenides DK 28 B 8.55–6)

Δέμας echoes μορφάς in the sense of outward appearance and bodily shape in general:[46] the naming of shapes supposes a primary separation of different types of bodily features, and this very separation requires criteria. Just as the shepherd recognises his goats through the help of marks, men set up signs to start separating out different kinds of bodies. Κατατίθημι is echoed here by τίθημι: the signs are established, and they also are a human institution. Σήματα are also set up independently, in order to separate two types of shapes. Setting up independent signs is not about establishing contraries but about separating out two different bodies both characterised by their peculiar features. The *krisis* will set up two shapes and oppose them, but this does not entail that this opposition follows the modality of contrariety. Separating two herds of cattle mingled together does not make contraries out of them: it only restores each herd's collective selfhood and independence. We may verify that the six adjectives given in the remaining lines, six signs to recognise bodies, respect this independence and progressively build up an opposition of bodies, where self-identity is of greater importance than the matching of contraries:

> on the one hand the aetherial fire of flame,
> mild, light, the same as itself in every direction,
> and not the same as the other. But that other too they set up by itself,
> being the opposite, ignorant night, with its dense and thick body.

> τῇ μὲν φλογὸς αἰθέριον πῦρ,
> ἤπιον ὄν, μέγ' ἐλαφρόν, ἑωυτῷ πάντοσε τωὐτόν,
> τῷ δ' ἑτέρῳ μὴ τωὐτόν· ἀτὰρ κἀκεῖνο κατ' αὐτό
> τἀντία νύκτ' ἀδαῆ, πυκινὸν δέμας ἐμβριθές τε. (Parmenides, DK 28 B 8.56–9)

In both Homer and Hesiod, the adjective ἤπιος has the meaning of something gentle, with no violent contrasts, and therefore something favourable. It makes fire feel like the familiar flame of a candle, gentle and soft, offering its shivering yet reassuring light in the darkness. This sign has no obvious contrary in the list of signs attributed to night. It might, however, have a counterpart in the fact that night is called ἀδαής. There is apparently only one occurrence of this adjective before Parmenides, in

---

[46] The fact that δέμας refers to outward appearance in general as opposed, for instance, to inner thought is clear from *Od.* 10.239–40. See the way Homeric descriptions of beautiful bodies associate δέμας, φυή and εἶδος (*Od.* 5.212–13, see also *Od.* 8.116 and *Il.* 1.112–15); δέμας refers to the body with an analogy to building (δέμω) whilst φυή does it with an analogy to growth (φύομαι) and εἶδος with reference to sight. See Chantraine 1980: 261–62. See also Xenophanes, DK 21 B 14.2 and 23.4.

Theognis: the poet there describes the ignorant chatter of the dinner guest whom everybody hates (ll. 296–97 West). But there is also an interesting use of this word in a chorus by Sophocles' *Philoctetes* (almost assuredly written after Parmenides' poem):

> Sleep, ignorant of sufferings, Sleep, ignorant of pains,
> may you, gently blowing, come to us, gentle,
> gentle lord!

> Ὕπν' ὀδύνας ἀδαής, Ὕπνε δ' ἀλγέων,
> εὐαὴς ἡμῖν ἔλθοις, <εὐαίων,>
> εὐαίων ὦναξ·

(Sophocles, *Philoctetes* 828–30)

Sleep does not recognise pain: it actually takes it away. Night is ignorant of the troubles of the day. Ἀδαής, understood in this way, would offer a counterpart to ἤπιος: we get two versions of being gentle and favourable – through mildness or through liberation – which identify two very distinct bodies in their very own idiosyncratic ways.

The body of night is also said to be πυκνός (or πυκινός) – like something made of closely fit stones or pieces of wood.[47] Trees can grow tight, intertwined like the twin olive trees that Odysseus found on the Island of Calypso.[48] This aspect of night has led some editors to want to keep ἀραιός for Fire, present in the manuscripts[49], for it is tempting to build a contrary opposition between dense and rare (ἀραιός/πυκνός).[50] But is Parmenides really looking for such contraries? Let us take a look at the one opposition that seems to work most obviously through contrariness: heavy and light. The flame of fire is αἰθέριος, aetherial: it reminds us of its celestial vocation. It goes well with ἐλαφρός, which seems to mean light as opposed to heavy, at least from Plato onwards, but has in earlier times various nuances to refer also to the swiftness of the feet or the quality of being bearable.[51] Ἐμβριθής, attributed to night, certainly means heavy,[52] but it is also contrasted with λεπτός as the fable of the trees and the weeds shows:[53] it is as much thick as

---

[47] See *Il.* 16.212–14.   [48] *Od.* 5.480: πυκνοὶ ἀλλήλοισιν ἔφυν ἐπαμοιβαδίς.

[49] The manuscripts of Simplicius repeatedly add ἀραιός and ἐλαφρός after ἤπιος, which metre does not allow (ἀραιός is not a dactyl). See the explanations by Frère 1987: 206. Ἤπιος is fit to open the verse with its long first syllable. Diels keeps ἐλαφρός as *lectio difficilior*, followed by most editors.

[50] See e.g. Karsten 1964, followed by Frère 1987: 206–7.

[51] See the occurrences gathered by Frère 1987: 207.

[52] See Herodotus on the weight of ropes, where the linen rope is heavier than the others (ἐμβριθέστερα ἦν τὰ λίνεα, 7.36) and Sophocles on the heaviness of necessity (ἢ τῆς ἀνάγκης οὐδὲν ἐμβριθέστερον, Fr. 757.3 Radt).

[53] Aesop, *Fables* 239–41 (Hausrath). The trees after the tempest wonder how the weeds, 'who are thin and weak' (οἱ δὲ λεπτοὶ καὶ ἀσθενεῖς ὄντες), were unharmed, whilst the trees, 'although they are strong and thick' (ἰσχυρὰ καὶ ἐμβριθῆ ὄντα), went down.

it is heavy, and the first nuance fits night better than the second. Parmenides plays here with adjectives that do not form clear enough oppositions, or maybe he stakes out too many[54] to build up a neat table of contraries, like the one attributed to the Pythagoreans by Aristotle.[55] The great divide produces not contraries but the opposition of two independent bodies, well established in their self-identities rather than through a relation of opposition. Here are two fundamental principles, based upon two sets of three properties, allowing humans to name two well-identified shapes: night and fire, the former ignorant, dense and thick, the latter celestial, gentle and light.

2.2.2   The Distribution of Shares – a Cosmogonical Process?

Fragment B 9 provides a subsequent step in the unfolding of the beautiful arrangement of words promised by the Goddess:

> And so, since all things have been named light and night,
> and since the names relative to the powers of these [of light and night] have
> been given to some things and to others . . .

> αὐτὰρ ἐπειδὴ πάντα φάος καὶ νὺξ ὀνόμασται
> καὶ τὰ κατὰ σφετέρας δυνάμεις ἐπὶ τοῖσί τε καὶ τοῖς . . .

> (Parmenides, DK 28 B 9.1–2)

The demiurgical dimension of language becomes explicit here. Because things have been given certain names, they have received the powers of the things referred to by these very names, i.e. light and night. To receive the names of fire and light is to receive a share of them. The implied practice is not that of marshalling troops, but of distributing shares, a common practice in the epic poems as far as loot, game, meat, and land are concerned, and a context in which the question of equality is significant.[56] There also seem to be two levels of this distribution through naming. First, *all things* have been named *light* and *night*. Secondly, the names *corresponding to* the respective powers of light and night have been given to things. It seems credible to identify this pair of light and night with the pair of fire and night, and to then identify their powers with the signs previously mentioned (once more: celestial, gentle and light; ignorant, dense and thick). As the distribution of words becomes a 'making-of-the-world',

---

[54] See the many oppositions between all the possible nuances of the signs of night and fire, summarised by Mourelatos 2008: 245 table 5A.
[55] See Arist. *Metaph.* 1.5.986a22–b2.   [56] See Borecký 1965 and Macé 2014.

signs become powers – capacities to act in a certain way or resist being acted upon. There are two levels in the distribution of names: everything has received the name of night and fire, but the various names relative to their different powers have been distributed differently. Maybe some things have received certain signs of fire rather than others (being lighter, or more glowing or gentler), because the proportion of fire and night distributed is different every time. How consistent is this diversified distribution of nominal powers with the universal distribution of the names of fire and night? We need first to make sure we have the right idea about the universality of the distribution of the two foundational names. Do we need to think that everything has received both the names of night and light? Or that everything has received either of them or at least one of them? This question seems to be answered by the third and fourth verses:

> everything is full of light and invisible night together,
> both of them equal, since nothing is part of neither of them.[57]

> πᾶν πλέον ἐστὶν ὁμοῦ φάεος καὶ νυκτὸς ἀφάντου
> ἴσων ἀμφοτέρων, ἐπεὶ οὐδετέρῳ μέτα μηδέν. (Parmenides, DK 28 B 9.3–4)

If each and everything is full of light and night *together* (ὁμοῦ), the inescapable answer to our previous questions is that everything has received a share of *both* (regardless of the respective proportion of each share in each individual nature). The number of shares of night and fire distributed is simply equal because everything has received a share of both, together. The last clause, however, introduces a nuance: looking at night and fire as a distributed sum of shares, it states that there is nothing that is not a part of at least one of them (since there is nothing that would not belong to either of them). The equal amount is only explained by the very fact that each and every thing has received a portion of each (regardless of the volume of the individual portion), but we might retain this further precision that in any case there is absolutely nothing that would not belong at least to one of them. This means that the equal number of shares could still be reached even if there were to be some exceptions of a few things being only part of one of them, as long as these exceptions are of equal number on

---

[57] There has been much discussion on how to construct ἐπεὶ οὐδετέρωι μέτα μηδέν. I follow Fränkel (1962: 412), who constructs the preposition μέτα with the dative, a frequent use in epic poetry. For a list of commentators having made this choice, and also different ones, see Bollack 1990: 26–27 n. 34. The main objection levelled against Fränkel by Mansfeld, followed by Bollack (Mansfeld 1964: 151–52; Bollack 1990: 26–27), is that night and fire are individual realities and that the use of μέτα with a singular dative goes for collective or multiple realities, such as armies. I think that night and fire, as sets of distributed shares, become collective entities.

both sides. This might help in answering the fundamental objection to this reading of B 9, as it has been developed by Jaap Mansfeld.[58] If one understands πᾶν as meaning each and every thing, and measures the equality of night and day by the fact that each and every thing has received a part of night and fire, then we have to understand that everything is a mixture of night and fire *together*, ὁμοῦ. What then are we to make of unmixed things, if any? Mansfeld names two: the corpses that consist in pure night according to Theophrastus (A 46, ll. 13–15) and the presence of pure fire in B 12:

> The narrower ones are indeed filled with pure fire,
> and next to these, others are full of night; then, a share of flame comes forward.

αἱ γὰρ στεινότεραι πλῆντο πυρὸς ἀκρήτοιο,
αἱ δ᾽ ἐπὶ ταῖς νυκτός, μετὰ δὲ φλογὸς ἵεται αἶσα·   (Parmenides, DK 28 B 12.1–2)

We shall come back to the corpse issue. Now there is no way the crowns of pure fire can fit in a world where everything is full of night and light. It is interesting to see the word αἶσα occur in this fragment, a word used to describe the share in the context of Archaic distributions.[59] It hints at B 9: the movement of this share of fire resembles a real version of the distribution of the name and power of light. This fits with the cosmogonical reading of this fragment in the light of Aëtius 2.7.1 (A 37), where the alternation of the crowns of pure night and pure fire are described as a pre-cosmogonical stage of the universe.[60] The cosmogony would actually consist in a motion starting from the central crown and producing a mixture of night and fire, as shares of night seem to move towards the centre and shares of fire towards the periphery. Without making an attempt to describe the genetic process itself, we could propose one possible preliminary test for our hypothesis. Has the resulting nature of everything that appears as a result of this process received a share of both night and fire?

2.3   The Resulting Natures: A Cosmology of Mixed Bodies

We now move to the third step of men's construction of nature, after the separation and the distribution. In B 19, we find another occurrence of the κατατίθημι–ὀνομάζειν association. The Goddess seems to conclude a description of how all things were born or grew according to opinions:

---

[58] Mansfeld 1964: 150–56.   [59] Cf. Borecký 1965.   [60] Cf. Bollack 1990.

This, for you, is how, according to opinion, these things grew and how they are now,
and how from this time onwards, having taken shape, they will perish:
to them men have assigned a name that distinguishes each.

οὕτω τοι κατὰ δόξαν ἔφυ τάδε καί νυν ἔασι
καὶ μετέπειτ᾽ ἀπὸ τοῦδε τελευτήσουσι τραφέντα·
τοῖς δ᾽ ὄνομ᾽ ἄνθρωποι κατέθεντ᾽ ἐπίσημον ἑκάστῳ.   (Parmenides, DK 28 B 19)

The establishing of names allows humans to mark and differentiate each being that comes to be and perishes. The use of φύω recalls B 10, where the Goddess has promised that her interlocutor will learn 'whence the sky has grown' (οὐρανὸν ... ἔνθεν ἔφυ) and B 11, where the earth, sun, moon, aether, the Milky Way in the sky, Olympus, and the stars all 'set out to come to be' (ὡρμήθησαν / γίγνεσθαι). B 19 seems to extend this to the way living beings will take shape[61] and die. The σήματα of B 10 would appear to correspond to the names given at B 19: to know how things grew is also to recognise the signs that have been allotted to each of them. The φύσις and ἔργα of B 10 – nature and the effects of the aether, the sun and the moon – seem to correspond to this ideal of knowing each and every thing in its nature and effects. B 10 thus features an Odyssean echo, reminding us of Hermes' revelation of the nature of the molu, this magical plant which has dark roots and milky white flowers.[62] Acquiring knowledge of the nature and effects of the aether, the sun and the moon would be to understand how they behave on the basis of the genetic process from which they emerged. Here is the final main test for our hypothesis: can all individual natures be explained by the shares of light and night granted through the process of their generation?

The description of the cosmogonical process by Aëtius might lead to the impression that the sun and the Milky Way are exhalations of fire only, whilst the moon would be what consisted of 'a mixture of both, of air and fire'.[63] But Aëtius corrects this impression: both the sun and the moon have appeared in the cosmogonical process as 'they were separated from the Milky Way' (ἐκ τοῦ γαλαξίου κύκλου ἀποκριθῆναι),[64] and the milky (γαλακτοειδὲς) colour of this circle is due to 'the mixture of dense and rare' (τὸ τοῦ πυκνοῦ καὶ τοῦ ἀραιοῦ μῖγμα).[65] The sun and the moon both come from that mixed stuff, the former from a rarer mix – which makes it hotter – and the latter from a denser one – which makes it

---

[61] For this use of τρέφω, with an analogy to curdling, see Demont 1978.   [62] *Od.* 10.302–6.
[63] Aëtius 2.7.1 = DK A 37: τοῦ δὲ πυρὸς ἀναπνοὴν τὸν ἥλιον καὶ τὸν γαλαξίαν κύκλον / συμμιγῆ δ᾽ ἐξ ἀμφοῖν εἶναι τὴν σελήνην, τοῦ τ᾽ ἀέρος καὶ τοῦ πυρός (Mansfeld and Runia 2010).
[64] Aëtius 2.20.15 = DK A 43.   [65] Aëtius 3.1.4 = DK A 43a.

colder.[66] All these celestial bodies did receive their shares of both night and fire. The proportion of these portions explains the variety of their properties.

It has been credited as an important step in the history of Greek astronomy that Parmenides came up with the idea that, despite having some fire in it, the moon does not shine by itself.[67] The proportion of darkness in the moon explains its earthy appearance, as well as the fact that it seems 'falsely appearing'.[68] Despite having fire in it, the moon cannot shine on its own: its fire is too mixed, too gentle. It needs the sun to light up. Hence the idea that it requires an alien light to shine in the night (νυκτιφαὲς ... ἀλλότριον φῶς, B 14). The specific combination of dark and light would also explain the behaviour of the moon, wandering in darkness in search of the sun (αἰεὶ παπταίνουσα πρὸς αὐγὰς ἠελίοιο, B 15), being able to catch it from time to time, in measures that will explain its changing appearance. Thus, mixture explains the moon in both its composition and its activity, shining in the darkness of a borrowed light because of a too significant share of darkness in its composition.

What about the sun? Does its specific mixed nature also explain its properties and actions? B 10 might yield something in this direction:

καθαρᾶς εὐαγέος ἠελίοιο
λαμπάδος ἔργ᾽ ἀΐδηλα

(Parmenides, DK 28 B 10.10–11)

The term ἀΐδηλος is variously translated. It has an active meaning ('make invisible', 'destroy') and a passive one ('what cannot be seen', 'the invisible', 'obscure').[69] In Homer the adjective is used with its active meaning to qualify the warrior gods such as Athena and Ares, the best human fighter (Achilles), or a fire which destroys everything: the phrase ἔργ᾽ ἀΐδηλα seems to combine the ideas of destruction and of being detestable.[70] But Hesiod uses the same expression to mean 'invisibility', when he speaks of the raven which goes up to reveal to Apollo some ἔργ᾽ ἀΐδηλα that had been extraordinarily hidden from the god who knows everything.[71] Ἀΐδηλα

---

[66] Aëtius 2.20.15 = DK A 43: τὸν μὲν ἀπὸ τοῦ ἀραιοτέρου μίγματος ὃ δὴ θερμόν, τὴν δὲ ἀπὸ τοῦ πυκνοτέρου ὅπερ ψυχρόν.

[67] See Graham 2013: Chapter 3.

[68] Aëtius 2.30.4 = Stob. *Ecl.* 1.26.1: <Παρμενίδης> διὰ τὸ παραμεμῖχθαι τῷ περὶ αὐτὴν πυρώδει τὸ ζοφῶδες, ὅθεν ψευδοφανῆ τὸν ἀστέρα καλεῖ.

[69] See the discussion of these two meanings and their various supporters by Mourelatos 2008: 237 n. 43.

[70] See all the pre-Parmenidean occurrences collected by Mourelatos 2008: 237 n. 44.

[71] Fr. 60.2–3 Merkelbach and West: 'He told long haired Phoebus some unseen deeds' (ἔφρασεν ἔργ᾽ ἀΐδηλα / Φοίβωι ἀκερσεκόμηι). The hidden deeds concern the unfaithfulness of Coronis to Apollo; see the scholion to Pindar, *Pythian* 3, where there is an insistence on the fact that Apollo knows

can also refer to the invisible things at stake whenever an offering is burning, in a striking contrast between the fire and the invisible dimension it relates to.[72] What reason could Parmenides have to call any activity of the sun 'invisible'? One hypothesis could be what has already been stated about the moon: the sun does something even when we do not see it – whilst invisible, the sun makes the moon shine with an alien light despite its wandering in darkness. So, most of the things that make up the contents of the universe, from the Milky Way to living beings on earth, would seem to have their bodies and actions explained by such mixtures of fire and night, a continuous mixture of specific proportions. The explanation of sensation and thought also seems to require a mixture (κρᾶσις) in the limbs of man (see B 16 and A 46).[73]

But does this extend to all things? At both extremes, we might still find bodies of pure fire and pure night: above the Milky Way, will the aether not be made of the shares of the purest fire? At the centre of the cold earth, whence all shares of air will have been expelled, shall we find pure night? Will the corpses of the deceased, losing their fiery part, be a portion of pure night, perceiving only darkness, silence and cold?[74] Maybe yes, but this does not necessarily constitute a serious objection to our hypothesis, as B 9 makes room for exceptions. Aether is said to be 'common' (ξυνός) in B 11, as is the earth in Homer's description of the distribution of cosmic shares between the sons of Cronos (*Il.* 15.187–93). It is probably so because it encompasses everything else. But the analysis of Archaic distribution practices allows the differentiation of two types of 'commons': the 'common' consisting in the fact that everybody has received the same share of something, the 'common' that is put to the side of the distribution, set aside as a reserve for all but not (yet) cut into individual portions, as is the earth in Homer.[75] So a general distribution of an equal number of shares of night and fire (equal in number, but always specific in proportions) would not be at odds with the simultaneous definition of reserves of both stuffs. It would, moreover, be complementary: just as both types of 'commons' are necessary to the good disposition of a political community, one could expect a world-order designed by human words to also display this very

---

everything (3.30: πάντα ἰσάντι νόῳ, text Maehler) – it is all the more amazing that any deed should have remained invisible to him.
[72] See Hes. *Op.* 755–56: 'When encountering burning victims, do not mock the invisible' (μηδ' ἱεροῖσιν ἐπ' αἰθομένοισι κυρήσας / μωμεύειν ἀίδηλα).
[73] See Cherubin (2005: 4–7) for a detailed explanation of the whole of sensation, not only sight, through the presence of light and night in everything.
[74] See Aëtius 5.30.4 = DK 28 A 46e.   [75] See Macé 2014.

character. We would then fall back on the rule described at B 9.4: some things, like the deepest earth and the corpses, or the pure aether, might only belong to one of the two realms of fire and night. Being symmetrical, they would not threaten the equality of night and fire, nor the common law for everything else, full of night and fire together.

I hope to have shown that there is a link between the nature of the criticism of human knowledge by Parmenides and the consistency of his reconstruction of the human picture of the universe. It is only because Parmenides reduces the epic claim for truth to the projection of human ideas on being that he is able to reconstruct a cosmogony and a cosmology on the basis of the use of human practices, such as marshalling troops and distribution of shares. Thus, Parmenides accomplishes the criticism of anthropologism developed by Xenophanes and expands it to the whole of cosmogony and cosmology, uncovering the practices of men at work behind the picture of the universe they would like us to believe. And we are expected from now on to refrain from following this path:

> It [*your mind*] will not cut being from holding on to being,
> neither scattering it in good order, in every way and in all directions,
> nor gathering it again.

> οὐ γὰρ ἀποτμήξει τὸ ἐὸν τοῦ ἐόντος ἔχεσθαι
> οὔτε σκιδνάμενον πάντῃ πάντως κατὰ κόσμον
> οὔτε συνιστάμενον.   (Parmenides, DK 28 B 4.2–4)

If we hesitate to translate κατὰ κόσμον here as 'across the universe', we may hear the epic sense of the phrase, as previously examined, and see in this fragment a statement on what mortals try to achieve through the cosmogonies they unfold in so many words. Humans thrive for order: they believe the demiurgic order of their words will distribute things κατὰ κόσμον, in good order, just as one distributes shares of loot or meat. We now understand exactly what this good order means: having first gathered together the two great bodies of fire and night, they 'scatter' shares of both of them to create all natures, so that each of them has received the exact proportion of night and fire that will explain its appearance and behaviour. But their words only display the order they have themselves put together, the order they like to find in their various properties and actions. The order and consistency of human accounts is the greatest cause of the deceit they nourish in everyone.

Parmenides uncovers the logic at work in the cosmogonies and cosmologies of poets and wise people – the projection of a human taste for order onto the whole universe. In doing so, he makes it explicit that the universe is something that is being put in order by clever mortals, exactly as armies and poems are. I suggest that Parmenides, in doing so, made it easier to extend the use of κόσμος beyond the realm of armies, costumes and songs to embrace the whole universe, as it is likely Empedocles and Philolaus did after him.[76] Overlooking the critical dimension of Parmenides' description of the illusions of mortal language, thinkers none-theless rushed in to build on the analogies brought to light by the Eleatic. Anaxagoras deepened the analogy between military order and the order of the universe.[77] A time for rich analogies to be drawn between human order and cosmic order had been opened – a time when human dancers started to imitate the motions of stars,[78] and Plato would come to think of the just soul and just city as reflections of the well-ordered cosmic soul.[79]

---

[76] See Horky in Chapter 1.   [77] See Macé and Therme 2013.

[78] See Chapter 9 of this volume by Gagné, tracking the 'metaphor stream' of astral choruses back to Euripides' tragedies.

[79] See the contributions of Brisson (Chapter 6) and Atack (Chapter 8) in this volume.

CHAPTER 3

Diakosmêsis

Malcolm Schofield

If you look up the word διακόσμησις in the Greek lexicon, you will find that the second sense or application listed in LSJ is given as: '*the orderly arrangement* of the Universe, esp. in the Pythagorean system'. The first reference given is to Chapter 5 – the Pythagorean chapter – of the first book of Aristotle's *Metaphysics* (1.5.986a6), although the next (to Plutarch's life of Pericles: *Per.* 4.4) relates to Anaxagoras, not the Pythagoreans, and the one after that to what sounds like a Stoic such as Cleanthes (Sextus Empiricus, *Against the Mathematicians* 9.27; cf. Cicero, *On the Nature of the Gods* 2.15). My first reaction to the implication in the lexicon entry is that this use of the word is especially common in ancient presentations or discussions of Pythagoreanism was incredulity – which further investigation has not dispelled.

Why the lexicographers took this view one can only guess. Perhaps they had noticed that Plato, the first surviving author to employ the expression at all, speaks – occasionally – of διακόσμησις only when writing about the ordering of human affairs; and that the instance in the *Metaphysics* is the sole use of it in this or indeed any sense in the authentic works of Aristotle, although like Plato he uses the verb διακοσμέω (from which the noun derives) in cosmological contexts from time to time, for example in comments on the systems of Anaximenes (*Physics* 8.9.265b32) and Empedocles (*On the Heavens* 1.10.280a20), and in describing the project of the first two books of his own *On the Heavens* (*Meteorologica* 1.1.338a22). Any inferences from an author's unique use of any particular word would, however, obviously constitute a shaky basis for the kind of claim LSJ make about διακόσμησις in its cosmological application.

Nonetheless, although the lexicon might set us off in a wrong direction with its remark about Pythagoreanism, thinking about the term διακόσμησις – or rather, the related expressions διακοσμέω, 'order' or 'arrange', and διάκοσμος (which seems to be the noun that most nearly corresponds to διακόσμησις in Presocratic usage) – will turn out to throw interesting light on the entire unfolding narrative of early Greek philoso-phy. A good place to begin exploration of the topic is with Anaxagoras, one of the major Presocratic thinkers of the mid fifth century BCE. Plutarch's mention of him in his life of Pericles will make a useful jumping off point.

Plutarch says of him that he was 'the first to make νοῦς, intellect, not τύχη, chance, or ἀνάγκη, necessity, the origin (ἀρχή) of διακόσμησις'.[1] As it happens, the passage that lies behind Plutarch's statement actually survives. It is Fragment B 12 in the standard[2] collection of Presocratic fragments, preserved as often by the late Neoplatonist commentator Simplicius, and the longest continuous stretch of Anaxagoras extant.[3] After explaining how intellect differs radically from everything else there is, and after outlining its exceptional powers and the way it exerts control over living things, Anaxagoras describes its initiation of the 'rotation' (περιχώρησις), the mechanism by which cosmic order was produced: this is how intellect 'ordered all things' (πάντα διεκόσμησε).[4]

This is not creation out of nothing. Intellect operates on a pre-existing reality. Its work consists in ordering and arranging what is there already, principally by causing separation of the hot from the cold, the dry from the wet, and so on. Hence Anaxagoras' choice of the verb διακοσμέω to convey the idea. The implication is that the ordered universe we inhabit is the product of intelligent design. Quite how design could be achieved by the mechanism of rotation Anaxagoras describes has always puzzled readers, from Plato and Aristotle (who both comment in explicit terms on their bafflement) to the present. But design is what Anaxagoras asserts – and indeed it would be hard to understand his conviction that cosmic order is the work of intellect if that were not the case.

Plutarch makes a contrast between Anaxagoras and other thinkers who explain διακόσμησις as the result of chance or necessity. He (or the source on which he draws) clearly has in mind the Presocratic Atomists Leucippus and Democritus, and their theory of how the random collisions and intertwinings of atoms moving through the void will inevitably from time to time, and at different points in infinite space, result in the genera-tion of an ordered universe (indeed – although Plutarch does not seem to be making this point – universes in the plural, in fact in infinite numbers). For Democritus, the junior member of the duo, there is evidence of a deliberate reaction against Anaxagoras' position. Diogenes Laertius quotes a report by Favorinus (contemporary and friend of Plutarch) to

---

[1] Plut. *Per.* 4.4. [2] Diels–Kranz, which is employed throughout this volume. [3] DK 59 B 12.
[4] See Simpl. *in Phys.* p. 156.21–29 Diels.

the effect that Democritus accused Anaxagoras of plagiarising from earlier thinkers his pronouncements on the sun and the moon, and poured abuse on his claims 'about the διακόσμησις and intellect'.[5] Moreover, there is reason to think that on one other specific matter Democritus' own stance was articulated in conscious opposition to Anaxagoras'.

The relevant passage in Anaxagoras occurs in his Fragment B 4. Here he seems to be proposing that other worlds than our own could be formed – indeed have been formed. He says that this is what we must suppose:[6]

> Humans were put together and the other animals, as many as have soul. And among the humans, cities have been established as communities and tech-nology has been developed, just as with us. And they have sun and moon and the rest, just as with us, and the earth grows for them all manner of plants, of which they garner what is beneficial into their habitation and put it to use. (Anaxagoras, DK 59 B 4)

In other words, these other worlds must be conceived as pretty well exactly the same as our own world, not just in having sun and moon and so forth the same as we do, but with human habitation and cultivation like ours too. Democritus had a very different view, as we learn from quite a detailed report in Hippolytus (*Refutation of All Heresies* 1.13.2):

> There are worlds unlimited in number and differing in size. In some there is no sun or moon, and in some they are larger than with us and in some more numerous. The intervals between the worlds are unequal. Here there are more worlds, there fewer; some are growing, some are at their peak, others are in decline; here they are coming into existence, there they are falling away. And some worlds are devoid of animals and plants and all moisture. (Democritus, DK 68 A 40)

Democritus' very specific insistence that in some worlds there is no sun or moon, and that even when there is, these will sometimes differ in size and number from our own, looks pointedly anti-Anaxagorean, as does also his no doubt related proposition about the biosphere. The implicit critique of Anaxagoras strikes one as rather powerful. It is not easy to discern or imagine the rationale for Anaxagoras' line on other worlds, certainly given that all we know of it is confined to a short passage in B 4. David Sedley in *Creationism and its Critics in Antiquity* made an interesting attempt to construe the passage as evidence of the teleologically oriented design of intellect as first cause.[7] It remains to be seen how much support his proposal will gather.

---

[5] Diog. Laert. 9.34–5 = Favorinus F 81 Amato.
[6] Simplicius reports the fragment verbatim (*in Phys.* p. 35.3–8 Diels).   [7] Sedley 2007: Chapter 1.

I suspect that what annoyed Democritus in Anaxagoras' theories was not only their substance, but his very use of the verb διακοσμέω itself. In Diogenes Laertius' catalogue of Democritus' writings, we find the following information about the book titles Thrasyllus (the author of Diogenes' catalogue of Plato's oeuvre also) included in the third of his so-called tetralogies:

> Great διάκοσμος (the school of Theophrastus maintains that this was a work of Leucippus); *Small* διάκοσμος; *Cosmography*; *On the planets*. (DK 68 A 33 = Diogenes Laertius 9.46)

Scholarship has pretty firmly and well-nigh unanimously accepted that Theophrastus' view on the authorship of *Great* διάκοσμος must be right. Theophrastus did serious work on the Presocratics, evidently read many of their works in the original, and had no particular known motive to falsify the evidence, whereas Thrasyllus – at work three hundred years later – had every reason to want to make his catalogue as impressive as possible, and in any case may have been unaware that the attribution to Democritus had been questioned by an eminent authority.

What will Leucippus have meant by talk of διάκοσμος? It seems unlikely that it is just an alternative for κόσμος, the standard word for a 'world' in Presocratic discourse.[8] The numerous doxographical reports which use κόσμος in discussing different aspects of atomist cosmology (the Hippolytus text just cited is a case in point) make it probable that this is how Leucippus and Democritus talked too, even though no verbatim quotations survive. One might expect that the different term διάκοσμος, whether or not Leucippus himself gave his work that designation (titles seem to have come in on a significant scale only later in the fifth century than Leucippus, who was probably roughly contemporary with Anaxagoras),[9] would have been employed to signify something different. One possibility worth considering is that it was an attempt to capture the idea that physics cannot restrict itself to talking about how a κόσμος comes into being and how it is structured. Physics must discuss the whole plurality of κόσμοι (in the plural). We may recall Homer's use of the verb διακοσμέω, in comparing the marshalling of the Greek troops before Troy into their different divisions 'here and here' (ἔνθα καὶ ἔνθα, perhaps capitalising on the distributive use of διά as preposition and as prefix in

---

[8] Or so – following e.g. Kahn 1960: Appendix 1 – I would suppose. But for an alternative view, see the discussions by Horky in Chapter 1 and Macé in Chapter 2.
[9] See Schmalzriedt 1970.

many verbs),[10] with the way goatherds divide flocks which have mingled at pasture (*Il.* 2.474–76),[11] although of course there is no separation from original mixture in atomism. So, I think the common translation of 'great διάκοσμος' as 'great world-system', if construed as expressing the idea I have just articulated, and as indicating a distribution of worlds while paradoxically subtracting any connotation of design or deliberate organisation, may well be on the right lines.

If we suppose that Leucippus used the word 'διάκοσμος' in his book to express the notion of such a chance system of worlds, whether or not he himself gave it that title, then Anaxagoras' appropriation of the verb διακοσμέω to describe organisation of a single such world, particularly as due to intellect as agent of such organisation, might well have been found provocative by Democritus. If, on the other hand, διάκοσμος talk in atomism is solely Democritean, then it is attractive to conjecture that it represented a conscious attempt on his part to put the terminology to a wholly different use from Anaxagoras'.

There has often been puzzlement about what the title *Small* διάκοσμος that was given to Democritus' own book was intended to indicate about its subject. My conjecture would be that the book dealt with the different kinds of arrangement of complexes of atoms at the microscopic level, explained in terms of variations in 'rhythm, touching, and turning' (ῥυσμῷ καὶ διαθιγῇ καὶ τροπῇ), as reported by Aristotle (*Metaphysics* I.4.985b4–18), and as elaborated in a number of other testimonia: in short, the system of microcosmic κόσμοι. We know from Theophrastus' *On Sense-Perception* that his explanation of why some things taste to us sweet, others bitter, or why some feel hard, others soft, and so on, made considerable appeal to just such explanations of microscopic arrangements of atoms. We know too that Thrasyllus grouped it with three unequivocally physical treatises.

It is sometimes supposed that by a 'small διάκοσμος' Democritus meant to be referring to man, rather as Aristotle implies that an animal can be viewed as a 'small κόσμος'.[12] The only concrete support for the suggestion available is a passage from the late and obscure Neoplatonist writer David, where he ascribes to Democritus (B 34) the doctrine pertaining to man as 'small κόσμος'.[13] But the ascription is not credible. The doctrine in question is clearly Platonist: it presupposes the tripartite division of the soul.

---

[10] See LSJ s.v. A.I.5.

[11] Interestingly, the whole section of Book 2 of the *Iliad* that we call 'the catalogue of ships' was sometimes named the διάκοσμος in antiquity, as by Strabo, *Geography* 12.3.5.

[12] Arist. *Phys.* 8.2.252b26.   [13] David, *Prol.* p. 38.14 Busse.

Somehow David must have heard that Democritus used an expression like 'small κόσμος', and applied his own Platonist repertoire of ideas to interpret it. His suggestion might have been more appropriately argued from the usage of the author – very likely late fifth century – of Book 1 of the Hippocratic treatise *de Victu*, who uses the verb διακοσμέω at several points. He tells us, for example, that fire has 'arranged fittingly all the parts of the body in imitation of the whole universe (τὸ πᾶν)' (*Vict.* 10.1).[14]

But the Hippocratic author's overall approach to physical explanation in general echoes Presocratic theories other than atomist, particularly Anaxagorean and Heraclitean. The human body would not be very likely to have been conceived by Atomists as replicating in a smaller version the structure of the universe itself. Thrasyllus' catalogue does, however, ascribe to Democritus a work *On the Nature of Man* (Diog. Laert. 9.46), and that if anywhere is where one might have expected to find a discussion of human physical constitution, although the catalogue gives it the alternative name *On Flesh*, which may suggest a narrower focus.[15] On the alternative interpretation proposed above, by entitling his book *Small διάκοσμος* Democritus will have advertised his intention to offer a fundamental theoretical treatment of the physics that he assumes valid for explaining how and why sensation works as it does – as a counterpart at that level to Leucippus' theory of the movement through void and consequent intermingling of atoms at the macroscopic level of cosmology.

On the evidence we have reviewed so far, the idea of διακόσμησις, and the use not of that term but of associated vocabulary – the verb διακοσμέω and the noun διάκοσμος – belong to a mid- to late-fifth-century context, and if Favorinus' report on Democritus is reliable, may have become a focal point in crystallising how the atomist cosmic vision diverges from Anaxagoras'. Are there any other traces of such a controversy in the evidence for cosmological thought of that time? The one figure who deserves consideration from this viewpoint is Diogenes of Apollonia, the last of the Presocratics to survive for us in any bulk. What Theophrastus (as summarised by Simplicius) said of him already encourages the expectation that he might be of particular interest for our question. 'Diogenes of Apollonia', we are told, 'pretty much the last of those who occupied themselves with these matters [i.e. physical enquiries], wrote for the most

---

[14] I am grateful to Stavros Kouloumentas for directing my attention to *de Victu*.

[15] The surviving testimonies on Democritus' treatment of biological questions are numerous but seem to be mostly concerned with the zoological sphere much more broadly (DK 68 A 139–63). These topics were presumably tackled primarily in the works known to the catalogue as *Explanations on Seeds, Plants, and Fruits* and the three books of *Explanations on Animals* (Diog. Laert. 9.47).

part jumbling up ideas, some of them along the lines of Anaxagoras, some of them those of Leucippus'.[16] But in his work *On Nature* – a book Simplicius says has 'reached me' – he is said to have made the more distinctive claim, neither Anaxagorean nor Leucippan, although not without Presocratic precedent, that air, infinite and eternal, constituted the basic nature of the universe.[17]

Among the extant fragments of Diogenes, the one that is most relevant to our present concerns is the long B 5, cited by Simplicius. A glance over the train of thought it articulates reveals that Diogenes' approach to cosmology represents what one might call Anaxagorean revisionism. The opening lines are obviously highly reminiscent of the beginning of Anaxagoras' B 12 on intellect. For Diogenes, too, intelligence is in the cosmic driving seat. But it is introduced as a predicate, not (as with Anaxagoras) as subject. Air (or what humans call air), the basic substance, is what governs and controls and is in everything, not intellect (as in Anaxagoras): air is what *has* νόησις, thinking or intelligence. That is the first and most obvious divergence from Anaxagoras. Only slightly less immediately apparent is another major difference: Diogenes makes no claim whatever about the way the world developed, nor about how (if it did) the process was initiated and controlled by air or what steers all things. All Diogenes' tenses in the relevant part of B 5 (reproduced verbatim by Simplicius: *in Phys.* p. 152.21–25 Diels) are present tenses (or in one instance a perfect tense). So he has no room or need for Anaxagoras' past tense διεκόσμησε, 'ordered', 'arranged'. He does talk of arranging or disposing, in the present tense. But he employs a different and less grandiose verb, in much more common use: διατίθημι, used by him not solely in B 5. Fragment B 3 focuses much more explicitly than does B 5 on cosmic order, and it concludes with the general remark that wherever one looks, then on reflection one will find that everything is 'arranged' in the finest possible way: the verb is the perfect participle διακείμενα (see Simplicius, *in Phys.* p. 152.15 Diels) – I think aspect of the perfect (i.e. present state), not past tense, is what is salient here. It is as though Diogenes wants entirely to sidestep any argument over the proper application of διακόσμησις talk.

*

So far we have been looking at instances of such talk in (or in relation to) mid- to late-fifth-century BCE thinkers. But the first recorded use of the vocabulary in Presocratic philosophy is the appearance of the word

---

[16] Simpl. *in Phys.* p. 25.1–3 Diels = DK 64 A 5.   [17] Simpl. *in Phys.* p. 25.4–8 Diels = DK 64 A 5.

διάκοσμος at the beginning of the δόξα section of Parmenides' poem.[18] At B 8.60 Parmenides' goddess undertakes to tell him 'the whole διάκοσμον ἐοικότα, for so no thought of mortals shall ever outstrip you'. Scholarship has agonised long and hard over the phrase διάκοσμον ἐοικότα, though the focus of the puzzling has been very much ἐοικότα rather than διάκοσμον. That debate has recently been reviewed in a full and careful discussion by Jenny Bryan in *Likeness and Likelihood in the Presocratics and Plato*, and any reader who wants to get closer to the issues at stake there needs to consult her study.[19] I find persuasive her proposal that while ἐοικότα is multi-faceted in the potentialities of its meaning here, there is a good case for seeing the forensic usage 'plausible' as the most salient in context, carrying with it the implication 'merely plausible'. What Parmenides seems to be doing at this juncture in the poem is rounding off the sequence of exposition begun at B 8.50–52, where the goddess announces the end of her treatment of ἀλήθείη, and the start of her presentation of mortal opinions.[20]

However that may be, for our purposes the thing to note is the suggestion of ring composition made by the clause ἐγὼ διάκοσμον ἐοικότα πάντα φατίζω, 'I declare the whole plausible διάκοσμος', which seems to constitute a sort of echo of the clause κόσμον ἐμῶν ἐπέων ἀπατηλὸν ἀκούων in line 52 ('listening to the deceptive ordering of my verses'), just as βροτῶν γνώμη ('thought of mortals') in line 61 corresponds in a way with δόξας ... βροτείας ('mortal opinions') in line 51. The 'ordering' represented by διάκοσμος is the arrangement of the constituents of the physical world which is going to be described in the part of the poem that follows. But Parmenides wants simultaneously to convey the implication that that arrangement is no more than the deceptive κόσμος, 'order', of the goddess's words or verses. It is simply a construction: a construction, line 61 in effect claims, that is superior to any other that has been or is likely to be devised, but a construction all the same. All there is to mortal belief or opinion – he is intimating – is a story about how things are: a story which can be told in different ways, but none of them actually capturing the way reality is in itself. διάκοσμος as cosmic order is nothing other than the way mortals – theologians and Presocratic physicists included or indeed

---

[18] See also Macé's discussion in Chapter 2.   [19] See Bryan 2012: Chapter 2.

[20] The extent of that expository passage between B 8.50–52 and 60–61 is uncertain. Simplicius gives us just lines 53–59 in his quotation of what he presents as a continuous sequence consisting of lines 50–61; but Theo Ebert argued a while ago that lines 34–41 really belong here (between line 54 and line 55), and John Palmer follows him in *Parmenides and Presocratic Philosophy* – and I am myself attracted to the proposal. See Ebert 1989, Palmer 2009: 139–40, 163–67, 352–54.

perhaps pre-eminently – decide to arrange their narrative. I suspect that the choice of διάκοσμον rather than κόσμον in line 60 is meant to issue a further linguistic reminder (beyond that already signalled in line 52) that κόσμος does not actually mean 'world' or 'world-order' – διάκοσμος, a merely human 'arrangement', is all it is.

I said: 'theologians and Presocratic physicists included'. It is evident that the cosmology Parmenides went on to expound designedly incorporated elements that echoed Hesiod and Anaximander (in his case, the theory of celestial bands posited to explain the appearance and movements of the sun, moon and stars, i.e. planets and fixed stars). And if we had fuller evidence of the earliest Greek cosmological speculation, very likely other echoes would be detectable. I suspect that Parmenides made the boast he did about the superiority of his own scheme precisely because he had contrived to incorporate from all the major thinkers and writers on such themes who had preceded him some headline feature or features of their cosmological schemes: creating out of them a sort of encyclopaedic system.

In calling that system a κόσμος or διάκοσμος; in stating or implying that it is not an order with any valid claim to objective reality, but a construction of 'my verses'; and in branding it 'deceptive' or 'plausible': in all this Parmenides must surely have been subjecting to critique one of the master concepts employed in early cosmology – the very notion of κόσμος itself. There is no direct evidence that the Milesians deployed the concept of κόσμος. But as Charles Kahn argued more than fifty years ago in *Anaximander and the Origins of Greek Cosmology*, the indirect evidence for Anaximander is very strong, in the very precise and unusual wording, 'all the heavens (οὐρανοί) and the worlds or world-orders (κόσμοι) within them', found in doxographical versions of Theophrastus' account of his views (preserved by Hippolytus and Simplicius).[21] 'This κόσμος did none of gods nor humans make', wrote Heraclitus (DK 22 B 30)[22] – which shows that by his time (somewhere at the end of the sixth and beginning of the fifth centuries) it was standard cosmological currency.[23] And incidentally, that puzzling formulation of his: 'did none of gods *nor humans* make'

---

[21] See Kahn 1960: 33–35, 46–53, 188–93, 219–30.

[22] I follow the text (from Plutarch and Simplicius) adopted in Kirk 1954: 307–24, which in my view remains in most respects the best treatment of B 30. Kahn 1979: 44 prints and translates Clement's text, dismissing as reflecting 'an inferior variant' – without consideration of Kirk's arguments – the inclusion by Plutarch and Simplicius of 'this' (τόνδε) and the omission of Clement's 'the same for all' (τὸν αὐτὸν ἁπάντων), both as applied to 'world' or 'world-order' (κόσμον).

[23] Any account of the origination or development of the use of κόσμος to mean 'world' or 'world-order' in which B 30 is not to figure as a key element will need to offer a convincing alternative interpretation of Heraclitus' saying.

suggests to me that as Parmenides had Anaximander's talk of κόσμος in his critical sights, Heraclitus in his turn might well have had Parmenides in his. For who else had ever claimed that κόσμος was a *human* invention except Parmenides?[24] The thesis enunciated in the sequel to Heraclitus' pronouncement – 'but it always was and is and will be: an ever-living fire, kindling in measures and being quenched in measures' – was of course designed to give an account of its nature that looked prima facie wholly counter-intuitive and had never been anticipated by any Greek thinker of any kind.

*

We started with the idea that the concept of διακόσμησις became a topic for disagreement and perhaps debate in the mid to late fifth century BCE, with Leucippus and Anaxagoras and Democritus. It now begins to look as though the debate may have started a generation or two earlier, with Parmenides and Heraclitus. Indeed, the issue turns out to encapsulate the basics of a good deal of the entire history of Presocratic thinking about cosmology. If I am right, the dialectic that it generated threw up simultaneously radically opposed views of the right way to explain how and why the κόσμος is as it is, and contestation of the very vocabulary of κόσμος and διάκοσμος in which the explanatory project was articulated.

Thus, one of the ways in which Parmenides attempted to undermine the assumptions on which previous cosmology relied was to prompt recognition that a κόσμος could be no more than the arrangement of the phenomena that some thinker was proposing. He put the point arrestingly by making or remaking κόσμος a κόσμος *of* something: of 'my verses' or 'my words', with their implication of a perspectival, subjective vantage point; and by substituting for κόσμος διάκοσμος: an 'arrangement', presupposing an arranger – emphatically marked by ἐγώ, 'I'. Can we detect any reaction to this particular element in his anti-cosmology? It is, of course, a commonplace of the study of the Presocratics that most of those whom we usually see as his heirs or successors for one reason or another rejected that general stance of his. My suggestion is that Heraclitus' B 30 is most plausibly interpreted as a rejection not only of all previous cosmology but of Parmenides' attempt to exhibit the notion of κόσμος itself as a merely human construct. B 30, like

---

[24] Kirk 1954: 311 observes that the formula οὔτε τις θεῶν οὔτε ἀνθρώπων is a 'polar expression with an all-inclusive sense' and suggests that 'its components are not to be taken separately'. He compares Homer, *Il.* 8.27, 14.342 and Xenophanes DK 21 B 23.1 – all, however, passages where what is said does make sense as applied to each component severally. The fact remains that gods had tradition-ally been considered responsible for cosmic creation, and Parmenides did – provocatively – make it a human fiction.

most of Heraclitus' maxims, sounds like a dogmatic pronouncement. But in some of his methodological and epistemological fragments, he has in effect pointed out to his readers or hearers that, if they think about it, they are perfectly well able to distinguish a perspectival, subjective vantage point from one that is universally and objectively valid, 'listening not to me but to the λόγος' (B 50). And they will then get some understanding of what it is that the λόγος discloses: which is not at all like what Parmenides' goddess has allegedly revealed to him. The Heraclitean assertion in B 30 has to be read as claiming to be reasoned denial of the view that κόσμος expresses no more than a subjective viewpoint. We all have the same κόσμος – and it is something real, or rather it is a process that has always been in existence and always will be. In other words, B 30 does not simply reject Parmenides' treatment of κόσμος as διάκοσμος, a construction, but does so out of methodological and epistemological considerations that are at least as deeply pondered as Parmenides' own.

If Leucippus himself talked of a διάκοσμος as well as of κόσμος, he will obviously have been assuming it to be something that was objectively the case, not some thinker's constructive arrangement of what is taken to be the case. Indeed, the Atomist use of the expression is applied to an arrangement that has no arranger of any kind: the 'great arrangement', the μέγας διάκοσμος, the system formed by all the worlds (κόσμοι) that were and are and will be, is what it is by virtue of what Plutarch called chance or necessity. So his talk of a μέγας διάκοσμος could be read as a further kind of reply – very different from Heraclitus' – to Parmenides' treatment of διάκοσμος as representing merely human perspective. However, in this instance we do not have the clue we do with Heraclitus' οὔτε ἀνθρώπων pointing to active engagement with Parmenides' thinking about κόσμος. It might just have been a case of appropriating Parmenides' vocabulary, for a different and positive purpose.

It makes a nice further episode in the story to suppose that in making intellect architect of the διακόσμησις of this or any other individual κόσμος, Anaxagoras was reclaiming the idea from Leucippus' use of διάκοσμος to convey the notion of a whole architectless system of an equally architectless system of κόσμοι; and to see Democritus as particularly riled in his turn by such an attempt on Anaxagoras' part to reorient διακόσμησις talk for an entirely different – and in Democritus' view entirely wrong-headed – purpose; and to see Diogenes of Apollonia as discreetly but emphatically rejecting the Anaxagorean idea of διακόσμησις for quite other reasons. Some ingredients in the narrative have more robust evidence in their favour than others. But that there was throughout the whole development from Parmenides on some preoccupation with the contested or contestable apparatus of κόσμος and διάκοσμος seems to me to be beyond question.

How big and strong a component was it in the way these thinkers talked and argued? The evidence we have been considering suggests that in describing the business of articulating 'mortal belief' as διάκοσμος, Parmenides bequeathed to his successors among the Presocratics an idea about the main agenda for physics and physical explanation: nothing other than διακόσμησις. It has clearly become a headline focus for Anaxagoras and the Atomists. Some might call them φυσικοί, others μετεωρόλογοι, but a label that would capture the principal focus of their explanatory agenda was precisely διακόσμησις. So far as we know, the other great fifth-century BCE physicist, Empedocles, did not himself use the noun διάκοσμος or the verb διακοσμέω, but his entire system of alternating periods of Love and Strife was very naturally characterised in terms of διακόσμησις, as for example by Diogenes Laertius (Diog. Laert. 8.76), while Aristotle enlivens his claim that the φυσιολόγοι organise (διακοσμοῦσιν) the whole of nature by taking the movement of like to like as their principle[25] with Empedocles' remark that the dog sits on the tiling because it is most like him (*Eth. Eud.* 7.1.1235a10–12: like him in colour, presumably). And although the Pythagoreans did not talk in these terms either, again so far as we know, it was natural enough for Aristotle to grasp for the word διακόσμησις – uniquely in his writings on physics and cosmology – in talking of the way they (he is thinking primarily of Philolaus) fitted what he speaks of as 'the attributes and parts of the heaven and the whole διακόσμησις' into their cosmic scheme of numbers and harmonies.

Here there is perhaps a further twist to the story. If one recalls Aristotle's observation a few lines later on about the Pythagoreans' invention of a counter-earth to make a tenth heavenly body, one begins to wonder whether talk of διακόσμησις here carries something of the same pejorative, perspectival force with which Parmenides invests the word διάκοσμος. After all, he had other more unambiguously neutral terminology at his disposal that he could have used instead: τάξις or σύνταξις or σύστασις, for example, rather than this sole instance of διακόσμησις in his surviving corpus. So perhaps this text of Aristotle with which we began our enquiry was the right place to end as well as begin it.[26]

---

[25] A principle to which Democritus too had resort (see Diog. Laert 9.31 and Sext. Emp. *Math.* 7.117 (= DK 68 B 164)), comparing the way seeds mass in a sieve, or pebbles on the seashore, with the way birds of a kind flock together.

[26] I am grateful for comments by a reader for the Press that have led to reformulations and revisions of one sort or another.

CHAPTER 4

Aristotle on Kosmos *and* Kosmoi

*Monte Ransome Johnson**

The concept of *kosmos* did not play the leading role in Aristotle's physics that it did in Pythagorean, Atomistic (Democritean or Epicurean), Platonic, or Stoic physics. Of course, Aristotle greatly influenced (or impeded, some would argue) the history of cosmology, but I contend that Aristotle does not even recognize the validity of, much less himself offer, a science of cosmology as such, meaning a science which takes the *kosmos* itself as the object of study, with its own phenomena to be explained, and its own principles that explain them. In a pretheoretical sense, *kosmos* just means "order," and Aristotle certainly has a concept of the order of the universe. But the term *kosmos* also played an important technical role in two aspects of his predecessor's accounts that Aristotle rejected and attacked: first, cosmogony and *kosmopoiia*, generation or creation of the *kosmos*; second, *diakosmêsis*, an account of a plurality of *kosmoi*.[1] Aristotle was extremely critical of accounts involving *kosmopoiia* and *diakosmêsis*, and he developed general dialectical strategies against them. In emphatically distinguishing his view from *all* his predecessors (including Plato), he prefers to use the terms *ho ouranos* (the heaven), *to holon* (the whole), and *to pan* (the totality) in preference to *ho kosmos* (the *kosmos* or world). There is usually no harm in speaking loosely of "Aristotle's cosmology" when referring to his concept of the order of nature and the *ouranos*. Nevertheless, it is important to see that Aristotle's theoretical philosophy offers something very different from

* I would like to acknowledge Phillip Horky, Tiberiu Popa, D. S. Hutchinson, Tanelli Kukkonen and an anonymous reader for offering written comments that very much helped me to improve this chapter.

[1] Note that both terms may be used generally: *kosmopoiia* includes not only intelligent design creationism but any account of the genesis of a *kosmos*; *diakosmêsis* includes not only the thesis of infinite *kosmoi* but any account of a plurality of *kosmoi*. Thus, although Aristotle focuses his discussions of *kosmopoiia* and *diakosmêsis* on creationist and atomist accounts, he uses the same terms in describing both Pythagorean and Anaxagorean cosmologies, which are importantly distinct from the Platonic and Democritean cosmologies.

what is offered by those of his predecessors for whom *kosmos* was a keyword.

While Aristotle was concerned to prove that the order of nature is singular and eternal, these issues arise in the course of what he calls "the science concerning nature" (ἡ περὶ φυσέως ἐπιστήμη) and not as the focus of a discourse about the *kosmos* (περὶ κόσμου). No argument in Aristotle's physics depends entirely on a theory of *kosmos*, and every argument about *kosmos* depends on Aristotle's account of nature (φύσις) and *ouranos*. In fact, the topic of *kosmos* hardly comes up in the eight books of Aristotle's *Physica*[2] except in the context of describing a rejected view. Aristotle's most sustained and explicit discussion of *kosmos* occurs in the first book of his work entitled *Peri ouranou*,[3] but again mostly in criticizing the cosmogonical and plurality of worlds theses of predecessors, including Empedocles, Anaxagoras, Democritus, and Plato. Nor again does *kosmos* play an important role in *Peri geneseôs kai phthoras*,[4] a work whose subject is the phenomena of generation and destruction. In the *Meteorologica*, the concept of *kosmos* is present, but in a peculiar way, as we will see.

I will try to show that Aristotle is dubious about if not dismissive of the enterprise that became "cosmology," and he seeks to refocus inquiry away from theses about the origin of the *kosmos* and the plurality of *kosmoi* to what he takes to be the singular eternal order of nature. In the conclusion I will briefly reflect on what I think are some unfortunate consequences of his position. But first the case will be made not only by a review of the relevant passages in the *Physica, Peri ouranou*, and *Meteorologica*, but also the *Peri kosmou*[5] (a spurious work in the Aristotle Corpus); the *Protrepticus*[6] and *Peri philosophias*[7] (early exoteric or popular dialogues of Aristotle surviving only in fragments) and the *Metaphysica*.[8] The exoteric works not only offer an improved context with which to interpret the main acroamatic works of the Aristotle Corpus, but they also show a pattern of argumentation about *kosmos* that was apparently adapted and deployed in them.

---

[2] Usually translated *Physics*. This chapter will cite works of Aristotle according to their Latin titles, following the conventions of this volume.

[3] Usually translated *On the Heavens*, although I will dispute this translation later in the chapter.

[4] Usually translated *On Generation and Corruption.*   [5] Usually translated *On the Universe.*

[6] Usually translated *Exhortation* [*to Philosophy*].   [7] Usually translated *On Philosophy.*

[8] Usually translated *Metaphysics.*

4.1 Pseudo-Aristotle, *Peri kosmou*

Although included in the Aristotle Corpus, the *Peri kosmou* is most likely the product of a philosophical popularizer of the late Hellenistic era (probably the first century BCE/CE), who composed "an Aristotelian rival of the Stoic treatises which bore the same title."[9] As Jaap Mansfeld explains, "the formula *peri (tou) kosmou* gradually became a common expression denoting an important field of inquiry, viz. the study of the *kosmos* as a whole."[10] Neither the titular expression nor the subject matter conceived as a field of inquiry seems to have crystalized until after Aristotle, apparently with the Stoics.

Although the *Peri kosmou* is in some sense Peripatetic in doctrine, Pseudo-Aristotle offers only a pat and dogmatic description of cosmological, geographical, and meteorological positions, displaying none of the diaporetic and apodeictic method characteristic of Aristotle, and thus is of limited help in understanding the Stagirite's views. Nevertheless, it will be useful to consider the quasi-Stoic definition of *kosmos* used by Pseudo-Aristotle, and to introduce Aristotle's own conception by way of comparison to both this and the Stoic definition. First, the classic Stoic definition:

> Chrysippus said that *kosmos* is (1) a structure consisting of *ouranos* and earth and of the natures in them. Or (2) the structure consisting of gods and humans and out of the things that have come to be for their sake.

> Κόσμον δ᾽ εἶναί φησιν ὁ Χρύσιππος σύστημα ἐξ οὐρανοῦ καὶ γῆς καὶ τῶν ἐν τούτοις φύσεων· ἢ τὸ ἐκ θεῶν καὶ ἀνθρώπων σύστημα καὶ ἐκ τῶν ἕνεκα τούτων γεγονότων. (*SVF* 2.527.1–3 = Arius Didymus Fr. 31)[11]

And now the very beginning of the philosophical part of *Peri kosmou* (at 391b9–12, just after the "address to Alexander"):

> *Kosmos*, then, is (1) a structure consisting of *ouranos* and earth and of the natures contained within them. And otherwise this is also called *kosmos*: (2) the order and also arrangement of the wholes,[12] protected by god and also through god.

---

[9] Mansfeld 1992: 392–99. Authors of Stoic treatises entitled *Peri kosmou* include Sphaerus, Chrysippus, Antipater, and Posidonius.

[10] Mansfeld 1992: 396. A recent review of the doctrine, language, style, geographical knowledge, and cultural-historical background concludes that the work was written by someone in the Peripatetic tradition who addressed it to Alexander the Great in order to lend it credibility and attributed it to Aristotle for the same reason (Thom 2014: 3–8). The exceptions to the consensus that the work is spurious are discussed by Thom (2014: 5 n. 15).

[11] Also referenced by Posidonius in his *Meteorology*, Fr. 14 Kidd = Diog. Laert. 7.138.

[12] English translations of τῶν ὅλων as singular, e.g., "the totality" (Furley, Thom), make more sense and are more consistent with Aristotle's definition: ἡ δὲ τοῦ ὅλου σύστασίς ἐστι κόσμος (280a21–

Κόσμος μὲν οὖν ἐστι σύστημα ἐξ οὐρανοῦ καὶ γῆς καὶ τῶν ἐν τούτοις περιεχομένων φύσεων. Λέγεται δὲ καὶ ἑτέρως κόσμος ἡ τῶν ὅλων τάξις τε καὶ διακόσμησις, ὑπὸ θεοῦ τε καὶ διὰ θεὸν φυλαττομένη.

Part (1) of Pseudo-Aristotle's definition is identical to part (1) of Chrysippus' and represents common ground between the Stoics and the Peripatetics: a singular *kosmos*, consisting of a singular *ouranos* and earth and the "natures" included in it. Part (2) of Pseudo-Aristotle's definition, however, seems to be an adaptation of part (2) of Chrysippus', so as to render a conception of *kosmos* acceptable to both Stoics and Peripatetics: instead of implying that the structure of the *kosmos* has *come to be* for the sake of gods and humans, the "order and arrangement of the wholes" is said to be "sustained" by and through a god.[13] The idea of generation of the *kosmos* and the anthropocentrism in the Stoic definition is absent from the pseudo-Aristotelian definition.

Pseudo-Aristotle's definition is not present in any extant work of the Aristotle Corpus, and with its strange reference to "the wholes" (τῶν ὅλων) which are somehow arranged into a *kosmos* it is reminiscent of the definition of *kosmos* attributed to Pythagoras in the doxographical tradition: "Pythagoras was the first to call the enclosure of the wholes [τῶν ὅλων] *kosmos* because of its inherent arrangement."[14] In Aristotle, such an explicit definition of *kosmos* in its own right is surprisingly hard to find; in the closest he comes, he refers to a singular whole (τοῦ ὅλου) and not to plural "wholes" (τῶν ὅλων): "the structuring of the whole is *kosmos* and *ouranos*" (ἡ δὲ τοῦ ὅλου σύστασίς ἐστι κόσμος καὶ οὐρανός).[15] The term "the whole" does not occur in Chrysippus' definition,[16] as it does appear in Aristotle's definition, and (in plural) in the second part of Pseudo-Aristotle's. As we will see, small terminological differences like this indicate very significant theoretical differences.

Aristotle's definition is both similar to and different from the Stoic and Neo-Pythagorean definitions in a couple of other ways. First, Aristotle uses the term σύστασις (structuring) where Chrysippus, Posidonius, and the author of *Peri kosmou* use the cognate term σύστημα (structure). It would

---

22). But the MSS all have the plural (not the singular τοῦ ὅλου). One sees here a distinctly Neo-Pythagorean expression and not a particularly Aristotelian one.

[13] Or "by and through gods" (plural) – the MSS differ here. [14] Aëtius 2.1.1, tr. after Horky.

[15] Arist. *Cael.* 1.10.280a21–22.

[16] Note that, according to Aëtius 2.1.7, the Stoics distinguished between "the totality" (*to pan*) and "the whole" (*to holon*), holding the former to include and the latter to exclude the infinite extra-mundial void posited in Stoic physics. Aristotle, who rejected the existence of a void (see below, n. 43), uses both terms synonymously with *ouranos*, his most comprehensive term.

be going too far to read too much into this terminological difference, I think, but it is worth noting that σύστημα is the term also used by a Hellenistic Pythagorean author in this exact context (but never in this context by Aristotle).[17] More importantly, the idea of "a structure consisting of *ouranos* and earth," which is present in both Chrysippus and Pseudo-Aristotle, is not present in Aristotle. Aristotle's "structuring" is "of the whole," and this defines *both kosmos* and *ouranos* (ἡ δὲ τοῦ ὅλου σύστασίς ἐστι κόσμος καὶ οὐρανός). The *kai* in the expression *kosmos kai ouranos* is epexegetic: Aristotle's singular *ouranos* includes the earth as a (vanishingly small) part, and so he does not conceive of the *kosmos* as a "structure consisting of *ouranos* and earth" which, put that way, emphasizes the importance of the earth in a context in which Aristotle instead minimizes it. This emphasis on the importance of earth in turn entails a more geocentric and thus anthropocentric and Stoicizing conception of physics than I think should be attributed to Aristotle, though it often has been, including by the author of *Peri kosmou.*[18]

Aristotle's all-embracing conception of *ouranos* is expressed in *Peri ouranou* 1.9 when, in the course of defining his own subject matter, he distinguishes three different senses of *ouranos.*

> (1) In one sense, then, we call the substance of the extreme revolution of the totality [τὴν οὐσίαν τὴν τῆς ἐσχάτης τοῦ παντὸς περιφορᾶς] *ouranos*, or that natural body [σῶμα φυσικὸν] whose place is the extreme circumference of the totality. We habitually and especially call the extreme or upper part *ouranos*, which we take to be the seat of all that is divine. (2) In another sense, we use this name for the body continuous with the extreme circumference which contains the moon, the sun, and some of the stars; these we say are in the *ouranos* [ἐν τῷ οὐρανῷ]. (3) In yet another sense we give this name to all body included within extreme circumference, since we

---

[17] Pseudo-Ocellus: "I refer to the whole [τὸ ὅλον] and the totality [τὸ πᾶν] as 'the entire *kosmos*' [τὸν σύμπαντα κόσμον]. For it obtained this name for this very reason, that it was thoroughly arranged [διακοσμηθείς] out of all things. After all, a system of the nature of the wholes [σύστημα τῆς τῶν ὅλων φύσεως] is consummate and perfect, since nothing is outside of the totality [τοῦ παντός]. For, if something exists, it is in the totality, and the totality is with it, and it comprehends all things with itself – some as parts, and others as outgrowths" (p. 127.11–16 Thesleff; tr. by Horky). Notice that Pseudo-Ocellus, like the author of the *Peri kosmou*, also speaks of "the wholes" in the plural. Thanks to Phillip Horky for the reference.

[18] For discussion and references, see Johnson 2005 and Sedley 2007. Aristotle does not fit neatly into either side of what Sedley, like many others, considers two "sides of the ancient debate" (2007: xvi), referred to as "creationism" and "atomism" (e.g., by Sedley), or (more often) "teleological" and "mechanistic" by others. I have recently argued that Aristotle embraces both "teleological" and "mechanistic" explanations (Johnson 2017), and I will argue here that Aristotle rejects both creationism (along with all forms of cosmogony) and atomism (along with all forms of the plurality of worlds thesis).

habitually call the whole and the totality *ouranos* [τὸ γὰρ ὅλον καὶ τὸ πᾶν εἰώθαμεν λέγειν οὐρανόν]. (Aristotle, *Cael.* 1.9.278b11–21)

Notice that Aristotle defines his overall subject matter as the *ouranos*, not the *kosmos*. In fact, it is possible to describe Aristotle's "whole" and "totality" without any reference to the term *kosmos* whatsoever – the term "universe" translates the philosophical concept perfectly. The first sense of *ouranos* refers to the extreme revolution or circumference of the totality; this is identical to the sphere of fixed stars, which Aristotle takes to be the outer limit of the spherical totality, and which we understand to be, mostly, the immediately visible portion of the Milky Way galaxy.[19] For the second sense, he also refers to outer space, moving inwards to include the planets, sun, and moon, roughly what we now call the "Solar system." For the third sense, he moves again further inward, including all body whatsoever (thus all fire, water, air, and earth), which he considers continuous and entirely contained in a single "centrifocal" *ouranos*.[20] In this context he speaks interchangeably of "the whole" (*to holon*), "the totality" (*to pan*), and *ouranos*. We can now begin to understand why Aristotle defined "the composition of the whole" as "*kosmos*, i.e., *ouranos*." Given his view of a singular *kosmos*, Aristotle can replace all talk of the *kosmos* with talk of *ouranos* (in the third, broad sense, meaning "universe"), and so he freely uses these terms interchangeably when describing his own position, usually preferring the term *ouranos*.[21] Note that, for this reason the title of the treatise *Peri ouranou* should be translated *On the Heaven* (as in the Latin: *De caelo*), and not (despite English idiom) *On the Heavens* – the use of the singular in the title of the treatise is significant. In fact, the translation *On the Universe* would better capture Aristotle's attempt to define the exact object of the study.

---

[19] All the stars visible to the naked eye turn out to be located within the Milky Way galaxy, except the Andromeda galaxy, the Large and Small Magellanic Clouds, and some of the historical supernovae. There is no evidence that Aristotle observed any of these phenomena.

[20] In the *Peri ouranou*, Aristotle employs a variety of expressions in connection with this third sense, such as the totality (*to pan*) (1.1.268a4; 1.7.275b30); the nature of the totality (*tês tou pantos phuseôs*) (1.2.268b11); the body of the totality (*to sôma tou pantos*) (1.7.275a17). The term "centrifocal" was introduced by Furley to distinguish Aristotle's theory from the "linear" or "parallel" theory of Anaximander and the Atomists (1989: 15).

[21] English translators of *Peri ouranou* including Furley and Stocks have introduced confusion by using the English word "world" as an ambiguous translation for several distinct Greek terms: *ho kosmos, ho ouranos, to pan, to holon*.

4.2 *Protrepticus*

Aristotle's dialogue *Protrepticus* offered an exhortation to philosophy, and specifically a defense of mathematical and theoretical philosophy in which there was enormous interest in the Academy of which Aristotle was a member when he wrote it. This kind of philosophy was in some sense inspired by the activities of "the Pythagoreans." In the *Protrepticus*, Aristotle offered the following explanation of why the Pythagoreans put so much value into the study of mathematics in relation to the *kosmos*:

> In all these things, probably, the Pythagoreans honored the effort put into mathematics, and coordinated it in various ways with the observation of the *kosmos* [πρὸς τὴν τοῦ κόσμου θεωρίαν], for example: by including in their reasoning the number that arises from the revolutions and their differences, by theorizing what is possible and impossible in the structuring of the *kosmos* [τῇ τοῦ κόσμου συστάσει] from what is mathematically possible and impossible, by conceiving the revolutions of *ouranos* [τὰς δὲ οὐρανίους περιφοράς] according to commensurate numbers with a cause, and by determining measures of the *ouranos* according to certain mathematical ratios, and generally putting together the natural science [φυσιολογία] which is predictive on the basis of mathematics, and putting the mathematical objects before the other theorems about the *kosmos* [τὰ περὶ τοῦ κόσμου θεωρήματα], as if they were principles. (Aristotle, *Protrepticus, apud* Iamblichus, *On the General Mathematical Science* 23, pp. 73.17–74.1 Festa-Klein)[22]

This is significant evidence that "the Pythagoreans" (Aristotle may be referring to some Pythagoreans contemporary with Philolaus of Croton, ca. 470–385 BCE) used the concept of the *kosmos* in the sense of "the world." Despite this enthusiastic description, however, Aristotle later seems reticent about the focus on *kosmos*, after he expresses a protreptic conclusion reached by Pythagoras:

> Pythagoras, according to this argument anyway, said rightly that it is for the sake of understanding and observing that every human being has been constructed by the god. But later, perhaps, one should inquire whether the object of this understanding is the *kosmos* or some other nature [ὁ κόσμος ἐστὶν ἤ τις ἑτέρα φύσις]. (Aristotle, *Protrepticus, apud* Iamblichus, *Protrepticus* 9, p. 51.6–9 Pistelli)[23]

---

[22] Translated by Hutchinson and Johnson (www.protrepticus.info). For the attribution of *DCMS* Chapter 23 to Aristotle's *Protrepticus*, see Merlan 1953 and Festugière 1956.

[23] Translated by Hutchinson and Johnson. For attribution of *Protr.* 9 to Aristotle, see Hutchinson and Johnson 2005: 258–62.

Notice that Aristotle is careful to distinguish between "the Pythagoreans" (to whom he attributes views about the *kosmos*) and Pythagoras himself.[24] The second passage calls into question whether the object of this philosophical speculation *should* be understood to be the *kosmos* (as the Pythagoreans apparently did) or "some other nature" (τις ἑτέρα φύσις). In the other surviving fragments of the *Protrepticus*, Aristotle repeatedly discusses nature as a cause, but does not seem to refer again to the *kosmos*.[25] As I will argue, this follows a typical pattern according to which Aristotle moves from a criticism of a predecessor's view about *kosmos* to his own account of nature, thus removing the debate to a field in which he occupies strong and well-defended positions.

4.3 *Metaphysica*

It is interesting to compare Aristotle's account of the Pythagoreans in the *Protrepticus* with the more ambivalent account in the *Metaphysica*:

> Since then all other things seemed in their entire nature to be modelled after numbers, and numbers seemed to be the first things in all of nature [πάσης τῆς φύσεως], they supposed the elements of numbers to be the elements of all things, and the whole *ouranos* [τὸν ὅλον οὐρανόν] to be a musical scale and a number. And all the properties of numbers and scales which they could show to agree with the effects and parts of the *ouranos* and with the whole arrangement [πρὸς τὰ τοῦ οὐρανοῦ πάθη καὶ μέρη καὶ πρὸς τὴν ὅλην διακόσμησιν], they collected and fitted into their scheme. (Aristotle, *Metaph.* 1.5.985b32–986a6, tr. after Ross)

Compared to the fragments of the *Protrepticus*, Aristotle's approach to Pythagorean speculation is, predictably, more cautious and critical in *Metaphysica* 1, where he alludes to the "harmony of the spheres" thesis ridiculed in *Peri ouranou* 2.9. The more critical approach is also reflected in other accounts of Pythagorean cosmology, such as *Peri ouranou* 2.2 and 2.13, which Aristotle concludes by saying that "they are not seeking the

---

[24] Although Pythagoras is by tradition credited with first using the term *kosmos* in the sense of "world" (Aëtius 2.1.1 = DK 14 Fr. 21), Carl Huffman has argued that in the Pythagorean tradition it is Philolaus who is most likely to have first used the term in this way (DK 44 B 1, 2, 6, and possibly 17; see the commentary of Huffman 1993: 97–98); note that this usage is as archaic as Empedocles' B 134, which is usually taken to be the earliest such usage. This and the rest of the evidence is reviewed by Horky in Chapter 13 of this volume; for further treatment of Aristotle's references to "the Pythagoreans," see Horky 2013: 3–36.

[25] Of course, an argument from silence cannot be probative in the context of a fragmentary text, but it is telling that in several extended passages in which Aristotle discusses nature the term *kosmos* does not appear (e.g., *apud* Iamblichus, *Protr.* 7, pp. 41.24–43.5 Pistelli, and 9, pp. 49.3–52.16 Pistelli).

accounts and the causes directed toward the things that appear, but rather drawing the things that appear toward one of their accounts and opinions, and trying to co-ordinate them" (συγκοσμεῖν).[26] The more positive and detailed account of the *Protrepticus* is thus valuable in filling out the overly brief description of the *Metaphysica*, describing several ways Pythagoreans related numbers to "the *ouranos* and the whole arrangement" (τὴν ὅλην διακόσμησιν). The term *diakosmêsis* appears in the authentic works in the Aristotle Corpus[27] as a noun only twice, here in the *Metaphysica* and once in an embryological context,[28] although it does appear in part (2) of Pseudo-Aristotle's definition of *kosmos*. The term is associated in Pythagoreanism with *kosmopoiia* (and its verbal forms), as in Aristotle's criticisms of the Pythagoreans at the end of the *Metaphysica*:

> It is absurd also to attribute generation to eternal things, or rather this is one of the things that is impossible. There need be no doubt whether the Pythagoreans attribute generation to them or not, for they obviously do ... But since they are *creating a kosmos* and wish to speak naturalistically [ἀλλ᾽ ἐπειδὴ κοσμοποιοῦσι καὶ φυσικῶς βούλονται λέγειν], it is fair to give some explanation of their account about nature [περὶ φύσεως]. (Aristotle, *Metaph.* 14.3.1091a12–20, tr. after Ross)

Aristotle in general is hostile to cosmogony and rejects the enterprise a priori.[29] What is evident here is not only his rejection of cosmogony but specifically his strategy of forcing the question about the generation or creation of the *kosmos* to be answered on the basis of a view about nature (περὶ φύσεως). This same strategy we see deployed against Anaxagoras. As with the Pythagoreans, Aristotle is extremely ambivalent in his treatment of Anaxagoras. On the one hand he congratulates Anaxagoras for saying "that intellect was present, just as in animals, so too in that which exists by nature – as the cause of the *kosmos* and all of its order (καὶ ἐν τῇ φύσει τὸν αἴτιον τοῦ κόσμου καὶ τῆς τάξεως πάσης): he seemed like a sober man in contrast with the idle talk of his predecessors" (1.3.984b15–18, tr. after Ross). On the other hand, thinkers like Anaxagoras only "got hold up to a certain point of two of the causes which we distinguished in our work about nature [περὶ φύσεως] – the matter and the source of movement – vaguely, however, and with no clearness" (1.4.985a10–13). Cosmogony is

---

[26] *Peri ouranou* 2.13.293a25–27, with reference to their hypothesis of the "counter-earth." See also Aristotle's criticism of Pythagorean cosmology in 2.2 (although he only refers to the term *kosmos* in that chapter in a technical aside about the transverse at 285b12).

[27] But the term was probably also used in *Peri philosophias*, Fr. 12b Ross (discussed in what follows).

[28] Arist. *GA* 2.4.740a8. This usage is due to Democritus and the Atomist embryological theory.

[29] Gregory 2007: 163–72.

exactly where Anaxagoras goes wrong: "Anaxagoras uses intellect as a device for his *creation of the kosmos* [μηχανῇ χρῆται τῷ νῷ πρὸς τὴν κοσμοποιΐαν] and when he is at a loss to say by (or for) what cause something necessarily is, then he mentions it" (1.4.985a18–20).

A fifth reference to *kosmos* in *Metaphysica* appears in the context of an attack on Protagorean relativism. Notice that Aristotle does not directly discuss the *kosmos* as such, but rather "the things that are in the *kosmos*," i.e., the *ouranos* in the narrow, first sense identified earlier in the chapter, meaning the outermost space.

> In general, it is absurd to make the fact that the things of this earth are observed to change and never remain in the same state the basis of our judgments about the truth. For in pursuing the truth one must start from the things that are always in the same state and suffer no change. Such are the things in the *kosmos* [τὰ κατὰ τὸν κόσμον]; for these do not appear to be now one way and then again another, but are manifestly always the same and share in no change. (Aristotle, *Metaph.* 11.6.1063a10–17, tr. after Ross)

This is a generalization of the argument made against Pythagorean and Anaxagorean cosmology: it is wrong to reason from the changeability of the things near earth to the changeability of everything (the universe), and those who do will be led astray in their account of nature, the *kosmos*, and even truth. It is in this critical dialectical context that all the references to *kosmos* appear in Aristotle's *Metaphysica*.

4.4 *Peri philosophias*

According to an argument attributed to Aristotle's dialogue *Peri philosophias*, Aristotle discussed two sources for humans' belief in the gods: (1) from the prophetic power of the soul in dreams; and (2) "from the things aloft [ἀπὸ τῶν μετεώρων] ... seeing by day the sun running his circular course, and by night the well-ordered [εὔτακτον] movement of the other stars, they came to think that there is a god who is the cause of such movement and such good order [εὐταξίας]."[30] In a related passage, Sextus expands on the second reason, comparing the "well-ordered [εὔτακτον] movement of the heavens [τῶν οὐρανίων]" to the "array of Greeks approaching the plains with much organization and order" (κόσμου καὶ τάξεως); one naturally infers an "organizer of this kind of order" (ὁ διατάσσων τὴν τοιαύτην τάξιν), a commander of such well-ordered

---

[30] Sext. Emp. *Math.* 9.20–23 = Aristotle Fr. 12a Ross, tr. after Ross.

forces, "Nestor or some Hero who knew how to organize [κοσμῆσαι] horses and bucklered warriors" (*Math.* 9.26–27, tr. after Ross). In both passages the word *kosmos* plainly refers to organization, i.e., order, including in the second, verbal usage, a quotation from Homer (*Il.* 2.554). These texts have been interpreted as showing Aristotle committed to supporting intelligent design creationism, in conjunction with a famous text in Cicero[31] recounting Aristotle's thought experiment about cave dwellers living in comfortable subterranean apartments furnished with the products of human art, who have heard by report and hearsay about divine power. If they were to go to the aboveground realm of nature, and see the grandeur and beauty of the stars, moon, and sun "their courses settled and immutable to all eternity; when they saw those things most certainly they would have judged both that there are gods and that these are the works of gods." Philo of Alexandria reports a similar argument:

> The most highly esteemed philosophers said it was from the *kosmos* and its parts and the powers inherent in these that we came to grasp their cause . . . if one comes into this *kosmos* as into a vast house or city, and sees the *ouranos* revolving in a circle and containing all things within them . . . he will surely reason that these things have not been framed without perfect skill, but that there both was and is a framer of this totality – God. (Philo of Alexandria, *Allegories of the Sacred Laws* 3.32.97–9 = Aristotle Fragment 13 Ross, tr. after Ross)

Even if all these arguments were attributable to Aristotle's *Peri philosophias*, they would not show that Aristotle himself advocated intelligent design creationism, as some have claimed.[32] First, the work *Peri philosophias* was a dialogue, and the speech reported by both Cicero and Philo could easily have been put in the voice of a Pythagorean or Platonic character, such as Heraclides of Pontus. Aristotle himself, speaking in his own voice, could have rejected the argument out of hand, or accepted part of it and criticized another part.[33] In fact, each piece of attributed evidence, including the most suspect one of Philo just quoted, only purports to explain the reason why people came to believe in gods, and what they happened to believe

---

[31] Cic. *Nat.D.* 2.37.95–6 = Aristotle Fr. 13 Ross, tr. by Ross.

[32] Jaeger 1923/1934 and Chroust 1973; see Johnson 2005: 259–62.

[33] Besides the fact that Aristotle absolutely rejects the creation or generation of the *ouranos*, there is the fact that the inferred concept of God as the organizer (ὁ διατάσσων) is explicitly rejected by Aristotle, e.g., in the conclusion of the *Eudemian Ethics*: οὐ γὰρ ἐπιτακτικῶς ἄρχων ὁ θεός (7.15.1249b13–14). Aristotle rejected the idea of gods intervening in nature as much as Epicurus did, and on this basis his concept of God has been fruitfully compared to theirs (Merlan 1967; Effe 1970: 157–62).

about the *ouranos* and the *kosmos*. To offer that anthropological theory entails no commitment whatsoever to the thesis that god created the *ouranos* or the *kosmos*, any more than the observation that some people believe in gods on the basis of the prophetic power of dreams entails that dreams have prophetic power. In fact, we know that Aristotle rejects both the prophetic power of dreams, and the idea that the *kosmos* or *ouranos* was created. In *Peri philosophias* Aristotle not only rejected creationism; he mocked it, as Philo reports:

> Aristotle . . . insisted that the *kosmos* is ungenerated and imperishable, and convicted of grave ungodliness those who maintained the opposite, who thought that the great visible god, which contains in truth sun and moon and the remaining pantheon of planets and unwandering stars, is no better than the work of human hands; he used to say in mockery . . . that in the past he had feared lest his house be destroyed by violent winds or extraordinary storms, or by time or lack of proper maintenance, but that now a greater danger hung over him, from those who by argument destroy the entire *kosmos*. (Philo of Alexandria, *De Aet. Mundi* 3.10–11 = Aristotle Fragment 18 Ross, tr. after Ross)

It is generally held that the arguments of *Peri philosophias* against the generation of the world were directed against Plato,[34] who held that although the *kosmos* will be everlasting, it was created by an intelligent designer; and also against the Atomists, who held that an infinite number of *kosmoi* are continually being generated and destroyed. Besides mocking the view that the *kosmos* could be destroyed (which mockery must have been directed against the Atomists), Aristotle also offered a number of apodeictic arguments (preserved by Philo, *Fragments* 19a–c) to the conclusion that the *kosmos* is eternal, meaning ungenerated and indestructible. For our purposes the most important of these is Fragment 19b, where Philo relates an argument drawn from Aristotle:

> If, then, the cause of destruction of the other animals is their unnatural order [ἡ παρὰ φύσιν τάξις], but in the *kosmos* each of its parts is situated according

---

[34] "When he began to work out his physical *methodoi*, cosmogony in the form in which it had flourished among the Presocratics was dead, while the new version which the *Timaeus* presented called for one more painstaking examination of its presuppositions" (Solmsen 1958: 266). Solmsen's account, which in general I find persuasive (and I agree with his conclusions), tends to over-emphasize the importance of Plato to Aristotle's positions on cosmogony: "by discrediting this last essay in cosmogony <sc. the *Timaeus*>, the whole effort was ruled out of court" (ibid.). But I will argue that the Democritean account is treated as a live option (i.e., an account to be refuted) throughout the Aristotle Corpus, and there is every reason to assume that his views were also at issue in the earlier dialogue *Peri philosophias*. In general, Aristotle considers Democritus a more advanced thinker on natural science than Plato (Johnson 2005: 104–12).

to nature and has had its proper place assigned to it, the *kosmos* may justly be called indestructible. (Philo, *De Aet. Mundi* 7.34 = Aristotle Fr. 19b Ross, tr. after Ross).

As Philo relates the argument, composite bodies are destroyed by being dissolved into their components; and dissolution is nothing but reduction to the natural state of the parts; plants, humans, and animals, which are compositions of earth, air, water, and fire, are unnatural according to this argument, and this is the reason they are perishable, because the elements, which in a composite body are prevented from reaching their natural place, will eventually be dissolved and return to their natural place. Now "the *kosmos* has no part in this disorder ... if it is perishing, its parts must now each be placed in the region unnatural to it. But this we cannot easily suppose" (Fr. 19b). Philo goes on to describe why earth, water, air, and fire should all be thought to be in their natural position, and even the phenomena of temporary dislocation show that these elements constantly return to their natural places.

A recent study has concluded that of all Aristotle's arguments against the generation or destructibility of the *kosmos* in *Peri philosophias*,

> 19b gives us perhaps the worst argument, because it is clear that for Aristotle the parts of the *kosmos* are not all in their natural positions. If they were, there would be concentric spheres of earth, water, air, and fire, with no mixing of the elements. The oddest part of this argument is that Aristotle recognizes that the parts of animals are not in their natural places, but he does not then recognize that animals are part of the *kosmos* and so not all parts of the *kosmos* are in the natural place. (Gregory 2007: 171)

I think that the argument can be salvaged by examining in detail this part of the argument:

> For humans are composed from the four elements, which in their entirety are part of the totality of *ouranos* [ἄνθρωποι γὰρ ἀπὸ τῶν τεττάρων στοιχείων, ἃ δὴ ὅλα τοῦ παντός ἐστιν οὐρανοῦ] – earth, water, air, and fire. Now these parts when mixed are robbed of their natural place. (Philo, *De Aet. Mundi* 6.29 = Aristotle Fr. 19b Ross, tr. after Ross).

English translations have followed Cumont in expunging οὐρανοῦ from the text; here I follow Bernays in keeping οὐρανοῦ and taking it with παντός, adding in support of this proposal that Aristotle uses this very expression in a related context at *Peri ouranou* 1.9: τοῦ παντὸς οὐρανοῦ (279a25). Keeping οὐρανοῦ in the text attributed to *Peri philosophias* requires interpreting the term in the third, broad sense identified by Aristotle: "we habitually call the whole and the totality *ouranos*"

(278b20–21), and interpreting the genitive inflection of τοῦ παντός οὐρανοῦ (in Philo's text) as partitive, so that the four Empedoclean bodies are understood in their entirety to form only "a part of the totality of *ouranos*." This in turn allows us to avoid an even more urgent problem than the one mentioned by Gregory: according to Aristotle, the totality does not consist only of the four elements – there is also what Aristotle calls "the primary body," the aether, the matter of the stars, planets, sun, and moon. This is by far the largest and most important part of the *ouranos* and the totality – the earth and its environment are as a point relative to the magnitude of the *ouranos*.[35] But this primary part of the *kosmos* would, absurdly, be ignored here if *ouranos* is deleted from Philo's text (or ignored). Aristotle had already affirmed the existence of the "primary" body, aether, in *Peri philosophias* (Fragments 21–2 Ross). This body, at least, can never be dislocated, and in fact it serves as the absolute limit of all the natural locations in the *kosmos*. What about the other bodies? Aristotle argued that humans and the other animals as composites of the four Empedoclean bodies are perishable. But the four elements as a whole are not perishable (because they are not composites but elements, and they are not destroyed upon dissolution of the composite but return to their natural places). Thus, to answer Gregory, even though animals are parts of the *kosmos* (i.e., the *ouranos* in the broad, third sense, meaning universe), the crucial point is that they are not the totality, and the cause of their perishability (being unnatural and temporary compositions of elements) does not affect either the system of four elements, or the *ouranos* in the narrower first and second senses (the fixed stars, and solar-lunar-planetary system), and so applies only to a vanishingly small part of the all-embracing *ouranos*. It would be poor form to extrapolate from the destructibility of the things around earth to the destructibility of everything, including the whole *ouranos*, as Aristotle argues in *Metaphysica* 11.6.1063a10–17 (referenced earlier).

I dwell on this argument because the passage represents an argumentative strategy Aristotle repeatedly deploys against all of his predecessors: they worked under the misapprehension that the *kosmos* and hence *ouranos* was generated; and the cause of this misapprehension was an insufficient grasp of the natural principles of simple bodies. The purpose of the rest of this chapter is to show the deployment of that argument in the acroamatic texts of the Aristotle Corpus.

---

[35] Arist. *Cael.* 2.14.279b30–298a20 and *Mete.* 1.14.352a17–28 (discussed in what follows).

4.5 *Physica*

In the early work *Topica*,[36] Aristotle's paradigm of a theoretical and "natural" dialectical problem is "whether the *kosmos* is eternal or not [πότερον ὁ κόσμος ἀίδιος ἤ οὔ]."[37] Aristotle explains that such problems arise because there are persuasive arguments on both sides of the issues, and because the issues "are so vast, and we find it difficult to give our reasons."[38] This should be compared with *On the Parts of Animals* 1.5.644b21–645a25, where Aristotle points out that the *remoteness* of the phenomena is the cause of difficulties in astronomical research, which reveals one of the comparative advantages of biological research.

As we have seen, the problem was hotly debated in the *Peri philosophias*. Despite the fact that this problem is a paradigm of a natural problem in the *Topica*, Aristotle does not address the problem "Is the *kosmos* eternal or not?" in the *Physica* itself – and in fact not until the final three chapters of *Peri ouranou* book 1.[39] He does note that "the writers on physics obviously do discuss … whether the earth and the *kosmos* are spherical or not" (*Physica* 2.2, 193b29–30). This is additional secondary evidence that the early Greek philosophers did discuss *kosmos* in the sense of "world."[40]

All the other references to *kosmos* in the *Physica* are in the context of the rejection of predecessors' cosmogonical views. In *Physica* 2.4, Empedocles is criticized for not explicitly discussing luck, even though he seems to assign it as a cause of motion ("separation") of air: "he says in his creation of the *kosmos* [ἐν τῇ κοσμοποιίᾳ] that "*it happened to run that way at that time, but it often ran otherwise*'"; he also tells us that most of the parts of animals came to be by luck" (196a22–24).[41] Immediately following this

---

[36] Usually translated *Topics*.

[37] Arist. *Top.* 1.11.104b9. Aristotle refers to the dialectical problem and proposition of whether or not the *kosmos* is eternal as an example of something that would be beneficial to know, not with a view to choice or avoidance, but "merely with a view to knowledge" (104b8); the question arises not in ethics or logic but in natural science (105b25). In a later handbook, the paradigm of a "physical" problem is "whether there is one *kosmos* or many" (πότερον εἶς κόσμος ἐστὶν ἤ πλείους) (*Divisiones Aristoteleae* 56.1).

[38] Arist. *Top.* 1.11.104b16.

[39] I will discuss the possibility that he wrote a work entitled *Peri kosmou geneseôs* later.

[40] See above, n. 24.

[41] Empedocles DK 31 B 53. A related point is made in *Peri geneseôs kai phthoras* (the only occurrence of the term *kosmos* in that work): "But, again, it is obvious that they <sc. the bodies> move. For though strife dissociated, it was not by strife that the aether was borne upwards. On the contrary he attributes their motion to something like luck (ὥσπερ ἀπὸ τύχης): 'for thus, as it ran, it happened to meet them then, though often otherwise' (= B 53); while at other times he says it is the nature (πεφυκέναι) of fire to be borne upwards, but (to quote his words), 'the aether sank down upon the earth with long roots' (= B 54). But at the same time, he also says that the *kosmos* (τὸν κόσμον) has

Aristotle accuses the Atomists of not making explicit their account of spontaneity, even though

> they ascribe to spontaneity the parts of animals and all the *kosmoi* [τῶν κόσμων πάντων]. They say that the vortex arose spontaneously, i.e. the motion that separated and established the totality in its present order [τὴν κίνησιν τὴν διακρίνασαν καὶ καταστήσασαν εἰς ταύτην τὴν τάξιν τὸ πᾶν]. (Aristotle, *Ph.* 2.4.196a25–28)

This is not the place to assess the veracity of Aristotle's interpretation, much less his criticism, of Empedocles and Democritus.[42] The important point for the present investigation is that Aristotle's entire discussion of the principles of natural science and of causation in *Physica* 2 makes no positive use of the concept of *kosmos* whatsoever.

The Atomists' views are mentioned as Aristotle explains why people believe in the existence of infinity: one reason is because of "what is outside the *ouranos*" (τὸ ἔξω τοῦ οὐρανοῦ): "if what is outside is infinite, it seems that body is also infinite, and that there are also infinite *kosmoi*" (3.4.203b25–26). Aristotle is explaining why people are led, wrongly, to the conclusion that infinity somehow actually exists. In Aristotle's view there is nothing "outside the *ouranos*" – literally nothing, no body, not even void – and so the affirmation of anything actually infinite is rejected.[43] A fortiori infinite *kosmoi* outside the *ouranos* are rejected.

The concept of *kosmos* appears in only three other significant passages of the *Physica*, all in Book 8, and all again in the context of the rejection of cosmogony. In the first, Aristotle asserts that *all* of his predecessors in natural science have been concerned with the problem of motion, because all have offered a cosmogony:

> The existence of motion is asserted by all who have anything to say about nature, because they all concern themselves with the creation of *kosmos* [τὸ κοσμοποιεῖν] and study the question of generation and destruction, processes which could not come to be without motion. But those who say that

a similar nature both now, in the reign of strife, as it was formerly, in the reign of love. What then is the first mover and the cause of motion?" (2.6.333b35–334a8, tr. after Joachim).

[42] On Aristotle's treatment of Empedocles, see Johnson 2005: 95–104; and for Democritus, see Johnson 2005: 104–12; 2009.

[43] Aristotle treats as similar the physicists who hold that there is an infinite body (or void) outside the *kosmos*: "But in respect of addition there cannot even potentially be an infinite which exceeds every assignable magnitude, unless it is accidentally infinite in fulfillment, as the physicists hold to be true of the outer body of the world (*to exo sôma tou kosmou*), whose substance is air or something of the kind" (*Ph.* 3.6.206b20–24). Nor is any void admitted within the *kosmos* (4.8.216b17–18). Thus Aristotle has no motivation, as the Stoics do, to support a distinction between *to pan* and *to holon* on the basis of the inclusion of void or not (see above, n. 16).

there are also infinite *kosmoi* [ἀπείρους κόσμους], some of which are in the process of becoming while others are in the process of being destroyed, assert that there is always motion. (Aristotle, *Ph.* 8.1.250b15–23)

In a later passage he makes an equally generally statement about "all who have ever said anything about motion":

> They all assign their principles of motion to things that impart motion of this kind. Thus separation and combination are motions in respect of place, and the motion imparted by love and strife takes these forms, the latter separating and the former combining. Anaxagoras, too, says that intellect, his first mover, separates. Similarly those who assert no cause of this kind but say that void accounts for motion – they also hold that the motion of natural substance is motion in respect of place ... The process of increase and decrease and alteration, they say, are effects of the combination and separation of atoms. It is the same too, with those who make out that the becoming or perishing of a thing is accounted for by rarity or density. For it is by combination and separation that these things are arranged [συγκρίσει γὰρ καὶ διακρίσει ταῦτα διακοσμοῦσιν]. (Aristotle, *Ph.* 8.9.265b16–32)

The term "arranged" translates the verbal form of the term *diakosmêsis*, which we saw used in the description of the Pythagorean cosmology in *Metaphysica* 1.5. In this passage Aristotle groups Empedocles, Anaxagoras, and the Atomists in a general criticism of *diakosmêsis*.[44] The predecessors' explanations of the present arrangement of the *kosmos* all reduce to locomotion, but none of them gives an adequate account of locomotion. Aristotle's general strategy against the enterprise of cosmogony depends on this reduction. All cosmogonies must give an account of the cause of change, since they hold that the *kosmos* has been generated, and generation is a kind of change. But their accounts of generation can all be reduced to locomotion, because they depend on separation and combination, and separation and combination depend on locomotion (e.g., of infinite atoms in infinite void).[45] The predecessors' accounts of locomotion are all weak:

[44] Both Leucippus and Democritus authored works entitled *Diakosmêsis*. These works must, then, have discussed how atoms in locomotion generate compounds, and how they undergo increase, decrease and alteration by a process of combination and separation of atoms. Leucippus' *Great Diakosmêsis* may have been an account of how our *kosmos* and the infinite *kosmoi* were generated by atomic processes, while Democritus's *Small Diakosmêsis* may have been a description of how plants, animals, and humans are generated by similar atomic processes. See Schofield, in Chapter 3 of this volume.

[45] It is interesting that although the Atomists recognized a plurality or infinity of *kosmoi*, they offer a unified account of motion (the cause of motion of the atoms in all possible worlds); whereas Aristotle, who insists on a singular *kosmos*, is forced to embrace a dualistic account of natural motion (the cause of motion in the sublunary region is essentially different from that in the superlunary).

in Empedocles' case, it amounts to "luck"; in Democritus' case "spontaneity";[46] Anaxagoras makes a notable advance with his "intellect." But none of these causes can be the primary intrinsic cause of all motion. That cause must be: "a principle or cause of being moved and being at rest in that to which it belongs primarily, in virtue of itself and not incidentally" (*Physica* 2.2.192b20–22). This is Aristotle's definition of nature. Things that exist by nature include all the plants and animals, all the simple bodies, and all the stars, sun, and moon (192b8–10). These things all have the causes of their motion in virtue of themselves, and not any other cause, and thus cannot have been caused to exist by anything else external, like luck, spontaneity, or intellect. Hence cosmogony is impossible, and what we should focus on is the eternality of the stars, planets, sun, and moon, and the natural cause of their continual motion. (For a related reason, we should abandon zoogony: Aristotle assumes that the forms of animals are eternal, just like the stars.) And so Aristotle in his natural science systematically works through the aethereal body and the elements, followed by their combinations in the spheres in which they mix (the meteorological and biological spheres), and gives an account of all the unchanging forms contained therein. Throughout he rejects the possibility that these things have been generated by some cosmic process other than nature itself, even those that continue to exist by transmutation (the four elements) or reproduction (living things).

4.6   *Peri ouranou*

Not surprisingly, *kosmos* is referred to more in *Peri ouranou* than in any other work of Aristotle. But even here, it is mostly in the context of the refutation of cosmogony and the plurality of worlds thesis.[47]

---

[46] The characterization of Democritus' view according to which the motions of the *kosmos* could have originated in the same way that animals originate locomotion, i.e., "spontaneously," is the third major context in *Physics* 8 in which Aristotle uses the concept of *kosmos*: "Now if this can occur in an animal, why should not the same be true of the totality [τὸ πᾶν]? If it can occur in a small *kosmos* it could also occur in a great *kosmos* [εἰ γὰρ ἐν μικρῷ κόσμῳ γίγνεται, καὶ ἐν μεγάλῳ]; and if it can occur in the *kosmos*, it could occur in the infinite; that is, if the infinite could as a whole possibly be in motion or at rest" (8.2.252b24–28). Of course, Aristotle is completely critical of this argument and of the whole conception that the motion of the *ouranos* ever had a beginning (see 8.3.253a7–21 and 8.6).

[47] Kukkonen offers an interpretation of *Peri ouranou* that is largely consistent with the interpretation offered here: "despite the tendency on the part of modern commentators to side with Alexander and to call Aristotle's *On the Heavens* his cosmology; the term *kosmos* does not appear to have any special significance in Aristotle's exposition in this particular treatise" (2014: 312; see below, n. 57, for an important difference between our interpretations). Kukkonen's study is especially useful for his detailed examination of the commentators, beginning with Alexander and Simplicius, and their influence on later commentators, including those in the Arabic tradition.

According to Simplicius, Alexander of Aphrodisias

> says that the subject of Aristotle's treatise *Peri ouranou* is the *kosmos* [περὶ
> κόσμου]. He says that *ouranos* is used in three senses by Aristotle in this
> work, to mean both the sphere of the fixed stars and the whole of the divine,
> revolving body, which in this book he also calls the "furthest *ouranos*" (with
> the adjective), and additionally, the *kosmos* [καὶ ἔτι μέντοι τὸν κόσμον], as
> Plato called it. (*in Phys.* p. 1.2–6 Diels, tr. Hankinson)

The reference is clearly to the passage in 1.9, quoted earlier, in which
Aristotle defines the third, broad sense of *ouranos*: "In yet another sense we
give the name to all body included within extreme circumference, since we
habitually call the whole and the totality *ouranos* [τὸ γὰρ ὅλον καὶ τὸ πᾶν
εἰώθαμεν λέγειν οὐρανόν]." The problem with Alexander's interpretation is
that the term *kosmos* is notably absent from that passage, and so it cannot
literally be evidence for the claim that *kosmos* is the actual subject of *Peri
ouranou*. In fact, what the passage shows is that Aristotle's comprehensive
account of the totality can be given without any reference to the concept of
kosmos whatsoever, and hence the name of the inquiry (and title of the
treatise) is *Peri ouranou* and not *Peri kosmou* (or *Kosmopoiia* or
Diakosmêsis). His focus is on the singularity and eternity of the universe.
Now it is true that for Aristotle the single and unique *ouranos*, since it is
identical with "the whole" and "the totality," is therefore identical with the
kosmos, and thus the investigation *Peri ouranou* subsumes the investigation
of the *kosmos*. There is nothing else that an investigation of *kosmos* could
have as its object, in Aristotle's view, other than the elements contained in
the *ouranos* (in the broad third sense meaning "universe"), since this is
identical with the totality of everything. Accordingly, the *Peri ouranou*
contains a comprehensive discussion of the primary body and the four
elements.[48] The descriptions of the movements of these bodies are the
subject matter of Aristotle's natural science, "the science concerned with
nature" as he describes it in the opening of *Peri ouranou* 1.1; he does not
even mention a "science concerned with the *kosmos*." For this reason, one
should avoid speaking loosely of Aristotle's "cosmology": yes, he has views
about the *kosmos* (about its shape, order, arrangement, eternality,

---

[48] As Simplicius says, "he clearly does not explain the *kosmos* in this treatise as Plato did in the *Timaeus* . . .
very little is said about the *kosmos* as a whole, and only such things as it has in common with the *ouranos*,
i.e. that it is eternal, limited in size, and single . . . But if anyone wishes to inspect Aristotle's theory of the
kosmos, it must be said that he presents his account of the *kosmos* in all of his physical treatises taken
together. . . . Aristotle himself does not say, either when setting out in summary in the third book of this
treatise what is said in it, or in the prelude to the *Meteorology*, that he has discussed the *kosmos*, or the
ouranos in the sense of the *kosmos*" (*in Phys.* pp.3.17–4.2 Diels, tr. after Hankinson).

singularity, etc.); but these views follow from his physics, his account of the principles, elements, and causes of nature and natural things, not from an account of the *kosmos* as such. It would be more accurate to speak of Aristotle's "ouranology" rather than his "cosmology," if we needed a specific term and were required to speak in anachronisms. In the predecessors and many successors, on the other hand, views about the origin of the *kosmos* or arrangement of *kosmoi* were used as the basis for explaining nature, and thus the term "cosmology" seems more or less apt. Aristotle's contribution to the history of cosmology as an independent science is largely critical and negative.

Aristotle only refers to *kosmos* in stating his own positive views twice in *Peri ouranou*: "It is plain from the foregoing that the *kosmos* is spherical" (Aristotle, *Cael.* 2.5.287b15); and "the order of the *kosmos* is in fact eternal [ἡ δέ γε τοῦ κόσμου τάξις ἀΐδιος]" (Aristotle, *Cael.* 2.14.296a33–34). In the second case, the context is the dispute about whether the earth moves or is immobile. In both cases the term *kosmos* could easily be replaced with *ouranos* (in the broad third sense) without any loss of meaning, as far as Aristotle is concerned. Every other reference to *kosmos* in the *Peri ouranou* occurs in the context of refuting cosmogony or plurality of worlds.

In the first book, after introducing his subject as the science of nature, bodies, and magnitudes (in Chapter 1), Aristotle argues for the following theses (in the chapters noted): that the primary body moves in a circle (Chapters 2–4), that no body is infinite (Chapters 5–7), that there cannot be more than one *ouranos* (Chapters 8 and 9), and that the *ouranos* is ungenerated and indestructible (Chapters 10–12 and 2.1). The term *kosmos* does not appear in the chapters in which Aristotle explains his own positive view (Chapters 1–4), that "there must necessarily be some simple body which moves naturally and in virtue of its own nature with a circular movement" (269a5–7, tr. Stocks). And the term *kosmos* appears only once in the course of Aristotle's argument (Chapters 5–7) against an infinite body: "The infinite, then, cannot revolve in a circle; nor could the *kosmos*, if it were infinite" (1.5.272a20).

The majority of the references to *kosmos* in *Peri ouranou* occur in the argument of 1.8 that there cannot be more than one *ouranos*. Aristotle anticipates the argument in 1.7 by distinguishing the question of the plurality of worlds from the question of an infinite body:

> After these things, one should investigate whether the totality [τὸ πᾶν], although not infinite with respect to body, is nevertheless great enough to admit more *ouranoi* [πλείους οὐρανούς]. For someone might well be

puzzled about whether, since the *kosmos* around us [ὁ περὶ ἡμᾶς κόσμος] is constituted as it is, nothing prevents there also being more than one, although not an infinite number. (Aristotle, *Cael.* 1.7.274a24–28)

Aristotle does not, here at least, accept even this limited plurality of *kosmoi*:

> We must now proceed to explain why there cannot be more *ouranoi* [πλείους οὐρανούς], the further question mentioned above. For it may be thought that we have not proved universal of bodies that none whatever can exist outside of the *kosmos* [ἐκτὸς εἶναι τοῦ κόσμου τοῦδε ὁτιοῦν αὐτῶν], and that our argument applied only to those of infinite extent. (Aristotle, *Cael.* 1.8.276a18–22)

Aristotle's argument to the conclusion that that there cannot be more than one *ouranos* depends on the principles of his doctrine of natural place, and thus his physics. According to the doctrine, each simple body (earth, water, air, fire, and aether) has a natural motion defined by its natural motion within the totality. Motion toward (or, in the case of aether, within) a natural place is natural, motion away from it is unnatural or "constrained"; these are conceived as opposites. Now Aristotle argues that since earth naturally moves to the center, and must have this nature wherever it exists, then if there are more *kosmoi*, the earth in one *kosmos* would naturally move to the center of both its own and another *kosmos*, but at the same time the earth in the other *kosmos* would move to the center of the first; this would result in motions at once natural and "by constraint," an absurdity.

> If, then, it is by constraint that earth moves from a certain place to the center here, its movement from here to there will be natural, and if earth from there rests here without constraint, its movement hither will be natural. And the natural movement in each case is one. Further, the *kosmoi*, being similar in nature to ours, must all be composed of the same bodies as it. (Aristotle, *Cael.* 1.8.276a27–31)

From these assumptions, Aristotle shows that the hypothesis of plural *kosmoi* is absurd, necessitating simultaneous natural and unnatural motion of the earth element in opposite directions in the two *kosmoi*. It is remarkable that in the course of the argument, Aristotle says that the point is made clear by "positioning the *kosmoi* in relation to one another," or what one translation describes as a "juxtaposition of the worlds" (Stocks). This seems to refer to a diagram depicting the hypothetical movement of an element of [E]arth with respect to two different spherical *kosmoi* centered on points (A) and (B), the circumferences of which meet at point X. Here is a schematic and hypothetical reconstruction:

$$[E] \rightarrow (A) \rightarrow X \rightarrow (B)$$

If E moves naturally toward the center of *kosmos* A, then since it has the same tendency relative to the center of *kosmos* B, it will continue to move in the direction of point X; but at that point it will be moving both "upwards" away from the center of *kosmos* A and "downwards" toward the center of *kosmos* B. This, however, is impossible because it is the nature of each element to move in exactly one direction relative to a center point, and toward different places in the totality.

> The particles of earth, then, in another *kosmos* [ἐν ἄλλῳ κόσμῳ] would move naturally also to our center and its fire to our circumference. This, however, is impossible, since, if it were true, earth must, in its own *kosmos*, move upwards, and fire to the center; in the same way the earth must move naturally away from the center when it moves toward the center of the other. This follows from positioning the *kosmoi* in relation to one another [τὸ τοὺς κόσμους οὕτω κεῖσθαι πρὸς ἀλλήλους]. For either we must refuse to admit the identical nature of the simple bodies in the plurality of *ouranoi* [ἐν τοῖς πλείοσιν οὐρανοῖς], or, admitting this, we must make the center and the extremity one as suggested. This being so, it follows that there cannot be more *kosmoi* than one [κόσμους πλείους ἑνός]. (Aristotle. *Cael.* 1.8.276b11–21.)

The thesis about natural motion is the sole basis of Aristotle's rejection of the plurality of worlds hypothesis in the *Peri ouranou*; if the doctrine of natural motion were abandoned, then the *reductio ad absurdum* argument against the plurality of worlds thesis would be baseless. And so Aristotle offers further arguments in this chapter in support of the doctrine: that the simple bodies cannot have different natures in different places or *kosmoi*; that all locomotion must be finite and defined by both start and end point; and there cannot possibly be an infinite speed. He also refers to arguments from earlier in book I (the argument that there is a primary body which naturally moves in a circle, demonstrated in 1.2–4). Moreover, he relates an apparently independent metaphysical argument: "The same could also be shown with the aid of the discussions which fall under First Philosophy, as well as from the nature of the circular movement, which must be eternal both here and in the other *kosmoi* [ἐν τοῖς ἄλλοις κόσμοις]" (1.8.277b9–12). But when one follows up the reference, evidently to *Metaphysica* 12.8, one finds an extremely compact argument to the conclusion that "there is only one *ouranos*" (εἷς ἄρα οὐρανὸς μόνος) (1074a38). I will not here digress to discuss the long history of commentary on this passage,[49] except to note that the entire argument is expressed without reference to *kosmos* at all but, as we might now expect, only *ouranos*.[50] The domain of this argument is *Peri ouranou*, not *Peri kosmou*. Also, note that Aristotle in the very next chapter of *Peri ouranou* elaborates a similar argument. He begins, aporetically, by constructing an argument in favor of plural *kosmoi* but in the end concludes that

> it is quite right to say that the formula of the shape apart from the material must be different from that of the shape in the material, and we may allow this to be true. We are not, however, therefore compelled to assert there to be more *kosmoi* [πλείους εἶναι κόσμους]. Such a plurality is in fact impossible since this one contains the entirety of material, as in fact it does. (Aristotle, *Cael.* 1.9.278a23–28)

It is, however, worth digressing to consider the epistemic implications of Aristotle's solution to this problem:

> a thing whose substance resides in a substratum of material can never come into being in the absence of all matter. Now the *ouranos* is certainly a particular and a material thing ... composed not of a part but of the whole of material. (Aristotle, *Cael.* 1.9.278b1–6, tr. after Stocks)

One obvious implication of the fact that the *ouranos* (in the third, broad sense, meaning the "universe") is a particular material thing is that it is sensible. But if it is sensible then it is not, as such, knowable: "what actual sensation apprehends is individuals, while what knowledge apprehends is universals."[51] In a way, then, the *ouranos* in the sense of *kosmos* is a sensible particular, not a knowable thing. What is knowable within the *kosmos* are the universal and eternal forms that are repeatedly generated in plural or infinite material things: the transmutation of the eternal elemental forms, and the reproduction of the eternal forms of living things. Aristotle also holds that the "eternal" cycles of the stars are knowable, but there is a problem in that the moon, sun, planets, and stars, insofar are they are particular, sensible

[49] Ross 1924: *ad loc.* and cxxxix–cxl provides a useful overview of the difficulties and the commentarial history.
[50] It is often said that *Metaphysics* 12 is a key text for Aristotle's cosmology (e.g., Wright 1995: 69), but this is only true if we are speaking loosely. It cannot literally be true, since the word *kosmos* does not appear in that book – the operative notions are order (*taxis*) and nature. Nevertheless, the term *kosmos* is frequently read into the text (e.g., the translation of *Metaph.* 12.10.1075a12–20 by Wright 1995: 70; this does not necessarily cause confusion).
[51] Arist. *An.* 2.5.417b22; cf. *APo.* 1.4 *passim*; 1.33.88b31; 2.5.417b22; *Metaph.* 13.9.1086b5; *EN* 6.6.1140b31.

things, would seem to be unsuitable as objects of knowledge as opposed to sensation.[52]

If Aristotle could conceive of our *ouranos* as one *kosmos* among many, then he could conceive of a general science of cosmology, which would explain how plural or infinite *ouranoi* and *kosmoi* are generated, just as his elemental transmutations and organic reproductions are infinitely generated. The motions of our moon and sun could be explained according to universal principles that apply to all cosmic bodies – to all stars, suns, moons, planets, and earths – and not just these particular ones we see with our own eyes. But Aristotle rejected this Democritean approach completely.

> From our arguments then it is evident not only that there is not, but also that there could never come to be, any bodily mass whatever outside the circumference. The total *kosmos* [ὁ πᾶς κόσμος], therefore, includes all its appropriate matter, which is, as we saw, natural sensible body. So that neither are there now, nor have there ever been, nor can there ever be formed more *ouranoi* [πλείους οὐρανοί], but this *ouranos* of ours is one and unique and perfect [εἷς καὶ μόνος καὶ τέλειος οὗτος οὐρανός ἐστιν]. (Aristotle. *Cael.* 1.9.279a6–11 tr. after Stocks).

Thus Aristotle concluded that the *kosmos* and *ouranos* must be identical, and it must also be singular and unique.[53] Having arrived at this conclusion, Aristotle moves on to his last major argument of *Peri ouranou* 1, which runs from 1.10–12, and includes 2.1: that the *ouranos* is eternal, i.e., ungenerated and indestructible.

I digress briefly to mention that, according to an ancient list, Aristotle wrote a work entitled *Peri kosmou geneseôs*. As Moraux (1951: 263–65) explained, the title is awkward since it seems to suggest Aristotle wrote "*About the generation of kosmos*" – but we know he rejected the generation

---

[52] For this reason, Aristotle subordinates the empirical science of "star-gazing" to mathematical astronomy in *APo.* 1.13; similarly, the empirical sciences of acoustics and meteorology are subordinated to mathematical sciences like arithmetic and geometry. This is necessary in order to secure universality of the principles by means of which the empirical phenomena are explained; see Johnson 2015: 175–77.

[53] For this reason, my interpretation, despite much agreement, differs from that of Kukkonen, who explains why "cosmological perspectives provide such an ill fit for the overall Aristotelian pattern of explanation and understanding" (2014: 327) as follows: "The first and most fundamental stumbling block, I submit, is that for Aristotle there simply is no world, conceived of as a single object, such as would admit of a unified investigation. The physical universe just is not a single being" (ibid.). In my view the problem is just the opposite: because he conceives of the *kosmos* as a single object identical to the visible *ouranos*, this *kosmos* cannot itself be the object of its own science; rather the objects of the relevant science have to be understood to be the generic substances that constitute the *ouranos* in the third, broad sense, namely: aether, fire, air, water, and earth. These are precisely the subject matter of *Peri ouranou* 1–4.

of the *kosmos*. One is thus tempted to read it as a polemical work *"Against the generation of kosmos"*; but in that case, as Moraux pointed out, we should expect the preposition *Pros* as opposed to *Peri*.[54] Setting that consideration aside, I speculate that *Peri ouranou* 1.10–12 + 2.1 may have circulated separately under the title *Peri kosmou geneseôs*, as these chapters form an apparently self-sufficient unit addressing the dialectical problem announced in the *Topica*, whether the *kosmos* is eternal, and specifically whether it came into being (as the cosmogonies have it). This is compatible with the interpretation of the arguments of *Peri ouranou* 1.10–12 and 2.1 as largely adapted from arguments in the *Peri philosophias* (as argued by Effe 1970: 20–23 and 132–39). I should point out that in this section of *Peri ouranou*, Aristotle begins with a review of earlier theories (1.10), and definition of key terms (1.11), followed by a series of proofs that the *ouranos* (and thus the *kosmos*) is finite, singular, eternal, ungenerated, and indestructible (1.12). The next chapter (2.1), which argues that this view of the *ouranos* is consistent with traditional views about the gods (unlike the predecessors' views), is linked with these chapters and may have been part of the lost work *Peri philosophias* as well.

Thus, *Peri ouranou* 1.10–12 has the structure of a self-contained diaporetic inquiry. Aristotle begins this inquiry with a review of previous theories:

> That it was generated all are agreed, but, generation over, some say that (1) it is eternal, others say that (2) it is destructible like any other natural formation; (3) others again, with Empedocles of Agrigentum and Heraclitus of Ephesus, believe that there is alternation in the destructive process, which takes now this direction, now that, and continues without end. (Aristotle, *Cael.* 1.10.279b14–17, tr. after Stocks)

The first crucial point is that Aristotle characterizes the debate as one about *ouranos*, not *kosmos*, and the second is that *all* of Aristotle's predecessors had argued that the *ouranos* was generated. So we see here Aristotle's exact contribution to the debate, and what sets him apart from *all* his predecessors: according to Aristotle the *ouranos* is ungenerated, indestructible, and eternal in both directions. Since he holds that the *kosmos* is identical with the eternal *ouranos* (in the broad, third sense of "universe"), he offers the classical version of the theory that has become known as steady-state cosmology, and his view would have to be opposed to intelligent design creationism, the big bang model, and any of the

---

[54] An anonymous reader for the Press usefully pointed out to me that the *Peri ideôn* seems to be a critical work (i.e., critical of the Platonic theory of forms). That is a good point, although its fragmentary status prohibits us from inferring anything with certainty about the meaning of the title.

multiple big bang models (big bang followed by big crunch, rebounding totality, etc.). Steady-state theory has been continuously defended since at least Aristotle, but has lately fallen out of favor in scientific cosmology almost as much as intelligent design creationism.

From Aristotle's point of view, then, the alternatives are as follows: (1) according to Plato, *ouranos* is indestructible; (2) according to Democritus it is destructible; and (3) according to Heraclitus and Empedocles it alternates between periods of generation and destruction. In the rest of 1.10, Aristotle employs the term *kosmos* in arguing against the first[55] and third views. In arguing against the cyclical model, he offers his own definition of *kosmos*:

> If the whole body [τὸ ὅλον σῶμα], which is a continuum, is so disposed and arranged [διατίθεται καὶ διακεκόσμηται] now in one way, but then in another, and if the system of the whole is *kosmos*, i.e. *ouranos* [ἡ δὲ τοῦ ὅλου σύστασίς ἐστι κόσμος καὶ οὐρανός], then it will not be the *kosmos* [ὁ κόσμος] that comes into being and is destroyed, but only its dispositions [αἱ διαθέσεις]. (Aristotle, *Cael.* 1.10.280a19–23))

This argument eliminates the third view, attributed to Heraclitus and Empedocles.

As for the second view, Simplicius, following Alexander of Aphrodisias, correctly identifies Democritus as the target of Aristotle's argument against a destructible totality:

> Those who talk of the *kosmos* as being generated and destroyed ... as if it were like any of the other composite things, would be Democritus and his circle. For just as, according to them, everything else is generated and destroyed, so too is each of the infinite number of *kosmoi*. (Simplicius, *in Cael.* p. 295.20–22 Heiberg)[56]

Simplicius quotes an invaluable passage from Aristotle's lost work *On Democritus* in which Democritus is said to speak "of this generative combination and of the separative destruction which is contrary to it not only in the case of animals, but also in that of plants and *kosmoi*, and in general in the case of all perceptible bodies."[57] The views of

---

[55] "Suppose that the *kosmos* was formed out of elements which were formerly otherwise conditioned than as they are now. Then if their condition was always so and could not have been otherwise, it could never have come into being. And if so, then, clearly, their condition must have been capable of change and not eternal: after combination therefore they will be dispersed, just as in the past after dispersion they came into combination, and this process either has been, or could have been, indefinitely repeated. But if this is so, it cannot be indestructible, and it does not matter whether the change of condition has actually occurred or remains a possibility" (Aristotle, *Cael.* 1.10.279b24-31, tr. after Stocks).

[56] Alexander of Aphrodisias Fr. 208, *apud* Simpl. *in Cael.* p. 294.27–31 Heiberg, tr. by Hankinson.

[57] Note that this passage confirms that it is Democritus that is the target of the argument at *Physics* 196a25–28 (referenced earlier in the chapter).

Democritus on the destructibility of the *kosmos* have already been discussed in the context of the refutation of the plurality of worlds thesis in 1.8–9. Democritean cosmology does not arise as an issue again until the discussion of corpuscular movement in Book 3. By that point, the theories of motion of Democritus and Plato are, remarkably, grouped and dismissed together.

> Leucippus and Democritus, who say that the primary bodies are in perpetual movement in the void or infinite, may be asked to explain the manner of their motion and the kind of movement which is natural to them. For if the various elements are constrained by one another to move as they do, each must still have a natural movement which the constrained contravenes, and the prime mover must cause motion not by constraint but naturally. If there is no ultimate natural cause of movement and each preceding term in the series is always moved by constraint, we shall have an infinite process.
>
> The same difficulty is involved even if it is supposed, as we read in the *Timaeus*, that before the *kosmos* was made the elements moved without order [ἀτάκτως].[58] Their movement must have been due either to constraint or to their nature. And if their movement was in accordance with nature [κατὰ φύσιν], a moment's consideration shows that there was already a *kosmos*. For the prime mover must cause motion in virtue of its own natural movement, and the other bodies, moving without constraint, as they came to rest in their proper places, would fall into the order in which they now stand, the heavy bodies moving toward the center and the light bodies away from it. But that is the order of their distribution in our *kosmos* [ταύτην δ' ὁ κόσμος ἔχει τὴν διάταξιν]. (Aristotle, *Cael.* 3.2.300b9–25, tr. after Stocks).

This sequence of dialectical argumentation is remarkable because Aristotle understands his doctrine of natural movement at once to undermine both Democritean and Platonic cosmogony. Here we see Aristotle himself clearly distinguishing his own views from those of Plato and Democritus – the two greatest influences on his natural philosophy. In Aristotle's view, nature explains order, and order the *kosmos*; this is the proper explanatory order. The principles of nature are primary and indemonstrable, they are responsible for and the basis of all explanation of order and *kosmos*. But since both Democritus and Plato fail to explain natural movement, their attempts to explain order and *kosmos* are doomed from the beginning. The fatal flaw in both cases is taking

---

[58] Cf. Pl. *Ti.* 30a5.

cosmogony as the starting point for explaining nature, and not nature as the starting point for explaining the *kosmos*.

The argument deployed against the Atomists is more developed and carefully argued. Aristotle argues that if infinite bodies in infinite void move with an infinite variety of motions (as opposed to with one or several definite kinds of motion), then a certain order would be impossible. But a certain order is necessary. Therefore, infinite bodies do not move with an infinite variety of motions.[59] Aristotle represents this as a self-sufficient refutation of Atomism. Crucial to Aristotle's argument is what he means by "a certain order" (τάξις τις). And that becomes clear in the following passage, in which order is explained by reference to a thing's nature:

> The disorderly is nothing other than the contrary to nature [τὸ ἀτάκτως οὐθέν ἐστιν ἕτερον ἢ τὸ παρὰ φύσιν], since the order proper to perceptible things is their nature [ἡ γὰρ τάξις ἡ οἰκεία τῶν αἰσθητῶν φύσις ἐστίν]. And there is also absurdity and impossibility in the notion that the disorderly movement is infinitely continued. For the nature of things is the nature which most of them possess for most of the time. Thus their view brings them into the contrary position that disorder is in accordance with nature [τὴν μὲν ἀταξίαν εἶναι κατὰ φύσιν], and the order i.e. the *kosmos*, is contrary to nature [τὴν δὲ τάξιν καὶ τὸν κόσμον παρὰ φύσιν]. But no natural fact can originate as luck has it. (Aristotle, *Cael.* 3.2.301a4-11, tr. after Stocks)

Again, we see Aristotle's method of explanation. Order is explained by nature ("the order proper to perceptible things is their nature"), and the *kosmos* just is the order of nature. The Atomists, postulating an infinite variety of motions, undermine order and embrace what is contrary to nature, making it impossible to explain the *kosmos*. Aristotle compares Anaxagoras's cosmogony favorably: his starting point is unmoved things (Arist. *Cael.* 3.2.300b31–301a13: ἐξ ἀκινήτων γὰρ ἄρχεται κοσμοποιεῖν). But Aristotle does not think Anaxagoras's position much better, since Aristotle considers cosmogony in general to be a pseudo-science. Even in the above argument we can see that the concept of *kosmos* is not essential to

---

[59] "The answer to the view that there are infinite bodies moving in an infinite is that, if the cause of movement is single, they must move with a single motion, and therefore not without order [οὐκ ἀτάκτως]; and if, on the other hand, the causes are of infinite variety, their motions too must be infinitely varied. For a finite number of causes would produce a kind of order [τάξις τις], since absence of order is not proved by diversity of direction in motions: indeed, even now we know that not all bodies, but only bodies of the same kind, have a common goal of movement" (3.2.300b32–301a3, tr. after Stocks).

the argument – it appears epexegetically with *taxis* (order), and it is the notion of order which does all the work in the argument.[60]

4.7   *Meteorologica*

In the opening words of the *Meteorologica*, Aristotle introduces and situates his topic by summarizing the contents of the *Physica* and *Peri ouranou*, and *Peri geneseôs kai phthoras*:

> We have previously spoken about the first causes of nature and about all natural change [περὶ μὲν οὖν τῶν πρώτων αἰτίων τῆς φύσεως καὶ περὶ πάσης κινήσεως φυσικῆς], and also about the stars having been arranged [διακεκοσμημένων] in accordance with the upper motion, and about the elements of the bodies (how many and what quality, and their transformation into one another), and about generation and destruction in general. (Aristotle, *Mete.* I.I.338a20–25)

Given the considerations in *Peri ouranou* just reviewed, it comes as no surprise that Aristotle reiterates that his own enquiry begins with an account of the principles of nature and natural change, and that precisely these are the first principles. The issue that arises for the present investigation is why Aristotle should choose to use the verb *diakosmeô* to refer to the discussions of *Peri ouranou* 1–2 since, as we have seen, Aristotle associates the term *diakosmêsis* with the Atomist plurality of *kosmoi* hypothesis.[61] Is it

---

[60] The following argument, attributed to the *Peri philosophias*, follows the same pattern of argument and method of explanation: "To Aristotle belongs the following: there is either one first principle, or many. If there is one, we have what we are looking for; if there are many, they are either ordered or disordered. Now if they are disordered, their products are more so, and the *kosmos* is not a *kosmos* but a disorganized thing (*akosmia*); besides, that which is contrary to nature belongs to that which is by nature non-existent. If, on the other hand, they are ordered, they were ordered either by themselves or by some other cause. But if they were ordered by themselves, they have something common that unites them, and that is the first principle" (Scholiast *in Proverb. Salomonis* = Fr. 17 Ross, tr. after Ross). But if this argument does belong to Aristotle, whether from *On Philosophy* or elsewhere, it is very important because it is the most explicit case I have seen which would show Aristotle making a positive argument on the basis of the nature of the *kosmos* itself, where this term is not attached to another term epexegetically, like *ouranos* or *taxis*. So he argues to the conclusion that there is a single principle of motion, because if there were several, they would have to be ordered by a single one (whether internal or external to themselves), or else be disordered, but they cannot be disordered because then "the *kosmos* would not be a *kosmos* but an *akosmia*." But then here again the argument ultimately depends for its warrant on a claim about nature: "that which is contrary to nature belongs to that which is by nature non-existent." The longer passage from *Peri ouranou* 3.2 quoted earlier explains what Aristotle means by nature here (which indicates that Democritus, like Plato, was a target in Aristotle's *Peri philosophias*, since the Atomist view is attacked in the parallel argument). In each case we see Aristotle adverting to his theory of nature in order to explain the *kosmos*.

[61] Schofield, in his chapter in this volume (Chapter 3), defines *diakosmêsis* as "an attempt to capture the idea that physics cannot restrict itself to talking about how a *kosmos* comes into being and how it is

possible that Aristotle could be referring to a *diakosmêsis* in his own sense – an account of an ordering or "organization" of a finite number of *kosmoi*? In what remains of this chapter I will suggest a way that he could be.

In the *Meteorologica*, Aristotle uses the expression "the *kosmos* around the upper motions" (ὁ περὶ τὰς ἄνω φορὰς κόσμος), to refer to the aetherial bodies in the places above the moon (i.e., outer space).[62] But he also on several occasions uses the expression "the whole *kosmos* around the earth" (ὁ δὴ περὶ τὴν γῆν ὅλος κόσμος), with reference to the natural places of the four Empedoclean elements (earth, air, water, and fire) which as a "whole *kosmos*" are located under the moon.[63] Furthermore, he uses the expression "the *kosmos* around the earth which is continuous with the motions <of the *ouranos*>" – this is of course the "meteorological" sphere.[64] These expressions, which refer to at least two different *kosmoi*, are not used in the *Peri ouranou*, and indicate either an earlier stage in Aristotle's regimentation of scientific concepts, or an adaptation of his diction for the specialized subject matter of meteorology.[65]

It would seem from these expressions that Aristotle is committed to a view about the relation between "the upper *kosmos*" (i.e., the stars, planets, sun, and moon) and "the lower *kosmos*" (the *kosmos* around the earth, composed of fire, air, water, and earth). This could explain why he used the term *diakosmeô* in describing the contents of the *Peri ouranou*. This clearly does not imply that he recognizes a plurality of worlds in the Atomist sense. As Aristotle recognizes exactly two *kosmoi* (which we have come to call the sublunary and the superlunary spheres, which are both

structured. Physics must discuss the whole arrangement of *kosmoi* (in the plural) – the organization of the entire system." This is useful, although the term "organization" is potentially misleading in describing the Democritean account of the arrangement of the plurality of *kosmoi*; indeed, if the infinite Democritean *kosmoi* could be shown to have an overall "organization," Aristotle's objections to his theory would lose much of their force.

[62] "We earlier discoursed about the first element, what quality its power is, and why it is that *the kosmos around the upper motions* is entirely full of that body" (ἡμῖν μὲν οὖν εἴρηται πρότερον περὶ τοῦ πρώτου στοιχείου, ποῖόν τι τὴν δύναμίν ἐστιν, καὶ διότι πᾶς ὁ περὶ τὰς ἄνω φορὰς κόσμος ἐκείνου τοῦ σώματος πλήρης ἐστί) (Arist. *Mete.* 1.3.339b18–19, tr. after Lee).

[63] In addition to Arist. *Cael.* 1.7.274a24-28 (discussed above), see also *Mete.* 1.7: "For we suppose that the dry and warm exhalation is the outermost part of the *kosmos* around the earth [τοῦ κόσμου τοῦ περὶ τὴν γῆν], which falls below the circular motion. It, and a great part of the air that is continuous with it below, is carried round the earth by the motion of the circular revolution" (Arist. *Mete.* 1.7.344a9–14, tr. after Lee). "For such is the motion of the *kosmos* around the earth [τοιαύτη γὰρ ἡ φορὰ τοῦ κόσμου τοῦ περὶ τὴν γῆν]" (1.7.344b11–12, tr. after Lee).

[64] "We have spoken concerning the things that come to be in the *kosmos* around the earth which is continuous with the motions <sc. of the *ouranos*> [περὶ μὲν οὖν τῶν γιγνομένων ἐν τῷ περὶ τὴν γῆν κόσμῳ τῷ συνεχεῖ ταῖς φοραῖς εἴρηται]" (*Mete.* 1.9.346b10–15, tr. after Lee).

[65] Kahn (1960: 99 and 109) argues that meteorology is a remarkably conservative line of inquiry from the tradition of Anaximander forward (see also Taub 2003: 9–10). If so, this may help explain why Aristotle in the *Meteorologica* seems to use the term *kosmos* more like his predecessors, and specifically more like Anaximander (see later).

centered round the earth, and which are completely bounded by a singular *ouranos*), his *diakosmêsis* consists precisely in an account of how these two *kosmoi* are arranged and causally related to one another. And Aristotle offers precisely such an account in *Meteorologica* 1.2:

> So the whole *kosmos* around the earth is made out of these bodies; concerning which one should grasp the occurrences that we claim to be effects. [ὁ δὴ περὶ τὴν γῆν ὅλος κόσμος ἐκ τούτων συνέστηκε τῶν σωμάτων· περὶ οὗ τὰ συμβαίνοντα πάθη φαμὲν εἶναι ληπτέον.] This necessarily has a certain continuity with the upper motions; consequently all its power is derived from them. For the originating principle of all motion must be deemed the first cause. Besides, that element is eternal and its motion has not an end with respect to its place, but is always at an end [ἡ μὲν ἀίδιος καὶ τέλος οὐκ ἔχουσα τῷ τόπῳ τῆς κινήσεως, ἀλλ᾽ ἀεὶ ἐν τέλει]; whereas all these other bodies have separate places which limit one another [ταῦτα δὲ τὰ σώματα πάντα πεπερασμένους διέστηκε τόπους ἀλλήλων]. So we must treat fire and earth and the elements like them as the material causes of the things that are generated (meaning by material what is subject and affected), but must assign causality in the sense of the originating principle of motion to the power of the eternally moving bodies. (Aristotle, *Mete.* 1.2.339a19–32, tr. after Lee)

The lower *kosmos* is continuous with the upper *kosmos*, and the things that happen in the lower *kosmos* are effects of the causes operating in the upper *kosmos*. In a sense the expression "the upper *kosmos*" refers to a *kosmos*, the one which consists exclusively of eternal aetherial bodies in constant circular motion, and which is not itself limited in its motion with respect to place, in distinction from "the lower *kosmos*," which is limited both below and above, consisting of the four elemental bodies that are constantly moved by the upper *kosmos*, thus generating and destroying living substances. There is a precedent for speaking this way. Anaximander seems to have used the plural terms *kosmoi* and *ouranoi* to indicate different regions or parts of the totality: "he says that it is neither water not any other of the so-called elements, but some other unbound nature from which been generated all the *ouranoi* and the *kosmoi* in them [ἀλλ᾽ ἑτέραν τινὰ φύσιν ἄπειρον, ἐξ ἧς ἅπαντας γίνεσθαι τοὺς οὐρανοὺς καὶ τοὺς ἐν αὐτοῖς κόσμους]".[66] Although there has been a tendency in later doxagraphic

---

[66] Anaximander DK 12 A 9 = Simpl. *in Phys.* p. 24.17–18 Diels. Notice the variant versions: "he said that the *apeiron* contained the whole cause of the generation and destruction of the world, from which he says that the *ouranoi* are separated off, and in general all the *kosmoi*, being *apeirous*" (A10 = Ps.-Plutarch, *Strom.* 2); "he said that the material principle of existing things was some nature coming under the heading of the *apeiron*, from which come into being the *ouranoi* and the *kosmos* in them" (A11 = Hippol. *Haer.* 1.6.2). Hippolytus's reference to a singular *kosmos* is probably inaccurate.

literature to conflate Anaximander's references to plural *kosmoi* and *ouranoi* with the Democritean plurality of worlds thesis, it has been persuasively argued by Charles Kahn that the *kosmoi* here must refer to "different departments or regions" of the totality, "some lower 'arrangements' of atmosphere or earth," and the *apeiron* or boundless "can thus surround both the *ouranoi* or *kosmoi* within the framework of the one and only world system."[67] This fits well with Aristotle's own usage. How closely Aristotle seems willing to follow Anaximander's way of speaking (in the *Meteorologica*, at least) is indicated by his remark that, whereas the lower *kosmos* is "bounded" or "limited" in respect of place, the upper *kosmos* is not so bounded (rather it *is* the boundary or limit itself for all the natural places). And in Book 2, Aristotle seems to be referring to Anaximander's theory when using the expression "the *kosmos* around the earth":

> they are met by the same difficulty as those who say that at first the earth itself was moist and the *kosmos* around the earth [τοῦ κόσμου τοῦ περὶ τὴν γῆν] was warmed by the sun, and so air was generated and the whole firmament grew, and the air caused winds and the solstices. (Aristotle, *Mete.* 2.2.355a21-25, tr. after Lee)

So it would seem reasonable to attribute to Aristotle the thesis there is not one *kosmos* but two, and they are, unlike Democritean *kosmoi*, tightly causally connected to one another (i.e., as mover to material). But in fact, Aristotle never uses the plural expression *kosmoi*, except with reference to the cosmogonies and plurality of worlds theories that he rejects, as we saw. So in the *Meteorologica* he usually uses expressions like "the upper place" instead of "the upper *kosmos*," even while he has no compunction about using the expressions "the *kosmos* around the earth" and "the lower *kosmos*" (τοῦ κάτω κόσμου).[68]

Whatever his own conception of *diakosmêsis*, Aristotle in no uncertain terms deploys his generic attack on cosmogony against meteorological arguments of his predecessors who "think the cause of such effects to be the transformation of the whole [τὴν τοῦ ὅλου μεταβολὴν] in the sense of a coming-to-be of the *ouranos* [ὡς γιγνομένου τοῦ οὐρανοῦ]."

---

[67] Kahn 1960: 48–49.

[68] "After the exposition of the difficulties involved, let us go on to state our own opinion, with a view at once to what follows and to what has already been said. *The upper* <place, *topos*> [τὸ ἄνω] as far as the moon we affirm to consist of a body distinct from both fire and from air, but varying in degree of purity and in kind, especially towards its limit on the side of the air, and of *the kosmos around the earth* [καὶ πρὸς τὸν περὶ τὴν γῆν κόσμον]. Now the circular motion of the first element and of the bodies it contains dissolves, and inflames by its motion, whatever part of *the lower kosmos* (τοῦ κάτω κόσμου) is nearest to it, and so generates heat" (Arist. *Mete.* 1.3.340b6–10, tr. after Lee).

We must not suppose that the cause of this is the coming-to-be of the *kosmos* [τὴν τοῦ κόσμου γένεσιν]. For it is ridiculous for the totality (τὸ πᾶν) to change by being transformed [μεταβολὰς κινεῖν] because of small and trifling things [διὰ μικρὰς καὶ ἀκαριαίας], when the bulk and size of the earth are surely as nothing in comparison with the whole *ouranos* [πρὸς τὸν ὅλον οὐρανόν]. (Aristotle, *Mete.* 1.14.352a17028, tr. after Lee).

Notice that in the context of this argument Aristotle makes it clear that he sees the entire earth and meteorological sphere ("the *kosmos* around the earth") to be a vanishingly small part of the whole universe, that is, the entire *ouranos* (in the third, broad sense). It is wrong, he thinks, to infer from the phenomena of generation and destruction in this *kosmos* – "the *kosmos* around here" – to the nature of the *ouranos* or the totality of the universe. This is the fundamental mistake, as he sees it, of all his predecessors, including Plato. He thinks they all get off on the wrong foot by attempting to explain the sea's saltiness (etc.) according to causes operating to bring the *kosmos* as a whole into existence. Aristotle's procedure is the opposite. He infers from the eternality of the *ouranos* the eternality of the sea. Aristotle complains that everyone thinks that the sea "has been generated, if the entire *kosmos* has been too [ὅτι γέγονεν, εἴπερ καὶ πᾶς ὁ κόσμος]; for they generate them at the same time." Against this he opposes the view: "if the totality is eternal [εἴπερ ἀΐδιον τὸ πᾶν], the same must be assumed for the sea." In this context he ridicules Democritus's views, comparing them to Aesop's fables.[69]

Given the importance of an account of the origin and history of the sea to modern oceanography and climatology, Aristotle's uncompromising rejection of an account of the origin of the sea seems unfortunate, but it is not the only unfortunate consequence of his thoroughgoing rejection of cosmogony. Even worse, he misses the value, universally recognized by modern cosmologists, of explanations for natural bodies and their motions (e.g., the elements) on the basis of an account of the origin and evolution of the *kosmos* (e.g., over a roughly 14-billion-year period). In a way, the generation and arrangement of the *kosmos* is explanatorily prior to the account of natural things and their movements, including the elements. Similarly, Aristotle failed to imagine the plurality of *kosmoi* in the sense of solar systems beyond the one bounded by the stars visible to us. The big bang and the existence of plural galaxies and "galactic clusters" consisting of countless solar systems beyond those visible to our naked eyes (not to mention the possibility of the multiverse, etc.) are absolutely essential to

[69] Arist. *Mete.* 2.3.356b4–12.

modern cosmology, and so in a way are the ancient projects of *kosmopoiia* and *diakosmêsis* initiated by Aristotle's predecessors.

I suggested earlier that Aristotle's philosophy of science discourages a science of cosmology, since he also holds that only universal propositions about natural kinds can be demonstrated, and particular sensible things are not the proper objects of natural science, and yet he vehemently argues that the universe is a singular and unique sensible thing (generically known as the *ouranos*). Thus, Aristotle's physics focuses on the generic forms of natural bodies and their various material and moving instantiations, especially as these are transformed or move regularly ("always or for the most part"), or are involved in regular cycles of reproduction. Aristotle stands out from all his predecessors by being the first philosopher to focus on zoology and psychology in his theoretical philosophy, and in so doing he saw a different picture and developed a different theory than his predecessors, who had focused on the natural history of our *kosmos* and of other possible *kosmoi*. Aristotle's change of focus was certainly productive for psychology and zoology, but his influence on the history of cosmology was much less successful. Aristotle was too dismissive of the views of his predecessors and too quick to embrace his own a priori argumentation against those who should rightly be considered the forerunners of scientific cosmology.

CHAPTER 5

Order and Orderliness
The Myth of 'Inner Beauty' in Plato

George Boys-Stones

5.1 Introduction

As Phillip Horky notes in the Introduction to this volume, the language of
the '*kosmos*' has normative as well as descriptive potential. But there are at
least two distinct ways in which this normative potential can be realised.
One is in the assessment of a unity or 'whole': the internal disposition of its
parts (if it has parts) may be what determines whether it is considered good
in its class or not.[1] But another is in the assessment of a *part*. In this case,
whether we consider the part 'good' or not may depend on the role that it
plays in the whole relative to which it is a part. Of course, some things are at
the same time both wholes and parts: that is, they have their own unity and
integrity, but also function as elements contributing to a larger system (a
cog in a clock for example; or a clock in a synchronised industrial
machine). In a well-designed system, one would typically expect that
there would be no conflict between what it was to be a good whole (a well-
structured cog) and a good part (a well-functioning piece of the clock).
Indeed, something which is both a whole and a part might inherit what it is
to be good in its kind (its normative structure) from what it is to play its
role in the good order of the greater entity relative to which it is a part.[2]

At least some ancient systems of ethics apply this thought to the realm of
moral value: they think of a human being as something that is both
a whole, but also a part contributing to some greater entity, the *kosmos*
itself. What it is to be a good, i.e. a well-ordered, human being depends in
this case on understanding the relationship of the human to the *kosmos*;
meanwhile the *kosmos* grounds ethical value by being a whole which is *not*

[1] Pauliina Remes in Chapter 7 of this volume, for example, considers Plotinus' account of the *kosmos*
from this point of view.
[2] This would presuppose just the kind of mereology that Verity Harte in fact reconstructs for Plato; see
Harte 2002: Chapter 4.

a part of something greater.[3] Among these systems, as I am going to argue, is the ethics of Plato: and I hope to show that a full appreciation of the fact can help us in our approach to some persistent puzzles about his ethical views, and also dispel some long-standing misapprehensions about his anthropology.

5.2 Plato and 'Inner Beauty'

The clearest example of an ancient ethical system that derives what is good for individuals within the *kosmos* from the role they play as parts *of* the *kosmos* is that of the Stoics. There is nothing arbitrary about the way they do this, either. The Stoics are creationists and determinists, and as such are committed to the position that what exists in the *kosmos* must be chosen according to god's plan for the *kosmos* as a whole; in other words, that the identity and success of any 'whole' *within* the *kosmos* is necessarily given by its purpose as a 'part' *of* the *kosmos*. In the case of a human being in particular, individual 'success' – in the form of virtue and happiness – ends up being defined in terms of a person's role in the cosmic economy.[4] If someone acts for themselves as a 'whole' without regard to their status as a cosmic part as well, it is impossible that they will achieve fulfilment as a human being because in effect they will not be acting as a human being at all. This is Epictetus' point in a famous analogy:

> I shall say that being clean is natural for the foot; but if you take it as a foot, and not as something independent, it will be appropriate for it to broach the mud and trample on thorns – and sometimes to be amputated for the sake of the whole. Otherwise, it is not a foot after all. (Epictetus, *Discourses* 2.5.24.2–6)

There is an important consequence of this way of viewing things. For the Stoics, it makes no sense to think of virtue as something belonging to the private as opposed to the public realm. True, virtue is a 'private' possession (and a fact about the individual *qua* whole), just in the sense that it is identified as the belief-system of the virtuous individual; but it will *count* as

---

[3] To pre-empt a worry that might arise when I apply this model to Plato, when I say that the order of the *kosmos* is the grounding for ethical value, I do not deny that the forms, and the form of the Good in particular, are the ultimate grounding for *value in general* – including the goodness of the *kosmos*. That there is good in the world is due to the form; but that there is goodness in, for example, paying debts or honouring parents (i.e. in ethically evaluable activity) is due, so described, to the cosmic system without which there would be no debts or parents.

[4] This is all the more clearly the case for the Stoics, who are nominalists, thinking that each thing is in a class of its own.

virtue only insofar as these beliefs determine choice and action in the public sphere – that is, in the activity of the individual *qua* cosmic part. So virtue to this extent is, for the Stoics, defined with an eye on 'public' activity, and is manifest in everything the virtuous person does. The Stoics mean it quite literally and quite seriously when they say that the virtuous person, and only the virtuous person, is manifestly beautiful.[5]

This conclusion – that the virtuous person is beautiful – immediately puts the Stoics at odds with Plato, on a standard picture of Plato. A standard account of Plato insists that Plato precisely makes virtue a matter of a person's private, or 'inner' life rather than what about them is publicly manifest. One proof-text alleged for this account is *Charmides* 154d–e. Socrates is introduced to Charmides and invited to agree that he is outstandingly beautiful – which he does, but not without an addition:

> 'By Hercules', I [Socrates] said: 'like you I think that he is peerless – if there is just one more small thing he has'.
> 'What is that?' said Critias.
> 'If he has a well-bred soul', I said (εἰ τὴν ψυχήν, ἦν δ' ἐγώ, τυγχάνει εὖ πεφυκώς). (Plato, *Charmides* 154d7–e1)

The state of Charmides' soul is something that the dialogue, then, is meant to explore. And exploration is necessary because, absent the appropriate external conditions for the display of virtue, it might be quite unclear from what is accessible of them in their public appearance whether someone is virtuous or not.

This is apparently the moral of the *Republic* as well:

> Justice isn't concerned with someone's doing his own externally, but with what is inside him, with what is truly himself and his own.
>
> Τὸ δέ γε ἀληθές, τοιοῦτόν τι ἦν, ὡς ἔοικεν, ἡ δικαιοσύνη ἀλλ' οὐ περὶ τὴν ἔξω πρᾶξιν τῶν αὑτοῦ, ἀλλὰ περὶ τὴν ἐντός, ὡς ἀληθῶς περὶ ἑαυτὸν καὶ τὰ ἑαυτοῦ κ.τ.λ. (Plato, *Republic* 443c9–d1)[6]

On one reading of the *Republic*, the essentially internal nature of virtue is what motivates the construction of a political utopia: its purpose is to help us to see what a virtuous person would look like in, as it were, their 'natural environment'. Conventional cities lack the mechanisms to give

---

[5] Plutarch's satirical remarks at *The Stoics Make Stranger Claims than the Poets* 1057e–58a make no sense if the claim was not seriously intended; and cf. *SVF* 3.568, where we are told that a sage can be grasped as such by perception.

[6] But cf. all of 443c–44e.

public recognition to inner virtue, and that makes it possible for virtuous people in them to pass unnoticed, or even seem vicious – and vice versa.

A case in point is Socrates – by his own account, the best political leader in Athens (*Grg.* 521d), although you might not think it to look at him. Socrates in fact is the paradigm case for the idea that a person's outward appearance *in general* may not be the best guide to their 'inner' character. Indeed, an analysis of the contrast between his outward appearance and his inner character – a contrast which takes Socrates' distinctive physiognomy as its starting point, so that it is phrased in terms of 'ugliness' versus 'beauty' – is thematised in one of the most famous passages in all Socratic literature, Alcibiades' speech in the *Symposium*:

> Isn't he just like a statue of Silenus? You know the kind of statue I mean; you'll find them in any shop in town. It's a Silenus sitting, his flute or his pipes in his hands, and it's hollow. It's split right down the middle, and inside it's full of tiny statues of the gods. (Plato, *Symposium* 215a6–b3)[7]

In a society too concerned with external appearances, we are told, it is one of Plato's most important ethical insights that we should think more about what people are like *on the inside*.[8]

That is the standard view. In what follows, however, I want to provide some evidence that this view of Plato is dangerously misleading; that the soul for Plato does not, in fact, represent a moral agent insulated from the sensible world which the body inhabits. What is more I want to argue that, when Plato talks about the 'beauty' of the soul, he does so not to contrast the private 'beauty' of the soul with the public (and inferior) beauty of the body: he does so because the *virtue* of the soul is in some distinctive way *publicly*

---

[7] Translations of the *Symposium* are taken (and where necessary adapted) from Nehamas and Woodruff 1989.

[8] The idea that Plato is interested in 'inner beauty' is so well established in the literature that it even comes to be used as a touchstone of Platonic authenticity. One of the principal considerations alleged against the authenticity of the *Hippias Major*, for example, is the fact that Socrates in that dialogue even *countenances* a definition of beauty which relies on its being a matter of outward appearance; see Pohlenz 1932: 56–57 and Edwards 1991: 162 with n. 5. Even Paul Woodruff (1982: 102), who ends up accepting the authenticity of *Hippias Major*, notes that it 'omits to use Socrates' conception of inner beauty, adumbrated in the *Charmides*' (154de). But 'inner beauty' is not a phrase to be found in Plato, despite his contrast between the beauty of the soul and the beauty of the body (in addition to *Charmides* 154e, see *Symposium* 210b8: ἐπιεικὴς ὢν τὴν ψυχήν; and *Republic* 444d12–e1: ἀρετὴ μὲν ἄρα, ὡς ἔοικεν, ὑγίειά τέ τις ἂν εἴη καὶ κάλλος καὶ εὐεξία ψυχῆς, κακία δὲ νόσος τε καὶ αἶσχος καὶ ἀσθένεια). Reason is an 'inner man' at *Republic* 589a–b; but, as Plotinus realised, this only opens the way to talk about the *intellectual* virtues as 'inner'; the virtues involving 'habit and training', i.e. Plotinus's 'political' virtues, are joint possessions of body and soul: *Ennead* 1.1.10.

manifest through the body,[9] so that a virtuous person actually is, quite literally, better looking.[10] Ultimately, I want to show, Plato may be closer to the Stoics on this matter than we usually think: that he does not locate ethical value in something private and internal, some fact about ourselves or some part of ourselves, merely as well-ordered 'wholes'; but, like the Stoics, grounds it in the public manifestations of our character, our contribution to the *kosmos* as parts. This will require us to revisit the *Symposium*.

5.3 Doubting Alcibiades

I should begin by emphasising that my argument is about the nature of virtue (the 'beauty of the soul'), and not about the nature of the soul as such. I make the point because one way in which one might argue that the soul's beauty is visible is to say that the body and soul are not distinct in the way normally – but not always – assumed for Plato.[11] Such a position would be grist to my mill, but it is not something I believe or rely on myself: I assume that, for Plato, the soul is distinct from the body, and that the body as such is visible while the soul as such is not. My argument is, however, that the question matters more to Platonic metaphysics than it does to Platonic ethics. The reason for this is simply that the soul's activity in the world is always in combination with the body, however one conceives of the soul. One might reasonably insist that the soul (rather than the body, or the soul–body combination) is what is properly identi-fied as the moral agent: but even so, its agency in the *kosmos* is expressed through the body.[12] And this, indeed, is how the 'beauty of the soul' (i.e. virtue) may be visible even though the soul itself is not: precisely and simply because, whenever the person acts, it is the soul operating through the body – and the body is visible.[13]

---

[9] In the case of Charmides, for example, note that it is not strictly the case that he is said to have an (invisible) beauty of soul but that he is beautiful/noble – πάνυ καλὸς καὶ ἀγαθός – *in respect of* his soul (*Charmides* 154e1–4). Voula Tsouna (whom I thank for useful discussion of this paper) will argue in forthcoming work against a common view that Charmides' definitions of *sōphrosynē* themselves turn 'inwards', from a form of activity (τὸ κοσμίως πάντα πράττειν καὶ ἡσυχῇ, 159b3) to an inner disposition (αἰδώς, 160e4).

[10] Other recent work to have given consideration to the aesthetic dimension of Plato's moral theory includes Moss 2005 and Lear 2006.

[11] See e.g. Gill 2000 and Carone 2005.

[12] For soul as the true locus of 'self' and the body as 'tool', see *Alc. I*. But this is not an argument that the soul is hidden in the body: the tool *reveals* the craftsman.

[13] For the idea, cf. Xen. *Mem.* 3.10.5 (the soul can be depicted, because a person having virtue can); *Cyrop.* 8.7.17 (Cyrus' soul is visible through what it does: οὐδὲ γὰρ νῦν τοι τὴν γ᾽ ἐμὴν ψυχὴν ἑωρᾶτε, ἀλλ᾽ οἷς διεπράττετο, τούτοις αὐτὴν ὡς οὖσαν κατεφωρᾶτε).

To be sure, this is not how Alcibiades asked us to think about the matter in the passage cited earlier. He clearly did intend a contrast between what is available to public assessment on the one hand, and what one might think of a person's soul independently of their outward appearance on the other. But it seems to me incautious at best to assume, as most commentators do, that Plato wants us to put our faith in Alcibiades' judgement. In fact, almost everything we know about Alcibiades problematises the assumption that he speaks for Plato when he speaks about Socrates. Alcibiades is here presented to us as someone who is young and vain; who, by his own admission, is a failure as a philosopher (cf. 216b–c). Indeed, he managed to miss the main philosophical discussion of the *Symposium*, including the culminating speech by Socrates; and in consequence of the diversions that caused him to miss them he is drunk.[14]

Plato is, of course, quite capable of having interlocutors unwittingly give voice to truths of which they are themselves unaware. But it is not just what Alcibiades has missed that ought to give us pause for thought in this case; it is also what he has succeeded in grasping. His distinction between the 'outer' and 'inner' person is not *even* an *unwitting truth*: it is a crudely expressed lesson in basic Socratic thought, namely that a human being is a combination of body and soul (and that the soul is the superior partner). That is all that Alcibiades is relying on in his speech. It may be no coincidence that the distinction between body and soul is the principal message of the dialogue named for Alcibiades (i.e. *Alc. I*);[15] but nor is it a coincidence that the *Alcibiades* was generally taken in antiquity as an elementary first step in Platonic philosophy. Alcibiades is not offering us a sophisticated insight into Socrates; he is rather demonstrating his own superficial grasp of basic Socratic anthropology. It is superficial because, having recognised the distinction between body and soul, Alcibiades goes on to talk as if virtue involves a dichotomous choice between investment in one or the other. He thinks of himself as invested in the body and things of the body,[16] and he assumes that the philosopher has a correspondingly exclusive investment in the soul. This is of a piece with his approach to philosophical progress. As Socrates puts it, Alcibiades talks as if he can

---

[14] On the uncertain status of Alcibiades' authority even, or especially, in praising Socrates, see Nightingale 1993: 123–27 and Lane 2007: 47–49. Both Nightingale and Lane see that Alcibiades' claim to reveal Socrates' 'inner' nature is part of what ought to make us suspicious.

[15] The significance of the point may be blunted, but it is by no means eliminated, for someone who doubts that Plato was himself the author of *Alc. I*.

[16] He might not even be right about that: his very ability to reflect on, and regret, the fact shows that his soul is more involved than he realises.

'trade up', giving others enjoyment of his body in return for embellishment of his soul – like Diomedes offering his bronze armour in exchange for the golden armour of Glaucus (218e).[17]

Alcibiades' assessment of Socrates, then, can be read as one that precisely misses the point, and does so in just the way that might be expected from a none-too-diligent philosophical tyro. But if we cannot rely on Alcibiades, then we should not start with him either. There are more credible philosophical guides to the nature of virtue in the *Symposium* – none more so than Diotima.

5.4 Hearing Diotima

But what difference, someone might ask, does it make to turn back to Diotima? Did she not make exactly the same sharp distinction between the 'outer' and 'inner' beauty of a person when she presented us with an aesthetic journey which leads, at a crucial point, from an interest in the 'outer' beauty of the body to the 'inner' beauty of the soul?

In fact, she did not: a closer look at the text will show how badly this misreads her intentions. Here is the relevant passage:

> A lover who goes about this matter correctly must begin in his youth to devote himself to beautiful bodies. First [πρῶτον μέν], if the leader leads aright, he should love one body and beget beautiful ideas there; then [ἔπειτα] he should realize that the beauty of any one body is brother to the beauty of any other and that if he is to pursue beauty of form he'd be very foolish not to think that the beauty of all bodies is one and the same. When he grasps this, he must become a lover of all beautiful bodies, and he must think that this wild gaping after just one body is a small thing and despise it. After this [μετὰ δὲ ταῦτα] he must think that the beauty of people's souls is more valuable than the beauty of their bodies, so that if someone is decent in his soul, even though he is scarcely blooming in his body, our lover must be content to love and care for him and to seek to give birth to such ideas as will make young men better; the result is that our lover will be forced to gaze at the beauty of ἐπιτηδεύματα καὶ νόμοι [ἵνα ἀναγκασθῇ αὖ θεάσασθαι τὸ ἐν τοῖς ἐπιτηδεύμασι καὶ τοῖς νόμοις καλὸν] and see that it is always of a similar kind, so that he will conclude that the beauty of the body is not, after all, of

---

[17] On my reading, then, Socrates does not 'own' the comparison to make the point in his own voice that the exchange is unfair; he uses it to describe how Alcibiades is thinking. But what Alcibiades fails to realise is that psychological beauty *involves* proper use of the body and that there is an essential incoherence in the thought that one can purchase virtue at the expense of unethical activity. (This works whether you think that what is unethical is his de facto prostitution of himself, or his attempt to lure Socrates into an exchange he himself believes to be unfair.)

so great moment. And next [μετὰ δὲ ταῦτα], his attention should be diverted from ἐπιτηδεύματα to the sciences; the result is that he will see the beauty of knowledge [ἵνα ἴδῃ αὖ ἐπιστημῶν κάλλος] (Plato, *Symposium* 210a4–c7)

I have left ἐπιτηδεύματα καὶ νόμοι untranslated here, because it turns out that the structure of the passage depends a good deal on what one takes the words to mean. Typically, they are understood to mean something like 'institutions and laws',[18] a translation which suggests that there are *five* distinct stages described in the ascent here: the beauty of (1) a single body, (2) many bodies, (3) soul, (4) these 'institutions and laws' and finally (5) the sciences.[19] Yet it should be obvious that it is only the *translation* of ἐπιτηδεύματα καὶ νόμοι this way which suggests that they constitute a distinct stage in the ascent. A new stage is not otherwise flagged for the reader; in fact, rather the opposite. The explicit terms by which every (other) stage is signalled for the reader are marked, with the Greek, in the translation above: *first* [a single body], *then* [multiple bodies], *after this* [the soul], *and next* [the sciences]. But what introduces the ἐπιτηδεύματα καὶ νόμοι, far from marking them off as a new step, actually assimilates them to the identical ontological level of what immediately precedes – the soul – by placing them within a result clause. We ascend to the consideration of the soul's beauty *with the result that* we are forced to see the beauty of ἐπιτηδεύματα καὶ νόμοι (ἵνα ἀναγκασθῇ αὖ θεάσασθαι, 210c3). Note that the context rules it out that this is just another way of expressing transition – either to a further sight on the same ontological level, or to a higher step of the ladder (as if one sees the beauty of the soul, and in so doing is inevitably catapulted along to something else). It is not just that Diotima uses the very same grammatical construction (with ἵνα) in the very next sentence, dealing with the final step on the route, where transition is out of the question. (After the ἐπιτηδεύματα καὶ νόμοι, she says, we ascend to the sciences *with the result that* we can see the beauty *of the sciences* – i.e. of *those very* sciences to which we have now ascended: ἵνα ἴδῃ αὖ

---

[18] So Jowett 1892 *ad loc.* Joyce 1935 *ad loc.* has 'laws and institutions'; Nehamas and Woodruff 1989 *ad loc.* has 'activities and laws'; Griffith 1986 *ad loc.* has 'customs and institutions'; Vlastos (1991: 140) has 'laws and practices'; Howatson and Sheffield 2008 *ad loc.* has 'human practices and laws'. Cf. Bett (2010: 131): 'among the things one contemplates in the course of the ascent are laws and ways of life (*epitêdeumata*, 201c3–4), the "beauty" of which must consist at least in part in their ethical excellence' (sc. as opposed to physical beauty); Sheffield (2012: 130 n. 23) mentions 'laws and practices'. A. Nehamas (2007: 110) glosses the phrase as 'a life devoted to politics'.

[19] This five-stage reading is already well established in antiquity: cf. e.g. Alcinous, *Didaskalikos* 157.11–21 and 165.27–34; Plotinus 1.3.2.9; 1.6.1.43; 5.9.2.7.

ἐπιστημῶν κάλλος, c7.) It is not just that nothing is said to explain what makes the putative transition here, but not elsewhere, automatic (ἀναγκασθῇ, c3). It is also the fact that Diotima says explicitly that it is the encounter with the beauty of ἐπιτηδεύματα καὶ νόμοι which leads us to think less of the beauty of the body (c5–6) – an unaccountable claim if she thinks that we have seen the soul as something distinct from both in the meantime.

So it seems to me compelling to suppose that the ἐπιτηδεύματα καὶ νόμοι are not an extra step on the route, after all, but are that about the soul in virtue of which the soul can be beautiful – in such a way that it is our awareness of *their* beauty in our encounter with the soul that leads us to forget about the beauty of the body. But if this is right, then they are certainly not 'institutions and laws'. The only available translation that makes any sense of the fact that they describe what we see when we see someone's soul is something like 'habits and customs'.[20] (We do not need to put too much weight on the pairing here, by the way: it could be that there is a distinction intended between νόμοι as 'habits of convention', e.g. whether one greets with a hand-shake or a kiss, as opposed to a broader category of habits of character, including such things as whether one habitually offers or withholds help; but the phrase seems to be something of an idiom, and apparently, in this context at least, a hendiadys for ἐπιτηδεύματα – 'habits' – on its own:[21] in any case, Diotima herself refers back to them only as ἐπιτηδεύματα – immediately at 210c6, and again, twice, in the summary of the passage at 211c – and neither she nor anyone else mentions νόμοι again.)

In case the foregoing considerations are not in themselves sufficient to prove that there are four steps in the 'ascent' passage and not five, there is further confirmation to come. A single Stephanus page after setting the ascent out in detail, Diotima summarises what she has said:

[20] I discuss the contribution of νόμοι in what follows; for the meaning of ἐπιτηδεύματα, see e.g. Plato, *Laws* 967e3 (τὰ τῶν ἠθῶν ἐπιτηδεύματα); and cf. the pertinent (albeit non-Platonic) maxim attributed to Thales by Diogenes Laertius (1.37): 'Don't beautify your face, but be beautiful in ἐπιτηδεύματα'.

[21] The same substitution, in the opposite direction, is made between *Gorgias* 474d4 (ἐπιτηδεύματα) and e6 (τοὺς νόμους καὶ τὰ ἐπιτηδεύματα). The pairing of ἐπιτηδεύματα and νόμοι is also found in a political context, in *Republic* 484b and 502b; and (possibly with remote reliance on the *Hippias Major*) in the account of beauty in the 'Aristotelian Divisions' (Diog. Laert. 3.89). Since it will be important to my argument that the ἐπιτηδεύματα καὶ νόμοι can be literally perceived, *Hippias Major* 298a–d (whatever one thinks of its authorship; see n. 8) is especially relevant, since here ἐπιτηδεύματα καὶ νόμοι can be seen and heard as well – a claim that is neither challenged nor allowed to stand as an obvious disqualification of the definition of beauty here as 'that which is pleasurable to sight and hearing'.

Starting from (1) individual beauties, the quest for the universal beauty must find him ever ascending, as if using a staircase, from one to (2) two, and from two to every lovely body, and from beautiful bodies to (3) beautiful ἐπιτηδεύματα [καὶ ἀπὸ τῶν καλῶν σωμάτων ἐπὶ τὰ καλὰ ἐπιτηδεύματα], from ἐπιτηδεύματα to (4) beautiful learning. (Plato, *Symposium* 211c1–6)

Two things are to be noted here. First, of course, that she lists four steps, consistently with my reading of the main description of the ascent, and not five. (The striking convergence of this list with a parallel discussion of what is καλός in the *Gorgias* makes it hard to argue that it is this passage, not the earlier one, which is the anomaly.)[22] But secondly, and at first sight perhaps most surprisingly, that the putative 'fifth' element not mentioned here is the soul.[23] So should we say that the soul is somehow being overlooked? If the ἐπιτηδεύματα in the main ascent passage are understood to be things distinct from the soul, then it is. But if one takes it that they are precisely what one sees when one sees the soul, then it is not. On my reading, Diotima's summary follows her original course quite precisely: from body, to bodies, to (soul manifest in) 'habits', to learning.

The upshot of all of this is that Diotima does not agree with Alcibiades. We do not move 'inwards' as we move up Diotima's ladder, certainly not at the level of the soul.[24] Rather, we move from an appreciation of the intrinsic beauty of a body, or bodies, to an appreciation of them *in action*.[25] There is no *exchange* of body for soul in Diotima's location of ethical value; there is the recognition that when the soul acts it is through

---

[22] *Gorgias* 474d–75a: σώματα (474d3), τά γε κατὰ τοὺς νόμους καὶ τὰ ἐπιτηδεύματα (e5–6), τὸ τῶν μαθημάτων κάλλος (e8–9). I have not found any parallel in the wider Platonic corpus for the idea that soul belongs as a separate item in the hierarchy of aesthetic value (as anything other, that is, than a correlative of ἐπιτηδεύματα καὶ νόμοι).

[23] This makes it almost impossibly awkward to translate ἐπιτηδεύματα as 'institutions' this time, and translators committed to distinguishing ἐπιτηδεύματα from soul in 210a–d are sometimes led to render the word in terms of individual activity here, even where they had used 'institutions' earlier: examples are Jowett 1892 ('fair practices') and Griffith 1986 *ad loc.* ('human behaviour').

[24] It might be argued that the final transition to the contemplation of the 'sciences' and the forms themselves involves a journey into the intellect (and cf. e.g. *Phaedrus* 249d, where beauty of the body which reminds the lover of the intellectual realm). But even in this case I assume that, although the objects of contemplation are not available to sense perception (as I wish to argue the ἐπιτηδεύματα still are), they are located *outside* the contemplating subject.

[25] It is something of a Platonic principle that a thing is more beautiful in action than in repose: cf. *Timaeus* 19b. Or maybe a Socratic principle, since it is shared by Xenophon: see *Symposium* 2.15 (notwithstanding 7.3–4, where a person is more beautiful in repose: this is the case here only if the movement has no purpose); *Memorabilia* 10.1 and 9–10. Cf., later on, Plotinus 6.7.22.27–36.

the body – and the claim that a body engaged in virtuous activity is more beautiful than *any* body that is not.[26]

5.5 Ethical Implications

It should not really come as a surprise that Plato is not interested in carving out a theory of 'inner beauty'. The *kosmos*, in the *Timaeus*, is the animal *par excellence*, yet nobody thinks to talk about the 'inner beauty' of the *kosmos*, or to suggest that the soul of the *kosmos* is more beautiful than what is manifest to the senses. Indeed, the *kosmos* is itself explicitly called the *most beautiful* of god's creations (κάλλιστος τῶν γεγονότων, *Timaeus* 29a). True, the soul is its *superior* part;[27] but the soul's superiority lies precisely in the fact that it is in virtue of its presence that the *whole* is beautiful.[28] As far as the *Timaeus* is concerned, it is not by cracking a thing open, as Alcibiades thought he had done with Socrates, that one discovers whether they are beautiful. It is by seeing how it goes about living.[29]

Here, though, is where it becomes important to reflect on the fact that 'living' and 'acting' are, when we consider wholes like human beings that are also parts, processes inevitably tied to their contexts. The same set of movements in one time and place might be appropriate and beautiful, but inappropriate, ugly and dysfunctional in another. In fact it is a more general principle in Plato that the beauty of a part, or of a whole which is also a part, is a function of the whole relative to which they are a part.[30] Most famously, in *Republic* 420c–d, Socrates considers why it is that the eyes, which are the most beautiful part of the body, do not possess the most beautiful colour;

[26] My claim is appreciably stronger, then, than positions like that of Lane (2007: 47–48), who notes that Alcibiades gives examples in which Socrates publicly displays virtues he had identified as hidden within; or that of Nehamas (2007), arguing that, at least sometimes in Plato, beauty of body accompanies beauty of soul and is never exchanged for it.

[27] Pl. *Ti.* 34c4–5: ὁ δὲ καὶ γενέσει καὶ ἀρετῇ προτέραν καὶ πρεσβυτέραν ψυχὴν σώματος ὡς δεσπότιν καὶ ἄρξουσαν (cf. *Laws* 727d–e for the superiority of the human soul to the body).

[28] Pl. *Ti.* 30b1–3: 'On reflection he [the Demiurge] found that *among things whose nature is to be visible* nothing lacking intellect would be more beautiful than something possessed of it – taking each as a whole; and nothing could have intellect without soul' (λογισάμενος οὖν ηὕρισκεν ἐκ τῶν κατὰ φύσιν ὁρατῶν οὐδὲν ἀνόητον τοῦ νοῦν ἔχοντος ὅλον ὅλου κάλλιον ἔσεσθαί ποτε ἔργον, νοῦν δ' αὖ χωρὶς ψυχῆς ἀδύνατον παραγενέσθαι τῳ).

[29] So, when Theodorus calls Theaetetus ugly and Socrates responds by saying that it is someone who *speaks* well who is beautiful (*Tht.* 185e), he might mean this without the equivocation readers usually hear in the word καλός.

[30] Cf. *Timaeus*, where the importance of seeing – and evaluating – things in context leads Plato consistently to privilege sight over the other senses. Indeed, he argues in the *Timaeus* that sight makes philosophy possible by revealing the mundane world to us in the context of the heavens, with the result that we start to find it, not messy and confusing, but beautiful and awe-inspiring (cf. 47a).

even sculptors do not try to improve on nature by painting them purple rather than black, he says. (A similar point is made at *Hippias Major* 290a–c, where the question is whether they would look better painted gold.) The answer of course is that eyes are what they are only because they are, first, parts (of the body) – and what is beautiful for them is not what is beautiful without qualification, but what makes for the most beautiful body. So it is, I suggest, with human beauty, or virtue. It is rooted in the activity of the human agent considered as part of the *kosmos*. Of course, this involves a certain internal structure, an 'orderliness', for the person considered as an independent 'whole' as well; but the internal order is only the necessary condition for the person to perform their prior purpose as part of the *kosmos*. We might go so far as to say that the *conditions* for virtue are internal, and we can certainly talk about a person's virtuous 'state'; but these are to be understood relative to a tendency to act a certain way, namely the way it takes to play one's role as a part of the *kosmos*. This is why someone's virtue is always outwardly manifest.[31]

This does not amount, sadly, to a theoretical account of how one identifies in particular circumstances what it is to play one's part well – but that is just to say that there is plenty left to the topic of ethics. (The Stoics too were to find that there is a limit to how far one can generalise or specify this in advance in any case: at a certain point one has to rely on the – aesthetic? – judgements made by the *sophos* from time to time as well.) But it does help us to approach two 'meta-ethical' difficulties that dog discussions of Plato.

(i) The first goes back to the definition of virtue as something to do with the internal health of the soul at *Republic* 443c–444a. It is a classic problem with this passage on the usual reading that the turn 'inwards' – the definition of virtue in terms of 'inner beauty' – seems to miss the point of the original question. This question was precisely about why we should think acting well towards other people is 'better' (ἄμεινόν ἐστιν, 357b1), not about how we should organise our inner life.[32]

One, relatively easy, answer to this question is to say that 'doing just things' (inter alia) 'profits us' (λυσιτελεῖ δίκαιά τε πράττειν, 445a1), and it does so because just actions help to create the order in the soul that constitutes our well-being (444d). But on my account, this is only part of the story – and on its own might leave one with the impression that Plato attributes purely instrumental value to just activity. But it is important to

---

[31] This is not to say that a person is *always* acting in an ethically evaluable way (perhaps vicious people sleep just the same way as the virtuous for example); it is only to say that on the basis of such cases we could make only defeasible aesthetic judgements.

[32] Cf. Sachs 1971 [orig. 1963].

add that the 'well-being' we are talking about here is in turn, and by definition, the disposition towards virtuous activity. In other words, virtuous activity 'profits' us by improving our internal state, but this only counts as 'profit' because, in virtue of our natures, our well-being involves the kind of internal state that issues in virtuous activity.[33] So acting well is very much part of what we recognise to be 'better' for us; Plato's point – which addresses an assumption behind the original challenge – is only that it is not the virtuous activity *on its own* that is better for us, but our involvement in it as its agent.

(ii) Plato *also* says, interestingly, that the actions of a just agent will coincide with actions that even outside Kallipolis are conventionally thought to be virtuous. For example, such a person would not rob a temple (442e). Indeed, the whole *Republic* seems to be motivated by intuitions that coincide with a great deal of conventional morality. But on the usual reading, it is pure stipulation for Plato to say that the choices of the virtuous agent *will* coincide with the conventional demands of justice. In fact, there is no way of knowing in advance what someone with a well-organised inner soul would do: for all we know, they might have all sorts of reasons to steal from a temple, or insult their parents from time to time.

On my account of virtue as activity that is manifest and beautiful, we can explain just how it is that conventional morality gets it right much of the time – but without removing the possibility that it can get it wrong in a way that makes philosophy such a desirable part of political leadership. If Plato holds the view that what is virtuous is as a matter of fact beautiful then of course – like beauty in general – we are going to find virtue attractive *even before we know what it is*. That is why law codes and moral conventions will tend to make appropriate identifications of virtue and vice, and it explains why, at the beginning of the *Republic*, Glaucon and Adeimantus clearly think it *desirable* that Socrates' theory of justice should save conventional morality from the attacks of someone like Thrasymachus even though, at this point, they have no *philosophical* reason to be invested in their vindication, and cannot see in them any basis for naked self-interest. Where virtue is concerned, we are all very much like the

---

[33] Note, by the way, that 443c (quoted earlier) does not say, as it is sometimes reported, that justice cannot be defined in terms of external action: it only says that the formula 'doing one's own' does not capture justice if it is applied to external actions rather than the internal workings of the soul. And *this* is worth saying not only to be clear about how the formula applies to the *just individual* rather than any individual considered as part of the *just city*, but also because there may have been people who actually did apply the formula to external actions in definitions of virtue: cf. *Charmides* 161b–62c.

sight-lovers of *Republic* 5 (475d): we respond to virtuous activity *as beautiful*, even before we can articulate the cosmic notions of harmony and good order that underpin it. Conversely, something like the act of temple-pillage strikes us as ugly in the way that a badly performed song might offend even an audience of musical illiterates – namely *because* of the technical failings of the performers, albeit these are not failings that the audience could articulate. Of course, this is not good enough for the philosopher: philosophers need to move beyond this 'dream-like' experience of beauty in order to get a concrete sense of the principle *in virtue of which* things are harmonious and attractive (476c). This indeed is what the *Republic* aims to do for virtue – the *Republic*, and perhaps the *Timaeus* too, whose exploration of the *kosmos* will, in the light of my argument, be its obvious sequel and the culmination of its argument. But it can start with aesthetic intuitions, and it can *expect* to see them largely vindicated, simply because virtue is as a matter of fact beautiful.[34]

Finally, the figure of Socrates can help here as well. In the normal telling of the *Symposium*, Socrates represents someone who is ugly in outward appearance, yet beautiful inside. I have wanted to claim that he may be ugly considered only as a 'whole' and not as a part; but in that sense an eye is ugly too. Socrates is actually *beautiful* in outward appearance just because his activity is virtuous. And it is not that people miss this – it is just that they cannot *understand* it, and end up convincing themselves it is wrong. But Socrates' being beautiful in fact explains the – otherwise unaccountable – *attraction* he exerts over those around him, including, of course, Alcibiades. Alcibiades cannot understand the attraction (rather as Glaucon cannot understand the attraction of virtue) and is let down by his meagre philosophical resources when he attempts to analyse it, with the consequence that he comes to suppose that Socrates is ugly (just as someone like Callicles can end up convincing himself that conventional virtue is, in fact, something unattractive). But, of course, he would never have begun his pursuit of the 'inner Socrates' if he had not been attracted by the public persona in the first place.[35]

---

[34] Note that this does not lead us immediately to the position that certain action-types are definitively and objectively virtuous (or vicious): any action-type will be beautiful or not relative in the first place to its own constitution (cf. Kamtekar 2010: 72), but ultimately to the cosmos as a whole, of which the constitution in its turn is a part. (By the same token, it is no objection to my account that people differ about what is virtuous as much as they do, just as the sight-lovers presumably have their disagreements over what is beautiful.) It may well turn out that there are action-types which are beautiful in all (or no) virtuous constitutions: but, if that would not be a surprise given the constraints of human and cosmic nature, it would also not be a trivial truth.

[35] A similar point is made by Lane 2007: 48.

CHAPTER 6

Polis as Kosmos *in Plato's* Laws

*Luc Brisson**

Zwei Dinge erfüllen das Gemüt mit immer
neuer und zunehmender Bewunderung und Ehrfurcht,
... Der bestirnte Himmel über mir, und das moralische Gesetz
in mir.

Two things fill the mind with ever-increasing wonder and awe
... : the starry heavens above me and the moral law within me.
Immanuel Kant, *Critique of Practical Reason* (AA.V.161)

The *Laws* are more than a legislative code, more than a work of
political philosophy. For they call for the realisation of a project
towards which Plato's work converges: to account for the ordering
(κόσμος)[1] of the whole of reality – individual, city and world. This
discourse (λόγος) in which the law (νόμος) consists derives its origin
from the intellect, which represents what is most akin in man's soul to
the divine (θεός) that rules the world. I would like to show here how in
the *Laws*, Plato brings an old project to its conclusion.[2] Hesiod's
Theogony describes the appearance of the world as the setting in
order of a primordial chaos through the successive engendering of
the gods who are to ensure that order. Beginning with the sixth
century BCE, however, the thinkers we call 'Presocratics' sought to

---

* I thank Phillip Sidney Horky who has generously read this chapter and helped me to improve it.
[1] This chapter is based on a lexicographical study of the occurrences of the term κόσμος, its derivatives
and its compounds in Plato's *Laws*; the number of occurrences was too long to be listed here. We do
not know the exact etymology of the word *kosmos*, although its meaning is clear: essentially, it
designates order, which could be defined as the arrangement of elements in a constant relation; and
beauty, which could be defined as symmetry, with these two meanings being, moreover, closely
related. Order implies regularity and permanence in motion; in objects it is manifested by proportion, which is at the origin of beauty. We can therefore understand why *kosmos*, transposed onto an
ethical level, is associated with moderation and justice. We can also understand how the term *kosmos*
came to designate all of reality, that is, the world. In a context in which there is no creation *ex nihilo*,
the appearance of the world could only be conceived as the setting in order of a primordial chaos.
[2] For political cosmology prior to Plato, see Chapter 8 of this volume, by Atack.

account for the process leading to the appearance of the world, man and city in a way that was, as it were, purely mechanistic. Plato took up this project[3] in the *Timaeus* and the *Laws*, but he modified it regarding two points: for him, not only the body is involved, but also the soul, provided with an intellect, a divinity which, however, cannot intervene to change the course of things. Above all, Plato expresses this order in mathematical terms. The city, which is to bring about the birth of the whole of virtue in all the human beings who constitute it, is organised by means of a legislation that takes the functioning of the world as its model; the opposition between *nomos* and *physis*, maintained by some sophists, therefore disappears, because the law (*nomos*) becomes the expression of *physis*.

6.1 The World: Order and Beauty

In the *Laws*, 'the supreme divinity is the world in its totality' (τὸν μέγιστον θεὸν καὶ ὅλον τὸν κόσμον).[4] This divinity, which, like all divinities,[5] is a living being endowed with a body and a soul, contains other divinities, in particular the celestial bodies, which are also divinities endowed with a soul. But the regularity and permanence of the motion of these celestial bodies, which are also living beings, are due to their soul, from which the order that reigns in the heavens derives.[6] The soul is responsible for all motions in the world,[7] both material and immaterial. As the principle and source of motion, the soul is neutral. It depends on its higher faculty, the intellect, for its goodness or evil. Associated with this intellect, the soul guides all things in uprightness and happiness; however, when it associates with irrationality, it produces all the effects contrary to the preceding ones.

> The whole question consists in knowing what kind of soul is in charge of the world . . . the whole course and movement of the heavens and all that is in them [ἡ σύμπασα οὐρανοῦ ὁδὸς ἅμα καὶ φορὰ καὶ τῶν ἐν αὐτῷ ὄντων ἁπάντων] reflect the motion and revolution and calculation of reason [νοῦ κινήσει καὶ περιφορᾷ καὶ λογισμοῖς ὁμοίαν φύσιν ἔχει], and operate in a corresponding fashion [καὶ συγγενῶς ἔρχεται], then clearly we have to admit that it is the best kind of soul that cares for the entire universe [τοῦ κόσμου παντός] and directs it along the best path. (Plato, *Laws* 897c4–9)

---

[3] See Macé 2008.   [4] Pl. *Leg.* 821a2. The καί is interpreted as epexegetic here.
[5] See Brisson 2003.
[6] Pl. *Leg.* 899b3–9. Translations of Plato's *Laws* are by T. J. Saunders, slightly modified.
[7] Pl. *Phaedr.* 245b–246a. On motions in *Laws* X, see Guéroult 1924, Skemp 1967, 1985, de Mahieu 1963, 1964, and Naddaf 1992, 1996.

The good soul is the principle of good, whereas the bad soul is at the source of evil. The soul that guides the world cannot help but be good.[8] This conclusion is important, for it allows us to understand that the world receives its motion from the soul that belongs to it, a soul that is, moreover, guided by a higher faculty, the intellect. We can therefore understand why ordered motion is associated with reason, whereas the irregularity of motion is associated with irrationality.[9] Note in this passage, transposing them from the negative to positive, the list of synonyms of κόσμος, which is itself associated with νοῦς: uniform (ὡσαύτως), regular (κατὰ τὰ αὐτά), at the same point in space or round the same centre (ἐν ταὐτῷ, περὶ ταὐτά), in the same relative position or in a single location (πρὸς ταὐτά, ἐν ἑνὶ φερομένη). In this context, motion can be in order (ἐν κόσμῳ), organised (ἐν τάξει) or planned (ἔν τινι λόγῳ). Quite naturally, reason is also linked to justice, and irrationality to injustice. This is why this god that is the world, whose movements are permanent and regular, is followed by Justice.[10]

It is within this world, moved by a soul led by the intellect, that Plato inscribes the city, endowed with a body and a soul that is provided with an intellect, like a living being capable of knowing and ordering itself by imitating divine perfection. Thus, the 'measure' of the city is no longer man, but the most important divinity – the world as a whole – whose soul is guided by the intellect. We can therefore better understand the importance of the law against atheists in Book X of the Laws, which reminds us that the city is inscribed within an animate, ordered world, whose perfection (that is, according to Plato, its divinity) imposes its order upon the city – it is both a part of the world and a model for it. The intellect of the city, its Nocturnal Council (nykterinos syllogos),[11] knows the world and can govern the city in accordance with this knowledge. And the same will hold

[8] Polemics have raged and continue to rage over the question of whether the good soul and the evil soul were exclusively human souls, or whether there might be a good soul of the world and an evil world soul, as Plutarch hypothesised. In my opinion, only the human soul can be evil. Hence, I agree with Cherniss 1954. See also Carone 1994–95, 1997.

[9] Pl. Leg. 898b5–8.

[10] Pl. Leg. 715e7–716a1. To be sure, the quotation of the Orphic verse in this passage applies to Zeus, who is accompanied by Dikê (Justice); but in Orphism this is the Zeus who, after having swallowed all that precedes him, regurgitates everything, bringing about the appearance of the world, which is assimilated to his own body.

[11] 'Nocturnal Council' is the traditional translation. But this translation is misleading. English 'Council' should translate Greek boulê and not syllogos. And nykterinos does not mean 'nocturnal': '[The nykterinos syllogos] must have a strict rule to meet daily from dawn until the sun is well up in the sky' (Leg. 951d6–57). More importantly, 'Nocturnal Council' has a sinister connotation. One thinks of the 'Night of Crystal' or the 'Night of the Long Knives' in June–July 1934, in Germany.

true for mankind. Man and the city will be well governed if they are ordered like the world, and, more precisely, like the celestial bodies.

6.2   The City and the World-Order

As in the *Republic* and the *Timaeus*, the city of the *Laws* is compared to a living being: it is like the world and a man. As such, the city is endowed with a body – its territory, its population and its wealth – and, in a sense, with a soul, which corresponds to the magistracies that must be led by the highest magistracy, corresponding to the intellect, i.e. the Nocturnal Council (964e1–965a4).[12] In order to understand this passage, one must remember the composition and the role of the Nocturnal Council. Within it, there are four groups of an indeterminate number of former magistrates (see 951d–e and 961a–c). And each of the older magistrates should present a young man who could be selected among the Country-Wardens. The Nocturnal Council, which includes citizens under the age of thirty, is rooted in reality, since all its members have a role in civil society, which consists in the surveillance and control of the laws and of the magistrates who apply them. Yet this rootedness ought not to make us forget that the essential function of the Nocturnal Council, although not cut off from politics, is nevertheless not political in the strict sense of the term. In order to define for the city a goal – virtue – that is consubstantial with knowledge, the members of the Council must submit to a programme of studies akin to that which must be undertaken in the *Republic* by those who are destined to become philosophers. In the case both of its body and of its soul, the city must be modelled after the best ordered living being, the world studied by the members of the Nocturnal Council.

6.2.1   *Politics as Care of the Soul in the* Laws

The starting point of every reflection on Plato's *Laws* must be the acknowledgement of its paradoxical position relative to the definition of politics. As early as Book I, the Athenian Stranger declares:

> So this insight into the nature and dispositions of a man's soul [τὸ γνῶναι τὰς φύσεις τε καὶ ἕξεις τῶν ψυχῶν] will rank as one of the most useful aids, available to the art which is concerned to foster a good character [τῇ τέχνῃ ἐκείνῃ ἧς ἐστιν ταῦτα θεραπεύειν] – the art of statesmanship, I take it [ἔστιν δέ που, φαμέν, ὡς οἶμαι, πολιτικῆς]. (Plato, *Laws* 650b6–9)

---

[12] See Brisson 2000.

This definition of politics as care of the soul recalls one of the remarks in the *Statesman* (308d–e), according to which political technique must distinguish the soul's good morals in order to weave them together. Above all, it takes up a definition recurrent in the dialogues that is already found particularly in the *Gorgias* (464b).[13]

In the first book of the *Laws*, these presuppositions introduce the thesis that will be developed throughout all twelve of its books: the goal of the law is to make the entire city achieve the totality of virtue.[14] This is affirmed explicitly at *Laws* 630d–632d, where this task is assigned to legislation, along with the specification of the hierarchy of goods that is to preside over the evaluation and choice of conducts in the city. In the course of its earthly existence, the soul lives in a body which itself requires an environment that enables its birth and promotes its harmonious development and reproduction. This is why politics must also take its body and environment into account, but not without the context of a hierarchy of goods to be pursued. This hierarchy places at its summit the divine goods known as the four cardinal virtues: moderation, courage, wisdom and justice. The dialogue will return to this point in Book III, where the Athenian Stranger repeats that excellence can only be achieved on the condition of preserving the order of priority of the three constitutive aspects of human living: care of the soul, of the body, and of goods or wealth (*Leg.* 631b–632a, 697a–c and 743d–e).

This is the classification whose priorities the legislator must follow. The dialogue itself will conform to it, moreover, since its plan follows this hierarchy of goods precisely by choosing, in the exposition of legislation (Books 6 to 12), to deal first with questions concerning the soul (by evoking at length the education of the citizens), then the body (dealing with food or physical violence), and finally possessions (then dealing with properties and exchanges). The Athenian Stranger specifies what the law must promote among the citizens: a reflective mastery over pleasures and pains, which makes the community of citizens possible. More exactly, the law must promote a community of (shared) feelings. This gives it a considerable field of extension, and explains, in a sense, why it alone can enable the city to achieve the totality of virtue.

---

[13] And in politics, the counterpart of gymnastics is legislation, and the part that corresponds to medicine is justice. See Pradeau 2002: 43–71.

[14] See the 'Introduction' in Brisson and Pradeau 2006.

6.2.1.1   A Two-fold Definition of Law

The term *nomos*, which we render by 'law', possesses a very large number of usages and meanings. From a strictly juridical viewpoint, the term is susceptible to designate both of the two realities which English distinguishes under the names of 'laws' and 'law': not only a particular law, but also the system of laws, that is, on the one hand, the ordered totality of the laws, and, on the other, the common principles on which they are all based, because the legislator has arranged his work in accordance with them. When *nomos* is used in its general sense, to name the totality of law, it also designates the totality of the particular prescriptions imposed upon the city, so much so that the term can be synonymous with *politeia* ('constitution'). This testifies to the interweaving of juridical and institutional considerations in the *Laws*, as well as to the way in which, for the Greeks, the discourse on law is always already a discourse on the civic community and its constitutional organisation.

On this point, Plato does not contravene the usages of his time, and chooses to link the fate of the city and that of its legislation, in order to fuse them together. This link is sealed right from the initial definition of *nomos* given in the *Laws*. The Athenian Stranger criticises the legislations of Crete and Sparta, which are oriented only towards courage, and think they can promote temperance by fleeing pleasures.[15] Not only does this fleeing not suffice to eliminate licentious morals, but it does not promote true courage, which is defined as the domination of pleasures and pains, owing to the control of fear, which is also defined as the expectation of future pains, and of confidence, furthermore defined as expectation of future pleasures.

'Law' is thus defined, generally speaking, as *rational calculation on the part of the soul*, which evaluates pleasures and pains and controls fear and confidence – a rational calculation that is imposed upon the entire city. Thus, it promotes temperance and courage under the guidance of rational calculation (*logismos*): and 'when this is expressed as a public decision of a state, it receives the name "law"' (ὃς γενόμενος δόγμα πόλεως κοινὸν νόμος ἐπωνόμασται).[16] The significance of this definition consists in the way it collects and announces the various meanings that the continuation of the dialogue will reserve for the law: first of all, it is a rational process, fashioned as such by an intellect at the same time as it is set forth in a rational, demonstrative way. This rational thought is then addressed to

---

[15] Pl. *Leg.* 636a–637b.   [16] Pl. *Leg.* 644d3–4.

the soul, which is capable of feeling both pleasures and pains, fear and confidence, but also of perceiving a rational process.[17]

This rational process or calculation in which the law consists is intended to provide to all citizens a judgement on what must be and must not be appreciated, that is, in this case, what is to be desired or rejected. The rational discourse that teaches all souls what pleasures and what pains they must praise or blame is in their interest: such is the first definition of law in the *Laws*.

6.2.1.2   Law as a Distribution of the Intellect

Yet this definition of 'law' is advanced against a second definition, which gives meaning to the *Laws* as a whole. The city's *nomos*, which is prescriptive, is in fact named after 'the distribution [*dianomê*] of the intellect' (τὴν τοῦ νοῦ διανομὴν ἐπονομάζοντας νόμον).[18] The legislator of the *Laws* thus has a two-fold task: (1) to establish a proportional order *in* the individual's soul, which means making the intellect reign and turning the citizens into rational beings, especially through the intermediary of education, and (2) to impose a proportional order *among* the citizens, by establishing the reign of the most meritorious and virtuous, that is, those who make the best use of their soul's highest faculty, the intellect (νοῦς), over those who are less so. Thus, guided by the most virtuous among them, the citizens too will be able to become virtuous, as the law recommends. The written laws serve as a tool for realising these tasks, and this is why a well-established law is understood as the 'distribution of the intellect'. This distribution concerns not only the orientation of conducts, but also of honours, and hence of

---

[17] See Saunders 1962. On this point I disagree with C. Bobonich, who, in *Plato's Utopia Recast* (Oxford 2002), maintains that the psychology of the *Laws* differs from that of the *Republic*, to which it is superior, especially owing to its political consequences. According to Bobonich, the soul in the *Republic* has parts which can be considered as agents in the full sense of the term; in the *Laws*, by contrast, diverse forces coexist within one and the same soul, which alone can be considered as an agent. Thus, knowledge and power would no longer be reserved to those whose intellect is capable of acquiring genuine knowledge. A. Laks has answered this interpretive position point by point in his *Médiation et coercition. Pour une lecture des Lois de Platon* (2005: 85–92). In Brisson 2005, I tried to show why the political consequences that could have derived from this new psychology are not to be found in the *Laws*. In fact, the real question is that of the interpretation of the representation of the soul in the *Republic*. When applied to the soul in the *Republic* and even in the *Timaeus*, the terms 'parts' or 'species' must not be understood as if the soul were a body. The soul is an incorporeal entity which, while remaining one, accomplishes certain functions when attached to a body, such as courage (*thumos*) and desire (*epithumia*), intended to ensure the survival and reproduction of that body. As such, these functions cannot be declared to be distinct from the entity constituted by the soul. In addition, the quality of the existence of the soul separated from the body which it inhabits temporarily depends on the care it has devoted to such-and-such a function.

[18] Pl. *Leg.* 714a1–2.

magistracies, i.e. the establishment of a power structure: this is why the law produces decrees in both these domains. In both cases, it must pertain to the principle that the intellect (νοῦς), the same as that which governs the *kosmos*, is to hold the first rank in mankind and in the city.

6.2.2   The Legislator and the Ordered Establishment of the Constitution

To proceed to the ordered distribution of the intellect in the city, the legislator must first establish the magistracies and then enact the laws that the magistrates will advance and enforce them.[19] The legislator must ensure order in the city, not merely to win victory at war, but to inaugurate within the city the harmony that will avoid civil war.[20] This helps to explain why the courage praised by Tyrtaeus is relegated to fourth place within the order of the divine virtues.[21] Note, moreover, that the legislator will seek help from a tyrant who is to preside over the choice of colonists and the primordial distribution of land.[22] But this tyrant will be marked by the quality of moderation (σωφροσύνη), a popular virtue that is not necessarily based on reason. Indeed, moderation will make him a *properly ordered* tyrant (τύραννου κοσμίου, *Leg.* 710d7), i.e. something like a dictator. Even so, this dictator should yield to the legislator and his legal decrees as soon as possible after the distribution of land.

The Athenian Stranger states that by establishing order in the city, the laws will make it happy.[23] It is by making human behaviour (*êthê*) orderly that the laws will make such civic happiness possible. Nevertheless, the Athenian Stranger notes that the laws will have to be constantly improved, so that this order may be successfully extended throughout the entire city.[24] To illustrate this improvement, the Athenian Stranger draws a comparison with painting: the goal is to try to *embellish* legislation, as a painter does with a painting.[25] The comparison of legislation to a pictorial work is a recurrent trope in Plato's dialogues, particularly in the *Laws* (see 734a, 737d, and 934b–c); but we find this image already at *Republic* 6 (501a), and in the *Timaeus* (19b–d).

---

[19] Pl. *Leg.* 751a4–b2. This programme had already been announced at 735a2–6.
[20] Pl. *Leg.* 628a9–b4.   [21] See Calvo 2000.   [22] Pl. *Leg.* 709e6–710a4.   [23] Pl. *Leg.* 718a6–b5.
[24] Pl. *Leg.* 769d1–e2.
[25] Cf. Pl. *Leg.* 769a7–b3: 'Suppose that one day somebody were to take it into his head to paint the most beautiful picture in the world, which would never deteriorate but always improve at his hands as the years went by. You realize that as the painter is not immortal, he won't achieve anything very permanent by lavishing such care and attention on his picture unless he leaves some successor to repair the ravages of time? Won't his successor also have to be able to supplement deficiencies in his master's skill and improve the picture by touching it up?'

6.2.2.1   *The Circular City and Its Body*

The city of the *Laws* is founded upon institutions and activities that are almost always counted or numbered in an orderly way and additionally undergo changes, either because they are places in which motions occur, or because they themselves are moved. Human beings and civic buildings, understood as environmentally conditioned, are bodies, i.e. mobile and multiple existents that must be limited and coordinated by various types of threshold and limit, and their motions and arrangements must be harmonised such that the whole they constitute may maintain its own overall equilibrium. Political work is rooted in a physics of motion and change, and it is reflected in a limited set of geometrical dispositions: their most vivid effect is reflected in the circular disposition of houses and most civic movements, and the city itself is constructed in a circle (the houses form a kind of urban rampart around the city centre; the villages are also apparently set out equidistant from the central town). The citizens are invited to traverse it in a circle, at the same time as civic life is itself marked by the repeated regularity of the annual calendar. Even the city's territory and the movement of its citizens are modelled on the figure and the movements of the cosmic bodies in heaven.

Unlike Athens, which was an imperial maritime and commercial power, the city fashioned in the *Laws* is an autarchic, agricultural city, situated inland.[26] It is constructed around an urban centre, a town where one finds the main governmental, deliberative, commercial, military and religious functions, surrounded by an agrarian territory.[27] The latter is not without habitations, since it contains villages, that is, supplementary housing. The city's territory is thus configured by circular envelopment, thanks to an arrangement that turns the city into an ordered whole, a world rationally fashioned by a technical intelligence which makes use of geometry and arithmetic to construct a regular order and provide stability to the movements of a changing material. This, indeed, is what makes the city akin to the world as described in the *Timaeus,* in the manner of a work or handicraft fashioned by the divine intellect.[28] The craftsmen of the constitution have as their model the god who has fashioned the world: political demiurgy imitates

---

[26] The place occupied by the entire territory is only described in brief. In response to the Athenian Stranger's questions, Clinias explains that the colony will be set up some fifteen kilometres from the sea, that it will not be adjacent to any city, and that it will occupy a hilly landscape, rather than a plain (*Leg.* 704b–d). These initial specifications authorise the Athenian to declare that the city will be able to be virtuous because commerce will be impossible, and the citizens will have to provide for their needs themselves.

[27] *Leg.* 745b–e.   [28] The verb is συνδιακοσμήσων at *Laws* 712b6. On this point, see Laks 1990.

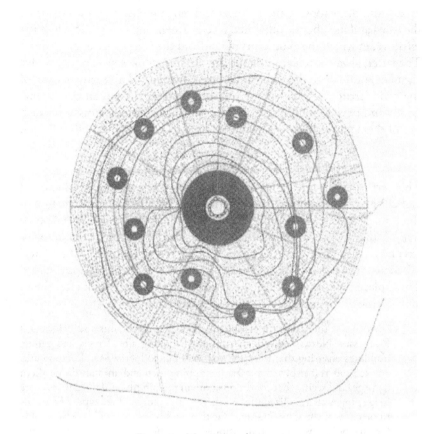

Figure 6.1 Magnesia and its territory.

cosmological demiurgy, and their works resemble each other. In its way, the
city of the Magnesians, endowed with a figure of circular appearance, is an
image of the perfect sphere constituted by the world.

The map above (see Figure 6.1) collocates the few elements found in the
description of Magnesia in Book 5 of the *Laws* (737e–747e).[29] In a civic
territory that ought to tend as much as possible towards circular geometrical perfection,[30] the founders of the city install successively, by concentric

[29] See also *Leg.* 848c–849a.
[30] The reason for the preference given to circular figures is two-fold, both morphological and kinetic:
circular geometry, when generalised, makes the various civic spaces homogeneous (the town is
circular, but so is the whole of the territory, and each of its twelve villages); and because it is always
self-identical, circular motion, in Plato's view, exhibits the most perfection.

expansion, the acropolis, the political and religious centre of the city, then the town and its suburbs, inhabited by craftsmen, and finally the rest of the territory, in which the allotments of land and the villages are to be found.[31] The latter, always circular in figure, are situated in the centre of the twelve segments into which the whole territory is divided.[32] This segmentation of the civic territory enables the establishment of twelve urban neighbour-hoods and twelve rural sectors, among which the citizens must live, each one of them possessing one townhouse and one house in one of the villages.

6.2.2.2   The Country-Wardens: Territorial Planning

This territory will not be left to itself; it has to be well maintained and embellished. To administer such a territory, Plato envisages the creation of three magistracies, responsible respectively for the countryside (χώρα or ἀγρός), the city (πόλις), or the town (ἄστυ) and for the town's marketplace (ἀγορά): they are the 'Country-Wardens' (ἀγρονόμοι),[33] the 'City-Wardens' (ἀστυνόμοι),[34] and the 'Market-Wardens' (ἀγορανόμοι).[35] These places will be embellished by magistrates who will look after them. This is true of the temples, the town, and marketplace:

> We can say, then, that the temples should have Attendants and Priests and Priestesses. Next, there are the duties of looking after streets and public buildings ensuring that they are well maintained [ὁδῶν δὲ καὶ οἰκοδομιῶν καὶ κόσμου τοῦ περὶ τὰ τοιαῦτα], stopping men and animals doing them damage, and seeing that conditions both in the suburbs and the city itself are in keeping with a civilized life. All these duties require three types of officials to be chosen: the City-Wardens (as they will be called) will be responsible for the points we've just mentioned, and the Market-Wardens for the correct conduct of the market [τὸ δὲ περὶ ἀγορᾶς κόσμον ἀγορανόμους]. Priests or Priestesses of temples who have hereditary priesthoods should not be turned out of office. But if (as is quite likely in a new foundation) few or no temples are thus provided for, the deficiencies must be made good by appointing Priests and Priestesses to be Attendants in the temples of the gods. (Plato, *Laws* 759a1–b4)

The most interesting group is that of the Country-Wardens. These magis-trates, whose mission is to guard the territory, are quite naturally described as 'guardians' (φρουροί). The five designated magistrates are called 'Commanders of the Guard' (φρουράρχοι); those whom they recruit are

---

[31] The circularity of these sets is emphasised: *Leg.* 746a, 778c and 848e.
[32] These segments thus have a circular morphology, identical to that of the city.
[33] Pl. *Leg.* 760a–763c. See Brisson 2003.   [34] Pl. *Leg.* 763c–e.   [35] Pl. *Leg.* 763c–764c.

called the 'young' (νεοί), those who are 'in the prime of life' (ἡβῶντες), and 'secret-servicemen' (κρυπτοί).[36]

The seventeen Country-Wardens, who make up one of the twelve groups so constituted, live in the villages, which are always located in the centre of each of the twelve sections of the countryside. The centre of each village is occupied by sanctuaries, and at its highest point, fortified installations are installed for the Country-Wardens. Throughout the two-year duration of their term, the Country-Wardens never cease moving from village to village throughout the territory. They change parts every month, going towards the right, that is, the East, during the first year, and towards the left, that is, the West, during the second year: thus, they will come to know the various parts of the territory at various seasons. Each group of guardians takes charge in turn of a section of the rural territory, over which it carries out its supervision for a month, before moving on to another section, and so on.[37] Their movements imitate those of the celestial bodies.

[36] *Leg.* 760a–b, 763b–c. This last term, which refers to a Lacedaemonian institution attributed to Lycurgus, has given rise to numerous commentaries. A scholium to the passage just quoted contributes the following specifications on the subject: 'A young man was sent outside of the town, with the order that he not let himself be seen for a specific period of time. He was therefore obliged to live by wandering through the mountains, sleeping with one eye open, in order not to get caught, without the use of servants and taking no provisions along with him. It was also another form of training for war, for each young man was sent forth naked, with the order to wander outside for a year in the mountains, and to feed himself by plunder and similar expedients, so as not to be visible to anyone. This is why it was called "cryptia" (the noun *krupteia* comes from the verb *kruptein*, "to hide, to hide oneself"), for those who were somewhere were punished.' This testimony does not contradict that provided by the *Life of Lycurgus* (28.3–4). The way of life of the *agronomoi*, except for the Helot hunt, is not disanalogous to that of the 'secret-servicemen'. Supervised by the Guardians of the Laws, their lives are austere and rough. The Country-Wardens cannot have a meal or spend the night outside their camp (*Leg.* 762b–c); he who does so without being so ordered or without necessity will incur blame, and will have his name exposed in the marketplace; anyone can strike him with impunity (762c–d). A commander guilty of such an infraction or who tolerates this kind of misbehaviour will incur an even more serious penalty, and will be banished from any post that deals with the youth. The importance accorded to good reputation seems once again to indicate the will to constitute an elite force. In addition, like the 'secret-servicemen', the Country-Wardens must do without servants, using local manpower only for public works. This is as far as the analogy goes: a rough way of life and military concerns. Perhaps Plato did not wish to transpose an institution with which he may not have been very familiar. He seems only to have limited himself to retaining the Spartan *krupteia* for the Country-Wardens because of the educational nature of the institution.

[37] There is a problem of consistency. At 760c2–3, we read τούτοις δὲ διακληρωθήτω τὰ μόρια τῆς χώρας κατὰ μῆνα ἕκαστα ἑκάστοις; whereas at 760b4–6, we read φυλὴ δὲ μία τῷ μορίῳ ἑκάστῳ ἐπικληρωθεῖσα κατ' ἐνιαυτὸν παρεχέτω πέντε. To remove the contradiction, several authors have condemned κατ' ἐνιαυτὸν, following E. B. England (1921) and R. G. Bury (1926). Another solution consists on making κατ' ἐνιαυτὸν depend on ἐπικληρωθεῖσα. See Piérart 2008. This would be a kind of lottery taking place every year, for the rotation of each group of Country-Wardens. If this were not the case, moreover, there would be a problem, for one and the same group would not rotate around the territory. Indeed, the same group would have to be present for two consecutive months in the first sector, either at the beginning or at the end of the first year.

The functions of the Country-Wardens are above all military and civic in nature. They must fortify the territory and protect it against incursions by neighbours by digging trenches, raising embankments and erecting fortified works. To lay out and embellish the territory, they must concern themselves with road-building and works of water supply and distribution; this activity is associated with the proper adornment (κοσμῶσι) of the natural environs, and the effect of their actions is the 'order and improvement' of the district (κόσμος τε καὶ ὠφελία τοῖς τόποις).[38] The City-Warden is expected do the same things in order to beautify the city.[39]

6.2.2.3 The Population: The Importance of Numbers

It seems strange that, in the city of the *Laws*, the number of households is 5,040. But this plan satisfies, in an economical way, the central requirements of Platonic political science and shows how much Plato privileges mathematical instruments to fashion his city in accordance with harmony, imitating the demiurge who, in the *Timaeus*, uses numbers and geometrical figures to fashion the soul and the body of the *kosmos* (*Ti.* 32b–37d).

What is calculated in the city's circular territory is not its surface, but its division into a precise number of lots, 5,040. This number, as the Athenian explains, has been chosen for its capacity to be divided by the largest number of divisors, to which we may add that it is also the product of the multiplication of the first seven numbers. Hence, says the Athenian, there are at least fifty-nine ways to divide the city, and these divisions are so many possible combinations for organising or distributing the elements of the city.[40] Plato gives a few examples, first among which is the division of the entire city and the territory that encircles it into twelve parts, each of which is under the protection of a god. This enables each household to be duplicated into two habitations, one in one of the twelve urban parts, the other in one of the twelve rural parts.[41] In addition to their function in the religious distribution and rationalisation of public life, these successive

---

[38] 'As for water that springs from the ground, the wardens must beautify the fountains and rivers that form by adorning them with trees and buildings [τά τε πηγαῖα ὕδατα, ἐάντε τὶς ποταμὸς ἐάντε καὶ κρήνη ᾖ, κοσμοῦντες φυτεύμασί τε καὶ οἰκοδομήμασιν εὐπρεπέστερα]; they must use drains to tap the individual streams and collect an abundant supply, and any grove or sacral enclosure which has been dedicated nearby must be embellished by having a perennial flow of water directed by irrigation into the very temples of the gods [τὰ ῥεύματα ἀφιέντες εἰς αὐτὰ τὰ τῶν θεῶν ἱερά, κοσμῶσι]' (Pl. *Leg.* 761b6–c5).

[39] 'In particular, the City-Wardens must ensure that the water which the Country-Wardens have transmitted and send on to them in good condition reaches the fountains pure and in sufficient quantities, so that it enhances the beauty and amenities of the city [ὅπως εἰς τὰς κρήνας ἱκανὰ καὶ καθαρὰ πορευόμενα, κοσμῇ τε ἅμα καὶ ὠφελῇ τὴν πόλιν]' (Pl. *Leg.* 763c4–d4).

[40] See Pl. *Leg.* 737e–738a. [41] Pl. *Leg.* 745b–e.

divisions play two political roles: first, and reflecting what may have been the great reform of Cleisthenes at Athens, the recomposition of the tribal distribution as a function of constitutional requirements;[42] second, and in a more Platonic perspective, the enabling of each citizen to belong both to the rural and to the urban parts of the city.[43] Through mediation according to the 'share', which, as will be shown, is the truly inalienable element of the city, Plato thus conceives of a means for the citizen, whoever he may be, to be associated with one of the city's divisions. He can also relate to the city, in a slightly different way, through participation in the assemblies and magistracies, either by administering one of its parts or a set of parts of the territory or the city, as is the case for the City-Wardens and the Country-Wardens,[44] or by virtue of being one of the 360 members of that 'one-fourteenth' of the city that sits at the primary council, and must thereby reside in the town.[45]

As we can see, on each occasion, it is *number* (ἀριθμός) that provides the citizen a means to attune his activity (and his travels) to the city – insofar as civic activity may involve him. The function of number is thus to limit and order terms that are indefinite and hard to master (the surface and appearance of the territory, but also human behaviour); it is the instrument of the proper arrangement and control of change. From this viewpoint, its function is the same as that of the law, and this is why the legislation constitutive of the city makes use of number as a tool. As we shall soon observe, legislating does not demand that one overlook the particular in the interest of a general prescription, but that one finds a means to arrange individuals and groups together. To legislate is to render proper measure,[46] that is, to make commensurable in the same place the manifold motions of all the constitutive elements of the city.[47]

---

[42] Cleisthenes was the great Athenian reformer at the very end of the sixth century BCE, and, if we can believe the testimonies of Herodotus and Aristotle, the real creator of democracy. Thus, he is said to have modified the number of tribes by creating one hundred 'demes', divided into thirty equal 'trittyes', themselves grouped together to form ten tribes. On this reform and the various kinds of rationalisation of the civic space in this period, see Lévêque and Vidal-Naquet 1964.

[43] In order to prevent the birth of an agrarian party or an urban party, as we have seen. Cleisthenes' reforms tended in this direction, although in a less radical sense, since each 'trittys' contained ten 'demes' from the city, ten from the inner territory and ten from the coast.

[44] Pl. *Leg.* 760a–764c. For instance, each of the twelve sections recruits five Country-Wardens, each of whom, in turn, selects twelve young apprentices. Throughout the year, both groups will travel around the twelve sections of the territory, in order to get to know it (and so that the best guardians of the territory may be chosen from among them).

[45] Pl. *Leg.* 756b–758d.   [46] Cf. Pl. *Leg.* 737e–738a and 757a–758a.

[47] This is the wish formulated by the Athenian Stranger at Pl. *Leg.* 746e, when he requires that the law ordain all things so that they may 'be commensurable and harmonious with one another' (πάντα ταῦτα ἔμμετρά τε καὶ ἀλλήλοις σύμφωνα δεῖ τόν γε νόμον τάττειν).

6.3   Ordering the Citizen: Education

The citizen, who does not work and does not engage in commerce, passes his entire life – from childhood to death – being educated, rather than making war. This way of life makes him ordered:

> Now that our citizens are assured of a moderate supply of necessities, and other people have taken over the skilled work,[48] what will be their way of life? Suppose that their farms have been entrusted to slaves who provide them with sufficient produce of the land to keep these men living in moderate comfort [ἀνθρώποις ζῶσι κοσμίως]; suppose they take their meals in separate messes, one for themselves, another nearby for their families, including their daughters and their daughters' mothers; assume the messes are presided over by officials, male and female as the case may be, who have the duty of dismissing their respective assemblies after the day's review and scrutiny of the diners' habits; and that when the official and his company have poured libations to whatever gods that day and night happen to be dedicated, they all duly go home. Now do such ordered ways of live leave them no pressing work to do, no genuinely appropriate occupation [τοῖς δὴ ταύτῃ κεκοσμημένοις ἆρα οὐδὲν λειπόμενόν ἐστιν ἀναγκαῖόν τε ἔργον καὶ παντάπασι προσῆκον]? (Plato, *Laws* 806d7–807a5)

It is education, based in a common way of life, that will ensure such proper ordering of the individual.

The *Laws* never cease to call for civic unity, affirming that a city is only virtuous insofar as it realises a community of thought and feelings among its citizens. In the legislation of the Magnesians, this goal is promoted by the institution of education, but also and more generally by public culture, which is made up of musical activities (above all, the various choruses, whose educational and political importance is considerable), obligatory military missions, and meals in common, in which all citizens must participate. Thanks to these various institutions and the community of morals they foster, the citizens will be truly united, breathing with a single breath like the members of a single chorus.[49]

6.3.1   Public Education: School

The goal which the legislator assigns himself is to inculcate life habits or behaviour, such that the law may become a way of life for the citizens,

---

[48] The territory must simply be large enough so that one may find in it enough to feed the entire city: *Leg.* 737c–d.

[49] For further reflections upon this theme in later Greek literature, see Chapter 9 of this volume, by Gagné.

involving both their body and their soul.[50] The diversity of ways of life is a threat against this unification of life habits under the guidance of the laws. In the same way – this is the argument that will take up this entire beginning of Book 7 – none of the customary practices is to be freed from the law, failing which transgressing the law risks becoming a habit itself.

The civic shaping of body and soul begins before birth[51] and continues until the age of three;[52] as soon as he ceases to be a nursling, the child is then removed from familial authority.[53] Education properly understood, which is public and compulsory,[54] begins at the age of six.[55] Placed in the responsibility of the Director of Education (supported by his assistants), who must be a Guardian of the Laws and plays a determinant role in the Nocturnal Council, education follows clearly formulated principles.[56] In the city of the *Laws*, education, based in cultural practice and physical exercise, is obligatory for girls and boys from the age of six, and it is supervised by magistrates.[57]

Girls are separated from boys by the age of six,[58] but they receive a similar education.[59] The choice of teachers, who are resident aliens since they receive a salary, is a function of the subjects they teach. Traditionally, these subjects were divided into those that concern the body[60] and those that concern the soul,[61] which therefore correspond to the whole domain of the Muses. Instruction is given in public buildings,[62] and begins at dawn,[63] the moment at which the Nocturnal Council meets. The study plan is detailed. It begins, of course, with learning how to read and write,[64] and quite naturally continues with everything concerning culture: poetry, music, dance and even theatre, comic and especially tragic.[65] Then comes mathematics, which are learned by playing.[66] Finally, there is astronomy, which plays a considerable role in the conduct of life, since it is by raising one's head and contemplating the regularity and permanence of the course of the stars that citizens will have available a model of good political organisation. The civic education of the *Laws* is modelled on the consistent motions of the heavenly bodies.[67]

---

[50] Pl. *Leg.* 788a–c. Specifically, 'correct' education in the law must demonstrate that it can make souls and bodies 'as beautiful and noble as possible' (ὡς κάλλιστα καὶ ἄριστα).
[51] Pl. *Leg.* 789e.   [52] Pl. *Leg.* 788d–793e.   [53] Pl. *Leg.* 793e.   [54] Pl. *Leg.* 804c–d.
[55] Pl. *Leg.* 794c–804c.   [56] Pl. *Leg.* 795d–e.   [57] Pl. *Leg.* 764c–d.   [58] Pl. *Leg.* 794c.
[59] Pl. *Leg.* 804d–806c.   [60] Pl. *Leg.* 795d–796e.   [61] Pl. *Leg.* 796e–804c.   [62] Pl. *Leg.* 804c–d.
[63] Pl. *Leg.* 808c–d.   [64] Pl. *Leg.* 809e–812a.   [65] Pl. *Leg.* 812a–817e.   [66] Pl. *Leg.* 817e–820e.
[67] Pl. *Leg.* 821a–822c.

6.3.2   Civic Education through Cultural and Physical Acculturation

One may say that so far, everything we've discussed has been theoretical. Yet we must also take practice into account, which must embrace the entire life of the citizens of Magnesia. Immediately after discussing astronomy, Plato evokes the benefits attached to the practice of hunting,[68] then, as we have seen, he continues as far as Book 8 with the description of the citizen's life as the prolongation of his education, particularly through civic festivals involving cultural and physical contests. Culture is strictly regimented, especially funerals and civic festivals;[69] even athletic contests are controlled.[70]

To make sense of this section of the *Laws*, one must understand that festivals and religious celebrations are expected to take place every day, because the calendar is oriented so that sacrifice be made every day in honour of a god or a demon, in the interest of the city.[71] Each month, however, a more important festival shall take place, which includes contests.[72] These physical[73] and musical[74] contests, presided over by magistrates, are a way of continuing conventional education throughout the life of the citizens, who will participate in them or constitute their audience. It is in this context, moreover, that the performances of the choruses of the Muses and of Apollo, which were so central to the programme of habituation found in Book 2, come into play.

6.3.3   Higher Education: Mathematics, Astronomy and Dialectic

Beyond these basic forms of acculturation there is higher education, to which the members of the Nocturnal Council must submit.[75] Unfortunately, the text of the *Laws* breaks off a few lines later. One may assume that the choice of the young members of the Nocturnal Council will take place in the context of the banquets mentioned in Book II, which, it seems, constituted a test. However, no specification is given concerning

---

[68] Pl. *Leg.* 822d–824a.   [69] Pl. *Leg.* 800d6–e6.   [70] Pl. *Leg.* 795e7–796a4.

[71] The festivals are regulated: 'In fact we also dealt pretty thoroughly with the role of the arts, although arrangements about reciters of poetry, and similar performers and the chorus-competitions obligatory at festivals, can wait till the gods and the minor deities have had their days and months and years allocated to them [κοσμηθήσονται τότε]; then we decide whether festivals should be held at two-year or four-year intervals, or whether the gods suggest some other pattern' (*Leg.* 834e2–835a1). 'Young boys, right from the early stages up to the age of military service, should be equipped with weapons and horses [μεθ' ὅπλων τε καὶ ἵππων ἀεὶ κοσμεῖσθαι δέον ἂν εἴη], whenever they parade and process in honour of any god; and when they supplicate the gods and sons of gods they must dance and march in step, sometimes briskly, sometimes slowly' (*Leg.* 796c4–d1).

[72] Pl. *Leg.* 828b–c.   [73] Pl. *Leg.* 828d–834d.   [74] Pl. *Leg.* 834d–835b.   [75] Pl. *Leg.* 968c–d.

the subjects to be learned, the moment to undertake them, or the duration of study.[76]

While we have no details concerning the last two topics, the author of the *Epinomis* seems to have concentrated on carrying out the first, and furthermore it seems that the programme that can be detected in the *Epinomis* corresponds roughly to the one found in Book 7 of the *Republic*:

Subject	*Republic 7*	*Epinomis*
Arithmetic	521b–526c	990c–d
Geometry	526 c–528a	990d
Stereometry	528a–530c	990d–e
Harmonics	530c–531c	991a–b
Astronomy	527c–528a	991b–c
Dialectics	531c–535a	99 c

The difference from the *Laws* comes from the fact that in the *Epinomis*, everything, including dialectics, is subordinated to astronomy, which is theology, because celestial bodies are visible gods; the intelligible does not come into consideration. In the *Epinomis*, the goal is to show that the programme of studies that will enable the members of the Nocturnal Council to acquire the wisdom which alone can ensure happiness culminates in the study of astronomy, which implies the study of numbers as its precursor and merges with theology, since the heavenly bodies are the gods most worthy of veneration.[77]

The question has been raised concerning what this passage is supposed to deal with; it seems to be an appendix on providence. In Book 10 of the *Laws*, three questions about the gods are envisaged, concerning their existence, their providence and their integrity.[78] The Athenian Stranger begins by dealing with the question of the gods' existence (885c–899d), then moves on to the question of providence (899d–905d), and finally to that of incorruptibility (905d–907b). Astronomy answers not only the first question, concerning the gods' existence (also see *Epinomis* 991c6–d4), but also the second question, which concerns providence (*Epinomis* 991d4–5). Providence is not presented as the intervention of an omnipotent being acting upon the world. The proof of the existence of such a providence (*Epinomis* 991e1–992a1), which assumes the appearance of fate and therefore leaves no room for chance (*Epinomis* 992a2–3), is situated in the

---

[76] It is interesting that the Athenian invites unknown 'others' to join him in the quest (*Leg.* 968b).
[77] Pl. *Leg.* 991e–992a.   [78] Cf. Pl. *Leg.* 885b.

regularity of phenomena, measured by time (including the Great Year), and ensured by the network of mathematical proportions that make up the unique system of the world, moved by a soul which the intellect controls with the help of numbers. Studying astronomy enables us to verify that this proof exists.

In the *Laws*, the Nocturnal Council (νυκτερινὸς ξύλλογος), which is the highest magistracy, is assimilated to the city's intellect, informed of everything in the city and trained in astronomy, i.e. in the movements of visible gods. We can therefore understand why it is described, in the last lines that have come down to us of the *Laws*, as a 'Divine Council' (θεῖος ξύλλογος).[79] Thanks to this Nocturnal Council, the city becomes aware, through knowledge and, in particular, through *astronomy*, that it too is an integral part of a *kosmos* that is not given over to chance. Owing to the order it reflects, and because of the activity of the soul (which is best because it is guided by the intellect), this part must follow the paths of the stars if it wishes to achieve virtue. For this very reason, virtue coincides with the contemplation of order in the world. This amounts to saying that in the city, as in man, one must discover the order, and therefore the beauty manifested by the world.

Ultimately, we may say that the *Laws* are a vast educational project intended to ensure, for all citizens, excellence of the body and, above all, the soul. The law, preceded by a preamble, is the privileged instrument for this goal, but teaching and practice, from conception to death, constitute its indispensable supports. Once the outlines of this divine and animate world have been sketched, the *Laws* install their own city within them, explaining that this city will be able to preserve its order and excellence only on the condition that its main magistrates be citizens who know what reality is, who distinguish themselves by their virtue and their intelligence, and who can therefore ensure the safeguarding of the city and its constitution. It is with this perspective that the Nocturnal Council is established.

This choice on Plato's part to defend the institution of an aristocratic regime, based not on birth, wealth or violence, but on *knowledge*, and endowed with a truly discretionary power, indicates that the project of the *Laws* exceeds merely political purposes. Indeed, at the same time as this work is less than a comprehensive political treatise, it is also much more: it reflects on ethics and pedagogy, the importance of which for the dialogue is easy to see; on anthropology and psychology – developed only in part – but also on the theory of knowledge and cosmo-theology, which constitute so

---

[79] Pl. *Leg.* 969b2.

many major chapters of the final books of the *Laws*. These topics were, however, not necessarily required for the constitutional project alone, which could have contented itself with more elementary ethical principles, or with an otherwise more cursory physics. The systematic aim of the *Laws* thus reveals itself to be much more ambitious than what we witness in other ancient works devoted to the genre of the constitution, since Plato undertakes to inscribe his constitutional and civic exposition in the midst of an explanation of the whole of reality: the dialogue reflects upon human and divine affairs, nature and the *kosmos* – as it does the knowledge we can have of them. This, of course, implies that the communal form of living known as 'the city' could not achieve perfection without possessing some understanding of reality. This is the thesis Plato defends in his *Laws*, as he had already done in various ways in other dialogues, especially in the *Republic*. But this is not everything: by treating all the topics we have just discussed, the *Laws* provides, as it were, the *reason why* it chooses opacity over clarity in presenting the political system: what authorises wise and virtuous governors to govern as they see fit and to select one another is nothing other than their knowledge of reality. The Platonic thesis that states the need to place power in the hands of the wisest citizens provides the best reason for the argument of the *Laws*: those who truly know reality, in its human, political and cosmic aspects – those who are enlightened – earn the right to legislate and to govern, i.e. to order the life of the citizens and the city after the movements of the sky.

CHAPTER 7

Relating to the World, Encountering the Other
Plotinus on Cosmic and Human Action

Pauliina Remes*

7.1 Introduction

Within Neoplatonism, the ancient ideal of god-likeness can take several forms. There is a competition with regards to which god exactly we should emulate: the perfect, ineffable and absolutely unified One, the origin of Goodness? Or perhaps the principle of multiplicity, being and intellection, the perfect and eternal Intellect? Or the complete Living God, the World-Soul ordering and moving the *kosmos*? All suggestions have their merits, and Plotinus most likely thought that all have, in addition to a causal role for the existence and features of human beings, another kind of vital explanatory role, as ends. They are all regulatory ideals of different kinds. The One makes human beings something unified, and is an ideal also for the unity of agency; the Intellect explains our humanity and rationality, and its perfect knowledge is a cognitive ideal for human beings to aspire to. And the *kosmos*, it may be argued, enjoys a privileged position, as the closest ideal entity that human beings can emulate.[1] Quoting Plato, Plotinus contends that association with the World-Soul's perfection makes our

* I am grateful to the audiences at four events: those at the conference on Cosmos in the Ancient World organised by Phillip Horky in Durham 21 September 2013; to James Wilberding and Svetla-Slaveva-Griffin at the University of Bochum seminar of ancient philosophy, also in 2013; to Tomas Ekenberg, Peter Myrdal and Frans Svensson for their comments at a workshop in Uppsala in December 2014; and finally to Ursula Coope, Erik Eliasson, Mika Perälä and Miira Tuominen, as well as other participants of the workshop on Issues on Ancient Ethics and Philosophy of Action, in January 2014 at the University of Helsinki.
[1] As Phillip Horky so aptly puts it in the Introduction, *kosmos*, in antiquity, refers to both a descriptive and a normative state or structure of reality. What differs are the myriad of usages in which it is put as an ideal. It is used not only to describe its own perfection but as a normative goal for other suitable entities. While it is perhaps more typical to use *kosmos* as an ideal for the organisation and unity of cities, as argued in several contributions to this volume (e.g. that of Luc Brisson, Chapter 6), the Neoplatonists see all entities higher and more perfect than the human soul, *kosmos* included, as both explanatory and ideal for individual human activities and aspirations. My focus in this chapter is the Plotinian World-Soul and its similarities and differences with its 'little sisters', the human souls. For

souls also more perfect, so that they can 'walk on high and direct the whole universe' (*Ennead* 4.8.2.19–22; cf. Pl. *Phdr.* 246c1–2 and *Ti.* 33c6–7). Unlike higher hypostases, the *kosmos* is a god that governs a particular body, the body of the universe. It is also, while itself transcendent to the temporal embodied realm, involved in temporality to the extent that its external activities take place in temporal succession. In the activities of the *kosmos*, the intelligible structures already present themselves as unfolded, both spatially (or materially) and in time.[2] Its life or peculiar mode of existence is thereby potentially closer to that of embodied human existence than that of a pure hypostasis Soul that has no direct relation to any body, or the eternal Intellect – not to speak of the altogether indivisible One beyond being.

This chapter focuses on Plotinus' philosophy of action[3] especially as regards the role and implications that his cosmology has for it. We shall first consider the *kosmos* and highlight especially those features that are relevant for human agency, character formation and development. This will be followed by a discussion of the aspects of human agency that make it structurally different from cosmic activity. These aspects are crucial, since they propose challenges, or, at minimum, restrictions for the use of *kosmos* as an ideal for human *telos*. I will elaborate especially on one major dissimilarity between cosmic and human agents, the idea of human action as directed outside the agent, encountering things in its exterior and being affected by them, and effecting, further, changes to that exterior. My interest is in the ways in which the whole notion of action involves an external world – situation, external bodies and circumstances, as well as other people, other moral agents. The main part of the chapter will argue that Plotinus is sensitive to the challenges these encounters pose to virtuous action. The focal occupation will be with a passage from *Ennead* 3.3: *On Providence* – an unusual kind of text, in terms of what we are accustomed to find in Plotinus. While it has in recent decades been amply shown that there is such a thing as Neoplatonic ethics, this ethics is not very practical in tone – it is predominantly metaphysical, and often considered as radically agent-centred. There is relatively little to learn, directly, about human

the view that this entity is an important step on the Plotinian road towards human gradual divinisation, see Armstrong 1976: 191.

[2] For the World-Soul (also as distinct from hypostasis Soul), see especially Caluori 2015: 112–20; Emilsson 2017: 154–58; and Helleman-Elgersma 1980.

[3] The chapter uses the term 'action', without problematising it, as a translation for Plotinus's terms *poësis, praxis* and *ergon*. In Remes 2017, I focus on giving a basis for a Plotinian theory of action and defend a view according to which all these Greek terms can indeed (at least in some of their usages) be brought under this contemporary heading – with necessary qualifications added.

moral encounters. Our central text, by contrast, will show a rare glimpse of Plotinus occupied with a more practical kind of ethics. The context of the passage concerns providential action-explanations, and while it affirms a reading according to which the moral qualities of the actions of a Plotinian agent flow from the virtuous state of her soul, it also treats human actions – or at the very least their consequences – as compromised by the relational, contextual and interpersonal nature of acting in the first place. Having articulated the particularities of human agency, the chapter will conclude with a reconsideration of *kosmos* as an ideal for human action.

7.2   Cosmic Ideal

Plotinus thinks that cosmic activity is perfect and orderly, and that it would be desirable for human activities to resemble this order and perfection as much as possible. *Kosmos* displays completeness. He lets the *kosmos* speak for itself:

> Since then, what has come into being is the whole universe [ὁ κόσμος ἐστὶν ὁ σύμπας], if you contemplate this, you might hear it say: 'A god made me, and I came from him perfect above all living things, and complete in myself and self-sufficient, lacking nothing, because all things are in me, plants and animals and the nature of all things that have come into being, and many gods, and populations of spirits, and good souls and men who are happy in their virtue. It is not true that the earth is adorned [κεκόσμηται] with all plants and every sort of animal, and the power of soul has reached to the sea, but all the air and aether and the whole heaven is without a share of soul, but up there are good souls, giving life to the stars and to the well-ordered everlasting circuit of heaven which in imitation of Intellect wisely circles round the same centre forever' [τῇ εὐτάκτῳ οὐρανοῦ καὶ αἰδίῳ περιφορᾷ νοῦ μιμήσει κύκλῳ φερομένη ἐμφρόνως περὶ ταὐτὸν ἀεί]. (Plotinus, *Ennead* 3.2.3.19–31; tr. Armstrong)

The order of *kosmos* encompasses everything in the perceptible universe: earth, sea and heavens. *Kosmos* describes itself further as complete (τέλειος l. 22), sufficient (ἱκανός l. 22) and self-sufficient (αὐτάρκης l. 22). These, of course, are terms that recur in ancient ethical discussions. The final or highest good is traditionally conceived of precisely in these terms: it is a good activity that is complete or final (τέλειος), an end beyond which there is no better end or activity. It is an activity for which other activities are done, choice-worthy for its own sake, and not instrumental for anything else. The term ἱκανός is used, among other things, by Plato in the *Philebus*, where he argues for a good that would not be dependent upon something other than itself (20b–23b, esp. 20d). Aristotle, likewise, talks of the final good as an unqualified end (ἁπλῶς τέλειον, *Eth. Nic.* 1.7.1097a30–34), and as self-sufficient (αὐτάρκης, e.g. *Eth. Nic.* 1.7.1097b7–8).[4]

Plotinus uses the same terms both in a cosmological context and in his ethical treatises. He describes the best possible life as perfect or complete life (τελεία ζωή), in which goodness is to be found within, and is not external to the agent (*Ennead* 1.4.3.30–34). A wise man (σπουδαῖος) is self-sufficient as regards goodness and happiness (*Ennead* 1.4.4.23–25). When considering, for instance, the way that the wise man deals with external circumstances and ill fortune, he paints a picture very close to that of the Stoics: virtue or the 'perfect life' is enough for happiness, and external things/goods are treated as necessities of the body. They do not properly belong to the virtuous man living the perfect life. *Kosmos*, then, embodies an ideal because its way of life is nearly paradigmatically self-sufficient and complete – there is no further life or activity that it would be lacking, nor can any external circumstances have effect upon it, because it comprises all of them in its own nature, leaving neither beauty nor power outside. These kinds of unified harmony and completeness are undeniably worthy of being ideals for human life and activity, and as such regulative of the ideal of selfhood and moral agency.

Besides completeness and its cognates, from the human point of view the other desirable feature of the *kosmos* is its orderliness. The whole of ancient literature displays connections with the notion of *kosmos* and the notion of order,[5] making the *kosmos*'s state ideal with regard to order and structure. Connections between the moral agent and the cosmic ideal derive probably from Plato's *Timaeus* where we already have a macrocosm – the universe – and a microcosm – the human being – displaying some similarities: the basic ingredients of the same and the different, and the co-existence of intelligible order and some feature of disorderliness (necessity in the cosmic level).[6] In the *Timaeus* (47a–c), the perfect and orderly revolutions of the stars have a beneficial impact on the microcosmic scale, namely on the soul that looks at them. The human soul that is shaken by the turbulence of the material world can benefit from looking at the harmony of the stellar motions. This perception will not only be aesthetically pleasing: the imitation of them will make the revolutions of the soul's own circular motions of the same and the different

---

[4] For self-sufficiency and completeness/finality in Plato and Aristotle, see Cooper 2003.
[5] On this topic, see Chapter 2 of this volume by Macé.
[6] For an interpretation of the *Timaeus*' notion of necessity as chaos or disorderliness, see Pettersson 2013: 18–30.

similar to those of the stars, namely well organised and harmonious. The imitated activity will thus also make the soul unshaken and orderly.[7]

Yet before assuming that Plotinus simply repeats the Timaean account, we would do well to recognise some dissimilarities in the two accounts. First, often, as in the treatise *On Providence* 1 (*Ennead* 3.2), Plotinus' point is actually not the same as Plato's in the *Timaeus*. Plotinus' concern is to answer an early version of the theodicy problem, namely why it is that there is evil and weakness in the parts of the *kosmos*, if the *kosmos* itself is a beautiful and harmonious whole. Ultimately, he will defend the perfection of the *kosmos* in which even lesser parts and evils have their own proper place within a providentially ordered whole. His moral concern is directly connected to this cosmological point about evil: it is not the case that the *kosmos* generates unqualified evil, so that we could relinquish responsibility for our actions to an external influence. Even evil may have a place within the whole world-order. But the same does not apply to the individual soul that is capable of generating evil. The responsibility of an individual soul as a part of the *kosmos* is to make the best of his or her own, partial, life. Whereas the *Timaeus* suggests assimilation of the microcosm – the individual soul – to the order of the macrocosm, Plotinus actually makes a point about difference of the part from the whole it belongs to, a feature that we will concentrate on in this chapter. Interestingly, it has been suggested that Plotinus appeals to differences of a bodily kind when explaining moral challenges of different kinds of items in the *kosmos*. As James Wilberding has argued, there are certain profound differences between the bodies of human agents and cosmic or heavenly 'agents': human bodies are simply more difficult to administer than the divine bodies.[8] They are not complete and harmonious wholes. It is this feature of human embodied agents as less than complete beings, as parts, that will have important repercussions for the activities – actions – that they generate.

7.3   Parts and Wholes in Action-Explanation

The *kosmos*, or the 'all' (*to pan*), is the totality of what there is, and thereby has no outside, nothing external to it, nothing to relate to or regard. It is whole, self-sufficient, lacking nothing, whereas its parts are precisely parts, having their own functions within the whole, and are thereby not able to,

---

[7] Also see Brisson's treatment of the imitation of the cosmic city in Plato's *Laws* and Boys-Stones' discussion of outer beauty and the manifestation of virtue in the *Symposium*, in their respective contributions to this volume (Chapters 6 and 5).

[8] Cf. Wilberding 2006: 48–68.

nor can be expected to, structurally imitate the whole. Human beings are parts, albeit admittedly rather special parts. Plotinus at one point refers to human souls as *kosmoi noêtoi*, intelligible universes: the particularity of the soul lies in its nature that is capable of reaching from the intelligible world above all the way down to the lower, bodily world (*Ennead* 3.4.3.21–27).[9] Yet even with their dynamic, extended, encompassing natures, individual souls are not as perfect as a World-Soul, or the hypostasis Soul, and by being embodied in the *kosmos*, they become agents that have a nature of a part. Being a part entails that there are things external to the individual. This aspect is already visible in the *Timaeus*, where the immortal soul becomes immediately torn and troubled once it is bound to the body, with material things coming in and out, thus giving rise to sensations (43a–b). This may sound as a trivial, or at best, familiar dualistic feature of Platonic anthropology, but for our understanding of action and agency it is crucial: it helps us to understand the nature of action as, by definition, a relationship between an agent and the external world. To explain certain crucial features of the nature of action in Plotinus' framework, let us keep in mind this 'part' ontology, and have a brief look at Plato's action-explanation.

The background of Plotinus' discussion on acting can be found in Plato's view of actions as always having two sides, the active and the passive, the agent and the patient. When something is done, then there is always also the other side of that doing, the being affected (*Grg.* 476b4–d2). Moreover, the quality of the passion always follows the quality of the action. To cut deeply implies that there is something that is deeply cut. There is a scholarly discussion on whether the active and the passive sides are identical or distinct activities/events for Plato.[10] For our purposes here it is enough to note that something external to the doer is a necessary part of the action-explanation, and that that something is affected in accordance with the thing affecting, the explanation thus privileging, via doing or acting, the role of the agent originating the activity. The quality of the action seems determined by the quality of the agent.[11]

Yet the vocabulary of 'patient' and of 'passivity' may mislead us here, for we may think that the Platonists would conceive this relationship always as exclusively one-directional. Recall the passage in Plato's *Cratylus* 386d–387b, where actions are attested at the same time as having a nature, or

---

[9] For a discussion of this passage, see Runia 1999.   [10] See Sedley 2003: 1–15.
[11] I am relying here especially on Thomas 2010. For an in-depth study of Plato on action, see Macé 2006, especially his nine propositions regarding action and passion (e.g. p. 32).

essence, of their own – there is a right way of acting in each and every activity – and as something relational. To cut well, Socrates says, it is important not to choose, aimlessly, whichever way to cut. One needs to take into account the tool of cutting. Moreover, should we want to burn something, we need to think of how the material burns naturally. To elaborate on his first example of cutting: it makes a difference for both the choice of knife and the choice of the way of cutting whether you cut meat, a tomato or very soft white bread. To succeed in cutting, the nature of the thing being cut has to be taken into account. Cutting is one-directional and asymmetric insofar as only one of the parties in the action is the one from which the activity is originated. Moreover, if the agent does not know how to cut, or has decided to cut badly, the right choice of knife does not help. Nonetheless, as regards the outcome of the cutting and its quality, there are two things that both have their own effect: the nature of the agent and the nature or qualities of the patient. To succeed in acting, this two-place ontology of action and its repercussions have to be acknowledged. While the example of cutting does not touch, directly, upon ethical behaviour, it does, of course, yield the teleological underpinning equally governing the cases more relevant for questions about virtue and vice soon to be discussed. In acting, there is a natural, that is, a successful way, and many unnatural, that is less successful or downright unsuccessful ways of trying to reach one's goal.[12] But diverse from the more straightforward realisation of one's own nature, in realisation of the natural way of acting, more than the agent's nature contributes to the action. The action and the effect upon the world that the person wants to achieve are primarily dependent upon the agent herself, her plans, ends and capacities, but secondarily also upon the objects in the world which are involved – that is, what is available in her surroundings, and the properties and potentialities of the available things. To sum up: actions are essentially world-involving.

Plotinus establishes that the category of doing (ποιητικόν) is other-directed and relative (πρὸς ἄλλον; πρός τι; *Ennead* 6.1.12.29–31). He distinguishes two kinds of action, the first kind in which the agent has in herself an independent or intransitive (ἔχειν ἐν αὑτῷ κίνησιν τὴν ἀπόλυτον παρ' αὑτοῦ) motion, and the second motion that originates in oneself and ends in another (τὴν τελευτῶσαν εἰς ἄλλο ἀπ' αὑτοῦ; *Ennead* 6.1.22.3–5). An example of the former is walking, which may or may not cause footprints, but is not done in order to cause footprints. The latter

---

[12] See also Sedley 2003: 56.

presumably includes all such actions that are done in order to effect some change or effect in the world.[13] It is these latter kinds of activities that we will especially focus on, but with regard to both, we can note that Plotinus seems at least to some extent to agree with Plato. Actions are, as Dominic O'Meara has put it, other-related, and involve a heteronomous dimension.[14] It is precisely for this reason, of course, that they make us vulnerable and can never yield secure happiness.

Now, Plotinus elaborates the idea of action as a relation to something external within an explicitly moral context in his treatises on providence (*Ennead* 3.2 and 3.3). In the former, we learn first that all parts within a *kosmos* are, because of their nature as parts, beings dependent upon and thereby in some sense hostile to one another:

> For from that true universe [ἐκ τοῦ κοσμοῦ τοῦ ἀληθινοῦ] which is one this universe comes into existence which is not truly one; for it is many and divided into multiplicity, and one part stands away from another and is alien to it, and there is not only friendship but also enmity because of the separation, and in their deficiency one part is of necessity at war with another. For the part does not govern/rule itself, but in being preserved is at war with the other by which is it preserved [οὐ γὰρ ἀρκεῖ αὐτῷ τὸ μέρος, ἀλλὰ σωζόμενον τῷ ἄλλῳ πολέμιόν ἐστιν ὑφ' σῴζεται]. (Plotinus, *Ennead* 3.2.2.1–7)

While it is not clear why dependence upon something external and alien to oneself would necessarily imply animosity, the text does establish a way in which any part, human beings included, in the *kosmos* must necessarily find itself in a situation in which it is not entirely self-controlling but supported, maintained in existence, or preserved in and by its relations to things external to it. I take this to mean that for as long as a human soul is in a human body, a completely self-sufficient and independent existence is beyond its capacities, save for some temporally limited moments of intellectual contemplation.

But human beings are not left in this situation entirely clueless. In the latter treatise, 3.3, Plotinus further establishes that evil actions, while happening according to necessity, are caused by the human beings themselves, not by providence. Human beings are the only principles in the *kosmos* endowed with not just a providential nature, as parts of the universe, but also their own individual principle of action. A similar point is made in a couple of places. Plotinus says, for instance, that without

---

[13] For Plotinus and action, see also Remes 2017, Emilsson 2007: 22–68 and Wilberding 2008.
[14] O'Meara 2003: 133.

the body, the soul is in absolute control and free, and outside the cosmic order of things, but when in the body, it is no longer always in control, as it forms part of an order of other things (*Ennead* 3.1.8.9–11). The individual free principle would seem to coincide with decision (προαίρεσις). For example, at 6.3.26 we have a three-fold distinction of motion: natural motion such as growth and diminution, technical motion (examples being building houses and ships) and finally prohairetic motion. Among the latter belong inspecting, learning, engaging in politics, speaking and acting. It seems that these activities help in creating a distance between us and any necessary or deterministic world-order, for it is in these activities that human beings truly differ from other cosmic agents, like the stars. Stars, while in many ways more perfect than human beings, especially as regards the fine qualities of their bodies, do not act willingly nor out of prohairesis (ἑκόντες; with προαίρεσις), but out of necessity (ἠναγκασμένοι; *Ennead* 2.3.2.16–3.4).

7.4 Moral Encounters

In the passage that provides the focal evidence for this chapter, Plotinus is interested especially in the effects or consequences of actions (*erga* at last mentioned), and what these consequences depend. He starts by distinguishing different ways in which evil or bad actions come to be, being adamant in holding people themselves responsible for their doings, and excluding any possibility of putting the blame on the cosmic order:

> So evil deeds [τὰ κακά] are consequences [ἑπόμενα], but follow from necessity; they come from us [i.e. caused by us], not necessitated by providence, but (I) we connect them, of our own accord, with the works of providence or works derived from providence, but are not able to link up what follows according to its wish [κατὰ βούλησιν], but do (II) according to the will of the people who act or (III) according to something else in the universe, which itself is acting *or* producing some effect [πάθος] in us in a way not according to the will of providence. (Plotinus, *Ennead* 3.3.5.33–40)

The text establishes, first, that evil deeds follow from necessity, but are not necessitated by providence. This is a technical Platonic distinction that accomplishes two things. First, it allows evil to deviate from everything that strives for intelligibility and goodness. All evil follows the other main principle of the *Timaeus*, necessity (Pl. *Ti.* 48a–b). Second, the fact that evil deeds come about in accordance with cosmic necessity in this sense does not mean that they would be necessitated in another sense: human beings are not fated to do evil things. Rather, the efficient cause of evil deeds lies in the agents, and not in the providential order, thus securing that responsibility lies within the agent.[15] Plotinus seems to locate three different origins for the evil in a happening in the world: (I) first he speaks generally about us as origins for evil. We can identify a case where the agent him- or herself wishes or wills evil, and evil comes to be in accordance of his or her wish. In the second formulation (II), we have a person that is, actually, a patient of evil. The evil deed in which he is involved, by which he is affected, is willed and caused by some other agent, someone else more actively engaged in acting, in doing. In the third (III) possibility, the evil is caused by something else in the universe, that is, we still have a passive agent, being involved in evil, but not effecting it according to his or her will or wish – not wanting it. This seems a slightly puzzling case. If an evil deed is never caused by providence, what is the origin of evil of this sort? One suggestion is cases where the origin of evil is still in human beings, but in a more distanced way: the evil in question (say, war) was caused by some people who attacked some country, but the particular hurt inflicted on this agent/patient was not caused directly by anyone. Examples of cases like this could be, say, a pestilence that followed a prolonged war, or a building badly built and collapsing on people. Note that these cases are not clearly actions (there is no teleologically directed causal origin directly present), but evil happenings, and effects of some other actions.

The distinction is fleshed out in the immediately following lines, where we get examples, and a more complicated picture, as virtue, and not merely vice or evil, also comes into the picture:

> For everything does not always produce the same effect when it encounters everything else [οὐ γὰρ τὸ αὐτὸ ποιεῖ πᾶν προσελθὸν παντί], but it produces the same effect when it encounters one thing and a different effect when it encounters another; as, for instance, the beauty of Helen produced one effect on Paris but Idomeneus was not affected in the same way; and when one thoroughly depraved human being [ἀκόλαστος] happens upon another, and both are beautiful, the effect is different from what follows when one self-controlled [σώφρον] beauty meets another; and something different again happens to the self-controlled beauty when he meets the depraved man, and again something different to the depraved one when he meets the self-controlled. And the action which proceeds from the depraved man is done neither by providence nor according to providence, whereas the action from a self-controlled one is not by providence, but by the agent

---

[15] For Neoplatonic conceptions of fate and providence, and the question of responsibility, see Adamson 2014.

himself, and in accordance with providence. (Plotinus, *Ennead* 3.3.5.40–49; tr. Armstrong modified)

Although Plotinus does not go deeper here into the interpretation of the intricacies of the causes of the Trojan War, it is evident that he uses the example of Paris and Helen, known to everyone in his audience,[16] as a device for showing, briefly, what relevance differences in moral character have in ethical encounters, and reminding, simultaneously, what long-term effects, even snowball effects, such encounters may have. He tries out different scenarios of encounters between human beings. The very first example seems to be fairly general: an agent, Paris, meeting Helen and being affected, in a certain way, by her beauty. Helen herself is here not depicted as an agent, but considered merely as a beautiful thing. Paris' encounter with beauty he had no will-power to resist brings about a great evil. The main issue here seems to be the question of Paris' moral character. If he had been self-controlled, like the chaste Idomeneus also frequenting Menelaus' household, invulnerable to the beauty of Helen, would there have been any Trojan War? Probably not.

But things get much more complicated later in the passage, just as they do in the interpretation of the causes of the Trojan War. Firstly, it is striking that at the level of the Greek, it seems that it is the beauty of Helen that works as the active side, producing an effect on Paris (τὸ τῆς Ἑλένης κάλλος πρὸς μὲν τὸν Πάριν ἄλλο εἰργάζετο; ll. 41–42). Rather than having a straightforward example of I (the evil being wished and caused by the agent), we could also have here an example of III (the evil befalls the agent without his active engagement, perhaps from the situation he finds himself in, without any causal agency involved). However, given the well-known story, it seems that after being affected by Helen's beauty, the point is that Paris did very much act as an agent himself, making decisions and actions that led to the events they did. So while Paris is a patient in the sense of encountering and sensing things in the world, as well as being affected by

---

[16] The example appears to have been commonly used by philosophers. Relevant earlier usages include at least those by Alexander of Aphrodisias, *in Metaph.* 3, p. 186.10 ed. Hayduck, and Alcinous, *Didask.* 26.2. The latter text uses the example to show that Paris acted voluntarily and that the soul has a power to act. He claims, further, that while the act is not fated, the consequences are: if Paris acts as he acts, the Greeks will go to war. The background is the Middle Platonist insistence on Plato's idea that a virtuous soul has no master. In the same spirit as both Middle Platonists and Alexander of Aphrodisias, Plotinus emphasises the causal role of the agent. He seems to draw a further conclusion, following the peripatetic tradition that connects the example to the question of the origin of the evil effects, the Trojan War. By providing the first premise – voluntarily – Paris is indirectly a cause of the Trojan War (say, a productive cause), even though he is not its efficient or immediate cause. For the example in Alcinous, see Dillon 1993: 161–62 and Reale 1990: 231–32.

them, he is also very much an agent by doing rash things that have their own, evil consequences.

But, as it happens, Helen was not merely a beauty; she was a person in her own right. As Plotinus goes on to explicate, within the effects that encounters between human beings have, the moral characters of both persons involved in the encounter have a role to play. Besides envisioning differences in effects due to the moral character of an agent originating the action, Plotinus entertains the idea of differences in effects due to the moral character of the other, more passive party involved. The scenarios between two moral characters encountering one another mentioned in the second section of the passage can be schematically divided into four, using the same example that Plotinus started with, that of Paris, Helen and Idomeneus:

	Depraved patient, liable to go along with someone else's suggestions	Self-controlled patient, not liable to succumb to anyone's evil suggestions	Resulting action
Depraved agent following his/her evil desires without regrets	Paris taking a willing Helen	Paris abducting an unwilling Helen	neither by providence nor according to providence
Self-controlled agent, following only good desires	Idomeneus meeting Helen?	Idomeneus meeting Helen?	not by providence but according to providence

We have already discussed Paris' agency, and concluded that he must stand, in the column, on the side of depraved agents. But just as the main story of Paris and Helen was known by everyone, so must the debated question of Helen's personal involvement have been familiar to Plotinus' audience. That is, did Helen go willingly with Paris or was she kidnapped? If she did go willingly, could the Trojan War have been prevented had she been a virtuous, self-controlled wife and mother? The encounter between Paris and Helen falls, depending upon which ancient sources one follows, either to the encounter between a depraved person lusting after a virtuous character (kidnapping), or to that of a depraved person lusting after the beauty of an equally depraved and thereby willing partner. According to most poetical descriptions, and in Euripides' *Trojan Women*, Helen was compliant, but according to Stesichorus and Euripides' *Helen*, she was forced.[17]

Given the example of the Trojan War, with its prolonged extension and devastating consequences to both Troy as well as to the Greek navy, it becomes by the end of the quote acutely clear what terrible consequences the encounters between two depraved characters – the remaining slot – can have not just for themselves, but for entire cities and armies. Plotinus does believe that providence, happily, evens such horrendous things out, securing that the proportions of good and evil remain, on the cosmic level, the same, and even that individual deeds receive, in time, their rewards and punishments (*Ennead* 3.2.13). From the point of view of the individual agent this should not, however, make much of a difference. Having the individual principle of self-originated agency within means, for Plotinus no less than it does for Aristotle, that people are responsible for their free or non-coerced actions as well as the direction of their character formation. Realising, therefore, one's own role as even a partial cause of the Trojan War is damning for the agent in question, quite regardless of the ways in which providence is able to accommodate the war into its grander scheme of things.

In order to come to full grasp of the implications of the passage under consideration, let us recall the simplified and perhaps somewhat radical agent-centred view referred to earlier, according to which an action unfolds automatically from a state of the soul. Plotinus' discussion here goes some way towards confirming an agent-centred moral view. The actions of a virtuous agent are all virtuous, and according to providence, because, as today we might put the thing after a lot of philosophising about action-explanation, the intention (or in our source material, the 'wish', βούλησις) of the agent flows from a virtuous soul. Regardless of what and whom the virtuous agent encounters, and quite independently of the outcome, the physical action and its effects or consequences in the world, she acts according to the best of her knowledge, and according to the virtuous state of her soul.[18] The example of Idomeneus enforces the already encountered view according to which, while actions are always encounters between two things, the character of the agent has the real causal power. Whether or not Helen was virtuous seems to have been somewhat irrelevant for Idomeneus, who did not succumb to her beauty and thereby did not cause any problems whatsoever.

---

[17] Gorgias' *Encomium of Helen*, which sparked, for its part, the discussion on Helen's blame, absolves her through another move, by appealing to a divine intervention (*Hel.* 6 and 19).

[18] This is the interpretation found, among others, in Wilberding 2008 and Emilsson 2012.

As we can also see in the table, the action's relations to the providential order – and thereby the responsibility issue – are also determined by the qualities of the agent: no real action is done by providence, since human beings, as we have seen, are the origins of their own actions. However, the actions of the virtuous soul are according to providence: echoing the Stoics, they are directed not only towards the individual good of the agent, but the good of the whole providence.[19]

Read carefully, however, the discussion also qualifies the agent-centred picture in two important ways: first, when considering the outcome of action – just as when Plato considered the outcome of cutting – the nature of the active part cannot be the only determining factor to take into account. The agent is reacting to some effect on her – or in the example of Paris, on him. Plotinus seems to regard beauty as an objective quality of Helen. A change in that quality – say, if the beauty of Helen were to have been ravaged by some terrible disease – does have great significance for what will happen in the encounter between someone potentially lusting after beautiful women and Helen herself, and thereby also indirectly for the consequences. Had Helen been ugly, the Greeks might not have gone to war at all. Second, remember the shifts in treatment of Paris, from someone who is affected by Helen, to a person who acts on his decisions and makes a mark in the history of the Trojan empire; and, of Helen, from a mindless object that Paris could take with him whether he wanted to or not, to someone who makes her own decisions. Plotinus seems to suggest that in human interaction we have two potential agents, and thereby two moral characters in play. Helen is not merely a passive personality, but an agent with an independent action-principle of her own, or at least she was potentially that. The whole notion of interaction means that in human encounters, if they last anything more than a moment, the interacting parties both take alternating roles as agents and patients. Some qualities of human beings are not merely existing or non-existing objects of the agent's desire or intentions, but qualities of the *character* of the other person in the situation. Such moral qualities as self-control are not merely potential objects for, or things encountered by, an agent, but they affect the other person from within, that is, her own decisions and behaviour in the situation, thus further complicating the interaction between the two parties in the relationship. And as soon as there are two causal origins for

---

[19] As George Boys-Stones argues in Chapter 5 of this volume, this way of thinking of virtue as not primarily inward-looking or private, but cosmically situated and publicly manifest, may not be original only to the Stoics, but originate already in Plato himself.

actions, the question of consequences and responsibilities also becomes more complicated.

Plotinus' psychological acuity thus established, there remain challenges for analysing actions with a model like this. One challenge is ontological: when looking at a moral encounter, we always have more actions than one. More precisely, it seems that in a situation where there are two active agents, we have to always postulate at least two actions. An action has to, as it were, always be looked at from two points of view; from the point of view of the active side, agent A causing an effect in the passive side, agent B, and given that agent B is not only a patient in the encounter but active herself, there is another action, her action, with its effects on agent A. In most moral encounters, there is always simultaneous double action going on in an event that someone might want to identify as one happening.

How problematic is this feature? In contemporary action-explanation, individuation of actions is famously problematic. As Elizabeth Anscombe[20] once put it, when a man moves his arm, operates the pump, replenishes the water supply and poisons the people, is he doing four different actions? It seems that actions can be described in a variety of ways, and either all good descriptions capture an action, and we have hopelessly many actions, or there must be a way of locating, among these descriptions, something such as basic actions, upon which other descriptions rest. There is, perhaps, something inherently problematic in individuation of actions: we seem to have too many of them. The ancient picture is not, of course, an answer to this very problem. Yet what it does, or did, was to impose some structure on what seems an endless variety of overlapping happenings in the world, by positing that an action is always accompanied by a passion, and by elevating one part of the relation to a decisive role: actions are the things that come about by someone causing them by wish or intention, as in case I earlier in the chapter. That is, crucial for identifying an action is to have a person in a proper causal role as the origin of the action. This kind of happening always has another kind of description, from the point of the view of the side that is affected, but the passive effect is not another action, but another side of the same action. If, however, there is another causally active agent, then there is also another action. While potentially multiplying actions in the sense of forcing us to find, in what someone might take to be one happening, as many actions as there are causing agents involved, the theory does suggest one clear axis for

---

[20] Anscombe 1957: 37.

us to track when trying to individuate actions: the causal origin of the activity involved.[21] (As for replenishing a water supply and poisoning the people, the ancient philosophers would appeal to ends: if the person did not intend to poison the people, at least that description fails to individuate an action of his. Anscombe's own solution uses some such insight to create a teleological structure between the different descriptions.)

7.5 Critical Circumstances – the Human Condition

We have one more slot in our table of moral encounters to consider. What are the consequences of the actions that result from an encounter between two self-controlled or virtuous agents? Would they always have it right, that is, would they effect only beauty and goodness in their surroundings? Our intuitions tell us that this is unlikely, unless they were to be floating in a vacuum or in the air, like Avicenna's floating man: even good people can indirectly cause harm, since they are neither omnipotent nor omniscient. We have already seen Plotinus establish that, as parts of the *kosmos*, human beings are not floating in a vacuum, that is, that they are actually dependent upon their surrounding things. There remains one more aspect of things external to the agent to be considered, namely this very notion of 'surroundings' or 'circumstances'. First, it allows that qualities of the actions – or at least their effects in the world – depend partly on the agent's object, like the quality of the thing being cut. Second, introducing such a notion helps us to understand the last alternative, III, according to which evil in an action can come about not through the agent, but in some other way, not wished by him, nor caused by some other agent. Take, for instance, Hector in the same war: surely Hector did nothing to stir up the war between the Greeks and the Trojans, and acted, on most accounts, virtuously. His was a situation – encounters with Achilles and others, the complex circumstances of which were so difficult and beyond his powers – in which the outcome of his choices does not merely display the virtuous state of his soul, but is heavily coloured by the characters of the people and situations he encountered.

While virtuousness may unfold, effortlessly, and maybe even necessarily, to the action of the virtuous agent, this does not seem to be the exhaustive origin for the qualities of the action. It is metaphysically possible that the

---

[21] Where this leaves, for instance, shared actions such as a band playing a song together is an interesting question that I cannot go into here. Given Plotinus' familiarity and recurring use of the example of an army, it is not entirely anachronistic to expect him to have a view on the matter.

effect is not like the cause.[22] Given the Platonic idea of the success of the natural action, and involving the right choice of instrument and a proper understanding of the qualities of the object, the virtuous person not only would have to be omniscient to act virtuously, but she would always have to obtain the naturally ideal manner of acting. In the Plotinus quote discussed earlier, the qualities of the actions themselves remain obscure, but as regards the consequences, he affirms a view according to which agents, while having some kind of causal role, cannot be in full control. Elsewhere he states once (*Ennead* 3.4.5.14) that the purpose/decision of the soul as a whole cannot be turned altogether aside by external chances – that is, that when a soul acts as an origin of an action in a unified manner, as a whole, then it must be in some measure and sense successful in what it attempts to cause. He seems perhaps overly optimistic that a wise person cannot entirely fail in her effects in the world, that is, that nothing purely bad can come out of a well-disposed soul. Yet he clearly acknowledges that the quality of the effects is not *exclusively* governed by the agent. The effects depend also upon the other part in a human relationship, and upon the circumstances more generally.

Plotinus does actually have a word for something like 'situation' or 'circumstances', one which he uses only a few times. The word is περιστατικῶς. Plotinus mentions it when he discusses φρόνησις, thus implying that practical wisdom is different in that its considerations happen in an environment, in circumstances (*Ennead* 1.2.7.21). This is all part of the human predicament: the soul's descent or coming to be in the body also involves directing its attention to itself as a part. In the (critical) circumstances it finds itself in, the soul starts to administer the individual it has become (*Ennead* 4.8.4.12–21; l.19; τὸ καθέκαστον μετὰ περιστάσεως διοικεῖ). The *kosmos*, as a whole that encompasses parts, forms the critical circumstances that each soul finds itself in.

In his ethical discussions, Plotinus connects the same word directly to his inquiry into the character of a virtuous man:

> The good man's activities [αἱ ἐνέργειαι] will not be hindered by changes of fortune, but will vary according to what change and chance brings [ἀλλὰ ἄλλαι ἂν κατ' ἄλλας γίγνοιντο τύχας]; but they will be all equally noble, and perhaps, finer for being adapted to circumstances [ὅσῳ περιστατικαί]. As for his theoretical activities, some of them which are concerned with particular points will possibly be hindered by circumstances [αἱ μὲν καθ'

---

[22] Ancient philosophers discuss such examples as rubbing the hands together and producing heat. See Sorabji 2004: 141–48.

ἕκαστα τάχα ἄν], those for instance which require research and investiga-tion. But the greatest study is always ready to hand and with him. (Plotinus, *Ennead* 1.4.13.1–6)

It is here that Plotinus provides one answer to the dilemma we noted earlier, whether the effects of the good man's choices display the goodness of his character. He endorses, again, the quite optimistic view that changes of fortune, no matter how severe, cannot prevent the virtuous man from acting altogether. At the same time, he allows that the circumstances will affect his activities. He is especially concerned with the problems that the external world proposes for doing research in peace and quiet. As anyone with children will know, theoretical activities are vulnerable to surroundings. What a virtuous man does will be noble, but he is not invulnerable to the circumstances – his activities vary in accordance with the context he encounters.

Note that Plotinus even says that a virtuous man's actions may be nobler if they happen in difficult circumstances, thus implying that there is something particularly fine about retaining one's virtue and concentration in the most difficult of circumstances. But what would be so fine about that? Should we not, rather, wish for as few difficulties and interruptions as possible, so that, e.g., philosophical enquiry would have as many good possibilities of advancing as possible? One clue is given in 1.9.13 where Plotinus argues against suicide – how it actually constitutes, in his mode of expression, a departure from the body, probably even in an emotional state, instead of a staying where one is; one should rather make the body depart. Circumstances come into the picture when Plotinus considers whether the feeling of beginning to go mad would be a good enough reason to commit suicide. Plotinus opts here also for the negative answer, claiming that the wise man understands the inevitability connected to his own looming madness, as part of the circumstances. Going mad is to be chosen, not because it would be desirable or noble itself, but because of the circum-stances. The life of the wise man becomes, thereby, a difficult balancing act: he will act virtuously and thereby cause good actions and generate goodness in his surroundings, but he will not make the mistake of thinking that he could cure everything in the providentially ordered, perfect *kosmos*, nor that he could entirely rise above it.

7.6 *Kosmos* as an Ideal for Human Behaviour

To assess the way that the *kosmos* is and is not an ideal for human beings, let us first take stock. Human beings, unlike the *kosmos*, are parts. They are

beings dependent on the other parts that form the compositional whole
they belong to. Acting is ontologically relational: in acting, human beings
effect changes in their external world. They also play the role of the patient
in these encounters when it is they that are affected. Acting and being
affected are asymmetrical insofar as the effects of actions are, to a large
degree, determined by the state and quality of the agent, the origin of the
action. But this causal origin is not exclusive in determining all the qualities
and consequences of the actions; the qualities of the encountered objects
also make a difference. The ethical realm is, moreover, particular in that it
is a realm of interpersonal relationships: it involves encounters between
two – or more – principles or origins of action, and thereby also more than
one character. The effects of such encounters become therefore much more
complex and even more dependent, in intricate ways, upon things outside
the agent herself. Finally, actions are cosmologically situational: actions are
done in circumstances that impose the dependency relationships within
the *kosmos* to the action-explanation.

There is an important ethical repercussion of this that I will only
mention here: becoming a virtuous person cannot be, for Plotinus, only
a matter of externalising the body and gazing upon the intelligible principles, even though this lies at the heart of the process of self-improvement.[23]
Moral virtue and development include, perhaps surprisingly, the ability to
see these dependencies not merely as obstacles to one's own decisions and
free activities, but as the parts of the framework to which one belongs, and
possibilities given to human beings by the providential order of the
kosmos.[24]

Having established the ontological and cosmological differences
between the *kosmos* and the human being, we may return to the issue of
the *kosmos*, and its activities, as a potential model or desirable ideal for
human beings. The *kosmos*'s soliloquy we started with will give us some
indications. The speech continues:

> Everything in me seeks after the good, but each attains it according to its
> own power [κατὰ δύναμιν τὴν ἑαυτῶν ἕκαστα]; for the whole heaven
> depends on it, and the whole of my soul, and the gods in my parts, and
> all animals and plants and whatever there is in me (if there is anything)
> which is thought to be without life. And some things appear to participate
> only in being, others in life, others more fully in life in that they have sense-
> perception, others at the next stage have reason, and others the fullness of

---

[23] Compare Epicurean 'gazing', as discussed by Shearin in Chapter 12 of this volume.
[24] This, of course, brings him once again close to Stoic philosophers.

life. One must not demand equal gifts [τὰ ἴσα] in things which are not equal. It is not finger's business to see, but this is the eye's function, and the finger's is something else – to be essentially finger and to have what belongs to it. (Plotinus, *Enneads* 3.2.3.31–41)

Orderliness, or a state of being well-adorned (from κοσμέω; *Ti.* 47d6; see Plot. *Ennead* 3.2.3.26) is described by the *kosmos* as a functional differentiation. Just as the finger and the eye have different functions and cannot try to fulfil the tasks of one another, the different beings in the *kosmos* have their own functions. This view of the *kosmos* also arises from Plato's *Timaeus*, and belongs to his general ontology. For Plato, a whole is more than a sum of its parts: it is a compositional whole, with compositional relations between the parts. These relations, and the functions that the parts have within the whole, create a unity, the whole, out of something that would otherwise not be a whole at all. There are two things about these kinds of wholes relevant here. First, they are made out of functionally differentiated parts (like letters in a syllable in the *Theaetetus* 203 c), having their own roles within the whole. These roles are determined by the purpose and structure of the whole, which brings us to the second relevant aspect: the unity or wholeness discussed is normative. As Verity Harte puts it, the thing is either good or not a whole at all.[25]

With regards to Plotinus' *kosmos*, we have seen that after establishing its completeness and perfection, the *kosmos* emphasises the different functions and powers within its parts, and how each strives after the good in its own manner and according to its own capacity. Associating with the World-Soul, 'being with it' (μετ' ἐκείνης at *Ennead* 4.8.2.19) is thus different from emulating a god that is distinct and unqualifiedly higher than oneself: *kosmos* is the totality of which one is oneself a part. We can conclude with some remarks on what the purport for the moral ideal of god-likeness could be. First, the idea that human beings also complement the *kosmos* with their own particular contributions is a continuation of the Aristotelian theme of different species having their own nature and task to fulfil. Just as horses do horse-like things, individual human beings do different things, according to their individual dispositions (*Ennead* 3.3.1.23–27). It is here that we see the true nobility of the Plotinian sage. While the directedness of the Platonic intelligible paradigms informs all the sage's choices, he is at the same time aware of the cosmic situation and his own role in it. This brings us to one of the most important aspects of what it means for Plotinus to act in accordance with providence. In Plotinus' view, using *prohairesis* of

---

[25] For Plato's ontology of wholes, see Harte 2002: 274.

one's own is not merely to have a principle of one's own reasoning to use as
one likes, but it is to use it with a vision of the whole. A true *prohairesis* is
not directed, for instance, to one's own limited being or body, but to the
whole, and one's purpose in it (*Ennead* 4.4.33.17, the dancer and dance-
analogy). It is for this reason that we could not possibly be exactly similar
agents to the *kosmos*. While the cosmic providence organises the whole
kosmos towards a harmonious structure in which everything has a place, it is
the task of the human being to come to grips with the particularities of his
own place and situation, and to make the best of that situation. This task is
thereby more partial and less perfect than anything that the visible *kosmos*
may be doing.[26]

Yet, if we are inclined to take the idea of the macrocosm being
ideal for the microcosm seriously, we may wish to push the isomorphism between agent and *kosmos* further. In the earlier quote, the
wholeness of *kosmos* is not merely a matter of inert pieces forming
a unity, but of different kinds of *activities* that strive for goodness in
their own different kinds of ways. The same could be said of a human
life: our lives include different kinds of activities, prompted by diverse
kinds of life situations. All of these are, in their unique ways, directed at
the good as their goal. Given that human acting in the moral sphere is in
3.3 analysed as relational, as involving the relation of affecting the other
part in the moral encounter, and 1.4 described as happening in different
circumstances requiring different kinds of measures, we may elaborate on
the regulative ideal of the cosmic activity as follows.

A complete and good life of a human agent involves understanding
what you can and cannot do in certain circumstances, with what
instruments best to attain your end in those situations. A parallel of
the wholeness of the cosmic activity on a human scale is a wholeness of
diverse human activities in which all have their own appropriate role.
In an Aristotelianising tenor, one might say that a good agent knows
how to shape a harmonious life where different activities have their
own place and proper, balanced proportion. She will have to eat and
drink, to take care of her dear ones and respond to the many difficulties that the ordinary life imposes upon her, and of course finding
enough time to contemplate and philosophise. In all these she will act
not only well, but so that the activities are properly and proportionally
well related to one another, creating a structured unity that is the whole
outflowing of her powers and activity.

---

[26] I have also argued for this in Remes 2006.

7.7   To Conclude

Perfection and completeness in human action cannot take the form of the inward-directed activity of the *kosmos*, which does not encounter anything external to it. Human acting is *ontologically relational*: action is a relation between the agent and the patient, a reaching out towards the world external to the agent. It is *cosmologically situational*, each part of the temporal *kosmos* being dependent upon other things in the same *kosmos*. Action is, furthermore, *morally interpersonal*, although in a way specific to antiquity, with an embedded asymmetry of the agent–patient governing the explanations.

The significance of the *kosmos* as a god-like ideal for human action lies, rather, in the unity it forms out of multiplicity, and, in this way, it displays the same structural features as the Intellect. The uniqueness of the *kosmos* lies in its exhibiting this wholeness in a way particular to its nature, as a composition of different temporally extended life-activities. It is in this way that it is able to function as an ideal appropriate for human acting.

Let us end with a final distinguishing feature of human moral life. Being a part does not imply only deficiency. Humans actually have one opportunity for a perfection denied to the *kosmos*. As Plotinus vividly puts it, providential order is like a commander ordering both her own army and that of the enemy, fitting together both good and evil things (*Ennead* 3.2.2.1–7). Human action may resemble that activity to the extent that it is, often enough, our task to recognise our weaknesses, use our strengths in the right places, and in general administer our different activities into as beautiful and harmonious a whole as is possible for us. But in the view of Plotinus, humans, or at least aspiring philosophers, should not be resigned to harmonising the good and the evil aspects in their nature. As parts, their fate neither needs, nor can be, to bear the evil of the *kosmos*. They are required, rather, to defeat the enemy. While they cannot control external objects, neither the instruments nor the circumstances of their actions, it is possible for them internally to always act in accordance with virtuous principles.

CHAPTER 8

Tradition and Innovation in the Kosmos–Polis Analogy

Carol Atack*

8.1 Introduction

The analogy between the divine order of the *kosmos* and the human order of the polis was well established in Greek thought, and the basis of a persistent but evolving political cosmology that attempted to link human and divine. The analogy is well attested in literary evidence, although the use of *kosmos*-derived terms in archaic political structures from several Greek cities in some cases predates the re-purposing of *kosmos* language by early philosophers.[1] These developments in the scope of *kosmos* language meant that this analogy underwent substantial change in the classical period, as philosophical ideas of nature and the divine challenged traditional formulations of one side of the analogy, and the development of the polis, and particularly radical Athenian democracy, challenged the other. Although the analogy is one that is fundamental to Greek thought, as Geoffrey Lloyd has shown, its origins lie much more firmly in the human end of the analogy, in the arrangement of forces by military leaders and in the anthropomorphism by which Greek gods were seen in terms of human leadership.[2]

One established view of the *kosmos*–polis analogy in Presocratic thought is that its use of the language of human justice, with the forces of the *kosmos*

* I would like to thank the participants in the 'Ancient Cosmos: Harmony among Worlds' conference for their papers and discussions that illuminated the concept of *kosmos*, the University of Durham for supporting my attendance at the event and Phil Horky and Malcolm Schofield for their helpful comments on drafts of this chapter. Parts of this chapter are drawn from my PhD research, funded by the Arts and Humanities Research Council.
[1] It also shows that *kosmos* terminology is first used at the human end of the analogy and migrates, under the influence of philosophers, to the divine/universal side. See Chantraine et al. 2009 *sv.* κόσμος, Kranz 1955: 13–16.
[2] Lloyd 1966: 172–209; Kranz 1938: 430–32. Jean-Pierre Vernant adds a further similarity, between the arrangement of objects around a central focus, whether the earth at the cosmic level or the agora at the polis level (Vernant 1983: 176–80).

conceptualised in terms of retribution and repayment, and with an emphasis on equality between such forces, imbued it with a democratic tinge.[3] For
example, Anaximander (DK 12 A 9–11), in an early testimony for this new
usage of *kosmos* language, describes the heavens and the world(s) within
them as subject to such forces.[4] But perhaps some caution should be
exercised in assimilating Presocratic cosmology to the politics of democratic Athens, rather than to broader models of political change operating
in a world with multiple possibilities for types of rule, and multiple models
of justice. A broader examination of the use of *kosmos* language in political
contexts, both in literary texts and in documentary sources, shows that the
analogy could be applied in many differing forms and in different political
contexts, but had a strong association with archaic and aristocratic
worldviews.

This chapter will therefore show that the *kosmos*–polis analogy was
contested, with a more democratic version briefly visible in the fifth
century BCE eventually losing out to a less democratic version, more
evident in both fourth-century texts and in political nomenclature that
persisted into the Hellenistic era. I will argue that, as the polis became
less aristocratic, alternative formulations of the analogy, such as those
found in Aristophanes' comedies, repositioned it in a democratic context. But the relationship of the comedic, democratic version to philosophical investigations into cosmology and cosmogony is not
straightforward. In fifth-century historiography the analogy retains its
links to political foundation by monarchs, although *kosmos* begins to be
used as a synonym for *politeia*; documentary evidence largely supports
this usage.

The fourth century BCE saw a new enthusiasm for the deployment
of *kosmos* imagery in political life, often in an archaising context,
a development that is evident in both documentary sources and in
the texts of political philosophers. Plato's reassessment of the *kosmos*–
polis analogy, which structures the interwoven accounts of the creation of the world and the downfall of Atlantis and primeval Athens in
his *Timaeus/Critias*, plays an important role. Plato's later political
thought connects the older use of *kosmos* language to new political
thinking, such as that displayed in the *Statesman* and the *Laws*, in
which the description of political arrangements is placed within

---

[3] Vlastos 1947. See also Horky's and Macé's contributions in Chapters 1 and 2.
[4] As in A 11: ἔφη τῶν ὄντων φύσιν τινὰ τοῦ ἀπείρου, ἐξ ἧς γίνεσθαι τοὺς οὐρανοὺς καὶ τὸν ἐν αὐτοῖς
κόσμον. Cf. Kahn 1960: 219–39; Kirk et al. 1983: 117–21; Kranz 1938: 433; and Schofield, Chapter 3 of
this volume.

a cosmological framework.[5] But there is also the possibility that *kosmos* terminology is revived because of its archaic and Homeric connotations, in a political climate which increasingly looked to the past, as in appeals to ancestral constitution models, and that both the Homeric and the philosophical resonances of *kosmos* language are in play.

8.2 Political Cosmology in Early Greek Poetry

Before early philosophers contemplated the basic stuff of what would later be identified as the *kosmos* or posited an intelligence guiding it, a pre-political and pre-philosophical version of the analogy developed in which human rulers and leaders were likened to gods, and parallels drawn between groups of aristocratic leaders and anthropomorphic Olympian gods, as well as their subjects.[6] Homeric epic emphasises this analogy, from the very beginning of the *Iliad*; Agamemnon, leader of the Greeks and supreme among the *basileis* who head each contingent of fighters, struggles for dominance over his not-quite equals, perhaps more than Zeus does in his analogous position as head of the Olympian gods.[7]

The traditional form of the *kosmos*–polis analogy represented by Homeric epic was inherently conservative, in placing Zeus and human *basileis* in the same position in each side of the analogy, controlling the ordering of overall and civic elements respectively.[8] The analogy took both the form

> Human ruler: human society :: Zeus: divine society

and also the form

> Human ruler (of *x*): human society *x* :: Zeus: natural world.

In the *Iliad*, while Agamemnon is introduced as *anax andrôn* (1.7) and *basilêi* (1.9), a title emphasised by focalisation through the god Apollo, he shares the title with Menelaus, his fellow son of Atreus; together, they are

---

[5] See Kahn 2009 on the cosmology of the *Statesman* myth and Kahn 2010 on the development of Plato's cosmology in the *Timaeus*; Luc Brisson explores the political cosmology of the *Laws* in Chapter 6 of this volume. See also Kranz 1955 and Szlezák 1996.

[6] See Vernant 1982: 23–37; Lloyd 1966: 172–209.

[7] Carlier 1984 provides the most detailed examination of Homeric kingship; Schofield 1986 investigates the political nature of Homeric society, in response to Finley 1954.

[8] Kranz suggests that this is more broadly true of Greek foundation myth, and that the names of the mythical kings Codrus (Athens) and Cadmus (Thebes) derive from the same etymological roots as *kosmos* (Kranz 1955: 8–9).

κοσμήτορε λαῶν (1.16), marshals of the forces or organisers of the people.[9] Ensuring an effective arrangement of troops for battle was perhaps the most important task of the *basileus* in the agonistic world of the *Iliad*. Titles such as *kosmetôr* have a primarily military meaning, a sense that persists into the classical world. The primary meaning of *kosmos* and related terms is 'orderly arrangement', and the ordering of troops by a general is the most obvious example of this.[10] Such acts of ordering are positively evaluated through this language, as in the common Homeric description of actions properly carried out or arrangements properly made εὖ κατὰ κόσμον (e.g. at *Il.* 11.48, 12.85, 24.622) and its negative form οὐ κατὰ κόσμον (e.g. at *Il.* 2.214, 5.759, *Od.* 14.363). David Elmer has shown that this extends to an aesthetic appreciation of proper arrangement, with the bard's arrangement of stories assessed as a *kosmos* just as the military arrangements of a king might be, as when Odysseus praises the bard Demodocus for his *kata kosmon* recital of a Trojan War narrative (*Od.* 8.487–91).[11]

In this version of the analogy, both the Achaeans and the Olympian gods have leaders, identified as kings, who control both their own forces directly and those of others through intermediate leaders, the other Achaean leaders and the other gods. The traditional view of kings in this model is summarised by Nestor's address to Agamemnon (*Il.* 9.96–102), which emphasises both the origin of Agamemnon's power, symbolised by his sceptre, with Zeus, and that its function is to manage justice and to give advice: 'you/are lord over many people, and Zeus has given into your hand the sceptre and rights of judgement, to be king over the people'.

Equally, the order can be disrupted, as it is by Thersites' intervention in the Achaeans' assembly (*Iliad* 2.211–42).[12] Thersites' speech disrupts the leaders; his words are disorderly (*akosma*, 2.214), and he speaks out of turn (*ou kata kosmon*, 2.215). Agamemnon's royal sceptre, on the other hand, handed down to him from Zeus, guarantees that his acts of ordering will be proper.

The connection between human world and divine *kosmos*, microcosm and macrocosm, is explored through the idea of kingship. Kings, as leaders and with their role as priests, mediate between human and divine. This relationship is not always successful, but the king still plays a part; Apollo's anger with Agamemnon affects all the Achaeans (*Il.* 1.43–52), while Zeus exploits Agamemnon's belief that he can interpret dreams as portents (*Il.* 2.1–47).

---

[9] As are Castor and Polydeuces (*Il.* 3.236).
[10] Cartledge 1998: 3–4. But the ordering of feasts and festivals is a use that continues to be important.
[11] Elmer 2010: 291–92.   [12] Elmer 2013: 93–97; Cartledge 2009: 34–36.

The *Odyssey* reflects a more positive account of the king's role in uniting human society with cosmic order. In its opening books we see examples of well-ordered societies headed by a good ruler, such as the court of Menelaus, in contrast with the failed order of Ithaca with its absent king and undisciplined suitors. Odysseus himself, in praising Penelope and her renown, introduces a simile where the presence of a good king and his actions (εὐηγεσίης) in providing good judgement (εὐδικίας) ensure a return to a golden-age situation where crops are abundant and food-sources plentiful, and the people prosper as a result:

> As of some excellent king who, as a blameless man and god-fearing [θεουδὴς] [and ruling as lord over many powerful people] (110) upholds the way of good government [εὐδικίας], and the black earth yields him barley and wheat, his trees are heavy with fruit, his sheepflocks continue to bear young, the sea gives him fish, because of his good leadership [εὐηγεσίης], and his people prosper [ἀρετῶσι] under him. (*Od.* 19.109–14; tr. after Lattimore)

Odysseus depicts a golden age distinct from the present situation he has found on Ithaca, where the lack of leadership caused by his absence is causing the depletion of resources by the suitors.[13]

Epic poetry is not the only genre in which *kosmos* language moves from a military context to a more political one. A similar process occurs in early Greek elegy, where the militaristic values of poets such as Theognis are appropriated and transformed by Solon, addressing the unstable political situation of sixth-century Athens.[14] One couplet, variously attributed to both Theognis and Solon, sets out the developing use of *kosmos* language to describe specifically political acts of ordering:

> I will adorn [κοσμήσω] my homeland, a shining city, neither turning it over to the people nor giving in to unjust men. (Theognis ll. 947–48 West, tr. by Gerber)

The object of the ordering is specifically described as a polis, in which unjust men oppose the demos.[15]

---

[13] Hesiod's *Works and Days* (*Op.* 225–37) also explores these ideas, but with greater emphasis on the possibility of bad rule. Hesiod's *Theogony* presents Zeus as king of the heavens (*Theog.* 71) and gods (*Theog.* 886), but also provides him with the kind of genealogy that a human king would demonstrate, giving him divine ancestry as the son of Cronus.

[14] Irwin 2005 provides a detailed study of Solon's incorporation of both elegy and epic in a new language of political exhortation for the Athenians. Plutarch was the first to argue that Solon's project ended in failure with the dissolution of his constitution under the Peisistratid tyranny (*Comp. Sol. et Publ.* 3.3); McGlew 1993: 87–123 explores this idea in detail.

[15] The poet invokes ship-of-state imagery to argue that political order (*kosmos*) is destroyed whenever the many prevent the skilled helmsman from maintaining control (Theognis ll. 675–79 West).

Solon continues this line of argument, using the *kosmos* analogy to hymn the virtues of good government to the Athenians. He links the activity of the poet to that of the law-giver, first presenting himself to the Athenians as someone who can set words in order as song (κόσμον ἐπέων ᾠδήν, Fr. 1.2 West).[16] Although Solon documents a changing political environment at Athens, in which collective action and interests dominate, he nonetheless presents himself as a uniquely placed arbitrator of political discord.[17] Solon's *Eunomia* (Fr. 4 West) criticises Athenian political behaviour, particularly that of the existing aristocratic and military elite.[18] The leaders are unable to conduct festivals in an orderly fashion (οὐδὲ παρούσας/ εὐφροσύνας κοσμεῖν δαιτὸς ἐν ἡσυχίη, 4.9–10); order is linked to quietude, itself a politicised concept.[19] Lawlessness (*Dysnomia*) and lawfulness (*Eunomia*) are personified and contrasted in terms of their effect upon the city (4.30–39).[20] The benefit of Eunomia to the community is that the proper order (*eukosma*) of everything is revealed:

> Lawfulness [Εὐνομίη] reveals all that is orderly [εὔκοσμα] and fitting
> And often places fetters around the unjust [ἀδίκοις]. (Solon 4.32–33 West; tr. by Gerber)

Further benefits of Eunomia include some that match those mentioned by Homer and Hesiod, such as the 'straightening out' of crooked judgements (εὐθύνει δὲ δίκας σκολιάς, 4.36); others include the suppression of the aristocratic vices of *hubris* and *koros* (greed).[21]

The process of ordering is linked to a specific set of political values, presided over by the concept of Dike as retributive justice, but the personification of lawfulness represents the role of law in collective political activity, and collective acts of political strife (*stasis*) such as divisive civil conflict (διχοστασίης, 4.37).[22] In Solon's version of the analogy, order is threatened and maintained by collective political acts as well as individual failings.[23]

---

[16] Plut. *Sol.* 8.2; see Noussia-Fantuzzi 2010: 211–12. The special status of the poet as creator, speaker and intermediary here resembles that of the king in Hesiod's *Theogony* 81–92.

[17] Fr. 5.5–6, cited in Arist. [*Ath. Pol.*] 11.2–12.1, summarising Solon's political views and actions.

[18] The poem has its own extensive literature: classic analyses of its political and philosophical content in Jaeger 1966a and Vlastos 1946, and more recent approaches in Lewis 2006 and Irwin 2005; detailed linguistic commentary in Noussia-Fantuzzi 2010.

[19] Vlastos 1946: 68–70. See later in the chapter for the use of festivals as models of the polis, and their association with ordering, in Thucydides and Plato.

[20] Ostwald 1969: 62–65 on the transformation of Eunomia from Hesiod's daughter of Zeus (*Theog.* 901–2) to Solon's more political concept.

[21] Raaflaub 2000: 40–42.   [22] Ostwald 1969: 65–69; Lewis 2006: 55–59.

[23] Vernant 1982: 92–101.

While Homer and Hesiod depicted the ruler, whether an individual king or an abstract respect for the law, as the source of good political order which is supported by Zeus (or other divine entities, such as the personifications of justice and lawfulness), Solon's use of *kosmos* imagery suggests developments that enable the analogy to be applied more precisely to the specific problem of stasis, or conflict between groups in the context of the polis. Solon combined the cosmological and military uses of *kosmos* language seen in other early poets to produce a polis-specific version of the analogy that fits the context of the polis in stasis. The benefit delivered by good order, whether under law or a powerful ruler, is the end of internal conflict within the polis, although, as Solon feared, the advent of tyranny remained a possibility.

8.3 Recalibrating the *Kosmos*–Polis Analogy in a Democratic Context

After the Athenian democratic project restarted in the fifth century, Solon's developments were taken forward by other writers with an Athenian focus and interest in processes of political change. Developments in the *kosmos*–polis analogy can be seen in the work of the historians Thucydides and Herodotus, with the term *kosmos* applied to the settled constitutional arrangements of a city. But the military sense persists in some uses of the word, and *kosmos* as order remains the outcome of a deliberate act by an authoritative individual such as a king or a general, even on occasion a leader identified as a tyrant. Absence of *kosmos*, on the other hand, is often attributed to failing collective endeavours, military and political, typically the loss of battle-order by an army facing defeat.

Thucydides' careful use of the verb *diakosmeô* suggests that significant acts of political ordering are properly performed by kings and founders. He uses it to describe Theseus' original synoecism of Athens from its originally separate constituent villages (διεκόσμησε τὴν χώραν ... ἓν βουλευτήριον ἀποδείξας καὶ πρυτανεῖον, ξυνῴκισε πάντας, 2.15.2), which emphasises the incorporation of separate cities with their own councils into a single unified political entity. It also identifies political arrangements made by Archelaus of Macedon (2.100.2), and the Athenian tyrants (6.54.5). His Archidamus of Sparta uses *kosmos* language in his speeches (1.84.3, 2.11.9), as does Pericles in the Funeral Speech (2.42.2, 2.46.1), perhaps another way in which Thucydides marks the Athenian general as a pseudo-monarch. Thucydides more broadly uses *kosmos* (either *kata kosmon* or *en kosmôi*) to describe proper arrangements, whether of constitutions and political order, or in the original military context. He also uses its negative form, *oudeni kosmôi*, to describe the loss of political order or disarray on the battlefield; whether in the Athenian plague (2.52.2), Corcyrean stasis (3.77.3) or the naval battles of the Sicilian expedition (7.23.3, 7.40.3, 7.84.3). Particularly in Book 8, *kosmos* becomes a standard term to describe a settled constitution (8.48.4, 8.67.3, 8.72.2; cf. 4.76.2).

Herodotus' political thought, embedded in his account of the rise and fall of empires, hints at the conflation of the *kosmos*–polis analogy that Plato's *Timaeus-Critias* displays. The presence of Presocratic thought within Herodotus' work has received somewhat less attention than his links with Hippocratic ideas, but the presence of ideas of cyclicality from Presocratic thinkers has long been identified. Both Heraclitus and Empedocles seem to be influences: Empedocles' cyclical account of the *kosmos* and life within it, moving between separation under strife and unity under love (DK 31 B 17.1–13, 16–17), bears some similarity to Herodotus' account of political cyclical change.[24] The condition of the quality of unity of political entities changes as they wax and wane in power, alternating between greatness and smallness (1.5.4, 1.207.2).[25] Political entities change between conditions of unity, in which internal strife is absent, and conditions of disunity, in which such strife and factionalism are present.

Herodotus' account of political cycles is best applied to the large-scale kingdoms and empires of the Near East; internal political activity within democratic Athens does not fit neatly into his framework, except as a counter-example. Athens' pattern of change between democracy and tyranny counters the structures of Near Eastern empire, a contrast that Herodotus is happy to draw in presenting the defeat of Persian armies by Athenian forces.[26]

But, as Vernant suggests, the classical city had no need of the divine king; the kings of Near Eastern *ethnos* states, however, were often perceived to be such kings.[27] Greek accounts of such kings (especially Herodotus'

---

[24] There are other points of contact between Empedocles and Herodotus, such as a shared interest in mystery religion and cycles of incarnation: Hdt. 2.123 on Egyptian and Dionysiac views on reincarnation, for example; Empedocles B 8, 9 and 115 on the causes of the cycle. Other readings of Herodotean cyclicality emphasise alternation, and links with Heraclitean flux. Cf. Immerwahr 1966: 152–54.

[25] Asheri 2007: 36–37.

[26] Herodotus initially presents cyclicality in the polis world in terms of hegemony passing between Athens and Sparta (1.56, followed by a comparison of the two cities), but later documents the changing quality of Athenian civic life with the advent of democracy (5.76).

[27] Vernant 1982: 38–48.

Histories) set them against the political arrangements of the fifth-century polis. In part this may be to explain exotic images of distant places to a Greek or specifically Athenian audience, but in one narrative, that of Deioces' foundation of the empire of the Medes (1.95–101), the contrast between the political foundation of an empire and a polis such as Athens is made explicit, while the ordering process is envisaged in cosmological terms.[28] Herodotus' account of Deioces and the Median Empire is problematic when considered as history rather than political myth: although there are places where it can be seen to have some contact with historical evidence, there is more convincing evidence of patterning and naming to construct an exemplary foundation narrative.[29]

Herodotus' account of Deioces' consolidation of the scattered Median villages into a single empire can be read alongside Empedocles' account of cyclical change, governed by the changing predominance of Love and Strife. Deioces comes to prominence when the Medes have been liberated from Assyrian domination (1.95.2). He gains a reputation for administering justice in his own village, and other communities seek his assistance, recognising that he is the only man who could provide this service (1.96.2–3). But Deioces declines to do so, and lawlessness ensues (1.97.2). The Medes gather together and, recognising that he is the only man who can secure justice and peace in the community, elect him to be their king, encouraged by his friends (1.97.3).

Deioces builds a new single settlement and palace complex, the *polisma* of Ecbatana (1.98.2–3). Here the *kosmos*–polis analogy becomes explicit in Near Eastern rather than Greek terms, although one should note that what is constructed is a *polisma*, by which Herodotus appears to mean a settlement that would be a polis if it were Greek, but is instead a 'polis-thing'.[30] He contrasts the *polisma* of Ecbatana with the polis of Athens. The circuit of walls is roughly the same size in both cases, but their function is different. Athens' circuit contains its citizens; Ecbatana's walls mark a boundary that excludes the populace, who are ordered to live outside (1.99.1).

---

[28] The importance of this episode in Greek political thought has been recognised by many commentators; while Asheri's commentary focuses on the problems of the narrative's historicity, others, notably Walter 2004 and Belloni 2006, recognise its purpose as a political myth depicting an 'original position' and the foundation of a society. See also Ward 2008 and Arieti 1995.

[29] In addition to Asheri 2007: 147–51, Helm 1981 and Wiesehöfer 2004 assess the problems of historicity of Deioces and his empire; Asheri *ad* 1.96.2 notes the prevalence of Δικ- words in this story of justice (including Deioces' name) and suspects a patterning process.

[30] Asheri 2007: 150; see also Horky 2009 on the incorporation of Persian and Chaldaean cosmology into Greek thought.

In this narrative, the citadel of Ecbatana takes the shape of a ziggurat, with its seven successive layers coloured to signify the seven planets of Chaldaean mythology (1.98.5–6); Deioces' palace and treasuries are placed on the topmost, innermost level, which is decorated with gold.[31] It becomes clear that Deioces is establishing a new and all-encompassing type of order, in which his position is equated to that of the sun in the *kosmos*. Arieti suggests that Deioces emphasises all this because unlike other kings of his time he cannot claim divine ancestry or status.[32]

However, for Herodotus the language of *kosmos* still relates to the human side of the analogy. The physical building and arrangement of space is echoed by the establishment of court protocols, described by Herodotus as a *kosmos* established for the first time (κόσμον τόνδε Δηιόκης πρῶτός ἐστι ὁ καταστησάμενος, 1.99.1).[33] The *kosmos* takes the form of a set of prescriptions governing interactions between ruler and ruled, limiting access to the ruler and preventing him from being seen. These prescriptions are established through an act of *diakosmêsis* that also secures his power (ταῦτα διεκόσμησε καὶ ἐκράτυνε ἑωυτὸν τῇ τυραννίδι, 1.100.1); he also makes arrangements (ἐκεκοσμέατο, 1.100.2) for the administration of justice.[34]

Empedocles' structure emphasises the benefits of the unification phase governed by Love, especially the point at which Love unites everything.[35] For the political analogy this process of unification is significant, but political unity can be presented as taking many forms. Is the ascendancy of Love in the political cycle best represented by unification under a single ruler, or by the acts of political deliberation and agreement through which he was elected to his post? Many readings of these fragments follow Vlastos in reading the description of succession of office-holding (DK 31 B 17.27–31) as indicating a democratic arrangement.[36] The Strasbourg fragment identifies this order as *kosmos*, although the suggestion that Love generates *kosmos* is a reconstruction.[37]

---

[31] One should also note the persistent linkage of gold with kingship in Herodotus' kingship narratives, cf. the tale of Egyptian pharaoh Amasis at 2.172, the origin myths of the Scythian kings (4.5–7); Kurke 1995 explores the 'language of metals' with an emphasis on the development of coinage.

[32] Arieti 1995: 121–22.

[33] Ascribing 'first finder' status to Deioces for the invention of court protocol is a further departure from historical probability (Asheri 2007: 150–51 points out that the Medes imitated the Assyrians).

[34] See Chapter 3 on *diakosmêsis*, in this volume.

[35] DK 31 B 35.3–6 and B 135: Graham 2005: 233–35 suggests that the interactions of love and strife have a military context, thus further linking *kosmos* language back to its military origins.

[36] Vlastos 1947; see also Horky 2016.   [37] Graham 2006: 350–53, 424–25.

Darius returns to this problem with his contribution to the constitutional debate (3.82), in which he argues that monarchy (and not the democracy suggested by his fellow-conspirator Otanes, 3.80) provides the ultimate form of political unification. Herodotus appears here to make more use of the thought of Heraclitus, with echoes of Heraclitean fragments underpinning the speech. For Darius it is clear that it is the exceptional character of the great leader which makes the process of unification possible. One great man is worth countless individuals (ἀνδρὸς γὰρ ἑνὸς τοῦ ἀρίστου οὐδὲν ἄμεινον ἂν φανείη, 3.82.2), echoing Heraclitus DK 22 B 49 (εἷς [ἐμοὶ] μύριοι, ἐὰν ἄριστος ἦι). This provides a solution to one problem for the *kosmos*–polis analogy, the need for a *basileus* to mirror the place of the god of the heavens (whether Zeus or Ahura Mazda) in the divine order. But it was a solution difficult to implement in the practical arrangements of the polis. One possible practical solution was to retain a *basileus* figure with attenuated power, as with the Spartan kings or the Athenian *basileus archôn*, who fulfilled the ritual aspects of this role but held no significant political power in his own right.[38]

The Athenian comic dramatist Aristophanes takes a different approach in depicting a democratic reimagining of the political and cosmic order. The Athenian citizen, with his capacity to dispense justice, considers himself the equal of Zeus and his mirror in the human order. While tragedy too offers parallels between human politics and divine ordering, Aristophanes' comedy makes inventive use of different intellectual approaches and provides some context for understanding how the traditional and newer models of the *kosmos* were related to each other within the political context of Athens.[39] For Aristophanes at least, the traditional cosmology is more closely linked to democratic thinking than newer ideas (which include those of both Presocratics and Sophists), usually presented as the opinion of intellectuals who pose a threat to the cohesion of the democratic city.

This equation is made explicit in the *Wasps*, where the elderly citizen Philocleon gleefully describes the power that jurors hold through analogies with kingship and with Zeus. The status of Zeus as king of the gods is

---

[38] Although the archonship did confer benefits, such as membership of the Areopagus Council, and presumably other opportunities for personal advancement. [Dem.] 59 recounts the story of an unqualified holder of the position, which suggests that it was inherently desirable within the framework of Athenian magistracies, even if conferring nothing like the power of a traditional king.

[39] Richard Seaford (especially in Seaford 2012) explores the construction of space and time in *kosmos* and city and their representation in tragedy, with an emphasis on Aeschylus and tragedy rather than comedy.

invoked to explain the status of the Athenian citizen. Aristophanes' characters address only gods, particularly Zeus, as *basileus*, whereas they address a wider range of gods, heroes and human masters as *anax*.[40] Philocleon compares his *archê* as Athenian citizen juror to that of a king:

> Right from the start I'll demonstrate [ἀποδείξω]
> that our sovereignty [τῆς ἡμετέρας . . . βασιλείας] is lesser than no other.
> (Aristophanes, *Wasps* 548–49, tr. after Henderson)

The king he has in mind is not a human king but Zeus, an ambiguous comparison in that this power is envisaged in destructive terms:[41]

> So don't I wield great authority [μεγάλην ἀρχήν], no less than that of Zeus?
> I'm even spoken of in the same way as Zeus. For instance, if we're in an uproar,
> every passer-by says, 'Zeus the King [ὦ Ζεῦ βασιλεῦ], the jury's really thundering!'   (Aristophanes, *Wasps* 619–24, tr. after Henderson)

The activities of the citizen jurors have the same impact as those of Zeus when he hurls his thunderbolt; when they create disturbance or become disorderly (as *thorubos* implies a disorderly group), the impact on those outside the courts is the same as that of divine thunder.

With this, Aristophanes subverts the traditional *kosmos*–polis analogy, presenting the ordinary democratic citizen claiming the role traditionally allotted to kings and claimed by law-givers such as Solon.

It is far from clear that Aristophanes endorses this view; his point seems to be that the replacement of divine justice and judgement by the whims of the angry but pliable elderly Wasps is risky and brings the danger of disturbance to the city. Aristophanes represents his character's position as an example or even distortion of the position that a pro-democrat might take in using the *kosmos*–polis analogy, an extreme and absurd claim that every Athenian citizen in the democracy is effectively Zeus.

The *Wasps* dramatises both the direct relationship of individual citizen to polis within the context of participatory democracy, through the contrasted father and son characters Philocleon and Bdelycleon, and competition between the different Athenian ideologies which they represent.[42] The

---

[40] Zeus as *basileus*: *Clouds* 2 and 153; *Wasps* 624, *Birds* 223, *Frogs* 1278, *Wealth* 1095: the Clouds as *pambasileiai*, *Clouds* 357: other gods as *wanax*: Apollo (*Birds* 80); Heracles (*Peace* 180, *Lysistrata* 296, *Acharnians* 94, *Frogs* 298); Poseidon (*Knights* 551).

[41] MacDowell 1971 *ad loc.* suggests that the reference to thunder has authoritarian overtones at 671 and *Acharnians* 531.

[42] Konstan 1985: 30–33; Carrière 2004: 67–68; Olson 1996: 145–49. Hutchinson 2011: 62–67 adds a differentiation between structure of oikos/polis relationship conceptualised by each.

father Philocleon is crafty and resourceful, as an Athenian citizen should be (which links him firmly to Odysseus), but also devoted to participation in the jury courts.[43] Although he is defeated in the *agôn*, and re-educated in the second half of the play through the in-house trial and attendance at an aristocratic-style symposium, his final rejection of the new lifestyle suggests that Aristophanes may have some affection for the traditional Athenian mentality that his character represents.

The son Bdelycleon, on the other hand, is described by the chorus as a hater of the city and the demos (ἄνδρα μισόπολιν, *Wasps* 411; μισόδημε, 473) and a proponent of tyranny (τυραννίς ἐστιν ἐμφανής, 417; 463–65) and monarchy (μοναρχίας ἐραστά, 473–74). His (oligarchical, anti-democratic) political sympathies are shown by his adoption of Spartan and Persian fashions (466 and 475–76), which he later attempts to impose on Philocleon as part of his re-education (1133–69). Just as Strepsiades and Pheidippides in the *Clouds* mapped different approaches to education, the father–son pair here shows the different attitudes to political participation that belonged to two competing ideologies.[44]

Philocleon delivers his own take on the *kosmos*–polis analogy. He regards his status as an active Athenian citizen as being comparable to that of a god, in particular to Zeus, king of the gods (619–27).[45] He claims that the (collective) power exercised by an Athenian juror is like that of a monarch (548–49), and unlike other forms of civic authority is not subject to scrutiny (587).[46] The idea of the king as a super-citizen, the person who most fully displays the qualities and capabilities of the ideal Athenian citizen, emerging in Euripides' plays of the same era, is pushed to its (comic) limits in the person of Philocleon. The citizen-king can be seen simultaneously as a god and a tyrant, just as Theseus' demos has been established in an ambivalent and undefined *monarchia* (Eur. *Supp.* 355). The use of Zeus as king and tyrant as a comparator for Athenian rulers was a familiar device in Old Comedy, at least discernible from fragments of Cratinus and Eupolis where Zeus and Pericles are linked.[47] Bdelycleon, however, rejects the idea of the citizen-king as instantiated in his father and the likes of the wasp jurors; he inverts and replaces it with the idea of citizen-slaves (*Wasps* 515–19) prostrating themselves to the demagogues

---

[43] Dover 1972: 125–27.　　[44] Whitman 1964: 143–66.　　[45] Davie 1979: 166.

[46] Philocleon's claim may be absurd because, when acting as a juror, he is one of a collective of Athenian citizens, without a monarch's individual power. But his claim underscores the tension between individual and collective that is under examination in this play.

[47] Bakola 2010: 223; Carrière 1979: 210 and 30–31; Cratinus, *Chirones* Fr. 258 K.–A.

(προσκυνεῖς, 516); Philocleon gloated that defendants have to supplicate him as a juror (ἱκετεύουσίν θ᾽ ὑποκύπτοντες, 555).

However, when Aristophanes does make explicit use of Presocratic cosmology, it is not voiced by his everyman characters, representatives of democracy, but by characters set in opposition to them or who present a danger to their activities. The characters Euripides (*Thesmophoriazusae*) and Socrates (*Clouds*) are both presented as outside the main currents of Athenian thought, and the objects of suspicion to fellow citizens. Strepsiades the Athenian is bemused by the cosmological thought and intellectual activity of Socrates and his fellow members of the Phrontisterion; the implication is that the education provided leads to the kind of sophistry displayed in the *agôn* between the two arguments. But, in the persons of the Clouds, traditional religion and cosmology assert themselves (although the Clouds themselves, as daughters of Zeus, remain something of an innovation). The *Clouds* presents an alternative cosmology which is revealed to be nothing more than a misinterpretation of the traditional one; the natural phenomena of the clouds, worshipped by intellectuals, are revealed to be the daughters of Zeus.

The Euripides of the *Thesmophoriazusae* is depicted as the adherent of new cosmological thinking, reverencing Aether as a deity and expounding cosmological theory, strongly reminiscent of accounts of primal separation in Presocratic cosmogonies, to explain his novel ideas (*Thesm.* 14–19).[48] Euripides' religious and cosmological views are presented in just enough detail that they can be contrasted with those of the other, more conventional, characters. His views in the prologue are sharply contrasted with those of the everyman character, the In-law, who opens the play with an invocation to Zeus (Ὦ Ζεύ, 1).[49] They also set him against the women of the play, participating in the traditional fertility rites of the Thesmophoria. New cosmological thinking is presented, in Aristophanes' world at least, as alien to the democratic city and its collective practices. On the other hand, the Athenian audience is expected to recognise allusions to cosmology; if Clements' interpretation is correct, sophisticated allusions to Empedocles'

---

[48] Ashley Clements makes a strong case for reading the *Thesmophoriazusae* as an exploration of philosophical and cosmological thought, interpreting Euripides' *mythos* of Aether and separation as a response to and reuse of Empedocles' cosmogony (Clements 2014: 22–27), contra Sedley 2007: 54 n. 73. But this brief reference could equally evoke the ideas of Diogenes of Apollonia (DK 64 B 2 and B 5), or even the Derveni papyrus (P. Derv. Col. XIII.4)

[49] Choosing the right god to swear by is emphasised in this play by the careful use of different gods by different characters, such as the goddesses Demeter and Aglauros for women or those pretending to be women. Euripides also swears by Zeus (71 and 1125) so has not completely abandoned traditional beliefs.

and Parmenides' cosmological thought could be understood by an
Athenian audience more sophisticated than the Athenians Aristophanes
presents on stage.[50]

The question remains as to whether there was a democratic discourse of
cosmology in which Presocratic ideas of cosmic balance and equity were
incorporated into the language of Athenian politics. Unfortunately, the
evidence for this, as for any complex theorising of Athenian democracy in
the fifth century, is no longer extant. Cynthia Farrar has attempted to
ground such a discourse in the thought of Protagoras and Atomists such as
Democritus, in a detailed exploration of the available evidence.[51] However,
some of the most compelling evidence for such an argument is in
Protagoras' great speech in Plato's dialogue, a fourth-century response to
Athenian political debate rather than a fifth-century contribution to it.

If the argument of the 'Great Speech' can be attributed to Protagoras (as
Farrar suggests that at least some of it can), we see first in its zoogony
a further instance of the theme of the Athenian everyman granted equal
powers to order his society. Prometheus and Epimetheus are commanded
to create order and divide capacities appropriately among living creatures
(προσέταξαν Προμηθεῖ καὶ Ἐπιμηθεῖ κοσμῆσαί τε καὶ νεῖμαι δυνάμεις
ἑκάστοις ὡς πρέπει, *Protagoras* 320d4–6).[52] But Epimetheus bungles the
distribution and leaves humans without natural capacity to protect themselves. While Prometheus' theft of fire and skill from the gods gives
humans some protection, their lack of political skill makes it impossible
for them to cooperate in communal defence. Eventually Zeus sends
Hermes to distribute the additional capacities of Justice and Shame to
humans, so that they can protect themselves by living in order and friendship in their *poleis* (ἵν᾽ εἶεν πόλεων κόσμοι τε καὶ δεσμοὶ φιλίας συναγωγοί,
322c2–3). Protagoras' analysis of his myth makes it clear that this political
skill given by Zeus was given to each citizen, not to expert leaders; it must
therefore include some capacity for creating order, rather than simply
continuing in the overall ordering.[53]

---

[50] Clements 2014: 77–87 goes on to argue that Euripides' presentation of cosmology in the prologue re-
enacts the mistaken thinking of mortals in Parmenides' *doxa* (e.g. Parmenides DK 28 B 10–11). Of
course, Aristophanes could present such details for the amusement of a small proportion of the
possible audience.

[51] Farrar 1988: 77–98.

[52] Cf. Diogenes of Apollonia DK 64 B 3 (ὥστε πάντων μέτρα ἔχειν ... διακείμενα ὡς ἀνυστὸν
κάλλιστα).

[53] The complex dramatic scenario of the dialogue, with the crowd of sophists, has already introduced
both senses of *kosmos*; the group moves ἐν κόσμῳ (Pl. *Prt.* 315b5–6) and also ἐν κύκλῳ (b7), like
troops manoeuvring on the battlefield, or a chorus on stage.

In presenting Athenian juror citizens as everyman a Zeus, Aristophanes supports the view that there is a fifth-century origin to such an argument, even if some details are modified in Plato's fourth-century purposes. It therefore seems that the *kosmos*–polis analogy was subject to innovation in Athenian discourse of the fifth century by changing the holder of the human position from that of a single ruler to that of an everyman citizen, granted power akin to that of Zeus over the natural world. This change to the analogy is more securely attested than the direct influence of Presocratic cosmological thought on practical politics, and the replacement of anthropomorphic gods by more abstract natural forces; the evidence of Aristophanes is that there was no easy contact between the two modes of thought.

However, fourth-century reinterpretations of the analogy changed this. While Aristophanes had depicted his Athenian everyman identifying himself with Zeus, more conservative fourth-century thinkers rejected this identification, turning instead to the possibilities of fusing new philosophical cosmologies with the existing *kosmos* language of archaic but revered ancient constitutions, and placing increasing emphasis on order established by leaders.

8.4 *Kosmos* in Early Civic Titles

The resurgence of *kosmos* language in fourth-century Greek political thought does not, however, seem to draw on the democratic possibilities of Presocratic thought found by Vlastos, even though apparently recognised as such by Aristophanes. Writers such as Plato take up *kosmos* language to draw together the idea of the macrocosm contained in the *kosmos*–polis analogy and with a nod to the continuing use of *kosmos* language in the political vocabulary of the archaic and aristocratic constitutions that became positive examples for such political theorists.

Kosmos language and imagery had never been restricted to literary texts, as they were embedded in the political language and structures of archaic cities and transmitted through documentation of *poleis* structures in historical and philosophical texts – more directly, through epigraphic evidence.[54] The presence of *kosmos* terms in the names of magistracies and priesthoods of such constitutions suggests that the idea that political leaders, typically kings and generals, were responsible for the ordering and arrangement of the people featured broadly in the Greek political

[54] See Gagarin 1986: 81–86.

imagination. In tune with the evidence from early poetry, such terminology clusters around religious and military organisation, and is particularly prevalent in Sparta and Cretan cities, political entities that were already seen as archaic and revered for being so in the fourth century BCE.[55] The nomenclature of magistracies and political arrangements made the *kosmos*–*polis* analogy explicit within aristocratic or mixed constitutional forms of government established prior to the re-purposing of *kosmos* language by philosophers, but often depending on the (Homeric) military sense of *kosmos*.

Sparta's political arrangements preserved archaic forms, such as the continuing dual kingship. Although the kings had relatively little political power (some kings being more successful than others) their authority was centred on military functions. As Aristotle notes in *Politics* 3.14, Spartan kingship served as a kind of powerful and permanent military command held through descent (στρατηγία τις αὐτοκρατόρων καὶ ἀίδιος, 3.14.1285b7–8; στρατηγία κατὰ γένος ἀίδιος, 1285b27–28). Aristotle identifies this as similar to Agememnon's kingship; as we saw in Homer, military organisation was frequently described using *kosmos* language; the Spartan king, especially when leading a campaign, was as much a *kosmetôr* as the mythical Dioscuri, and Menelaus from whom he claimed descent.

However, Herodotus' account of Spartan kingship brings out another aspect of Spartan kingship, its religious aspect as a hereditary priesthood. The Spartan kings served as priests of Zeus Ouraneus and Zeus Lacedaemoneus (*Histories* 6.56.1), linking them to Zeus and linking Zeus to the city. They also had a special status with the Delphic Oracle, which granted them privileged access to the oracle and thus another channel of communication with the gods (6.57.2–4). In contrast to Herodotus' interest in Spartan kingship, Aristotle emphasises the limits to royal power in Sparta exercised by the ephors, although he does not regard this as a positive influence, but a demagogic corruption of what would otherwise have been an aristocracy (*Pol.* 2.9.1270b13–17). Even so, Aristotle's focus on the political and military aspects of kingship results in his undervaluing the religious function of the kings

<hr>

[55] Crete is somewhat problematic, as its many distinct *poleis* are occasionally collapsed into a single 'Cretan constitution' when invoked as an exemplar in political thought contexts. There was a confederation of the cities in the fourth century BCE, but prior to this the cities had their own constitutions, although these may have contained common or interchangeable elements. See Perlman 1992 and Huxley 1971.

within Spartan society, according to Paul Cartledge.[56] The kings' function in communicating with the gods on behalf of the city was fundamental to their role, and explains how they could be seen to hold the Zeus-analogous position in the Spartan *politeia*.[57] Pausanias' description of the temple of Zeus Cosmetas provides further evidence linking cosmic ordering to the kings (*Description of Greece* 3.17.4). This was the main temple of Zeus on the Spartan acropolis, and again seems to have had a military aspect, in that it served as a repository for dedications by victorious Spartan generals (and not just kings). Two of its statues of Victory were dedicated by the naval commander Lysander, one after his victory over Athens at Aegospotami. Herodotus also problematises the presence of this apparently non-Greek (in his taxonomy) office within a Greek polis structure, drawing comparisons with Asia (6.58.2), Persia (6.59) and Egypt (6.60) in his attempt to understand Sparta and to present it as somehow 'other' in comparison with more typical *poleis*.

The central role of the king in such versions of the analogy would prove problematic for classical *poleis* such as Athens where such rule in practice was bound with the negative form of tyranny. One solution to this problem was to place the city's cosmic ordering in the mythical past, so that a founder king, colonist or synoecist could perform this role within the political imaginary, without entrusting such power to a real leader. The attenuated power of the remaining 'kings' of Greek cities, whether the dual kings of Sparta or the *basileus archôn* of Athens, shows the power remaining in this language. However, the use of *kosmos* language in the political terminology of Greek cities suggests that it was more prevalent in cities like Sparta which retained archaic aspects to their constitutions or were aristocracies rather than democracies. Outside the Greek mainland, cities in Crete and western Greece used a variety of *kosmos*-based terms to identify their senior magistrates. These were the types of constitution that would come to be highly praised in the fourth-century discourse of 'ancestral constitutions'; the presence of *kosmos* language effectively serves as an indicator that this is not a democratic *politeia*.

Kosmos language in the titles of magistrates was a feature of several older Cretan *politeiai*, with the fifth-century BCE Gortyn law codes and other

---

[56] Cartledge 2001: 55–67.
[57] Cf. Parker 1989 and Xen. *Lac.* 13.2–5, 15.2–3. Plato in his account of Spartan kingship places great emphasis on military and political arrangements made by the kings, again with frequent use of the verb *diakosmeô*; although this is an important term throughout the *Laws*, nowhere is it more frequently used than this section (685b4, 686a3, 687a5, introduced at 626a1 and 677c8).

early legal inscriptions providing firm evidence for this.[58] In Gortyn, a senior board of magistrates were titled the *kosmoi*.[59] Although there is no full description of the function of this magistracy, the surviving fragments of the Gortyn codes report their role in managing or preventing disputes over the transmission of property, handling issues such as the remarriage of heiresses, a function handled in Athens by the archons and in Sparta by the kings.[60] They were not to participate in legal action during their term of office.[61] Other evidence suggests that they handled a range of administrative functions that maintained legal and political order, and that there might be restrictions on holding the powerful office (as at Dreros).[62] Aristotle identifies the *kosmoi* as military leaders and substitutes for former kings (2.10.1272a8–10). This reinforces the close link drawn in Athenian political thought between Cretan constitutions and Sparta; Crete was seen as a possible origin of the Spartan constitution, and the same good and bad qualities were found in both.[63] This linkage perhaps explains some of the willingness by fourth-century analysts to treat Sparta as an example of both *eunomia* and *eukosmia*, with the *kosmos* language of Cretan politics being transferred to Sparta.

Both the implication of the code itself (Col. I.51–55) and Aristotle's discussion ('They choose the *kosmoi* not from all but from certain *genē*', *Pol.* 2.10.1272a33–34) suggest that the office of *kosmos* at Gortyn (and so probably in other cities) was restricted to certain classes, tribes or other social groups, as might be expected in an aristocratic constitution.[64]

---

[58] Cf. Willetts 1967: 10–11; Spyridakis 1969; Perlman 1992; Gagarin and Perlman 2016: 67–73. For the Gortyn Law Codes, I employ the edition of Willetts 1967 (checked against Gagarin and Perlman 2016). Other Cretan cities for which there is epigraphic evidence for *kosmoi* in the archaic period include Dreros (DHR 1 450/*SEG* 27.620; see Gagarin and Perlman 2016: 200–207); Lyttos (*SEG* 35.991); and Axos (Koerner 105). The terminology enjoyed a resurgence in the Hellenistic period, for which abundant epigraphic evidence survives: Willetts 1955: 117–44. In the third century BCE, Itanos, a city controlled by the Ptolemies, had *kosmetores* (*IC* 3.IV.3.22, 4.14, 6.8, 7.34; see Spyridakis 1970 and Willetts 1955: 126–28).

[59] They are also referred to using the participle *kosmiontes*, as at Col. I.50–51 Willetts (cf. Gagarin and Perlman 2016: 338–45) and using the verb *kosmeô* at Col. V.5–6 Willetts.

[60] Cols. VIII.53–IX.1 Willetts; Willetts 1967: 26–27, 32; Gagarin and Perlman 2016: 397–99. Willetts points out that the *kosmoi* manage situations that deviate from the normal practice, cf. Willetts 1955: 105–10.

[61] I.51–5; Willetts 1967: 57, Gagarin and Perlman 2016: 344–45.

[62] Dreros DHR 1; see Gagarin 1986: 81–83, Gagarin and Perlman 2016: 203–5. Willetts 1967: 108–15 surveys evidence from the fifth century for the legal functions of *kosmoi*.

[63] Aristotle *Politics* 2.9.1270b22–23: 'it seems and indeed it is said that in most respects the *politeia* of the Spartans copies the Cretan *politeia*'; Plato's Athenian Stranger describes the laws of Sparta and Crete as 'brothers' (*Laws* 682e10–683a2), at the start of an argument in which the Spartan constitution develops in an iterative process rather than through a single founding event attributable to Lycurgus alone.

[64] Spyridakis 1969.

Aristotle is concerned that this results in a narrow section of interests represented in the Gerousia, a council made up of former *kosmoi*. He also describes complex mechanisms by which the authority of the *kosmoi* could be bypassed, effective temporary dissolutions of the *politeia* (1272b1–16). But while the full details of the function of the *kosmoi*, their selection and the limits to their power, remain unknown, their special status within the polis and their role in stabilising distributive justice links them to the functions of the archaic *basileis*, even if they do not hold that title.

Beyond Crete, the Italian polis of Locri also used *kosmos* language in its political nomenclature, with a magistrate or magistrates titled *kosmopolis*. Its original, aristocratic, constitution was also regarded as an ancient one, the work of legendary law-giver Zaleucus.[65] Aristotle mentions it briefly in rounding up such constitutions in *Politics* 2 (*Pol.* 2.7.1266b19), but it was also the subject of a now-lost *politeia*. However, although Locri was an ancient polis, it underwent significant upheaval in the fourth century BCE, when it was ruled by the tyrant Dionysius II of Syracuse during his exile from his home city; he was expelled in 346, leading to a period of stasis resulting in the establishment of a new, more democratic constitution. It is probable that references by Polybius to a magistrate called the *kosmopolis* (12.16.6) are linked to this original aristocratic constitution. Polybius describes a case in which two young men were disputing the ownership of a slave, each claiming that the other had stolen the slave. The court called in the *kosmopolis* to adjudicate, and the *kosmopolis* decreed that the case should be tried according to the laws of Zaleucus, which meant that the plaintiff and the *kosmopolis* presented their interpretations of the law to the Thousand (the council of Locri) each with a noose around his neck, with the loser being hanged. The harsh retributive justice in this story does suggest either an old origin or determined archaism; however, as Walbank notes, many epigraphic references to this magistracy are from the later Roman period.[66] Significantly, the character Timaeus in Plato's *Timaeus* is presented as a leading citizen of Locri; he has held the greatest offices (τὰς μεγίστας μὲν ἀρχάς τε καὶ τιμὰς τῶν ἐν τῇ πόλει) in

---

[65] Arist. Frs. 547–48 (Rose³), Hansen and Nielsen 2004: 275. The Sicilian historian Timaeus doubted the existence of Zaleucus (*FGrH* 566 F 130).

[66] The reference occurs in a fragment of Polybius Book 12, in which Polybius criticises another historian (most likely Timaeus of Tauromenium, *FGrH* 566, but possibly Ephorus). Walbank (1957–79: Vol. 2, 363) cites Roman-era inscriptions from Thasos (*IG* xii.8.386 and 459), Lyttos (*IC* I Lyttos 55) and Cibyra (*IGR* iv.908), suggesting that the title from Locri influenced other constitutions.

a city of superlative lawfulness (εὐνομωτάτης ... πόλεως, *Ti.* 20a1–5).[67]
If the office of *kosmopolis* existed in this early period, Timaeus may even
have held it. Plato presents Timaeus as someone who has both held the
highest political office and reached the peak of philosophical activity, an
unusual combination that perhaps makes him the closest to
a philosopher-king of any character in the dialogues.[68] Timaeus also
describes the activities of the demiurge; *demiourgos* itself was a title of
magistrates, equivalent to the Cretan *kosmos*, in some cities.[69]

8.5 Fourth-Century BCE Responses

It is in the fourth century BCE that a connection between Presocratic
cosmology and traditional usage becomes more apparent in political
use of the *kosmos*–polis analogy. Thus, Plato adopts the language of
Cretan constitutions for his cosmology in the *Timaeus*, and also to
describe the institutional arrangements of Atlantis in the *Critias*.
Isocrates uses *kosmos* language when praising the ancestral constitution
of Athens.[70] Although there is an increasing literary use of the analogy,
however, it is unclear whether authors other than Plato are using the
philosophical connotations of *kosmos* language, or simply appealing to
the Homeric and heroic idea of the leader as the marshal of order.
Peter Rhodes suggests that the concept of *kosmos* is linked with Sparta,
citing Herodotus' report of claims that the Delphic Oracle gave
Lycurgus the present Spartan *politeia* (τὸν νῦν κατεστεῶτα κόσμον,
1.65.4) as established via the Delphic Oracle's advice.[71] As with the
Protagoras, the importance of *kosmos* is signalled in the dramatic
introduction; Socrates announces that he is arranged for the speeches,
a line that is usually translated using the 'adorn' or 'decorate' sense

[67] Cf. Pind. *Ol.* 10.13. Lampert and Planeaux (1998: 90–95) explore this while attempting to determine the dramatic date of the dialogue; they acknowledge that Plato's character Timaeus may be either historical or fictional. Cf. Timaeus *FGrH* 566 F 130; Ephorus *FGrH* 70 F 139; Diod. Sic. 12.20.1.
[68] So in the sense that Timaeus is one, the philosopher-kings have not entirely disappeared from *Timaeus-Critias*, even though they are absent from the apparent recap of the *Republic* at *Ti.* 17c1–19a9.
[69] Willetts 1955: 124–26, citing inscriptions from Polyrhenia (*IC* 2.23.7, third century BCE) and Olous (*IC* I 22.4, third and second centuries BCE).
[70] Isoc. *Panath.* 116 (ὅ τε κόσμος ὁ τῆς πολιτείας τῆς πρότερον ὑπαρχούσης), *Areopag.* 66 and 70; cf. *kosmos* as orderly lifestyle: *Antid.* 228 (κοσμιώτατα ζῶντας), 144 (κοσμίως καὶ τεταγμένως βεβιωκότα) and 162 (κοσμιώτερον βεβιωκέναι), and the use of *kosmos* language for monarchical arrangements (*Ad Nic.* 31, *Nic.* 38).
[71] Rhodes 1993: 504–5; Kurt Raaflaub, surveying the political ideas of early philosophers, also identifies this use of *kosmos* as Doric (Raaflaub 2000: 50 n. 61).

that *kosmeô* has when used to describe the appearance of individuals (κεκοσμημένος, *Ti.* 20c1).[72]

Kosmos language begins to appear in a broader range of contexts in Athenian politics, in published courtroom speeches and documentary sources. Demosthenes often uses *kosmos* as a synonym for *politeia*; a typical phrase is πᾶς ὁ τῆς πόλεως καὶ τῶν νόμων κόσμος (Dem. 25.19).[73] The rhetorical impact of these formulae is to suggest the enormity of the disorder threatened by the conduct of the accused.

In Athens, however, fourth-century sources record an official not named in earlier accounts, in an institution whose history before the mid fourth century is not well attested. Aristotle notes the arrangements for the military training of young men about to come of age, the ephebes, who are managed by officials known as *kosmêtai* (*Ath. Pol.* 42.2).[74] This must point to the original sense of *kosmos* language, the domain of military ordering. There are no references to this role prior to Aristotle's text, but this was an office that flourished in Hellenistic Athens and into the Roman period; the question of whether the formal *ephebeia* existed prior to Athenian reforms of the mid fourth century remains disputed.[75] These later *kosmêtai* were honoured with statues.[76] However, the metaphorical use of *kosmos* language to describe different kinds of order, especially public behaviour that depends on personal self-control, also features in fourth-century texts. *Eukosmia* is linked to philosophical approaches in that it seems to be one of the concerns of education (Pl. *Prt.* 325e1, Xen. *Cyr.* 1.2.4). The city-soul and city-*kosmos* analogies can be collapsed; *kosmos* imagery can be used to describe the macrocosm, the polis or the personal order of its citizens and their property.

Aeschines uses *eukosmia* to describe the personal qualities of good order and self-control that were lacking in Timarchus, qualities guaranteed by the laws on education (*In Ti.* 8.4); Aeschines also refers to laws established by Solon to regulate the *eukosmia* of speakers in the assembly (*In Ctes.* 2.5),

---

[72] A further link here is that the dialogues are set during the Athenian festival of the Great Panathenaea, the procession for which is described using *kosmos* language by Thucydides; the tyrants order the procession, which is in effect a microcosm of Athenian society (1.20.2, 6.57.1) (cf. Solon Fr. 4.9–10 West, above). The speeches of *Timaeus* and *Critias* permit Socrates to review alternative constructions of Athens.

[73] Further examples are 26.27, 13.28 and possibly 60.24, but Demosthenes also uses the term to mean good order of character (27.10, 18.216, 60.36), and the orderly arrangement of material goods (50.7, 50.34).

[74] Rhodes 1993: 504–5; Kranz 1955: 29–30.

[75] *RO* 88; Rhodes and Osborne 2003: 440–49 gives the background to renewed fourth-century enthusiasm for military training and for the use of *kosmos* language.

[76] Some of these statues survive in Athens; see Graindor 1915.

and the behaviour of women (*In Ti.* 183.2); the regulation of a variety of forms of public behaviour, conduct in the agora or the behaviour of women and children, is also named *eukosmia* by Aristotle in the *Politics* (*Pol.* 4.15.1299b16 and b19).

That both the Homeric/heroic and the philosophical senses of *kosmos* as ordering were in play can be seen in the parallel accounts of Plato's *Timaeus* and *Critias*. In these dialogues, the eponymous narrators describe the ordering of the *kosmos* and the life it contains, and the political arrangements of two cities. The relationship between the political narrative of the *Critias* and the cosmogonic narrative of the *Timaeus* is now receiving more scholarly attention than it has in the past, with more recent philosophical surveys of the *Timaeus* accepting that the relationship between these disparate parts may have some purpose.[77]

While a full survey of the complex cosmogony of the *Timaeus* is beyond the scope of this chapter, it is possible to highlight some interesting points of contact in the use of *kosmos* language in the narratives of both dialogues. The role of Timaeus himself as a magistrate of a city which used *kosmos* language in its political titles has already been noted. Such language is repeated throughout his speech, both in the use of *kosmos* as a noun to describe the universe created by the demiurge, and also in the use of verbs for ordering. Timaeus is aware that the same thing is sometimes called 'the entire heaven' and sometimes the '*kosmos*', and may have other names (*Ti.* 28b), and he uses them somewhat interchangeably throughout his long account of its creation. Timaeus is clear about who performs acts of ordering that result in the generation of the *kosmos* and the life forms within it. Acts of *diakosmêsis* are performed by the demiurge in making the heaven (37d5) and the principal substances from which it was constructed (69c1), and the universe is identified as something that has been ordered (διακοσμηθὲν, 53a7). The demiurge hands on the task of creating secondary life forms to the *daimones*, and their work too is described as *diakosmêsis*, for example in creating the mouths of living creatures (75d7).

However, in line with the use of *diakosmeô* by historians, Critias too makes much use of the verb in his account of the creation of primeval Athens and Atlantis. In this mytho-historical narrative, this verb identifies the work of divine agents in ordering societies. According to the Egyptian priest who reveals Athens' true history to Solon, the goddess was

---

[77] Osborne 1996: 185–91 suggests that the two dialogues represent different levels of intellectual activity; Johansen 1998, now Johansen 2004 and Broadie 2012, continue this process. For Plato's *Laws*, see Chapter 6 of this volume, by Brisson.

responsible for the arrangement and foundation of the city (ταύτην οὖν δὴ τότε σύμπασαν τὴν διακόσμησιν καὶ σύνταξιν ἡ θεὸς προτέρους ὑμᾶς διακοσμήσασα κατῴκισεν, *Ti.* 24c4–5). Great emphasis is placed on the inculcation of virtue in the citizens, suggesting that *eukosmia* is also the outcome of this process. Poseidon, in turn, arranges the land of Atlantis after his own taste (διεκόσμησεν, *Criti.* 113e3), and its political arrangements are described as τὰ ... διακοσμηθέντα (119c1–2). The true farmers of Athens also set the land in order (111e2).[78]

8.6 Conclusion

The connection between the command of Zeus over the universe and the ruler over his city was a natural analogy for early Greek thought. Developments in both the conceptualisation of the universe, and growing interest in its origins, provided a new way for the analogy to be used, but it was the replacement of Zeus by the Athenian or ordinary citizen, in Aristophanes' plays, or Zeus's gift of judging capacity to such citizens, in the accounts given to Protagoras by Plato, that show one way in which the analogy could be redeployed in the context of democratic Athens. Both Plato and Aristophanes, however, are somewhat hostile to this use of the analogy and present it as a problematic claim made by participants in and partisans of democracy. Aristophanes provides further evidence that novel cosmological thought was not linked to democratic Athens.

Plato's inventive reuse of the analogy, using it to link his cosmology and political thought in the *Timaeus-Critias*, and echoed in the *Laws*, draws on the political language not of Athenian democracy but of the conservative and aristocratic constitutions of Cretan cities that persisted from archaic times. By combining the *kosmos*–polis analogy with the city-soul analogy, other fourth-century writers developed a *kosmos*–soul analogy that provided a powerful critique of character to deploy in rhetorical contexts. Plato's contemporaries thus used *kosmos* language conservatively, describing the ordering of the individual soul in exceptional individuals (or the lack of such ordering, in the case of Aeschines' Timarchus). The triple analogy between soul, city and *kosmos* thus provided a route by which the exceptional individual could be further praised as an exemplar for imitation. The rich use of *kosmos* language by fourth-century BCE writers thus combines both tradition and innovation in the *kosmos*–polis analogy.

---

[78] For earlier uses of διακοσμέω, see Chapter 3 in this volume.

CHAPTER 9

Cosmic Choruses
Metaphor and Performance

Renaud Gagné*

9.1 Introduction

The movement of the stars is a powerful provocation for reflection on the nature of the world. The awesome difference in scale that separates human perception from the changing patterns of the night sky has always invited a sustained flow of thought and meaning. Nothing is more ubiquitous and visible than the shining stars in the darkness. But vision alone cannot discern the course of the celestial bodies. Progressing at a pace that escapes the eye, the stars move beyond the capacity of our senses. The domains of time and space they occupy are radically other. Yet the alternation of the days and the seasons marks their inexorable change of position. Following regular principles of recurrence, the invisible movement of the stars points to the existence of a hidden order of things. It embodies the very notion of *kosmos*.[1]

For many centuries, ancient Greek culture imagined the movement of the stars as a choral dance. The dance of the heavenly bodies was pictured as the archetype of every other *choros*.[2] That figure of the astral chorus was revisited again and again in different contexts. It was appropriated by authors across the genres and given new meanings and resonances in a long chain of creative reconfigurations. Images of the *kosmos* channelled by this figure from the domain of poetic performance could be made to reflect on any number of aspects of the world or human activity. The

* The research for this chapter has benefited from the generous support of the Swedish Collegium for Advanced Study (SCAS) in Uppsala, the Riksbankens Jubileumsfond and the Leverhulme Trust. Different versions of the text were presented at Cambridge, Princeton and Durham. I would like to thank the people present at those occasions, together with Neil Hopkinson and David Konstan, for their comments and criticism.
[1] Cf. the contributions of Brisson (Chapter 6), Sauron (Chapter 11) and Shearin (Chapter 12) to this volume.
[2] See e.g. schol. Theoc. 13.25. Cf. Mullen 1982: 225–30.

'tenor' of the metaphor, to use I. A. Richards's venerable but still handy terminology – the stars – pointed to a stable, universally known phenomenon and a potent symbol of higher realms. The 'vehicle' of the metaphor – choral dance – is an even more flexible referent and an index to the whole register of collective action.[3] While the distinctive unity of the metaphor makes it a recognisable element of meaning over time, the great adaptability of the image allowed for productive play and open-ended experimentation.[4] The astral chorus is a precious witness for investigations into the *imaginaire* of *kosmos* and the many shades of its variations.

The history of poetic metaphors is notoriously difficult to follow properly.[5] Their trajectories ebb and flow in myriad directions through occasions, texts and genres. More pointedly, the dense potential of meaning generated by the metaphorical conflation of concepts rarely maps well, if at all, on the schematic templates of scholarship when extended periods of time are involved. The approaches that emphasise system tend to present static, synchronic snapshots with little consideration for change and variation. And the approaches that emphasise change and evolution almost invariably produce linear narratives with a stratigraphy and a clear teleology. There, origins are written with the end in mind, and the space in between uses the distance that separates the two to tell a story. The old semantic understandings of metaphor are particularly prone to that teleological trap. The situational, pragmatic approaches, on the other hand, usually fail to move beyond the specificities of the individual statement, while the now dominant cognitive interpretations, for all their promise, tend to take all the texture out to get straight to the conceptual mapping at hand.[6] Those cognitive approaches, however fancy the charts and Venn diagrams, often end up reducing the metaphorical figure to the most banal implications of its most banal expressions in speech. Drawing from all these methods, I suspect I will reproduce and further many of their defects. But the contrastive approach I will use here, based on close parallels and long-distance comparisons, will seek to combine their strengths, and aim

---

[3] Richards 1936.

[4] Cf. the *kosmos*–polis analogy studied by Carol Atack in Chapter 8 of this volume.

[5] See e.g. Gibbs 2008: 197–307, and especially Shen 2008; Forceville and Urios-Aparisi 2009; cf. Pilkington 2000, Kövecses 2005, Porat and Shen 2015. Lakoff and Turner 1989, notoriously, did not have the same success as Lakoff and Johnson 1980. See also the *Metaphor Map of English* project: http://mappingmetaphor.arts.gla.ac.uk/. Matzner's stimulating new book (Matzner 2016) repositions metonymy at the centre of the equation.

[6] That being said, cognitive approaches that successfully integrate context, culture and rhetorical depth are becoming more and more common; a particularly rich overview of such work can be found in Short 2014.

for something slightly different: the variations that explore latent aspects of the same metaphorical stream. By 'metaphorical stream', I mean the recurrent presence of analogous, comparable patterns in the deployment of the metaphor.

A persistent feature of astral chorus metaphors is the metapoetic resonance it is given by authors. That is the metaphorical stream I will follow here. The perfect chorus of the heavens is a model that poets went back to numerous times to consider the nature and the limits of their art, and each portrayal of that dialogue can be made to serve as a commentary on all others. This chapter will compare various unrelated, self-reflexive usages of the astral chorus metaphor in three genres of poetry, and briefly consider how the specificities of one illuminate the other. Each case furthers the contours of the series, and the series gives greater relief to the texture of each case. A vision of the cosmic order is used in all three texts to reflect on the boundaries of poetic representation.

It will be useful to start right away with a first example:

Κωμάζω χρύσειον ἐς ἑσπερίων χορὸν ἄστρων
λεύσσων, οὐδ' ἄλλων λὰξ ἐβάρυν' ὀάρους·
στέψας δ' ἀνθόβολον κρατὸς τρίχα τὴν κελαδεινὴν
πηκτίδα μουσοπόλοις χερσὶν ἐπηρέθισα.
καὶ τάδε δρῶν εὔκοσμον ἔχω βίον· οὐδὲ γὰρ αὐτὸς
κόσμος ἄνευθε λύρης ἔπλετο καὶ στεφάνου.

I keep revel, gazing at the golden dance of the stars of evening, nor do I rudely disturb the converse of others. Tossing my hair that scatters flowers, I awake with musical fingers the deep-toned lyre. And in doing so I lead an orderly life, for the order of the universe itself lacks not a Lyre and a Crown. (tr. Paton)

That short epigram is a once famous text from the (probably) Augustan poet Marcus Argentarius (*Anth. Pal.* 9.270 = G.-P. XXVI).[7] So famous, in fact, that the great Marguerite Yourcenar's celebrated anthology of Greek poetry, *La couronne et la lyre*, was named after it.[8] The first person singular of the poem channels the vivid perspective of a person engaged in a figurative *kômos*. As far as we can tell, he is alone in the night. The ἄλλοι of line 2 refers to everybody else, the company that he refuses to trouble with his heavy foot – λὰξ ἐβάρυν' – a usage of the verb that might have connotations of drunkenness in the context of Argentarius' persona as

---

[7] On Argentarius more generally, see still Small 1951 and Höschele and Konstan, n.d.
[8] Yourcenar 1979.

a reveller.⁹ There is a problem with the transmitted text, and the ὅρος of the manuscripts cannot be accepted.¹⁰ The χορούς of Planudes is interesting, but I prefer the ὀάρους proposed by Orelli, which – and here I disagree with Gow – makes perfect sense in the figurative language of Argentarius. ὀάρους can be read as pointing to the proximity of close friends, or it can be understood on an erotic level, the soft chatter of sexual encounters rejected by this peculiar *kômos* of one. It can also be taken on a metapoetical level, as a reference to the songs of others, the songs that the poet wants to have no share in.¹¹ All these meanings are possible – there is no good reason to choose one and exclude the others. Here as elsewhere (if ἐβάρυν' ὀάρους is indeed the correct reading), Argentarius is building bridges between the facets of words and encouraging us to combine complementary layers of reference in the elliptical epigram.

The poem's rejection of noise furthers the theme of the silent spectacle. It is the company of the stars that the poet opposes to this dismissal of the ἄλλων ὄαροι. He is looking at them – λεύσσων – and that gaze reflects on the whole of the text. The stars form a golden chorus, a shining, desirable dance that the poet is viewing from afar. His own dance and song establish a direct link to that of the ἀστέρες above, a link that is emphatically underlined in the last verse of the text.¹² The crown that the poet wears on his head mirrors the constellation above. The lyre he holds in his hands also echoes a constellation. That correspondence informs the commanding presence of κωμάζω, the verb placed at the beginning of the first line. At the heart of the meaning of κωμάζειν is the idea of a disordered collective movement, of a progression towards a destination, and that progression obviously involves the spectacle that the poet is seeing. His eyes are turned to the night sky, opposed to the heavy foot of human interaction. κωμάζειν is a verb you normally do not use in the first person singular.¹³ If the *kômos*

---

⁹ *Anth. Pal.* 6.248 = XXII G.-P.; *Anth. Pal.* 9.229 = G.-P. XXIV; *Anth. Pal.* 9.246 = G.-P. XXV; *Anth. Pal.* 11.26 = G.-P. XXVII; *Anth. Pal.* 11.28 = G.-P. XXX; *Anth. Pal.* 7.384 = G.-P. XXXI.

¹⁰ See G.-P., vol. 2, pp. 180–81.

¹¹ In the *Anthology* alone, see *Anth. Pal.* 4.3.130; 5.3.4; 9.358.2; 9.362.16; 9.381.10; 9.385.6; 10.68.4; 16.202.2; 16.272.2.

¹² Cf. the references stars in *Anth. Pal.* 5.16 = I G.-P. and *Anth. Pal.* 5.105 = VII G.-P.

¹³ Meleager (*Anth. Pal.* 12.85) provides one of only two attestations of κωμάζω outside of the lexicographical tradition. That dense epigram is built on the theme of the foreign lover's plight, freshly off the boat and already possessed by desire, a suppliant party of one longing to be received by the *oinopotai* on the shore. The other literary attestation of κωμάζω is in Euripides' *Alcestis* (831). There, Heracles mocks his own solitary revel in a house beset by grief. That usage of κωμάζω insists on the unseemly nature of such a lone carousal. Cf. Alexis Fr. 244 K.-A.; *Anth. Pal.* 5.112 (Philodemus); 9.21 (adespoton); 9.406 (Antigonus of Carystus); Aristophanes Fr. 63.71 *CGF*. Apart from the comically tinged passage from the *Alcestis*, all those examples of κωμάζειν in the first person singular come from comedy or epigrams.

evokes a group, that of Argentarius is, strikingly, a dance of one. He is on his way, and as he advances, he claims to be already participating in what lies ahead. The question is: what is involved in that participation?

Perhaps distance is what is underlined. The energetic shaking of the head that sends the flowers of the crown tumbling down to the ground links the act of κωμάζειν to a precise action, as does the vivid image of the musical hands rousing a song with the plectrum.[14] The pointed, meaningful gesture in action is a characteristic trope in the miniatures drawn by Argentarius.[15] Here, its evocation of the rapid motion involved in the poet's solitary *kômos* creates a tangible scene for us to imagine. The flowers tumbling down, the music ascending, the rhythm of the feet on the ground: a live presence is given shape. This forms a stark contrast with the silent immobility of the stars in the sky. The astral chorus moves on such a different scale that the clash between the two forms of dance provokes an open question: what should we do with the poet's claim that his life's measure and order reproduce the measure and order of the dance above?

One possible reading is to have the scene portray an ironic jest. The idea that the poet's wild *kômos* can be equated with a βίος εὔκοσμος, that ecstatic shunning of human company by one lone individual has any relation to the serene, unreachable isolation of the astral chorus, could, in that view, be understood as another tongue-in-cheek game of wit by the clever epigrammatist, a man otherwise known for his great interest in the ὄαροι of others, erotic and otherwise.[16] The golden chorus of stars, on that account, stands for everything that Argentarius is not, a foil for his disordered earthly revel.[17]

But a more straightforward reading is also possible, obviously. Rather than see the distance between the poet's *kômos* and the astral chorus as an ironic statement of opposition, we can opt to take the scene of the epigram at face value. That is, the poet does exactly as he claims. Looking at the ordered sky in a moment of exaltation, he expresses a profound statement of communion with the movements of the *kosmos*. The instant we are shown reflects on the whole of the poet's life, the βίος that he mentions. It

---

[14] The στέψας of line 3 is, characteristically, picked up by the στεφάνου at the end of the poem; see Small 1951: 87; Höschele and Konstan, n.d. The image of the *stephanos* evokes further connotations of poetic anthology and triumph.

[15] See e.g. *Anth. Pal.* 9.161 = XV G.-P.

[16] Cf. Kindl 1991; Hendry 1991, 1997; Gagné and Höschele 2009.

[17] Another pun on the name Argentarius? See Höschele and Konstan, n.d. (on *Anth. Pal.* 5.16 = I G.-P.).

is the link between the performance of the *kômos* here and now – τάδε δρῶν, the δρώμενα we are made witnesses to – and the *kômos* of his life that is involved in his vision of the stars. As long as the *kômos* goes on, his βίος remains in communion with the astral dance, imperfect as it is. The moment commemorated in the epigram contains the poet's entire existence. His refusal to participate in the chatter of others is a declaration of poetic independence. The poet's dance is looking up above, he is not concerned with the *profanum vulgus* of other mortals. His song stands alone, dwarfed by the night sky. The silent dance above is the model that guides his life, something that evokes the ideal of total participation in the cosmic rhythms that govern the universe. The poet's *kômos* is on its way, and the golden chorus is there to receive it, the ultimate destination and victory.[18] The astral chorus (χορὸς ἄστρων), in that reading, is not only the poet's source of inspiration, but the cosmic whole he will rejoin at the end of his life's *kômos*. The astral chorus stands as the keystone of the poet's reflection on the nature of his art and his existence.

Whatever reading we adopt, and the short comments I have just made are of course far from exhausting the interpretations of this rich little poem, the silent, immobile chorus of the night sky is used here to embody the awesome wonder of cosmic order, the radical otherness that separates the imperceptible pace of its dance from the quick step of mortal movement and the question of a man's place in its rhythms. The combination of music, dance and celebration; the sensual, tactile quality of the human body in movement; the place of the single dancing body in the company of other men; the paradigmatic authority of the cosmic *molpê*; the relation between the disordered ecstasy of the individual and the harmonious whole of the universe; the echo of one dance's rhythms into another dance: everything the epigram has to say about itself depends on the semantic register of the chorus.

This condensed, deeply original metapoetic vision is built entirely around the notion of chorality. If, as Michael Silk argues, one of the primary features of a metaphor is, I quote, 'to exploit the associations, including the contrary associations, of the vehicle (i.e. of its given terminology), beyond any limited point or ground of comparison', then what we have in the epigram is a profound exercise in thinking the extent of metaphor.[19] The transfer of attributes is mapped in both directions at once. Choral performance, the idea of the body in collective movement, is

---

[18] For the theme of receiving the *kômos*, see e.g. Heath 1988; Eckerman 2010; Agócs et al. 2012.
[19] Silk 2003: 126.

emphatically thematised here, fixed in the visual evocation of the text and reimagined as a figurative foil/model for the poet's own art. The metaphorical substitution of our figure makes us look straight at an absence. High above in the aether, the χορὸς ἄστρων is the ultimate, distant source of all poetic imitation. It is both visible and elusive at the same time. The epigram brilliantly captures the paradox of the star chorus metaphor, which relies on the incongruous opposition between the remoteness of the heavenly bodies and the almost tangible immediacy of imagined performance. The creative inscription of the astral figure in the text redefines a chorality that explores the boundaries of the poet's art.

The very specific programme of the epigrammatist expressed in this piece revisits a trope which had by then acquired a long history. I have started this chapter with a discussion of that poem because it does not fit with the general narrative on the astral chorus we find in the scholarship.[20] Astral choruses, of course, appear in a great variety of sources and contexts, many scores of passages and genres, and they remained a staple of Greek representations of cosmic order through the centuries. That profoundly resonant metaphor embeds a certain idea of cosmic harmony in the shape of one of the most culturally specific, distinctive religious and poetic institutions of ancient Greek culture.[21] Scholarship on this striking figure of the Greek imagination has focused very actively on the notions of order and *kosmos* expressed in the image, its many links with the evolution of philosophical cosmology and astronomical theories about the movement of the stars, and conjecture about mystery cults. The astral chorus, when it is mentioned, is usually read as an index to a more or less linear trajectory of intellectual history.

Plato is the main interlocutor for that story; the powerful and rich portraits of the astral chorus found in the *Timaeus*, *Republic*, *Phaedrus* and the *Laws* have pride of place in that narrative, and the Church Fathers are the stated destination of the trajectory, especially the influential portraits of the astral chorus found in texts like Gregory of Nazianzus' *Orations*. James Miller's monumental *Measure of Wisdom* (1986), the most extensive study devoted to the cosmic dance in Classical and Christian antiquity, is a perfect illustration of that type of investigation. Theology is the backbone of the discussion, which remains centred on the explicit, more theoretical texts that can help trace the path from Plato to

[20] Key works include Lawler 1960; de Vries 1976; Mullen 1982: 225–30; Miller 1986; Montanari 1989; D'Alfonso 1993; Whitmarsh 2004; Csapo 2008, 2009; Ferrari 2008; Steiner 2011: 315–18; cf. Sachs 1937: 124–31; and Gibbon 1972: 241–44.
[21] See e.g. Athanassaki and Bowie 2011 and Francis 2012.

Patristics, what Miller calls the 'Academic Millenium'. More strictly poetic texts like Marcus Argentarius' epigram play next to no role in the story, except as antecedents or foils. The astral choruses that do not fit that narrative of intellectual history are, at best, mentioned in passing, if at all, or dismissed as so many *lieux communs*, dead metaphors or mere ornamental aesthetics.

In parallel to that dismissal of a large portion of the relevant material, what has all but disappeared from consideration in actual discussions of the topic is the chorality of the chorus. Essentially reduced to form, the chorus per se mostly points to the perfection of the circle in that scholarship, it is cast as the ideal embodiment of harmony and order.[22] The astral element of the metaphor, in other words, is totally dominating the way it is read. The *tenor*, to use I. A. Richards's terminology again, completely eclipses the *vehicle*, and the semantics of the figure are subordinated to a theological narrative of cosmic order. The poetic resonances generated by the tension between the choruses are lost in the operation. What I propose to do here is revisit some poetic passages where the astral chorus plays a determinant role, with an eye to the echoes of chorality. How does the idea of choral *performance* inform the charge of the cosmic metaphor? How is the synaesthetic combination of song and dance reflected in textual representations of the astral *molpê*?

The idea of choral poetry was recurrently asked to embody the essence of mimesis.[23] The astral chorus asserts itself as the paradigm of *choreia*, and the self-reflexive concerns of poetry are often directly solicited by this figure. The astral chorus embodies the supreme motion, the model of all harmony. Does the extensive mimetic register of choral poetry have anything to do with the many correspondences and equivalences that link the many representations of the χορὸς ἄστρων? Can the cultural memory of choral movement inscribed in the archive of literature affect the trajectories of the metaphor, even long after the actual performances that are referenced had faded away? How is genre involved? Over and beyond its importance for the history of philosophy and theology, the astral chorus offers a privileged focus for exploring the limits of poetic representation in the texts where it appears.

The rest of this chapter will contrast two other texts in quick succession. These texts are from different genres and different periods. What unites

---

[22] For the ideal circularity of the chorus, see Davidson 1996; cf. Lech 2009. For the ideal sphericity of cosmic and divine imagination, see Sedley, 2017; cf. Ath. 489c–d.

[23] See e.g. Hes. *Theog.* 1–115, with Clay 1988 and Goslin 2010; *Hom. Hymn Apol.* 156–64, with Lonsdale 1994–95 and Peponi 2009; cf. Carruesco 2012, 2016.

them is the fact that all three of the passages discussed here give shape to
a poetic programme, a statement about the nature of song where the star
chorus serves as a key element of the text's claims on representation. After
the miniature epigram of the Augustan elegist, we will briefly look at the
extensive elaboration of a mammoth late-antique epic. Going back to the
other end of the chronological spectrum, the last example will come from
a tragedy of Euripides, a text both anterior to Plato and grounded in the
pragmatics of actual choral performance. Beyond the pleasure of *poikilia*,
and the fact that each of these passages is interesting in and of itself, I have
deliberately chosen texts from different genres and periods to set different
representations of figurative choral performance side-by-side in contrast.
While the first text projects its evocation of chorality on the vivid scene of
a situation in movement before the mind's eye, the second locates its χορὸς
ἄστρων on the static surface of a shield ecphrasis.[24] The last text also
concerns a programmatic shield ecphrasis with a prominent astral chorus,
but that one, in contrast to the two others, is conveyed *by* choral dance and
song itself. All three explore the nature of poetic vision through a metaphor
of performance. Contrasting visions of the cosmic order, and of the cosmic
order's relation to human song, are refracted in these vignettes of the astral
chorus. The common metaphorical stream found in each case can be used
to better tease out the implications and resonance of each image. In order
to escape the familiar fallacy of the linear narrative, where origins and
destination govern everything else, the texts chosen have no direct relation
to each other, and they are not placed in chronological order. This is
a method well adapted to the fragmentary nature of our evidence, and
maybe it can allow for readings slightly less constrained by historicism.

Placed right in the middle of the massive poem of Nonnus of Panopolis,
the culmination of the second beginning of the great, monumental swan-
song of ancient Greek epic, the ecphrasis of the shield (ἀσπίς) of Dionysus
in Book 25 of the *Dionysiaca* provides another example of an astral chorus
that hardly fits in the general narrative of scholarship and invites us to
consider the force of the metaphor on its own terms. The text is almost 200
lines long (25.380–572).[25]

---

[24] The term 'ecphrasis' has been subjected to a barrage of redefinitions in recent years. For recent
debates about its correct usage and scope, see e.g. Webb 1999 and 2009 and Squire 2013. Cf. Graf
1995, Elsner 2002, Bram 2006, Bartsch and Elsner 2007, Francis 2009 and Zeitlin 2013.
[25] On the shield of Dionysus, see e.g. Hopkinson 1994: 22–24; Shorrock 2001: 70–71 and 174–77;
Lovatt 2013: 195–97 and 351; and Spanoudakis 2014a; cf. Miguélez-Cavero 2008: 283–309; Agnosini
2010; Faber 2016: 445–48 and 457–59; and Maciver 2016: 538–43.

The textualisation of performance we see at play there through the figure of choral movement creatively adapts a very old trope to its own purposes. A polar opposite to the minimalist aesthetics of epigram, the gargantuan expanses of the *Dionysiaca* are immeasurably more complex, and I will have to limit myself here to a few very brief remarks. First, it is important to note that the whole world does indeed dance in this text. Choral words and imagery, more specifically, are impressively abundant in the epic, appearing in more than 250 passages – that is, quite a lot more than a few times in every book – and they involve most aspects of the god's action.[26] Many choral genres are indexed and referenced, most notably tragedy, and the memory of their place in the canon and the rhetorical handbooks integrated to the learned, encyclopaedic epic.[27] The dances of Dionysus in the *Dionysiaca* present a deep intertextual fabric; the great struggles of order and divine upheaval are recurrently thought through the movements of earlier rhythm, where the memory of the chorus has pride of place. Dance in Late Antiquity is not all about pantomime.[28]

The heart of this choral activity is the χορὸς ἄστρων, prominently mentioned more than ten times in the text as the ultimate embodiment of the cosmic order, the regular movement of a collectivity of overarching powers.[29] In Book 1 already, where we first encounter it, its dance disrupted by the war in heaven, and in Book 2, the challenge presented by Typhon to the cosmic order is imagined as a battle for control of the astral chorus, and

[26] Nonnus, *Dion.* 1.13; 3.25; 3.63; 3.71; 3.110; 3.421; 4.82; 4.323; 5.88; 5.100; 5.104; 5.11; 5.116; 5.119; 5.184; 5.186; 6.49; 6.50; 6.121; 6.149; 6.264; 7.17; 7.46; 7.53; 8.27; 8.228; 8.334; 8.371; 9.118; 9.163; 9.202; 9.238; 9.263; 9.285; 10.240; 11.331; 11.456; 11.505; 11.509; 12.118; 12.261; 12.337; 12.383; 13.7; 13.157; 13.503–506; 14.28–32; 14.230; 14.249; 14.287; 14.389; 15.52; 15.67; 15.103; 16.56; 16.67; 16.127; 16.289; 16.401; 17.115; 17.383; 18.52; 18.99; 18.122; 18.143; 18.145; 18.148; 18.151; 19.5; 19.36; 19.119; 19.154; 19.166; 19.178–180; 19.198; 19.211; 19.221; 19.225; 19.268; 19.277; 19.299; 19.307; 19.342; 20.24; 20.47; 20.89; 20.91; 20.238; 20.278; 20.304; 20.341–343; 21.84; 21.185; 21.192; 21.252; 21.253; 21.293; 21.295; 22.5; 22.29; 22.44; 22.60; 23.124; 24.123; 24.193; 24.261; 24.348; 25.241; 25.286; 25.338; 25.389; 25.420; 25.429; 26.193; 26.263; 26.268; 27.50; 27.119; 27.167; 27.173; 27.214; 27.260; 28.36; 28.44; 28.290; 28.296; 28.328; 29.219; 29.242; 29.248; 30.2; 30.118; 30.121; 30.124; 31.223; 32.7; 33.103; 33.230; 33.249; 33.304; 34.117; 34.150; 35.92; 35.112; 35.145; 35.337; 35.347; 35.354; 36.256; 36.439; 36.453; 37.664; 37.742; 38.311; 38.335; 38.407; 40.239; 40.476; 41.7; 41.196; 41.225; 42.161; 42.359; 43.5; 43.74; 43.170; 43.243; 43.260; 43.390; 43.419; 44.4; 44.8; 44.29; 44.54; 44.124–125; 44.222; 45.24–26; 45.32; 45.36; 45.42; 45.57; 45.62; 45.160; 45.190; 45.218; 45.226; 45.273; 46.81; 46.93; 46.120; 46.143; 46.145; 46.148–155; 46.167; 46.173; 47.4; 47.11; 47.14; 47.28; 47.34; 47.37; 47.116; 47.273; 47.291; 47.324; 47.374; 47.457–469; 47.477; 47.727; 47.729–730; 48.193; 48.209; 48.281; 48.639–642; 48.671; 48.880; 48.959–961; 48.967; cf. Peek 1968–75 sv. χορός.
[27] For the *Dionysiaca*'s encyclopaedic engagement with genres and texts, see Shorrock 2011, Lasek 2016 and Acosta-Hughes 2016.
[28] The authoritative analysis of performance and pantomime in Late Antiquity will long remain Webb 2008; cf. Peponi 2013.
[29] See Miguélez-Cavero 2013.

the text repeatedly brings that crucial figure back to the fore.[30] The χορὸς ἄστρων is the fragile axis of the world.

The juxtaposition of this cosmic chorus and the exuberant disruption of Dionysiac chorality is emphasised again and again in the epic. A central concern of the poem is the tension generated by the new god's immense power, and its relation to the power of other gods, most notably the stable order of Olympus.[31] The threat of cosmic conflict, a fundamental disruption of the dance, is never far from the surface, as the first books establish early on for the rest of the poem. That is the ultimate charge inscribed in the image. At the end of the day, how one reads this figure ultimately depends on where one stands in relation to 'la questione nonniana', to take Enrico Livrea's phrase.[32] As the dominant nature of the *Dionysiaca*'s religious stance will remain matter for open-ended controversy in the foreseeable future, it's advisable to remain prudent here.

But whatever position one adopts on that question, the tension between the triumphant chorality of Dionysus and the movement of the stars is a feature of the poem that commands attention. Written over the Iliadic shield of Achilles at more than a thousand years of distance, the shield of Dionysus is a particularly resonant location for exploring this tension between the dances in Nonnus' poem.[33] If the *Iliad*'s shield of Achilles traces a focus for evoking the value and the struggles of humanity in the great cosmic whole, a canvas for contemplating the mortality of the hero and the work of the artisan poet, the shield of Dionysus serves as an instrument for illustrating the challenges of new divinity, the internal struggles of a fading memory of live polytheism, and the baroque artistry of Nonnus.[34] In a section where Nonnus presents his work explicitly as a rival to Homer, and νέοισι καὶ ἀρχεγόνοισιν ἐρίζων (25.27), directly confronting the model of all ecphrasis was basically a necessity.[35]

The first thing to note about that shield is that it is primarily an astral shield. It is referred to as the αἰθέρος ἀστερόεσσα ἀσπίς before the start of

---

[30] Nonnus, *Dion.* 1.230; 2.228; 2.352; see Braden 1974, Vian 1993 and Aringer 2012. Cf. Nonnus, *Dion.* 9.238; 21.253; 27.50; 32.7; 35.337; 38.311; 38.335.

[31] See Miguélez-Cavero 2008: 282.

[32] Livrea 1987, 2003. See e.g. Keydell 1931, Bogner 1934, Chuvin 1986, Vian 1994, Accorinti 1995, Liebeschuetz 1996, Fayant 1998, Shorrock 2011 and Dijkstra 2016. See the excellent analysis of Massa 2014 for the immediate antecedents. For a Christianising reading of the shield of Dionysus, see Spanoudakis 2013, 2014a. For ecphrasis in Nonnus, see Kröll 2013.

[33] See e.g. Baumbach 2007 and Squire 2013.

[34] For an overview of approaches to the Iliadic shield of Achilles, see e.g. D'Acunto and Palmisciano 2009 and Lecoq 2010.

[35] For the intricate details of Nonnus' deep engagement with Homer, see e.g. Hopkinson 1994: 9–42; Shorrock 2011: 44–50 and 67–104; and Bannert and Kröll 2016; cf. Fincher 2017.

the ecphrasis proper (25.352). The chorus of stars is the first prominent element of the shield to be described. As it progresses centrifugally from the χορὸς ἄστρων, the ecphrasis constantly returns to it, marking the astral dance as the organising principle of a meandering description. The chorus of stars is placed at the centre of the shield, circling around the earth and the sea.[36] Verses 387–412 describe it in detail, following the seven zones of the aether.[37] It serves as an index to the vast astrological apparatus of the entire poem.[38] The chorus is inscribed by the hand of Hephaistos, κεχαραγμένον, on the bended sky (389). The scene foregrounds the gleam of the metal as an artificial rendering of astral light, and it never loses an opportunity to remind us that the shield is a *made* object, *poiêton*, that it is static, dependent on the qualities of the material, the will of the artisan and the shared knowledge of the audience. The paraphrases and strong, direct references to Aratus which punctuate the whole passage reinforce that point on the poetic level. This is an imitation of an imitation, a sophisticated celebration of *poikilia* and meta-artistry.[39] The emphatic, repeated allusions to Apollonius of Rhodes' ecphrasis of Jason's cloak (*Argonautica* 730–68), for instance, a *locus classicus* of metapoetic imagery, function on exactly that level.[40]

The building of the walls of Thebes (*Dionysiaca* 25.414–28) is the only other figure of the shield to have a precise visual position on the object, this time on the main surface of the *aspis*. Circular, like the chorus of stars, it answers the centre of the shield by taking on the same form, and the seven doors of the wall answer the seven zones of the aether, all of which echo the seven years of the war. Contrary to the perfect cosmic circle of the stars, the circle of the walls is unfinished, it is work in progress. The seven doors are shown in the process of construction (κτιζομένων, 417). Facticity is emphasised (ποιητήν περ ἐοῦσαν, 422), and the form of the illusion constantly put forward. The stone is deceitful (ψευδήμονι νευρῇ, 425). You would say (φαίης, 421) that it is moving, even though it is immobile (ἀκινήτης, 423). Although it jumps without sound (κοῦφος) and the lyre is silent (σιγαλέη, 424), the artistry of the object invites you to listen for something that is not there.[41] This is an ecphrasis that goes out of its way to deny the synaesthesia

---

[36] Nonnus, *Dion.* 25.387–90: ἧς ἐνὶ μέσσῳ / ἐν μὲν γαῖαν ἔτευξε περίδρομον, ἀμφὶ δὲ γαίῃ / οὐρανὸν ἐσφαίρωσε χορῷ κεχαραγμένον ἄστρων, / καὶ χθονὶ πόντον ἔτευξεν ὁμόζυγον·
[37] A set of clear references to Aratus is listed in Vian 1990: 261–62.
[38] See still Stegemann 1930; cf. Bogner 1934: 327–29, Chuvin 2003: 10, 12 and 39, and Miguélez-Cavero 2008: 243–45.
[39] See, more generally, Fauth 1981. Cf. Miguélez-Cavero 2008: 139–45 and 162–68.
[40] Vian 1990: 262; see e.g. Bulloch 2006 and Mason 2016.   [41] Cf. Gigli Piccardi 1985: 156.

that plays such a fundamental role in earlier traditions of ecphrasis, from the *Iliad* onwards.[42] At the centre of the circle of the wall in construction, as if it were superimposed upon the chorus of stars, rather than one circle inserted within the other, Amphion plays the lyre, with the seven strings echoing the seven zones of the zodiac and seven doors of the city, and the blocks fly at the sound of the magical rhythm.[43] 'As if charmed', says the text, 'even though it is represented on a shield' (421). The static movement of the blocks is described on the model of a chorus. It is circular, ἕλιξ, a typical choral word.[44] The flying stone dances, ἐχόρευε. The *molpê* of the city in construction, in other words, is a direct parallel to the chorus of stars. One chorus answers the other; the unfinished dance of Thebes and the perfect dance of the cosmos structure the space of the Dionysiac ecphrasis.

Other scenes on the shield are less precisely located, but their echoes are clear. The rape of Ganymede (429–50), an event that connects the worlds of men and gods, is placed 'where the glittering *choros* of stars is', and the event is shown in two moments. First, we see the boy being carried to Olympus in the claws of Zeus as an eagle, and then Ganymede at the banquet, serving nectar to the gods from the *kratêr*.[45] The first scene, in other words, represents the elevation of a mortal to the realm of the astral chorus, and the second, an overcoming of the competition and rivalry rife in the community of the gods.

The following scene takes on a completely different register (451–552). Like the building of Thebes, it depicts an image that refers to the origins of Dionysus, but this time Lydia, the other nominal birthplace of the god.[46] This is done through representations of Maeonia, the serpent Moriê, the giant Damasen and Tylos, the Lydian man who died and was reborn, another fundamental transgression of boundaries. Without saying anything about the images and the way they are crafted, the text launches into an extended narrative involving all four characters. We do not have space to go into the details of that extended narrative, but let's just note that it is longer than the whole of the rest of the ecphrasis. There is no hint of an indication that any of it is included on the shield, beyond the four characters, leading to a complete blurring of categories. The boundaries of representation are dissolved. Where does the shield begin, where does it end? The text leaves that question wide open.

[42] See e.g. Porter 2013: 20–22.   [43] Hopkinson 1994: 24.   [44] Csapo 1999–2000: 419–24.
[45] See Lovatt 2013: 189–91; for Zeus in the *Dionysiaca*, see Kuhlmann 1999.
[46] Cf. Hadjittofi 2010.

Different *modes* of representation are thus juxtaposed to great effect.[47] The contrast between that narrative episode and the part of the ecphrasis which precedes it is striking. The contrast is reinforced by the fact that the following and last part of the ecphrasis returns to an emphasis on the material limits and facticity of the visual representation.[48] The scene, which is not located precisely anywhere on the shield, shows Cybele-Rhea, after childbirth, holding the stone that is to be passed off as Zeus.[49] We then see her give the stone to Cronos, Cronos swallow it whole and then vomit his many children.

In keeping with the earlier sections of the shield, the text foregrounds the fact that this is an image engraved by the artist, that Cybele-Rhea is a semblance, that her arms are made and that the rock itself is a deceitful, non-representational imitation of birth (554), a μιμηλὴ ἀχάρακτος λοχείη, if we accept the manuscript reading.[50] An extravagant mise-en-abyme of the ecphrasis as a whole, in other words. This is made even more significant by the thematic resonance of that episode for the passage. The fact is that Cybele-Rhea is the one character who gives the shield to Dionysus through Attis.[51] The birth of Zeus and the liberation of the gods from their father, the last episode described on the shield, is of course the event that ultimately establishes the cosmic order that the astral chorus embodies. The universe, in other words, is based on the deceitful power of an imitation. The birth of Zeus, more importantly, is obviously set up as a parallel to the birth of Dionysus. But how are they linked? Is one an echo of the other? Is the chorus of the Theban wall in construction there to defend the chorus of stars? Or is the immense power of the new god a challenge, a new dispensation about to breach the walls? The birth of Zeus, after all, led to the overthrow of his father's power. Or is this all, as some think, a parodic foil to the very different power of the one true God, the other new divinity who is never named but never absent from this text?

If all these questions can be raised, the main thread of the narrative within the poem does invite us to see the shield as a confirmation of

---

[47] See Gigli Piccardi 1985.

[48] For the idea of poetic facticity in the larger visual aesthetics context, see Agosti 2006, 2014.

[49] Nonnus, *Dion.* 25.553–59: καὶ Κυβέλη κεχάρακτο νεητόκος, οἷά τε κόλπῳ / μιμηλὴν ἀχάρακτον ἐλαφρίζουσα λοχείην / πήχεσι ποιητοῖσι, καὶ ἀστόργῳ παρακοίτῃ / λαϊνέην ὠδῖνα δολοπλόκος / ὤρεγε Ῥείη, / ὀκριόεν βαρὺ δεῖπνον· ὁ δὲ τροχοειδέα μορφὴν / ἔκρυφε μάρμαρον υἷα πατὴρ / θοινήτορι λαιμῷ, / ἄλλου ψευδομένοιο Διὸς δέμας εἰλαπινάζων. For representations of divinity in the *Dionysiaca* more generally, see Miguélez-Cavero 2008.

[50] Vian's emendation to μιμηλὴν **ἀλόχευτον** . . . λοχείην (1990: 269) is unnecessary. For the recurrent theme of significant rocks in the *Dionysiaca*, see Frangoulis 2003.

[51] Nonnus, *Dion.* 25.326–29; 25.352–60.

Dionysus' place in the pantheon of his father's *kosmos*. A work of Hephaestos, it is presented as an Olympian emblem, and a necessary tool for negating the opposition of Hera and Ares. In other words, a condition for the integration of Dionysus in the pantheon. Just a few lines before the beginning of the ecphrasis, furthermore, in line 241, we had been reminded of Dionysus' exploit in killing the cosmic monster Alpos, a Typhon-like creature, who threatened the chorus of stars with the height of his hundred serpent heads.[52] Deriades, the Indian king who opposes Dionysus in the poem, is emphatically identified as an enemy of Zeus and the chorus of stars.[53] By accepting the shield, in other words, Dionysus confirms his position as the champion of the χορὸς ἄστρων, subordinating his dance to another. The gift of the astral shield by Attis in Book 25 echoes the gift of the astral chiton by Heracles Astrochitôn in Book 40, the two most prominent moments marking Dionysus' apotheosis and progression towards the cosmic dance.[54]

Placed at the very centre of the poem, the ἀσπίς brings together the ordered dance of the stars with the new dances of the mad god. Structured by the idea of chorality, the shield inscribes the integration of Dionysus into the pantheon through the notion of rhythmic movement. But are we able to see anything beyond the static, silent representation of the dance? Although Attis had mentioned the presence of Oceanus on the shield (l. 360), leading us to expect something similar to what we know from *Iliad* 18, we never actually get to see it in the ecphrasis, thus reinforcing the impression of a strong contrast between this unruly vision and the comparatively disciplined, symmetrical Homeric model. The clear suggestion of the text is that Oceanus is the generic sea, the πόντος, which is placed in the middle of the ἀσπίς. Oceanus, that is, is encircled by the chorus of stars. The shield of Dionysus, in other words, has no rim, in strong contrast to the shield of Achilles, and every other single shield ecphrasis of Greek literature.[55] Unbounded by rim or narrative space, the ecphrasis spills in many directions and registers at once, and constantly calls into question its own status, and that of the poem as a whole by extension. The circular shield, we are told at the end of Book 25, is observed and admired by the bacchants who make a circle (ἐκυκλώσαντο) around it under the

---

[52] Nonnus, *Dion.* 25.236–41: καὶ γὰρ ἐμὸς Διόνυσος ἑῷ ταμεσίχροϊ κισσῷ / Ἄλπον ἀπηλοίησε, θεημάχον υἱὸν ἀρούρης, / Ἄλπον ἐχιδναίοις ἑκατὸν κομόωντα καρήνοις, / Ἠελίου ψαύοντα καὶ αὐερύοντα Σελήνην, / ἀστραίην πλοκάμοισι περιθλίβοντα χορείην.

[53] Nonnus, *Dion.* 21.253; cf. Hadjittofi 2016: 135–42.

[54] Nonnus, *Dion.* 40.577–78; Cf. 38.291–300.   [55] See e.g. Becker 1995: 147–48.

night sky.[56] A static chorus of bacchants is contemplating the static circles of the choral shield, further calling into question the boundaries between viewer and viewed, reality and representation, and the elusive nature of the god's power. The limits of poetic representation are brilliantly solicited in this passage through the metaphorical figure of the astral chorus, which is fully integrated into the specific aesthetic and semantic horizon of the poem.

Privileging philosophy or mystery cults in reading this text would be indefensible. The fact that this passage hardly fits the philosophical narrative that follows the astral chorus from Plato to Patristics explains its relative neglect at the hands of scholarship on the question. At the other end of the chronological spectrum, that part of the narrative that precedes Plato has received somewhat more attention, as one would expect. The antecedents of Plato, in the standard view, obviously all lead up to him, and they are consequently defined as organic precursors in contrast to the explicit discussions of the philosopher. Without going into the fraught question of dancing stars in Alcman, especially the relatively recent, stimulating and controversial book of Gloria Ferrari, I think it preferable here to consider an example from tragedy, the main locus for the appearance of star choruses before Plato.[57] As it plays a determinant role in Eric Csapo's important 'Star Choruses: Eleusis, Orphism and New Musical Imagery and Dance', I will focus on the first stasimon of Euripides' *Electra* (432–86).

Following Miller, Csapo argues that the star choruses we see in late tragedy derive from the dialogue of ritual and Presocratic speculation.[58] In other words, the χορὸς ἄστρων of tragedy is a reflection of something else, an element of meaning that owes its resonances and connotations to a reality outside the text. That reality, he believes, is essentially a cultic one, and what we have in the image of the astral dance is an evocation of

---

[56] Nonnus, *Dion.* 25.563–67: τοῖα μὲν ἐργοπόνοιο πολύτροπα δαίδαλα τέχνης / εἶχεν ἐνυαλίη πολυδαίδαλος ἀσπὶς Ὀλύμπου / Βακχιάς, ἣν ὁρόωντες ἐθάμβεον ἄλλος ἐπ' ἄλλῳ, / καὶ σάκεος τροχόεντος ἐκυκλώσαντο φορῆα, / ἔμπυρον αἰνήσαντες Ὀλύμπιον ἐσχαρεῶνα.

[57] Ferrari 2008; see e.g. Calame 2011. Cf. West 1967: 11–15.

[58] Csapo 2008: 285: 'But it was not until the second half of the fifth century and especially the last quarter that the star chorus begins to appear with any frequency in Greek poetry. In the last decades of the fifth century we find recurrent use of the image in music, and all in the choral odes of Attic tragedy. In these odes the influence of Eleusian mystery cult is explicit and the influence of Dionysian mystery cult palpable.' Also see p. 286: 'Tragedy developed an interest in round dance under the influence of dithyramb and for the same reason. Euripides in particular was prone to project cultic choruses, particularly cultic choruses of a Dionysian flavor, and most particularly the mythic archetypes of Dionysian cultic choruses. Among the latter, star choruses are supreme, because most mythical and most archetypal.'

that origin. It is an image that had 'a mystical aura from the beginning'.[59]
A nexus of cultic dances from Eleusis and the Dionysiac Mysteries is
associated to fragments of theology ascribed to early Pythagoreans and
Orphism concerning the movements of the heavens and the aetherial
afterlife of souls, and Csapo maintains that the astral choruses of late
tragedy largely reflect that cluster of mystical ideas and practices. For
him, the prime consideration is the evolution of the dithyramb in
the second half of the fifth century BCE.[60] Here as elsewhere, he argues
for a renewed Classical dithyramb profoundly intertwined with the ideas
and aesthetics of Eleusinian and Dionysiac mystery cults, as well as Orphic
notions of aetherial souls and astral immortality. That Late Classical
dithyrambic register he reconstructs is what lies behind the dancing stars
of the tragic corpus. The appropriation of the dithyramb by the revolu-
tionary artists of New Music, their attempt to inscribe a Dionysiac cultic
revival at the heart of their spectacle and their interest in mystical eschatol-
ogy are, according to Csapo, the fundamental factors at play behind the
cluster of star choruses found in tragedy. On our way to Plato's ideas, in
other words, the first body of texts of any real importance is shown to
derive directly from cult and the imagination of ritual, an organic antecedent to philosophical developments – something like a movement *vom
Mythos zum Logos*.

   Csapo's article is an impressive feat of scholarship and the case it makes
is enticing. But I have to note some disagreements with the general frame
of interpretation it conjures to explain the chorus of stars in tragedy. I will
limit myself to a few brief observations. First, the role it gives to Orphism
depends on a model of Orphism that I cannot share. The identification of
a nexus of ideas and practices that can be labelled as specifically 'Orphic' in
the late fifth century is highly controversial, and no real consensus has
managed to emerge since the devastating critique of Ivan Linforth's *The
Arts of Orpheus* in 1941. My inclination is to limit the usage of this term to
the rare occasions where the texts signal in the direction of Orpheus,
beyond the generic register of *teletai* and secrecy, or a putative set of
esoteric doctrines about guilt. I see no such signals in the tragic record of
star choruses. There is, in my opinion, no solid reason for believing that the
star choruses of tragedy have anything to do with Orphism, whatever we
want Orphism to mean.

   More importantly, the nexus of Dionysiac revival, mystery cults and
mystic theology posited as a background by Csapo's article for the tragic

imagery of the star chorus is based on an elaborate historical scenario. While this scenario does not derive from the evidence at hand, it provides the overarching context for making sense of the evidence. The danger in such situations is to have a system shaping the conclusions. Accepting that this composite nexus of Dionysiac revival, mystery cults and mystic theology is operative and that it is anterior, in that shape, to what we find in tragedy, is a premise that cannot be taken for granted. And why should all the relevant passages of tragedy derive from a ritual source outside of tragedy? The primacy of cultic roots and ritual origins is a storied mirage. While some references to astral choruses in tragedy are indeed in dialogue with the imagery of *teletai*, without necessarily deriving from them, like the χοραγὸς ἄστρων of Sophocles' *Antigone*, others, like the first stasimon of the *Electra*, are not so clearly situated.[61]

A third general point to make is that, by emphasising the common characteristics of New Music and the dithyramb in the choral odes that concern us, the specificities of the individual texts, and their specific usage of astral chorality, all but disappear behind the larger narrative. The first stasimon of Euripides' *Electra* is a case in point.

The first thing to note about the ode is that it is firmly set in the evolution of the play. Although the opposite used to be taken for granted not that long ago, it is now a truism to observe that the first stasimon of the *Electra* deepens and foreshadows many thematic developments of the tragedy.[62] Following the general move away from Walter Kranz's ideas about the independent dithyrambic ode of late-fifth-century tragedy, people have repeatedly shown how the song serves as a transition point in the play, from the celebratory tone of joy at the news of Orestes' survival to the sombre prefiguration of the violence to come.[63] The glorious evocation of the Trojan expedition and the rich, wondrous arms of the foremost warrior commanded by Electra's father mark a stark contrast with the miserable condition in which we see her in the first part of the play.[64] But the Trojan vision of the ode becomes progressively more ominous, as the weapons are populated with female monsters who prepare the way for the horrors ahead.[65] Part of the song's integration into the play is its dialogue with the second stasimon, the other paradigmatic report from the past heard by the chorus in the tragedy. The striking presence of

---

[61] Soph. *Ant.* 1146; cf. De Vries 1976.
[62] See already Walsh 1977, Mulryne 1977: 41–43 and Marshall 1980.
[63] See Kranz 1933, Panagl 1971, Morwood 1981 and Hose 1991: 103–6.
[64] For the game of echoes between Achilles and Orestes on the shield, see Mulryne 1977: 36–38.
[65] See e.g. O'Brien 1964.

a chorus of stars in both odes reinforces that link between the two songs.[66] The movement of the χορὸς ἄστρων in the play comes to embody the cosmic echoes of transgression. But rather than those larger issues, what I want to focus on now is the resonance of the star chorus imagery in the song itself.

The star chorus of the first stasimon appears at the heart of an ecphrasis of the shield of Achilles, and any attempt to make sense of it must ground the analysis in the particular logic of that ecphrasis. Here, as elsewhere, the striking metaphor of the star chorus is deeply embedded, and the only way to unpack it properly is to zoom in on the passage. The adaptation of the figure to the tragedy differs markedly from what we've seen in the two preceding poems, and it can be illuminated by them.

In *Metapoetry in Euripides*, Isabelle Torrance is right to insist on the many intertextual links that attach this ecphrasis to other shield ecphraseis of epic and tragedy, and I will not add to her discussion of the issue here.[67] The one point I want to make in that regard is that we should not just look at this ecphrasis in terms of a *text* in dialogue with other *texts*, but we have to think of it three-dimensionally. Contrary to what we have in Nonnus, this is a choral ecphrasis, bodies in movement. There is also a fundamental difference between this ecphrasis and the embroidered tapestries of the *Ion*, for instance, or the shields of the *Seven Against Thebes* and the *Phoenissae*.[68] With the notable exception of Froma Zeitlin's seminal work and Marco Fantuzzi's excellent recent piece on choral ecphrasis, the abundant amount of work written on tragic ecphrasis tends to avoid that question.[69] Considerations of performance are crucial for us to understand the experience of the image described in the song, and we lose the whole texture of the passage if we do not integrate them in our reading. Choral self-referentiality and choral projection are important elements of the equation, but they only go so far in making sense of the visual imagery of such choral ecphrasis.[70] There is a fundamental difference between the reference to the dance of another chorus by a chorus and the representation of a visual metaphor of dance in a choral ecphrasis. The construction of an object through dance and song is a very distinctive form of synaesthetic representation.

---

[66] Stars in the second *stasimon*: Eur. *El.* 727–32; see Csapo 2008: 279 and Gagné and Hopman 2013a: 9–10 and 12.

[67] Torrance 2013: 76–82; cf. King 1980 and Gartziou-Tatti 2004.

[68] See Zeitlin 1982 and Goff 1988.   [69] Zeitlin 1994 and Fantuzzi 2018.

[70] Henrichs 1994–95; cf. Martin 2007 and Peponi 2009.

The χοροὶ ἄστρων of line 467 are placed at the end of the ode's shield ecphrasis. The chorus of Pleiades and the chorus of Hyades dance around the sun, whose position is identified emphatically as right ἐν μέσωι of the round surface. The sun is presented as a κύκλος. *Phaethôn*, it does one thing: shine. The action of the verb κατέλαμπε, strikingly, is carried by the agency of the winged steeds, ἵπποις πτεροέσσαις. The gleam of Helios, in other words, is synaesthetically expressed through the notion of rapid movement.[71] In parallel to the framing shield, the circular shape of the sun obviously reflects on the physical presence of the chorus in movement here. This, of course, very possibly has something to do with the *kuklios choros* of dithyramb, but there is no reason to reduce the presence of that shape in the text and in performance to a dialogue between the genres.[72] The tragic chorus was as free in its movements as it was in its words, and the range of possibles is too broad for us to zoom in on any particular one.[73] Hunting for the precise details of stagecraft and choreography in the tragic text, as if they contained stage directions that are only waiting to be rediscovered, is a notoriously thankless game of smoke and mirrors. It would be absurd to propose a reconstruction defending this scenario in opposition to that, in order to reconstruct the minutiae of choral dance in the first stasimon of the *Electra*. But some points are worth making.

The emphasis on the movement of the circular sun, and its spectacular effect on vision, invites a three-dimensional perspective. This is an image that is conveyed by more than words. It is mediated by bodies in movement, where the forms in the orchestra, whatever they might have been, and the forms of the song are interlocked in a web of correspondences, oppositions, parallels and echoes. The circular movement of the sun is embodied here and now before our eyes, given a physical support.[74] Choral ecphrasis cannot simply be equated to choral projection. It reconfigures the possibilities of poetic visual representation through movement. The first stasimon of the *Electra* pushes those possibilities as far as they can go.

The dominant feature of that dazzling display of choral mimesis is similarity in difference. The circle of the individual sun is followed by the choruses of many stars, a passage from the singular to the plural predicated on the ability of the *molpê* to embody one register of aetherial movement after another in the blink of an eye. The abruptness of the

---

[71] See Cropp 1988: 132.
[72] D'Angour 1997, Ceccarelli 2013 and Franklin 2013; cf. still Ferri 1932–33.
[73] See Davidson 1986 and Csapo 2008: 282–84.
[74] Cf. the rich visual interactions of stage and heavens in Roman theatre explored by Robert Germany in Chapter 10.

transition is underlined by the fact that two different choruses of stars are evoked at the end of line 467. The sudden focus on Hector's eyes, with which the ecphrasis of the shield ends, involves another displacement of location and perspective, acting as an invitation to consider the object as a whole.[75] The word τροπαῖοι transfers the force of the movement from the turning of the dance to the rout of the enemy.

This rapid succession of moving concentric circles in the aether is what constitutes the inside of the shield. The ecphrasis is presented in two sections, one concerned with the inside of the shield, the other with its rim. The two sections are placed on both sides of a strophic division (464). The first word of the image, the adjective περιδρόμωι at line 458, already evokes movement at the edge of the object. The choice of the rather uncommon word ἴτυς to describe the shield reinforces the notion of the object's circularity, after the κύκλωι of line 455, and proleptically intro- duces connotations of the chariot wheel in movement.[76] But the most striking aspect of the first section of the choral ecphrasis is the trajectory of Perseus and Hermes flying over the sea with the head of the Gorgon in hand.[77] The focus on the winged sandals, as in the case of the winged horses of the sun's chariot, allows for the evocation of a link between the figurative movement of ecphrasis and the movement of the feet onstage. More significantly, the movement described by the ecphrasis is a trajectory, that of one, and then two characters around a circle. The noun περίδρομος can refer to the orbit of stars, or the lap of a race.[78] The outer rim of the shield, in other words, the fundamental delimitation of the object, is nominally empty space. Visual art can hardly represent such a trajectory, and textual ecphrasis tends to fill the space of its circles, like the Oceanus of *Iliad* 18 or the *choros* that precedes it.[79] In choral ecphrasis, that trajectory can be embodied by the dancers, and the course of the movement enacted onstage. The spectacle of the shield in song and dance offers a self- consciously distinctive range of visual experiences in motion, quite unlike any other form of ecphrasis.

Alone among the images of the ode, the shield is presented as the object of an oral report, something that the chorus heard from an anonymous man returning from Troy.[80] The entire ecphrasis, that is, gives shape to that rumour. While the infinitives of the second strophe remain governed by ἔκλυον (457; 460), not letting us forget that the embodied vision

[75] See Denniston 1939: 107.   [76] *LfgrE* sv. ἴτυς (Nordheider).   [77] See Morin 2004.
[78] The *LSJ* cites Aët. 2.1.4 and Cass. Dio 49.43.   [79] H. *Il.* 18.590–608.
[80] Eur. *El.* 452–53: Ἰλιόθεν δ' ἔκλυόν τινος ἐν λιμέσιν / Ναυπλίοις βεβῶτος; cf. Gagné and Hopman 2013a: 10–11.

performed onstage is the expression of that spoken account, the indicatives of the second antistrophe (464; 472) are not subordinated. Far from a claim of superiority on the reports of the past, this framing undermines the idea that the chorus might have some privileged knowledge about that glorious past. Like everybody else in the play, it can only rely on hearsay. But it can animate it, give it a tangible shape that no words can convey. The fact that the dazzling spectacle of ecphrasis that is seen in the ode is the echo of something that has been heard adds yet another facet to the mimesis of the stasimon, and attaches it to the theme of the treacherous, shifting rumours that recur throughout the play. Another thing it does is emphasise the dependence of the song on the stories that came before, and problematise the perspective of the viewing audience.

The choral ecphrasis of the shield of Achilles immediately announces itself as a dialogue with the shield of *Iliad* 18. Yet the presentation of the arms in the first antistrophe already signals that this is something different: we will not be shown an image from Homer. In the *Nereids* of Aeschylus, we know that the arms of Achilles were presented to him by the chorus at Troy, and it is difficult to imagine that some form of referential play with the text of Aeschylus is not also going on here, but we have no way of knowing what it might have been.[81] Whatever the case, when the chorus announces that it will describe the famous shield, κλεινᾶς ἀσπίδος, the audience is surely expecting interaction with other texts (455). The proleptic *deixis* of τοιάδε σήματα orients this experimentation towards the performance of vision (456).[82]

The first image we see is emphatically not Iliadic. There is no Perseus holding the Gorgon's head on the shield of *Iliad* 18. The scene described on the shield, it should also be noted, can hardly be seen to refer to the *gorgoneion* of the Athena Parthenos shield, where the head's central configuration has nothing to do with the circular motion of Perseus described in the ode.[83] It is an image that points in a different direction, towards the Hesiodic shield of Heracles, where we see, prominently figured, Perseus run from the Gorgons with his winged sandals, with the head of Medusa on his back.[84] The Hesiodic shield is also called an ἴτυς (314). The shield of the *Electra* gestures to all its prominent predecessors.

The second part of the ecphrasis, the surface of the shield, does engage directly with the dominant Iliadic model, but it does not simply reproduce

---

[81] Torrance 2013: 78; cf. Lowenstam 1993.
[82] See e.g. Calame 2004: 711, with Denniston 1939: 106.   [83] Csapo 2009: 102–3.
[84] Hes. [*Sc.*] 228–37.

it. In *Iliad* 18, the sun and stars are placed in the middle of the ἀσπίς (483–89), with the Pleiades and Hyades named explicitly.[85] The correspondence is an obvious, direct allusive activation. But it is there to signal difference at the same time as similarity. In the *Iliad*, the stars at the centre of the shield are placed at the very beginning of the ecphrasis, whereas they appear at the end of the description in the *Electra*. In Homer, their movement is implied, fixed. What really comes out of a comparison between the two passages, more importantly, is the contrast between the packed exuberance of the epic shield and the rapid minimalism of the choral passage. All the vivid portraits of the social world that populate the Homeric ἀσπίς are absent from the *Electra*. That absence reinforces the programmatic presence of the figures on the rim, a saviour hero travelling with a protector god, holding the severed head of a female monster. In contrast with the gluttonous narrative expansion that we just saw in Nonnus, the choral shield of the *Electra* is built on focus and contraction.

The presence of the stars at the centre of the shield is what holds the link between the two passages. In the Iliadic text, the edge of the shield, right next to the circular movement of Oceanus on the rim, is occupied by a circular *choros*.[86] The youths who dance around the outer edge of the ἀσπίς in the *Iliad* have disappeared in the *Electra*, but the notion of their choral movement is inscribed in the χορὸς ἄστρων, thus conflating the centre and the edge of the epic shield in one image. More stunningly, the dance-space of the Homeric passage is taken over by the actual performance space of the orchestra, and the dancing youths of the epic embodied here and now for all to see in the successive figures of the choral ecphrasis. Picking on the new resonances of the old Iliadic image, the shield of Achilles is literally brought to life by the new tragic spectacle. Poetic vitality is translated to kinetic force, and the forms of the mind's eye reimagined through the *schêmata* of bodies in movement. The perceptual blending enabled by the astral chorus metaphor generates a dazzling image of imbricated visions. Building on the hallowed models of Homer and Hesiod, pushing the possibilities of dramatic representation beyond the shield descriptions of Aeschylus' *Seven* and his own *Phoenissae*, Euripides experiments with the boundaries of dramatic representation in this ode by

---

[85] See e.g. Hardie 1985: 12–17. The Pleiades, as is often remarked, have a special and long-standing association to choral dance. The Bear constellation is shown to be 'circling in its place' in the Iliadic shield, and, alone, 'it has no part in the baths of Ocean' (Πληϊάδας θ᾽ Ὑάδας τε τό τε σθένος Ὠρίωνος / Ἄρκτόν θ᾽, ἥν καὶ Ἅμαξαν ἐπίκλησιν καλέουσιν, / ἥ τ᾽ αὐτοῦ στρέφεται καί τ᾽ Ὠρίωνα δοκεύει, / οἴη δ᾽ ἄμμορός ἐστι λοετρῶν Ὠκεανοῖο (H. *Il.* 18.485–88; tr. by Murray).

[86] See e.g. Lonsdale 1995.

fully exploiting the mediating potential of choral performance. The chorus of stars is the principal axis of this visual experience, and the ideal icon for the supremely imperfect mimesis claimed by tragedy in its imperial engagement with tradition.

Here, as in Argentarius' epigram and Nonnus' shield ecphrasis, the metaphor of the χορὸς ἄστρων allows the poet to channel reflection on the nature of his art. The chorality of the dancing stars metaphor, the ultimate paradigm of cosmic rhythm, held a vast range of poetic connotations, it opened up many prospective layers of 'semantic stretch', to use Geoffrey Lloyd's useful term.[87] Any attempt to make sense of that image of chorality must of course start from the specific hermeneutic logic of the passage in which it is inscribed. But it is only by contrasting various expressions of the metaphor in comparable usages that the more general outlines and texture can really start to emerge. A key figure of cosmic harmony was revisited time and again to ponder the limits of poetic representation. Absolute model and imperfect reflection: exploring the gap between the two drew from common stores of latent meaning. The striking image of the astral chorus was, among many other things, a powerful catalyst for thinking mimesis in action. Projecting itself onto the *kosmos*, the idea of the choral dance could also reflect the *kosmos* back on song itself.

[87] Lloyd 2003.

CHAPTER 10

All the World's a Stage
Contemplatio Mundi in Roman Theatre

Robert Germany

The Romans render θεωρεῖν as *contemplari*, θεωρία as *contemplatio*. This translation, proceding from the spirit of the Roman language and thus of the Roman *Dasein*, obliterates at a single stroke that which is essential in the import of the Greek words. For *contemplari* means to section off and bound. *Templum* is the Greek τέμενος, which arises from a totally different experience than θεωρεῖν. τέμνειν means cut, divide.

Martin Heidegger[1]

10.1 Introduction

Heidegger's distinction between Roman *contemplatio* and Greek θεωρία points to a subtle but important difference all too often lost in the philosophical and Christian tradition of treating the former as a straightforward calque for the latter.[2] The Latin word does indeed rest on a religious category and conceptual world at variance with its Greek "equivalent." The noun *contemplatio* is unattested before Cicero, but the verb *contemplari* (or *contemplare*) goes back to the earliest Latin writers, and as Varro and others explain, the "temples" at play in this word are none other than the augural *templa* of the Roman ritual of auspication.[3] If the

[1] M. Heidegger, *Wissenschaft und Besinnung*, 1954 (VA 50): "Die Römer übersetzen θεωρεῖν durch contemplari, θεωρία durch contemplatio. Diese Übersetzung, die aus dem Geist der römischen Sprache und d. h. des römischen Daseins kommt, bringt das Wesenhafte dessen, was die griechischen Worte sagen, mit einem Schlag zum Verschwinden. Denn contemplari heißt: etwas in einem Abschnitt einteilen und darin umzäunen. Templum ist das griechische τέμενος, das einer ganz anderen Erfahrung entspringt als das θεωρεῖν. Τέμνειν heißt: schneiden, abteilen."

[2] On Heidegger's *Augenblick* and its complex debt to Aristotelian θεωρία, see McNeill 1999. Bénatouïl and Bonazzi 2012 is a good recent survey of the Hellenistic philosophical cult of θεωρία/*contemplatio* and its Neoplatonic and Christian *Nachleben*, but here as usual the Greek and Latin terms are generally assumed to be interchangeable.

[3] Varro (*Ling.* 7.9) traces both *templum* and *contemplare* to *tueri* (on which, see later in the chapter), but Festus (Paulus), *Gloss. Lat.* 34, derives the verb from the noun: "Contemplari dictum a templo, id est

intent gaze of the augur watching for an interpretable sign in the skies provided the Romans with a handy metaphor for the special kind of looking implied in *contemplatio*, there was also an interesting similarity in the way space was cut and then spectated in Roman theatre. These two institutions, the taking of auspices in through contemplation of the *kosmos* (i.e., the *mundus*) and the production of plays, have not generally been connected in scholarship on Republican culture, but I shall argue here that there is a surprising structural homology between these symbolic spatial systems, one that emerges as a preoccupation of the plays themselves. There are scattered hints of interest in augural contemplation across the fragments of early Roman drama, but I hope to show more particularly that Plautus, for one, was aware of this happy parallel and ready to exploit it in his comedies. I shall also cast a brief glance at later refashioning of this motif in the philosophy and drama of Seneca.

10.2 Θεωρία and *Contemplatio*: Religious, Philosophical, and Theatrical

From at least the sixth century BCE, Greek *poleis* would send public delegates to religious events in other cities, where they would act as official spectators (θεωροί), returning home afterwards to make a report of what they saw.[4] The philosopher or the mystic likewise undertakes a kind of journey into the far country of truth, a sojourn from which he may return to make a report of his vision for the rest of us, so it is not hard to see how this tradition would find the concept of spectatorial embassy (θεωρία) so useful a metaphor for its own activity. But before the philosophers ever laid their claim on the metaphor of θεωρία, it had already been appropriated by Greek drama, as the spectators in fifth-century Athenian theatre (θεαταί) could be figured as θεωροί.[5] They too went on an imaginative journey through space and time and saw some amazing sights and then returned to present-day Athens where they might be expected to bring with them the wisdom won on their travels to other worlds. Thus theatre first and later philosophy, with their overlapping but different uses of the category

loco, qui ab omni parte aspici, vel ex quo omnis pars videri potest, quem antiqui templum nominabant."

[4] Alongside this civic institution, individuals could also undertake θεωρία, on which see Bill 1901: 199; Ker 2000: 310; and Nightingale 2004: 47–49. This dual public–private character amounts to a further similarity to Roman augury, which was sponsored by the state but was also conducted privately (Cic. *Div.* 1.16).

[5] See Rutherford 1998: 135; Goldhill 1999: 5–8; Monoson 2000: 206–26; and (somewhat contra) Nightingale 2004: 49–52.

θεωρία, can both be described as anchoring themselves in the metaphorical register of the same Greek ritual practice.

Laboring in the shadow of Fraenkel's magisterial work, the study of Roman comedy has often concerned itself with *plautinisches im Plautus*, the elucidation of which elements in the plays were carried over from the Greek originals and which elements are native to Italian soil. For the most part scholars have not looked for deep resonances between Roman theatre and Roman religion. Why would they, after all, since *palliata*, at least, announces its Greekness at every turn? But if my argument here is right, we have missed an echo of Italian ritual practice in Roman comedy. The metaphor is drawn from auspication, rather than pilgrimage, but *contemplatio* is every bit as distinctively Roman as θεωρία is Greek, and to the extent that the relevant ritual metaphor lives on in theatre and in philosophy, there may be abiding differences between θεωρία and *contemplatio*, for the former is closer to tourism and the latter is more like television. If the Athenian θεατής is a θεωρός, then he takes an imaginitive journey to a distant land. The Roman spectator analogized to the auspicant sits safely in his own city and watches an alien *mundus* through a temporary window cut into space.

The details of the practice of auspication in ancient Rome are a matter of scholarly dispute, but Livy's description of the inauguration of Numa Pompilius gives some sense of the procedure (1.18). The augur sat on a stone on the Arx facing south holding the *lituus*, the distinctive wand of his office, in his right hand, and with it he "marked out the regions [of the sky] from east to west" (*regiones ab oriente ad occasum determinavit*), defining the southern part of the heavens as right and the northern as left. Then he fixed upon a distant point as a *signum*, transferred the *lituus* to his left hand and setting his right hand on Numa's head made his prayer to Jupiter that if it be heaven's will that Numa should be king he would reveal it by sure signs "within those boundaries which I have traced" (*inter eos fines quos feci*). The augur described the *auspicia* he wanted sent, they were sent, and Numa, now shown to be king, "came down from the temple" (*de templo descendit*). This *templum* Livy refers to, sometimes called an *auguraculum*, is the place where the auspicant sits and watches, waiting for the birds or other heavenly signs to reveal themselves, but this was not the only *templum* in play. We know from multiple ancient sources that the patch of sky blocked out by the augur was also called a *templum*.[6] For example,

---

[6] Naevius may have the earliest attestation. Probus (*ad Ecl.* 6.31) says Ennius made Anchises an augur and Naevius likewise in the first book of the *Bellum Punicum*: "Postquam avem aspexit in

Servius: *templum dicitur locus manu auguris designatus in aere, post quem factum ilico captantur auguria.*[7] So the auspicant sat in one temple, a *templum in terris*, and gazed expectantly at another, a *templum in caelo.*[8] The former was made of permanent materials and the latter was drawn up each time for the nonce.[9] The semantic connection between these two uses of the same word seems to be that both involve a cutting (the Indoeuropean *tem-* root).[10] A line is ritually traced out demarcating a space that is literally "spoken out and freed" (*effatum et liberatum*) from the surrounding continuum.[11] The piece of space thus cut out is free to take on a new significance, charged in fact as the zone of signification, the screen in the sky at which the auspicant stares and waits for a message from the gods. Varro (*Ling.* 7.9) even offers an etymology connecting *templum/contemplatio* with *tueor*. This is, for us, an obviously false etymology, but it shows something of the radical association of temples in the Roman mind with this kind of intent watching.

This basic configuration – sitting in one temple and watching another – bears a remarkable resemblance to the shape of theatrical practice in the middle Republic. The Imperial architectural habit of combining monumental stone theatres with temples was, of course, years in the future, but the close association of temple and *ludi scaenici* seems to go back at least to the third century BCE.[12] As Hanson and others have long suggested and Goldberg has now conclusively shown, Plautus's temporary stages will have been erected directly in front of a temple with the audience sitting directly on the temple steps and pronaos.[13] As Cicero tells us, the plays at

---

templo Anchisa, / sacra in mensa Penatium ordine ponuntur; / immolabat auream victimam pulchram" (= Naev. *fr.com.* 3).

[7] Serv. *ad A.* 1.92. Some scholars (e.g. Taylor 2000: 21) have argued that the augural *templum in caelo* is not a part but rather the whole sky. This Servian testimony would seem to contradict such a view.

[8] For how these *templi* effectively constitute distinct *mundi*, see later.

[9] Did the internal structure of the permanent temple give shape to the temple above, or was the former built to conform to the structure assumed to exist naturally in the latter? Torelli 1995a investigates a Republican augural temple at Bantia where there were six *cippi* arranged to correspond to subdivisions of the celestial temple. One *cippus* seems to be for the god Nocturnus and another for Sol, two deities similarly juxtaposed, as Torelli notes (107–8), in Plautus (*Amph.* 272–82).

[10] Like Heidegger, quoted earlier, Linderski 1986: 2264 f. 466 follows Ernout-Meillet, but he gives a summary of other (speculative or discredited) theories as well. Interesting among them, for our thesis, is Weinstock 1932, which argues that the original sense of *templum* was *Brett, Balken*. By synecdoche then the meaning would transfer from the cross-beam to "*die aus diesen Brettern gebaute Hütte*" (108) and finally to the field of observation from this building. Weinstock points to ancient testimony of *templum* as "wooden cross-beam," and even if he is wrong about the etymological causality, this alternative sense of *templum* amounts to a tantalizing further connection with the wooden stage.

[11] Beard et al. 1998: 22.

[12] For private cosmic spaces in Imperial Rome, see Sauron's contribution to this volume, Chapter 11.

[13] Hanson 1959; Goldberg 1998.

the Ludi Megalenses were staged *in ipso Matris magnae conspectu* (*Har. resp.* 24), and this was probably the case for other games as well, with some variation depending on the festival occasion and the practical suitability of the relevant deity's temple to serve such a purpose.[14] To be sure, this was not an augural temple, but it was a temple nonetheless, and it is worth noting its permanent character, the seated posture of the spectators, and their gaze trained at a target outside the boundaries of the temple itself. The stage would not be called a temple, in spite of its altar, but its emphatically temporary character and its highly stylized code system for constructing spatial relationships onstage and off render it a similarly legible spatial register.

The stage and the *templum* of augural spectation were not only alike in being delimited in spatial extension and even cut off from the surrounding continuum, they were also alike in being similarly bounded in time. The *templum in caelo* must be redesignated for each observation, and the Roman stage was reconstructed and torn down afresh for every *ludi*. This temporary character of both stage and aerial temple is in contrast to the permanent temples in which the augur and the theatrical audience sat. There is another sense, though, in which the *templum in caelo* is temporally bounded. Apart from the temple not outlasting a single consultation, the efficacy of any given auspices was limited to a single day. Likewise, for both public and private affairs, one had to take the auspices on the day one wanted to do the task in question, and at the end of the day the auspices, whether good or bad, were understood to expire.[15] However long the procedure of taking the auspices required (and one assumes it would be somewhat variable, depending on how cooperative the birds were), the augury asserted a claim in time a little beyond the performance of the ritual, but only up to the limit of a single day. Similarly, a Roman comedy might require only a couple hours to perform and the story-time subtended by the plot could last somewhat longer, not, however, more than a single day. This, at any rate, seems to be one of the "rules" of the genre, the so-called Unity of Time.[16] The Roman stage is thus a temporary cut in space, both in the sense that it will be dismantled after the show and in the sense that the fictional world onto which it opens a window is itself literally ephemeral.

The spatial construction of the play's world had another echo with the augural temple in the semantic overlay between the various senses of the

---

[14] Marshall 2006: 42 speculates that the steps of the temples of Saturn and Concordia may have been used this way too.
[15] Catalano 1960: 42–45.   [16] Schwindt 1994, Dunsch 2005, Germany 2014.

word *templum* and those of the word *mundus*. Varro tells us there are three kinds of *templum*: in the sky, on the earth, and under the earth (*Ling.* 7.6). He mentions auspication specifically with reference to the earthly *templum*, but when he describes the celestial *templum* he is clearly thinking of auspication as well, since he assumes it is viewed facing south (*Ling.* 7.7): "of that *templum* there are said to be four parts, the left from the east, the right from the west, in front the southern, and behind the northern." This sounds very much like how he describes the *mundus* elsewhere (Festus, *Gloss. Lat.* 454): "When you look south from the shrine of the gods towards the left are the eastern parts of the *mundus*, on the right the western. I believe the practice is that they judge auspices on the left to be better than on the right." *Mundus* could refer to the celestial vault above (OLD *mundus*³ 1), the terrestrial world around us (OLD *mundus*³ 2), and alongside these maximally expansive senses of the word, a more limited subterranean *mundus* (OLD *mundus*⁴), a kind of underground vault or pit, sealed on most days by a stone lid called the *lapis manalis*, but opened up three times a year (August 24, October 5, and November 8) with the eldritch proclamation *mundus patet*.[17] On these days the dead were said to wander among the living, as the door between the upper and lower worlds was opened. This subterranean world is a kind of mapping or mirroring of the heavenly sphere, like the subterranean *templum* which Varro dubs *a similitudine* (*Ling.* 7.6). As Cato says, "The name is transferred to the *mundus* from that *mundus* which is above us; for the shape of it, as I have found out from those who have entered it, is like the other" (Festus, *Gloss. Lat.* 144).

This subterranean *mundus*, or the opening to it at any rate, is usually identified with the Umbilicus Urbis in the Forum and connected to Plutarch's description of the foundation of Rome:[18]

> A circular trench was dug around the Comitium, and inside it was placed a first-fruits offering of all natural and customary necessities. Finally, each of those participating brought a sample of his native soil to place inside the trench and add to the mix. They call this trench, as they do heaven, by the name *mundus*. Then they marked out the city around this, as a circle from a center.

> βόθρος γὰρ ὠρύγη περὶ τὸ νῦν Κομίτιον κυκλοτερής, ἀπαρχαί τε πάντων, ὅσοις νόμῳ μὲν ὡς καλοῖς ἐχρῶντο, φύσει δ' ὡς ἀναγκαίοις, ἀπετέθησαν ἐνταῦθα. καὶ τέλος ἐξ ἧς ἀφῖκτο γῆς ἕκαστος ὀλίγην κομίζων μοῖραν ἔβαλλον εἰς ταὐτὸ καὶ συνεμείγνυον. καλοῦσι δὲ τὸν βόθρον τοῦτον ᾧ καὶ

---

[17] Fowler 1912.   [18] See Humm 2004: 50 for discussion and references to earlier scholarship.

τὸν ὄλυμπον ὀνόματι μοῦνδον. εἶθ᾽ ὥσπερ κύκλον κέντρῳ περιέγραψαν τὴν πόλιν. (Plutarch, *Life of Romulus* 11)

This *mundus* is multiply isomorphic: it is circular like both the notional city surrounding it and the universe surrounding that city. It establishes, at the level of shape, the *urbs/orbis* homology that runs from Varro down to the current pope. Its boundary is set by cutting or digging, just like the boundary of its urban mapping, and yet it functions as a microcosm not only because it shares the form of the larger world, but because it shares its substance. The gathering of soils from the native lands of the founders implies more than just synoecism; it also suggests that the *mundus* is always already consubstantial with Rome's *imperium*. At the belly button of the Roman city one finds a self-contained "world" of multiple reference between here, above, and below and of pointed ambiguity on earth. As Mircea Éliade noted, "ce *mundus* était le lieu d'intersection des trois niveaux cosmiques."[19] Yet we can go further: not only does the earth meet the sky and the underworld on this spot, but also within the terrestrial level, various non-Roman geographical alterities are made to intersect just here. Like the similarly tripartite *templum* more generally, this *mundus* is cut off and ritually freed from its surrounding space and allowed to be a world unto itself.

10.3   Comedy: Plautus

Roman augury was an impressive science and public event, and the promise of a window onto divine sanction or the future is always hard to ignore, so it is no surprise that the language of auspication should come up often in Roman comedy, since the everyday talk of the audience too must have taken frequent recourse to this thematic register. More remarkable, perhaps, is how often the auspication references in Roman comedy pertain to the events of the play itself. So, for example, in the *Rudens*, when the pimp Labrax is unexpectedly forced to deal with Trachalio, the slave of the lover of one of the girls he has captured, he complains (*Rud.* 717): *non hodie isti rei auspicavi, ut cum furcifero fabuler.* Indeed, Trachalio is probably one of the last people he expected to see in this play, set as it is, exceptionally, on the remote shore of Cyrene, far from the *furcifer*'s home in Athens, where most comedies are set.[20] Of course, we are not to understand that he

<hr/>

[19] Éliade 1964: 315.
[20] On the peculiarly Roman resonance of Labrax's exile (and the significance of justice catching up to him there), see Leigh 2010.

literally took auspices to this effect; he is merely talking about his expectations, but he casts the *Erwartungshorizont* for this play's "today" in the metaphor of auspication. In the *Mercator* we meet the horny old man Demipho at the beginning of Act Two when he reports a prophetic dream in which he comes into possession of a beautiful she-goat and gives her into the care of a monkey who becomes angry at him because of the inconvenience. Then a kid appears and announces that he has stolen the she-goat and leaves Demipho weeping. After describing this dream Demipho immediately begins to interpret it by trying to figure out who each figure represents: the she-goat must be the lovely new slave girl he has just fallen for, of this much he is sure. The audience meanwhile is playing the same interpretive game, based on everything that was revealed in Act One.[21] At this moment Lysimachus comes onstage shouting back into his house instructions to castrate a he-goat who has been making trouble. "I don't like that omen or *auspicium*," says Demipho in an aside, "I'm afraid my wife my will castrate me like the he-goat and take for herself the part of the monkey" (*Merc.* 274–76).[22]

Compare the scene in Act Four of *Cistellaria*, where Halisca comes out praying for the gods' help and then the audience's to find the lost casket (*Cist.* 678–81): "Good people, my spectators (*mei spectatores*), give me some sign (*indicium*), if anyone saw who stole it away or picked it up and whether they set off this way or that. I'm no better off for questioning and troubling these folks, who take delight in a woman's travails." She sets about looking for tracks, then falls to ruminating on the paradoxical consequences for herself of the loss of the casket that gives her play its title (*nulla est, neque ego sum usquam. perdita perdidit me*, 686). Eventually she summons herself back to task (693–94): *Halisca, hoc age, ad terram aspice et despice, / oculis investiges, astute augura.* The metatheatrical theme of trying to figure the play out is even clearer here than in the *Rudens* and *Mercator* passages, this time, though, it is not about predicting the future

---

[21] On the dream as a puzzle (for the audience as much as for Demipho), see Marshall 2010: 67. For a survey of scholarship on this dream, see Augoustakis 2008: 40–42.

[22] Once again, this is not a real *auspicium* but another kind of sign, and it might be objected that unlike the procedure for formally taking auspices described earlier in the chapter, Demipho is simply noting an omen that comes up on the fly. Modern scholars distinguish between impetrative auspices (the intentionally sought kind) and oblative auspices, which pop up unbidden without the auspicant having to follow any preparatory procedure. However, this distinction, as useful as it is for us in classifying these phenomena, is unattested before Servius (*ad Aen.* 6.190), so perhaps we are safe in seeing a slippage between these types of auspication in Plautus. In any case, Demipho assumes that the manner of another character's stage entrance could be read, like an *auspicium*, and interpreted in continuity with his prophetic dream of the day's events.

but reading a present reality and drawing the spectators directly into the question as a possible source of a sign. Little does she know it, but Halisca has an internal audience, Lampadio and Phanostrata, who are even now reading her behavior and identifying her as the one who lost the casket by her movement onstage (*certe eccam; eum locum signat*, 696).[23] "He went this way," Halisca cries to herself in pursuit of her ever more metatheatrical quarry, "I see the trace of his comic slipper in the dust" (*socci video / vestigium in pulvere*, 697–98). She goes on to reconstruct the blocking of the previous scene's stage movement, and then she discovers that he may still be somewhere very near indeed and perhaps she should direct her contemplation to the stage: "But he went off this way. I'll watch for him. He went from here to here and never left from here" (*sed is hac abiit. contemplabor. hinc huc iit, hinc nusquam abiit*, 702).[24]

Nine times in the extant corpus Plautus uses the phrase *in mundo*.[25] This strange expression is sometimes translated as "ready" or "to hand" and explained as deriving from the adjective *mundus, -a, -um* (OLD[1] 4 makes this connection), but apart from the fact that such a phrase as "in the neat" would seem forced in relation to the concept of readiness or availability, such a nominalization, *mundum*, is otherwise totally unattested. Long ago, Gulick 1896 argued that the phrase *in mundo* is not from the adjective, but from the noun *mundus*, the celestial zone of auspication, and that it means something like "on the augural horizon," or perhaps as we might say "on the cards." In the *Asinaria*, for example, Libanus comes onstage exhorting himself to come up with a plan to save his master. He is pondering where he should get the cash, whom he should trick, where he should steer the jollyboat of the play; just then he gets a sign from above (*Asin.* 258–66):

> I've got my auspices, my auguries! The birds allow full choice of destination
> [*impetritum, inauguratumst: quovis admittunt aves*]. Woodpecker and crow
> on the left, raven and owl on the right, they all say it's so! I'll follow your

[23] Rather than serving their generically usual purpose of confirming the identity of the long-lost-but-now-found child, the tokens of recognition in the casket are a sign to Phanostrata that her search for her daughter is near its end, if only she follows the casket to its owner. See Manuwald 2004: 145. Thus the theme of interpretation around the *cistellaria* is a two-way street, as Halisca tracks her (internal) audience and they track her.

[24] This metatheatrical play with successful or failed interpretation and the motif of having a role in a comic plot comes up glancingly in the *Captivi*. Aristophontes has been temporarily freed, just long enough to come onstage and spoil everything for Tyndarus, when he fails to catch on to the play-within-the-play until it is too late. Now that Hegio is herding him offstage and back to his former condition, his parting lines reveal the limits of his role in this comedy: "I predicted myself out of chains [*exauspicavi ex vinclis*]. Now I understand that I must repredict myself back into them" (*nunc intellego redauspicandum esse in catenas denuo*, 766–77).

[25] *Asin.* 264, 316; *Cas.* 565; *Epid.* 618; *Per.* 45; *Poen.* 783; *Pseud.* 499, 500; *Stich.* 477.

advice for sure. But what's this? The woodpecker tapping on an elm? Coincidence? I think not! One thing I know for sure from the augury of that woodpecker: there's rods *in mundo* either for me or for the steward Saurea. But what's that? Leonida running up out of breath? I'm afraid he's bringing bad omen for my tricksy treacheries.

Obviously, Libanus is not saying the elm rods are "ready" ("in the tidy"?); he is forecasting them on the basis of the woodpecker's behavior. After a bit of back and forth, Leonida comes up with a great plan, one sure to make them both worthy of crucifixion, and Libanus exclaims, "Ah, that's it! I was wondering why my shoulders have been itching all this time. They've begun to say sooth, that there's a whipping for them *in mundo*" (315–16). Leonida's plan turns out to involve an intrigue, where he plays Saurea, and he asks Libanus to take it easy if he has to punch him in the jaw a little bit. "You won't lay a finger on me, if you're smart," says Libanus, "or you'll find you've changed your name today with bad auspices" (373–74).

Consider Epidicus, the hero of his own play, who comes onstage in Act Two to fleece the old men and assures Stratippocles, still back in the house, "Don't worry. I'm coming out here with clear auspices, a bird on the left" (181–82). He is right, of course, the day and the auspices are his, as he seems to realize in Act Three when he refers to the transfer of money happening <*meo*> *auspicio* (343) and as Stratippocles understands when he attributes the successful outcome to the *virtute atque auspicio Epidici* (381). But by Act Five things have become quite a bit more complicated for poor Epidicus, and it is not clear how a happy ending could still be in store. "Even if Jupiter brings himself and eleven other gods besides," he moans, "they won't be able to rescue Epidicus from crucifixion" (610). He has seen the old men preparing the instruments of his torture, but Stratippocles says, "Don't worry" (the same thing Epidicus had said to him before). "Naturally," fires back Epidicus wryly, "since I've got liberty *in mundo*" (618). Whether he is just being sarcastic or making the more philosophical point that death, at least, will bring freedom, it is clear that the metaphor of auspication has turned sour for him.

Likewise, in the *Stichus* the parasite Gelasimus comes onstage proclaiming:

> I've come outside with the best of auspices today [*auspicio hodie optumo*]: a weasel ran off with a mouse right before my feet. What a windfall of an omen! Completely clear to me [*spectatum*]. For just as the weasel found sustenance for itself today, I hope to do so too. This is what the augury portends. (*Stich.* 459–63)

Just then he notices the young spender Epignomus and figures this must be his promised meal ticket. He greets him and begins fishing for an

invitation to dinner. The conceit of this scene is that Gelasimus is generously inviting Epignomus to dinner at his own (that is, Epignomus')
house, an offer Epignomus presumably cannot refuse. Epignomus sees
through this absurdity, of course, and politely declines the paradoxical
invitation. "Don't get mad," says Gelasimus. "You should say yes. I do have
something [*nescioquid*] *in mundo*" (476–77). There is a nice irony here. To
the extent that *in mundo* can mean something as bland as "in store" and
nescioquid can refer to something one does, in fact, already know, this
sentence could be spoken by someone who really is inviting a friend to
dinner. But, of course, *nescio quid* can also resolve back into "some
I-don't-know-what" and in fact alongside Gelasimus' putative promise
that something is up for dinner, he is also saying that he has something
(he does not yet know what) on the augural horizon. None of this works,
and poor Gelasimus is left alone with only the indication that maybe he can
help with the leftovers tomorrow (*cras*, 496), in other words, definitely not
in this play. "I'm done for," he realizes, "completely unmoored. It's all one
Gelasimus less than it was. Never again shall I trust a weasel. I don't know
a fickler beast. Ten times a day it changes its place, and I staked my life on
auspices from it?" (497–502). In Act Three of the *Poenulus* the pimp Lycus
reports that the soothsayers have just given him bad omens, but surely they
must be wrong, since things have been turning out so well for him, but
even as he says this Agorastocles and his *advocati* are spying on him. They
confront him, things get tense, and he curses them (783): "Woe to your
life!" "That's <*in*> *mundo* for your life!" they fire back, thus echoing the
prophecy he thought he had escaped. At the beginning of the *Persa*, as soon
as Sagaristio agrees to help Toxilus try to find money, the latter is exultant:
nempe habeo in mundo (45). This assurance is neatly balanced by the pimp's
lament when he finally does give up the money that today was predicted to
be a profitable day: *lucro faciundo auspicavi in hunc diem* (689). In the
Pseudolus when the hero is asked why he did not keep Simo apprised of his
son's affair he replies, "I knew the mill was *in mundo* for me if I said
anything" (499). Simo fires back: "didn't you know the mill was *in mundo*
for you when you kept it hidden?" Pseudolus answers that he did, but that
"the one punishment was at hand and the other was further off, the one
present and the other a few days away." These *dieculae* (503) are more than
enough to postpone any punishment past the boundary set by the Unity of
Time, the one-day limit of every Plautine world.

  In all these hints that the world of the play is a *mundus* unto itself, cut off
from the surrounding world like the augural *mundus* in the sky and with an
alien soil like the *mundus* in the Forum, one sees an instance of the

peculiarly Roman fascination with the paradoxical geography of the stage and the wormhole that seems to surround its fictional location. For instance, the prologue of the *Menaechmi* explains that the "here" of the stage is "nowhere, unless it's where it's supposed to be" (*nusquam . . . nisi ubi factum dicitur*, 10). Usually it is Athens, he admits, but the setting can change just like the fictional residents who live onstage, and today "here" is Epidamnus. He even offers, for a fee of course, to take care of other business in Epidamnus if anyone in the audience needs his services (51–53). There is a similar conceit in the *Casina*. The prologue explains that a father and son are in competition for the love of a slave girl, the eponymous heroine, Casina. In an attempt to secure permanent access to the girl, the father, Lysidamus, has prompted a loyal slave to seek her hand in a sham marriage. Meanwhile the son has exactly the same idea and puts forward his own proxy. To make matters more complex still, Lysidamus' wife has learned about all this and, because of her jealous desire to thwart her husband's happiness, has become her son's best friend and champion of his cause with Casina. Thus the play revolves around the overt contest between two slaves and the covert contest between the master and matron of the house. To keep the focus on the dispute between man and wife, the son is left entirely out of the picture. As the prologue says (*Cas.* 64–66): "Don't wait around for him; today, in this comedy, he won't be returning to the city. Plautus didn't want him to and severed a bridge that was in his way." The playwright could have left the *adulescens* totally out of account, or if he did not want his audience wondering why the lad was not around to see to his own love life, he could easily enough have come up with a plausible excuse for his absence, one that did not involve Plautus himself coming in, like the animator's eraser in *Duck Amuck* chasing poor Daffy around. The bridge he destroys has no existence apart from this line, was only invented to be cut.[26] But this move not only reminds us of the utter fictiveness of the play's reality, it also generates a sense of the Athens of this comedy cut off from the rest of the world, or at least no more accessible than Plautus wants. An audience member may interfere with the performance, but genuinely breaking into the play world from without would be a feat of a different kind. Here too the Unity of Time is part of this game: a broken bridge will not stop true love forever, but it will slow it down

---

[26] O'Bryhim (1989: 82) reads *hodie in hac comoedia* as an indication that in Diphilus' original, the young lover did return, but as Sharrock (2009: 37 n. 48) rightly notes, this detour is "typical Plautine messing" and probably not secure evidence of the content of his Greek source. Either way, though, the bridge is invoked solely to serve as a functional absence, a nonbridge that marks Plautus' intervention as an act of quarantine, rendering the world of the play *effatum et liberatum*.

enough to keep the boy offstage for today (*hodie*, 64), and as both Plautus and his audience understand, that will be enough. The play world's temporal boundary is as impassable as a river without a bridge and as hard as the edge of the stage.

The prologue's closing shot returns to this theme in a subtler form. He describes Casina herself:

> She'll be found to be chaste and proper, a good Athenian girl, she won't do anything naughty, that's for sure, at least not in this comedy. Soon enough, once the play's over, if someone gives her money I imagine she'll be ready to wed without waiting for auspices. (81–86)

Casina may not be that kind of girl, but the actress who plays her probably is, and with a little cash down there will not be any standing on ceremony (*non manebit auspices*, 86). The trouble is, of course, you may have a hard time finding her once the play is done. Female roles were played by male actors, so if you do rush into things with this heroine, you will find yourself in exactly the same position as the slave of Lysidamus does in Act Five, when he thinks he is bedding Casina only to find that his rival has been substituted at the last moment for the lovely Casina, and he is tricked into going to bed with a man in drag.[27] The further irony, regarding the boundary between fictive world and reality, is that Casina herself never actually appears in the play. So not only is there no actress, there is no actor.[28] Returning to the parallel between theatre and augury, we can affirm that the Casina who will not wait for *auspices* is a Casina who does not exist at all.

The language of auspication makes one more notable appearance in this play. At the end of Act Three, Scene One, Lysidamus has set everything up to his advantage and departs to take care of some quick business in the forum, crowing in expectation of the opportunity he will soon have to bring his love affair to fulfillment. He leaves the stage empty and some time has evidently passed when his wife enters for Scene Two. She has

---

[27] Gold 1998 reads Chalinus' cross-dressing as the focus for the play's destabilization of gender essentialism, since "Casina's" existence as a woman and an onstage character is all performance, fooling only Olympio, Alcesimus, and Lysidamus. My reading of the prologue is thus an expansion of her take on this later scene, since the audience is teasingly invited to make a mistake parallel to that made by the comedy's dupes.

[28] Ehlers 1998 suggests that there was "*Wahrscheinlich*" (192), a mute, maskless actress/prostitute onstage during the prologue, and that she was seriously being offered up to the audience for sex work after the show. Otherwise, he wonders, would her total absence from the play not be a confusing disappointment: "*Eine reine Posse also, einen flauen Witz für männliche Zuschauer?*" (190). I suspect that the interest of this scene is somewhat more sophisticated than that.

uncovered the plan and immediately begins to undermine all his arrangements. When he returns to the stage in Scene Three she is waiting for him,
and he finds that everything has changed in his absence; the balance of
power has shifted, and his chance has passed:

> Total stupidity, in my opinion, for any lover to go to the forum, who has the
> object of his affections *in mundo* for that day. I've been stupid and done just
> that: I've frittered away the day standing as advocate for some relative of
> mine. (563–67)

When Lysidamus squanders his lucky day with Casina by spending it in
the forum, he is also missing his chance to control events onstage.[29] The
kinsman who detains him in the forum too long turns out to have the same
essential role as the broken bridge that keeps his son out of the play
altogether. It is too late now; Casina is not *in mundo* after all. Or rather,
perhaps, building on what we said earlier, she never really was "in the
world" at all.

10.4 Tragedy: Seneca's *Agamemnon*

Looking beyond Plautus, the usual frustration in studies of early Roman
theatre obtains: we have so little else, apart from Terence, that it is hard
to determine how consistent a theme of Roman drama augural *contemplatio* was. The fact that Terence seems less interested in auspication
than Plautus may be explained by the presumption that he stays closer
to the spirit of his Greek originals, which would have no particular
reason to play in this metaphorical register. The phrase *in mundo* is
attested twice in Caecilius (Frs 276 and 278 Ribbeck), but it is hard to
tell much about the context from what little remains. There is
a tantalizing fragment of Ennius, not from a drama, but perhaps in
the paratragic register: *contemplor / inde loci liquidas pilatasque aetheris
oras* ("From that place I contemplate the bright and piled shores of
heaven," *Sat.* 2.3–4). Servius auctus explains the strange word *pilatas*
here: *cum firmas et stabiles significaret quasi pilis fultas* (*ad A.* 12.121). But
surely Ennius' shores of heaven are supported on piles not, in the first
instance, because they are firm and stable, but rather lofty. In any case
they are the object of contemplation from some particular place and,

---

[29] Typically in ancient theatre, the stage is marked as masculine space and the house is feminine, but as
Andrews 2004 points out in the *Casina*, the female characters will seize control of the outside world
and pen the men inside together, thus inverting the usual semantic configuration of space.

like the temporary wooden stage of Ennius' day, held up by stanchions.[30]

It is the collocation of *contemplare* and *templum* that prompts Varro to cite Ennius's *Medea* 240 in his discussion of augural temples (*Ling.* 7.9): *asta atque Athenas anticum opulentum oppidum / contempla et templum Cereris ad laevam aspice* ("Stand and contemplate the ancient, rich town of Athens and behold the temple of Ceres on the left").[31] This *templum* is not an augural temple, of course, nor is it the direct grammatical object of *contempla*, but it is certainly part of the *oppidum* and the pointed object of spectation (*aspice*), and the figura etymologica with *contempla* is striking. Cicero's characterization of Ennius' *Medea* as a word-for-word translation of Euripides (*de Fin.* 1.4) is a slight exaggeration, but most of the fragments we have of it do indeed hew pretty closely to the Greek original. So the change of setting in this fragment from Corinth to Athens is hard to explain. Jocelyn (1967: 344) submitted that these lines are from a second Ennian tragedy about Medea, an Athenian sequel, but there is no sign that any ancient writer knew of more than one play. Vahlen (1903: ccviii) suggested that Ennius fused the plot of Euripides' *Medea* with his *Aegeus* for a monster tragedy that began in Corinth and ended in Athens, but such a scene change would be totally unique in Roman tragedy. Various scholars have proposed that there was only one play, set in Corinth, but that these lines might come from a scene in which Medea (Plank 1807: 97–98) or the chorus (Ladewig 1848: 16) or Aegeus (Pascal 1899: 3; Drabkin 1937: 13) or Jason (Arcellaschi 1990: 55) imagines Medea's future home in Athens. This last possibility may be the most plausible and particularly suggestive for our thesis, in that a character is expected to look at Corinthian space and imaginatively "contemplate" Athens, just as the audience looks at Roman space and reads it as Corinth.

This imaginative preview of Medea's destination (if that is what it is) would be similar to the most famous moment of *contemplatio mundi* in Republican literature, one that had an incalculably vast impact on later Roman, medieval, and early modern cosmologies: Cicero's *Somnium Scipionis*.[32] Earlier in *On the Republic* Scipio acknowledges the importance

---

[30] Consider also Ennius's *Euhemerus* (Fr. 5 G.-M.), where Pan led Saturn up to the mountain called Sky's Pillar (*Caeli Stel<l>a*, 99) from which he looked out (*contemplatus est*) far and wide. He built an altar to Sky there, at which Jupiter later sacrificed, and "from this place he looked up to what we call the sky and that thing called aether, which was beyond the world" (*in eo loco suspexit in caelum quod nunc nos nominamus, idque quod supra mundum erat, quod aether vocabatur*).

[31] The first line of this fragment is given by Nonius (p. 469.34).

[32] There has been much recent work on travel and visual perspective in the *Somnium Scipionis*. See especially Stevens 2006, Schweizer-Vüllers 2011, and Zanini 2012.

of auspication in the founding and maintenance of Rome (*Rep.* 2.16), and just before the dream, when Scipio meets Masinissa, the African prince casts his eyes heavenward (*suspexit ad caelum*, 6.9) and gives thanks to the celestial bodies among whom his guest will soon be soaring. But once the dream begins Scipio inverts the direction of contemplation and looks down on Carthage from the bright starry vault (*de excelso et pleno stellarum, illustri et claro quodam loco*, 6.11). From this unusual perspective, the earth is at the center of the universal *templum*, but both the divine *templum* and the earth are objects of Scipio's gaze (*templum ... quod conspicis ... globum, quem in hoc templo medium vides*, 6.15). But the heavenly *templa* are also Scipio's destination (*aspicis, quae in templa veneris*, 6.17), just as they once were Romulus' (*haec ipsa in templa penetravit*, 6.24). Here too *mundus* functions as a synonym of *templum* (6.13, 17, 18, 19, and 26). Scipio wants to keep on contemplating the earth (*sedem etiam nunc hominum ac domum contemplari*, 6.20), but he is gently admonished to train his gaze upwards to the regions that are, in fact, his destiny. Cicero seems to be building on the rich heritage of the Roman construction of *contemplatio mundi*, but Scipio's dream represents a somewhat more complicated version of *contemplatio* and a departure from the structure I am investigating here, in that the contemplator is on the move, like the Greek θεωρός, into the realms that are the usual object of contemplative spectation. His contempla-tion is not only a journey, however, but also a preview of his later destination, both immediately, in the case of Carthage (*videsne illam urbem ... ad quam tu oppugnandam nunc venis*, 6.11), and more remotely, of his final abode in celestial regions, when contemplation itself will have played its part in liberating the soul from the body (*contemplans quam maxime se a corpore abstrahet*, 6.29). If, as I have argued above, the ritual complex that gives birth to the Greek for-mulation of θεωρία is essentially peregrine, whereas Roman *contempla-tio*, with its roots in augural spectation, is correspondingly stationary, then Cicero is here working from a fundamentally Greek conception of contemplation-as-journey, but one that has been Romanized, not just by the play of temples and worlds, but by the conceit that the object of vision seen on that journey is yet another place where one has still to go.

Despite its psychagogic drama, though, Cicero's dialogic text is not a play. For a significant continuation of the tragic corpus we must skip ahead to Seneca and leave early Roman theatre far behind; however, the analogy of theatrical spectation with reading signs in the heavens is not just a Plautine quirk but deep in the Roman associative matrix of *contemplatio mundi*, and the theme outlives Republican drama.[33] In various places Seneca expresses the idea, familiar from Xenophon, Plato, Aristotle, and many others, that man's upright stature has destined him peculiarly for gazing on the heavens. In Cicero's *On the Nature of the Gods* (2.140) this ability to look up at the sky makes the human race *spectatores* of the celestial *spectaculum*, so the theatrical metaphor of this activity is already explicit a hundred years before Seneca. But Seneca continues this anthropological tradition and in the *On Leisure* (5.4) he refers to our natural design as being specifically to enable our *contemplatio* of the heavens.[34] As he says in *Epistle* 64.6: "For me anyway the *contemplatio* of wisdom tends to take up a lot of time; I gaze upon it in wonder just as I sometimes gaze on the firmament [*mundus*], which I often behold like a first-time theatregoer [*spectator novus*]."

Seneca's drama is particularly rich in the theme of metatheatrical *contemplatio mundi*, but unlike Plautus, who usually invokes the auspicant's gaze for a momentary gag, Seneca tends to integrate it into his construction in a more fundamental way, with consequences that ramify through the whole play.[35] So rather than attempting a full survey of his deployment of this motif, I shall focus here on one play, the *Agamemnon*. The ghost of Thyestes opens the tragedy, announcing his arrival from the gloomy pit of Tartarus and greeting the ancient threshold of the house of Pelops: *hinc auspicari regium capiti decus / mos est Pelasgis* ("From here the Pelasgians are wont to take auspices regarding the royal diadem for the head," *Ag.* 8–9). He means that this is where they inaugurate their reign, of course, but as Tarrant notes, this is an intrusion into a putatively Greek context, of the Roman practice of taking auspices, missing only the *fasces*.[36] From this spot (*hinc*) Thyestes himself will soon be pronouncing prophecies for the crown: "I see the royal head [*regium video caput*, 46] split by the heavy blow of an ax." He claims that his own evil deeds while he lived inverted nature (*versa natura est retro*, 34) and confounded day with night (*miscui nocti diem*, 36), and at the end of the prologue he realizes that his presence is

---

[33] The permanent theatres of the late Republic and the Empire will not, of course, have suggested the same parallel of ephemerality with the augural *mundus* as was natural for the older temporary stages, but there may have been other ways in which these monumental structures could signal their resonance with the heavens. See Aktüre 2008: 96.

[34] Küppers 1996.

[35] Also see Shearin's discussion of the sublime gaze for Stoics and Epicureans in Chapter 12.

[36] Tarrant 1976: 165.

delaying the arrival of Phoebus, so he retires back to the world below with the exhortation, "Give back the day to the world" (*redde iam mundo diem*, 56).

Clytemnestra picks up the theme of the delinquent sun and its connection to Thyestes and to this play. Aegisthus boasts Thyestes as his father, and Clytemnestra adds that he might as well throw in grandfather. He redirects around the sticky subject of his incestuous parentage by claiming that Phoebus is, after all, his ancestor. "Do you call [*vocas*, 295] Phoebus the source of your unspeakable family," she asks, "whom you drove [*expulistis*, 297] from the sky when he pulled back his reins in sudden night?" The addressee of *vocas* is singular and that of *expulistis* plural, and she means to refer principally to the Thyestean feast, but as Thyestes' ghost has already hinted and as we shall soon see, her indictment is relevant to Aegisthus and this play too. The examination of heaven for signs of the gods' sanction or lack thereof is a major theme of Eurybates' extended description of the storm that gathered and broke over the Greek forces as they departed from Troy, and the *mundus* was ripped out from its foundations and it seemed the *caelum* was broken and the gods falling from it as chaos enveloped the earth.[37] Eurybates ends his 160-line monologue with the return of Phoebus and the revelation of the night's destruction, and then Clytemnestra announces the arrival of the "crazed priestess of Phoebus" (*effrena Phoebas*, 588).

The gaze cast from the stage or the world of the play up to the heavens is now reoriented, as Cassandra regards the scene from her dislocated perspective:

> Where am I? Fled is the gladsome light, deep night covers my eyes and the sky lies hid in darkness. But look! The day flashes forth with double sun, and double Argos raises twin palaces. Are these the groves of Ida I see? (726–30)

There is an echo here of the *Bacchae*'s ecstatic Pentheus, seeing double Thebes in his enthusiastic intoxication, but Cassandra's dual vision seems to be split between Troy and Argos, as the apparitions she describes both reveal the hidden truth about the latter and superimpose images of the former. The conceit that Cassandra looks at Argive space and, in the manner of a theatrical spectator, sees Troy is nothing new in Roman drama, as we noted a similar phenomenon earlier in the chapter, in the *Menaechmi*'s intermural hopscotch between Rome and Epidamus and

---

[37] The messenger's cosmic perspective is one of the epic elements of this speech, on which see Baertschi 2010.

(perhaps) in the vision of Athens from Corinth in Ennius' *Medea*, but her role as "Beobachterin und Prophetin" (Riemer 1997: 142) brings Cassandra into even closer alignment with the Roman contemplative auspicant. After Agamemnon's entrance her bifocal perspective between the two cities continues, and of course her blurring is all insight. Agamemnon asks, "Do you think you're seeing Ilium?" "Yes, and Priam too," she answers ominously. "This is not Troy," he objects, to which she replies, "Where Helen is, I think Troy" (*Ag.* 794–95).[38]

Just before this scene with Agamemnon, in a remarkable apostrophe, Cassandra addresses the dead and exhorts them:

> Draw back for a while the covering of the dark vault,
> So the flitting throng of Phrygians may gaze on Mycenae.
> Behold, wretches. Fate is inverted.
>
> reserate paulum terga nigrantis poli,
> levis ut Mycenas turba prospiciat Phrygum.
> spectate, miseri: fata se vertunt retro.   (Seneca, *Agamemnon* 756–58)

This last phrase echoes the claim of Thyestes' ghost in the prologue about his own behavior inverting nature (*versa natura est retro*, 34). Cassandra does not refer to the abode of the dead as a *mundus*, but *nigrans polus* seems like a close equivalent, and she imagines it enclosed by a removable cover, just like the *mundus* that gets opened three times a year in Rome. She addresses the *levis turba Phrygum* as a theatrical audience (*spectate*), but these lines are performed in Rome, before a Roman audience claiming descent from Phrygian Aeneas, and when Cassandra imagines them as watching the stage from another world she is speaking the old language of theatrical *contemplatio*.[39]

The chorus now picks up the running theme of Phoebus unnaturally absent, singing this time about the conception of Hercules, when the law of the *mundus* was broken and the hours of night twinned (812–17). The spinning *mundus* stood still for that child who would mount heaven (*caelum*, 828). As the chorus continues its description of Hercules' life it comes eventually to his final labor, the hound of the nether regions dragged

---

[38] On the theme of history's cyclicity in the *Agamemnon*, see Boyle 1983: 200–202.

[39] The "performance question" – whether these plays were ever publicly staged or only meant for salon reading – is still debated in some quarters, though the evidence for public performance is very strong (Sutton 1986). In any case, for our purposes, it is enough to say that they are written "as if" to be staged (Kohn 2013: 13) and that they are Roman tragedies, coming at the end of a long history of that genre. Even if, as seems unlikely, they were mere closet dramas, they were still constructed in the semiotic traditions developed out of real theatrical practice in Rome, so the *levis turba Phrygum* addressed by Cassandra here remains at least notionally the Roman audience.

to the world above (*tractus ad caelum canis inferorum*, 859). Of course, Hercules did not bring Cerberus to heaven but to Eurystheus, so this use of *caelum* amounts to a focalization of our world, as sky, from the perspective of the underworld, once again very much like Cassandra's description of the dead contemplating the play. Cassandra herself, virtually dead already, now sees the murder of Agamemnon with vision never so clear and gladly takes the role of spectator (*spectemus*, 875). For one last time in the tragedy a character notes the sun's delay, as Cassandra makes explicit the connection that Thyestes' ghost and Clytemnestra have hinted at: *stat ecce Titan, dubius e medio die / suane currat an Thyestea via* (908–9).

One of Kant's better-known aphorisms, chosen by his friends for inscription on his tombstone, runs, "Two things fill the mind with ever new and waxing wonder and awe, the more often and steadily they are considered: the starry heavens above me and the moral law within me."[40] Both of Kant's two things, and indeed the relationship between them, are elucidated in Seneca's work. The primary images for the philosophical life in antiquity are, as Günther Bien has noted, the *Himmelsbetrachter* and the *Glücksforscher*.[41] In Thales and the other Presocratics the former is dominant, and in the Hellenistic schools the latter, but it is probably true that neither is ever completely absent. The intellectual heritage that runs from Aristotle to Theophrastus to Menander makes of the New Comic stage a kind of laboratory of Peripatetic ethics, a screen against which the audience may study the trajectories of vice. But if the Hellenistic audience was one of *Glücksforscher*, translation into Latin and into spatial sensibilities informed by Roman culture made for an audience of *Himmelsbetrachter*. The structural parallels between augural *contemplatio* and theatrical spectation were too good not to be exploited by Plautus and presumably other early Roman playwrights, so that Seneca found himself the inheritor of richly overlapping traditions of analogy between dramatized philosophical θεωρία and theatrical *contemplatio mundi*.

---

[40] *Kritik der praktischen Vernunft* (AA.V.161): "Zwei Dinge erfüllen das Gemüt mit immer neuer und zunehmender Bewunderung und Ehrfurcht, je öfter und anhaltender sich das Nachdenken damit beschäftigt: Der bestirnte Himmel über mir, und das moralische Gesetz in mir."

[41] Bien 1982.

CHAPTER II

The Architectural Representation of the Kosmos from Varro to Hadrian

Gilles Sauron

11.1 Introduction

My contribution to this volume concerns various Roman architectural set-tings whose composition reflects a desire to represent the *kosmos* in different ways. Sometimes, in private spaces, they integrate one person or the owner surrounded by a few chosen friends in a specific arrangement, and sometimes they offer to an outside viewer a cosmic vision, especially to celebrate the universal power of Rome or the apotheosis of an emperor. It is furthermore significant that the monumental arch was used in two cases as an architectural symbol of the world-order. Interestingly, we do not see explicit representa-tions of the astronomical nature of the *kosmos*, as, for example, the armillary spheres, which were known in Rome from the time of the sack of Syracuse by Marcellus, around 213 BCE.[1] What concerns us here is the fact that the *kosmos* is not evoked on its own behalf, in a disinterested way and with scientific purposes, but its evocation is always conditioned by a message, which may be philosophical, ideological or political. In this chapter, I aim to discuss such evocations only by reference to the arrangements of private space, which often correspond to what I call the 'lived *kosmos*'. In this way, it is a question of Plato's cosmology, as it has been presented by Cicero in the *Dream of Scipio* (*Somnium Scipionis*) and in the first book of *Tusculan Disputations*.[2]

11.2 The Aviarium of Varro

The description that Varro himself offers of the aviary he had built in his villa at Casinum (in the foothills of the current Monte Cassino), has been

---

[1] Cic. *Rep.* 1.21. See Gundel 1972 and Brendl 1977.
[2] See the discussions of Plato's cosmology in the contributions of Brisson (Chapter 6) and Atack (Chapter 8).

studied, both philologically and historically, by Georges Seure, who benefited from a graphical reconstruction by the talented architect Charles de
Anges.[3] As was shown by Seure, Varro's aviary was probably built around
80 BCE. For this project, Varro was inspired by two recent architectural
models: the temple of Fortune of the Day, built by Catulus in Rome,[4] and
the Tower of the Winds, the masterpiece of the architect Andronicus of
Cyrrhus, which remains one of the best-preserved monuments in Athens,[5]
and whose fame in antiquity was also celebrated in a description of
Vitruvius (*De arch.* 1.6.4). Varro's structure in his villa at Casinum was a
dining room placed inside an aviary. His guests were required first to take a
path through a rectangular square, observing on either side water and cages
of birds; next, they were settled on a circular bench inside a rotunda
converted into a birdcage through a concentric double colonnade. The
intercolumnations of the two colonnades were closed by fillets. Once they
were finally lying on the benches, what could they see? They were inserted
into a system of visual contradiction.[6] If Varro's guests turned their gaze to
the interior of the dome from which the rotunda was crowned (and that
Varro called *hemisphaerium*), they saw at its centre the random and inchoate
movement of a needle connected to a weathervane, but on the lower circle
of the dome they could observe the regular and circular movement of a star
that indicated the hours. Around them, they could see the birds in their
well-lit cage, but if they gazed upon the central part of the rotunda, located
below, they saw ducks wading in a pond (*stagnum*), an environment both
dark and damp, centred on a 'small island' supporting the pillar around
which pivoted a tambourine-shaped table. For any reader of the *Somnium
Scipionis* in the *Republic* or the first book of *Tusculans* by Cicero – who was
a friend of Varro and a guest at the villa Casinum – the meaning of this
arrangement would have been evident. The guests found themselves in the
middle of an evocation of the *kosmos*, placed exactly at the boundary
between the supralunar world (indicated by the star animated by a uniform
circular motion) and the part of the world beneath the moon (the small
point consisting of the island in the centre and the lower part of the building
is obviously the Earth, 'which astronomers consider in the middle of the
world, which, compared with the entire celestial system, resembles a point,
they call κέντρον' (Cic. *Tusc.* 1.40)). Connected to the 'small island'
representing the Earth, the tambourine-shaped table (*tympanum*) recalls

[3] Varro, *Rust.* 3.5.9–17. Cf. Seure and des Anges 1932.
[4] Identified in the temple B of the excavations at Largo Argentina in Rome by Boyancé 1940.
[5] Cf. von Freeden 1983.   [6] See my study in Sauron 2007a: 143–53.

the association made by Varro of the *tympanon* with the terrestrial disc, as the emblem of the Mother of the Gods (Magna Mater), which he identified with Tellus (Earth): 'the fact that it has a tambourine means it is the Earth' (Fr. 267 Cardauns = Aug. *De civ. D.* 7.24: *quod tympanum habeat, significari esse orbem terrae*). Given that the environment in which the Earth bathes is the part of the sky 'which is damp and dark due to exhalations of the Earth' (Cic. *Tusc.*, 1.43), we can assume that it is the place for meteors, reflected here in the dark 'swamp' (*stagnum*), which can be found again under the weathervane evoking the wind. Guests may have understood that birds bathed in light in a circular space represented souls in heaven, while the ducks paddling on the *stagnum* would be thought to represent impure souls to whom access to heaven was prohibited, or at least postponed.[7] In Varro's aviary, the guests were therefore arranged on a bench which included symbolically the lunar sphere, for in the famous *Dream* written by Cicero, Scipio Aemilianus meets Aemilius Paulus and Scipio Africanus within the Milky Way.[8]

As for the rectangular square that allowed access to the circular aviary, it was to symbolise the view of the *kosmos* from the Earth. Lucienne Deschamps had the ingenious idea of applying here the geometric figures described by Varro.[9] Varro says, indeed, that it features a rectangular square dimension of seventy-two by forty-eight feet, which are both multiples of eight, and the Pythagoreans made this first cube (2^3) the number of Cybele (Kybele, Κυβέλη), the goddess who, as we have seen, Varro likened to the Earth. Varro's diners see, to the right and the left, first long rectangular pools, then bird cages representing the first wetland meteors that surround the Earth. Beyond that, there is the supralunar area, which was associated with immortality by Cicero. The trail (*semita*) they took has been compared by Lucienne Deschamps with an injunction of Pythagoras, reported to us by Iamblichus: 'Forsake the main roads [τὰς λεωφόρους ὁδοὺς ἐκκλίνων]; take the trail [διὰ τῶν ἀτραπῶν βάδιζε]!' (*VP* 105). Cicero had indeed counted the number of diners at Casinum who had settled there in the spring of 44 BCE, accusing them of having transformed into a place of debauchery what had 'before' been reserved 'for discussions, meditation, writing' (*Phil.* 2.105), where 'Roman law, history, philosophy, science' were treated. We can speculate that it was while stationed inside

---

[7] Varro Fr. 226 Cardauns = Aug. *De civ. D.* 7.6; Cic. *Rep.* 6.29.
[8] Ibid. For the activity of *contemplatio mundi* in the *Dream of Scipio*, see the contribution of Robert Germany (Chapter 10).
[9] Deschamps 1987.

Varro's aviary that Cicero directed a contemplative gaze in all directions and had the idea of composing the *Somnium Scipionis*.

11.3   The Frescoes of the 'Second Pompeian Style'

We find the same kind of development in some private contemporary decors. The main source of evidence used by scholars in their interpretation of the advanced phase of the 'second Pompeian style' (phases Ib and Ic of H. G. Beyen) corresponds to the years 80–44 BCE: the decoration of *cubiculum* M of the so-called villa of P. Fannius Synistor in the Metropolitan Museum of Art in New York.[10] It shows perspectival views through architectural pilasters framing, or shrines located on, a podium painted in trompe-l'oeil below the four sides of the room. It has long been recognised that this representation constitutes a transposition of the *pros-kenion* of Hellenistic Greek theatres, in which scenographic paintings reproduced sets of palaces and temples for tragedies, contemporary buildings for comedies and natural vistas for satirical dramas.[11] But we can also see that the stage sets referred to the structure of the *kosmos*, and that if the actors on the stage were indeed to have lived in front of this *proskenion* – here we might recall the Cynics' σκηνὴ ὁ βίος – they also would have lived in an environment that indicated their place in the *kosmos*.[12] I will present only one example here: the decoration of the side walls of the alcove of *cubiculum* M. We see a rotunda, what the Greeks called a θόλος, placed within a peristyle. A strange thing that has not been highlighted by George M. A. Hanfmann is that the sky can be seen between the columns of the peristyle, a feature that probably aims to reproduce a real device. What does this colonnade without a roof mean for the economy of the representation? No doubt the sanctuary which it defines is a heavenly space, far above the clouds. We think of a famous passage in Homer's *Odyssey* describing the visit of the gods on Olympus (*Od.* 6.42–45), which would come to be analysed by the Platonist Plutarch according to the true nature of the gods (*Per.* 39), after having been imitated by Lucretius in his Epicurean description of the homes of the gods (Lucr. 3.18–22). Olympus is there described in these terms: 'the gods always remain constant. Nor do winds shake, nor does rain wet or snow fall there, but it still deploys a cloudless serenity and dazzling white reigns everywhere.' It is also worth considering a curious passage in his dialogue *On the Orator* (3.180), where

---

[10]   See Sauron 2007b: 23–36.   [11]   See Beyen 1957.
[12]   Compare Robert Germany's account of the cosmology of the comic and tragic stage in Chapter 10.

Cicero imagines the Temple of Capitoline Jupiter in heaven, far above the clouds and weather, and claims that even in this case it should retain its roof 'because without it, the monument seems to have lost its dignity' (*nullam sine fastigio dignitatem habiturum fuisse uideatur*). This probably means that the image of the *cubiculum* at Boscoreale does not show a true sanctuary, but instead reproduces some scenography used as the backdrop for a tragedy and symbolically evokes what was called in Rome a 'heavenly temple'. The great Roman national poet Ennius spoke in his *Annals* of 'blue temples of the sky' (En. *Ann.* Fr. 48 Skutsch: *caeli caerula templa*, Fr. 54–55 Skutsch: *caerula caeli templa*), and in one of his tragedies of the 'very high temples of heaven' (Fr. CLXI Jocelyn: *templa caeli summa*), a formulation that Terence borrowed literally (*Eun.* 590). We note, however, that the rotunda has retained its roof – as if the author of the image, who was not necessarily the artist responsible for its execution, was inspired to the letter by the text of Cicero! But it is a surprise to discover that the rotunda is empty, as if it is waiting for a newly arrived deity to reach the sky. As the pattern of the heavenly and empty rotunda is repeated exactly at both ends of the alcove, and thus originally framed the bed that was there, we hardly see as a future occupant of the heavenly temple anyone but the owner of the villa who slept here – or at least his soul. But, beyond this scenic decoration (*scaena*), it is the heavenly destiny of his soul that the creator of this painting's *kosmos* evoked, and the empty rotunda located inside the peristyle which the roofless colonnades could be thought to symbolise is the heavenly home of a soul still exiled on Earth, what Plato called 'the home of the star to which it is assigned' (*Ti.* 44b: τὴν τοῦ συννόμου ... οἴκησιν ἄστρου), a formula transposed by Cicero with a similar metaphor, explaining that the soul must 'reach heaven like home' (*Tusc.* 1.24: *in caelum quasi in domicilium suum peruenire*). Because the word οἴκησις, which means 'home', is used by the author of the *Phaedo* (114d) and of the *Timaeus* (44b) to designate the star where a pure and worthy soul will reach heaven after death, Cicero, in the first book of *Tusculan Disputations* devoted to death, translated it into Latin several times and in the same context as its model with the words *domicilium* or *domus* (Cic. *Tusc.* 1.24, 51, 58, 118), whereas only once does he apply the word *domicilium* to the body – only to describe it as *tam insolitum tamque perturbatum* (Cic. *Tusc.* 1.58)![13] Also consider the widespread belief at the time that sleep is the time when the soul comes into contact with the gods, the dead and in

---

[13] Concerning cosmology and the nature of the soul in Plato's *Timaeus*, see the contributions of Horky (Chapter 1), Boys-Stones (Chapter 5), Brisson (Chapter 6) and Remes (Chapter 7).

general, the afterlife. At the time the frescoes of interest to us were made, testimonies multiply about the prophetic dreams experienced by members of the Roman nobility, e.g. Sulla (Plut. *Sulla* 9.7–8); Lucullus (Plut. *Luc.* 12.2– 4); Catulus (Suet. *Aug.* 94.12); and Pompey (Lucan, *B.Civ.* 7.9–12, Plut. *Pomp.* 68.2, Appian, *B.Civ.* 2.69). But, above all, there are many examples in Greek and Roman literary tradition, probably on the model of the myth of Er in Plato's *Republic*, of dream evocations in which the sleeper has received a vision of the beyond, including the vision of Empedotimus the Syracusan in a famous text of Heraclides of Pontus, which Varro translated in one of his Menippean Satires (Fr. 57 Schütrumpf = Varro Fr. 557 Cèbe), and especially Cicero's *Dream of Scipio*.

We should also mention many other frescoes belonging to the 'second Pompeian style' from the mid first century BC, at the time when Cicero owned property in the territory of Pompeii. I am thinking in particular of the megalography of Boscoreale, which is represented behind the image of a celebration banquet of the gods (Dionysus, Venus, the Graces) juxtaposed on the back wall, representing the human condition shared throughout terrestrial life and the soul's hope for return to heaven. Terrestrial life is evoked by the presence of one or, perhaps, two statues of the goddess Fortune, to the left of the image of Venus. The changing and unpredictable activity of Fortune, presented here on the left wall, is discussed by the philosopher Demetrius of Phalerum in his treatise Περὶ τύχης, which was fully quoted by Polybius (29.21) and Diodorus Siculus (31.10), as an allegory of Macedonia's domination of Persia.[14] The promise of an eternal stay in heaven for loving souls is symbolised by the divinities to the right of Venus, Eros ('desire') and Psyche ('soul'), and by the illustrated theme on the right wall, the representation of a poet (a woman holding a stringed instrument) – which could be the most famous female poet of all, Sappho – followed by a likely illustration of one of her poems that presented the history of Cepheus, Cassiopeia, Andromeda and Perseus, four heroes whose constellations adorned the sky.[15] Just as the guests had settled into Varro's *aviarium*, guests of the owner of the Boscoreale's villa would have attended banquets amidst a decor evoking the situation of man in the *kosmos*.

Of all the extant examples of this brilliant phase of the second Pompeian style, it is worth lingering on the one that adorns the great hall of the Villa Poppea in Torre Annunziata/Oplontis, which appears as number 15 on the

---

[14] Frs 82A and 82B Fortenbaugh and Schütrumpf.   [15] See Sauron 2007b: 73–86.

maps published by De Franciscis.[16] It seems to me that this offers a rare example of a 'memory image' on the model of mnemonic processes described by the anonymous author of the *Rhetorica ad Herennium* (3.16–24) and Cicero (*Orat.* 2.351–54). In the foreground, there is a kind of front stage, on which are distributed images (laurel branches, peacocks, paintings evoking a peaceful edge of the inhabited sea), while in the background appears a park surrounded with porticos, amidst a tripod whose basin is surmounted by three stars that stand out against the blue sky. The theatrical scenery in the foreground seems to symbolise human life, in the sense of *skênê bios*, perhaps the life of M. Pupius Piso, who was consul in 61 BCE: the peaceful shore could allude to the pacification of the seas through the piratical war led by Pompey in 67 BCE, in which Piso participated (Appian, *Mith.* 95); the laurel could be thought to refer to his Hispanic triumph (Asconius, *in Cornelianam*, p. 60 Clark); and peacocks may refer to his activity of breeding these birds in the island of Planasia (Varro, *Rust.* 3.6.2). The strange basin with three stars in the background shows the imagery we see on money issued by L. Manlius Torquatus in 65 BCE, where we see two stars flanking an amphora over a tripod (*RRC* 411, 1a–b). A. Alföldi had seen in the two stars the symbol of the Dioscuri identified with the constellation of Gemini, and F. Chapouthier had seen in the amphora a symbol of a thriving maritime trade, as the constellation Gemini was a privileged point of reference for sailors.[17] I assume that the three stars symbolise the astral apotheosis of M. Pupius Piso within the constellation Gemini, basing my argument on one hand on two verses of Ovid (*Am.* 2.16.13–14: 'Not even if I were to be placed between Castor and Pollux, would I be willing to live in a part of the sky without you' [*Non ego, si medius Polluce et Castore ponar, / in caeli sine te parte fuisse uelim*]), and on a passage from the Sphaera Graecanica of Nigidius Figulus, where the Dioscuri 'received the honor of the constellation Gemini because they are said to have been the first to pacify the sea from pirates' (Nigidius Figulus, Fr. 91 Swoboda = *Sphaera Graecanica*, Fr. 9 Liuzzi: *Castorem et Pollucem Tyndaridas Geminorum honore decoratos, quod ii principes dicantur mare tutum <a> praedonibus maleficiisque pacatum reddidisse*).

The evocations of the *kosmos* made at the end of the Republican period briefly described here, including Varro's aviary and allegorical frescoes of the 'second Pompeian style', are primarily interested in the position occupied by man within the order of the world.

---

[16] Ibid., 98–128.

[17] See Alföldi 1975: 184–85, pl. 28 (3–8, 12) and 29 (1–8, 10–12) and Chapouthier 1935: 4, 150 n. 1, 315–16.

11.4   Tiberius' Cave at Sperlonga

Let us now examine the imperial residence, the court (*praetorium*), that Tiberius had in Spelunca, now known as Sperlonga, on the southern coast of Lazio, south of Terracina. The remains of this villa pose many problems, which mainly reflect difficulties in obtaining the chronology of the architectural developments and interpretation of the arrangement of the sculptures. Here I focus only on the latter. We know that the cave was part of the space of the villa, the famous cave where Tiberius almost lost his life in 26 CE due to a collapse of stones from the arch. The emperor was saved by his praetorian prefect Sejanus (Tac. *Ann.* 4.59; Suet. *Tib.* 39). This cave featured very important architectural developments since it included a large pool for fish breeding, rectangular at the front of its overture and circular on the inside, while a room for repose was built inside the cave at the bottom of a sort of vestibule under an artificial arch. The carved decoration located inside the cave could be seen from two points of view: on the one hand from the *triclinium* which was built inside the rectangular part of the pool, and which was turned towards the inside the cave; and from the *cubiculum* located inside the cave. The sculptural decoration consisted of four marble groups on a Homeric theme, where the figure of Odysseus dominates – hence, Bernard Andreae spoke of a 'marble *Odyssey*'.[18] These representations of the blinding of Polyphemus, located at the bottom of the cave on the edge of the circular pool; of the attack of the ship of Odysseus by Scylla, placed internally; and at both ends of the circular basins, near the *triclinium*, the 'Pasquino Group' representing the rescue of the Homeric hero Patroclus' corpse by one of his fellows; and the abduction of Palladion by Odysseus and Diomedes. To justify the presence of such a setting, we can consider Homeric geography,[19] as the site of the villa was considered one of the ancient Amynclae (Tac. *Ann.* 4.59), founded by the Dioscuri, and it was close to the mountain dedicated to Circe and Formiae that can be identified with the country of the Laestrygonians (Pliny, *HN* 3.59). There may be some reference to the supposed Stoicism of Tiberius, in the character of Odysseus, who is represented at least three times in the space of the cave, possibly as the embodiment of virtues in the Portico.[20] For several decades, Andreae has attempted to justify this by setting an alleged Odyssean ancestry of Tiberius,[21] a strange idea that has been vigorously contested by Nikolaus Himmelmann.[22]

---

[18] See Andreae 1994.   [19] Cf. Kunze 1996: 164.   [20] See Lavagne 1988: 550ff.
[21] Andreae 1994: 139.   [22] See Himmelmann 1995.

The interpretation I have proposed of Sperlonga's decoration[23] is based primarily on what we know about the main impression that it must have offered to the viewer, hypothetically that of Tiberius. Now, we know, thanks to all the various sources we have about Tiberius, that his most intimate concern was his passion for astrology, which originated in his childhood, owing to a flattering prediction of the astrologer (*mathematicus*) Scribonius (Suet. *Tib.* 14.3), and which persisted through his voluntary exile in the island of Rhodes and the decisive encounter with the astrologer Thrasyllus (Suet. *Tib.* 14.6). What did Tiberius observe in the cave? First, he saw the roof of a cave carved out over a circular basin. The Ennian metaphor of the concavity of the sky, as I mentioned earlier, was revitalised at the end of the *Republic* by the famous phrase *cauernae Caeli* ('caves of the sky') that we found in the Menippean Satires of Varro (Fr. 275 Cèbe); twice in Cicero, both in his translation of the *Phenomena* of Aratus (*Aratea* 252 ed. Soubiran) and in his poem *De consulatu suo* (II.5 ed. Soubiran); and again three times in the poem of Lucretius (*DRN* 4.171 and 391, and 6.252). Proclus linked the circle to heaven in his commentary of the first book of Euclid's *Elements*, where plane figures are placed in relation to the different parts of the universe (compare def. XV and XVI, p. 147 Friedlein). The interpretation of the Sperlonga's cave as an image of the sky is confirmed by the presence of a statue of Ganymede taken to heaven by the eagle of Jupiter, which was placed over the opening of the cave probably by Domitian, who was a fervent admirer of Tiberius and who had reproduced the decoration of Sperlonga in his property at Alba.[24] Concerning the decoration of the cave, there was not only the sculptural image of Odysseus, as Andreae has noted, but, most importantly, there was also an astrological representation.

The starting point of this exegesis is located inside the group involving the blinding of Polyphemus, where there was a ram. The ram, or Aries, is also a zodiacal constellation, considered at the time of Tiberius as the first of the series of twelve signs, as evidenced throughout the life of Tiberius in the writings of Vitruvius, Hyginus, Manilius and Germanicus. If an image of the zodiac is projected onto the structural arrangement of the cave, starting with the Polyphemus group and its representation of the constellation Taurus on the large longitudinal axis of the decoration, we note that Tiberius was situated under the sign of the heliacal rising of his birth date (16 November 42 BCE), the Scorpio, when he attended a banquet in the *triclinium*, just as he was under the sign of the heliacal rising of its adoption

---

[23] See Sauron 1991 and, more recently, Sauron 2009: 155–95.   [24] See Balland 1967.

by Augustus (26 June 4 CE), the Cancer, when he was sitting in the *cubiculum*. Now, if the ram is also thought to represent the flock of the Cyclops in the Homeric narrative, so too must every other sculptural group of the cave provide the analogous elements, both for its arrangement according to the zodiacal circle and for the representations it contains. Now if the group placed near the centre of the circular basin, signed by the same three Rhodian artists Pliny considered to be the authors of Laocoon, represents from a mythological point of view the episode of the attack of the ship of Ulysses by Scylla, then it should be noted, given the astrological exegesis that interests us now, first, that it is the only set of sculptures visible from the *cubiculum*, where the projection of the zodiac reveals the Cancer; second, that it contained the poop of a vessel evoking probably the constellation of the Stern (Puppis) or the ship Argo (Argo Nauis), which the astrologer Teucer considered at that time a *paranatellon* of Cancer; and finally that the six dogs that arise out of the belly of the monster evoke the Canis Minor (Procyon) and Canis Major (Canicula, Canis), the former of which Manilius considered the *paranatellon* of Cancer (*Astronomica*, 5.197–205).[25] The same relationship seems to exist between the last two sculpted groups and the zodiacal constellation situated where the *triclinium* was. The very strange decor of Patroclus' helmet (fawn, bird/snake, centaur) can be interpreted as the image of the constellations near Scorpio: Bird (Avis) or Raven (Corvus) on the tail of Hydra (Hydra and Hydrus), the Centaur (Centaurus), and the Beast (Fera, Bestia, Quadrupes). This helps to explain the insistence in the decor on the figure of Odysseus, and there are an additional two reasons to link Odysseus with Tiberius. First, Odysseus was a navigator hero and therefore a perfect connoisseur of the starry sky. The astronomical knowledge of the Homeric hero was indeed highlighted by Polybius (9.16.1), by the Stoic Heraclitus (*Homeric Allegories* 70.6), and by Eustathius (*Od.* 1389); and, second, Odysseus was an island hero, the king of the island of Ithaca. I have already focused on Tiberius's purported obsession with island retreats, which ends up being treated with contempt (Cass. Dio 58.5).

11.5   The Cenatio Rotunda of Nero

I will write just a few words about the famous circular dining room of Nero, for the reason that its arrangement is still largely unknown. The

---

[25] According to Servius, the Canis Major was considered the parantellon of Cancer by the other astrologers (*apud* Virgil, *Georgics* 1.218: *Canis paranatellon est Cancri*).

famous Domus Aurea of Nero was conceived as a microcosm, as Yves
Perrin has justly underlined.[26] Indeed, according to Suetonius (*Nero* 31) it
included 'a room of water similar to a pond' (*stagnum instar*), 'surrounded
by houses in the shape of cities' (*circumsaeptum aedificiis ad urbium
speciem*), 'and moreover an area of countryside, where there were farmings,
vineyards, pastures and forests' (*rura insuper aruis atque uinetis et pascuis
siluisque uaria*), 'containing a multitude of domestic and wild animals of
any kind' (*cum multitudine omnis generis pecudum et ferarum*). Obviously,
the cosmic theme was exalted by the famous Cenatio Rotunda, because, of
all the dining rooms, 'the principal one was round, and it spun around
continually, day and night, as the world does' (*praecipua cenationum
rotunda, quae perpetuo diebus ac noctibus uice mundi circumageretur*). We
know that, as part of a work of the Soprintendenza Archeologica di Roma
of 2009, the French archaeologist Françoise Villedieu discovered on the
Palatine impressive remains that could be those of the rotating dining
room of Nero's palace. It is a firm substructure, which could have supported the circular floor of the dining room and allowed it to turn
regularly, through both hydraulics and types of ball-bearing devices.
Since then, a research programme has been established by Camille
Jullian Centre of Aix-en-Provence, the École Française of Rome, the
Research Institute of Ancient Architecture, and the AnHiMA laboratory
of the University Panthéon-Sorbonne. They are trying to establish whether
the remains are those of the famous Cenatio Rotunda, and consequently
whether they were part of the innovations designed by the architects of
Nero, Severus and Celer (Tac. *Ann.* 15.42). It is also important to understand precisely the mechanism that made the platform of the dining room
turn. At the time of writing, this research programme is under way.

11.6   The Teatro Marittimo of Hadrian's Villa in Tivoli

The monument in the history of ancient Roman architecture that best
illustrates an attempt to take the *kosmos* as a building model is the
Pantheon, as it was rebuilt by Hadrian, or at least its latest reconstruction
completed by Hadrian.[27] We know the formula of Cassius Dio (53.27),
which considers its dome as an image of the sky (θολοειδὲς ὂν τῷ οὐρανῷ
προσέοικεν). The silence of our sources will probably leave open forever

---

[26] See Perrin 1987.
[27] The subject of its construction and reconstruction is a topic of current research. See e.g. Hetland
    2009.

the question of whether the new temple contained the statues of the seven planetary gods, as has long been assumed. In any case, the fact that the building contained a complete sphere, half-constructed (as the dome) and half-implied (since the diameter of the dome was equal to the height of the temple in its centre), and the fact that an *oculus* with a diameter of 9 metres, drilled in the centre of the dome, works as a real sundial – the same type Vitruvius named *hemisphaerium* – have rendered this monument the model of countless religious buildings which, throughout history, celebrate the link between heaven and earth, divinity and humanity. But I would like to emphasise another monument that belonged to the private domain of the Emperor: the famous Teatro Marittimo in the villa of the emperor at Tivoli. It is a small house, constructed on a circular island located in the centre of a basin, which was itself surrounded by a circular portico and connected by two bridges to the island. In his important paper published in 1985,[28] Mathias Ueblacker analysed the various opinions known about this unusual arrangement, which is not even mentioned in the brief description of the villa we find in the *Historia Augusta*: some scholars have thought the building was an aviary, on the same model as the aviary of Varro at Casinum (Gothein, Hülsen); or an imitation of the sanctuary of Osiris in Abydos (van Leeuw); or an imitation of Sparta's market, the Platanistas, on the pretext that it was connected by two bridges to the mainland (Sebastiani, Gusman); or an evocation of the Atlantis of Plato (Herter); or the Blessed Isles (Kapossy).[29] More recently, Filippo Coarelli has been inclined to see in this structure an imitation of the arrangement of Dionysius of Syracuse's bedroom (Cic. *Tusc.* 5.59: *Et cum fossam latam cubiculari lecto circumdedisset eiusque fossae transitum ponticulo ligneo coniunxisset, eum ipsum, cum forem cubiculi clauserat, detorquebat*). Coarelli made the same comparison with Augustus's room on the Palatine, called 'Syracusan' because it was the place where Augustus lived in seclusion on the pattern of Dionysius's room (Suet. *Aug.* 72.2: *Si quando quid secreto aut sine interpellatione agere proposuisset, erat illi locus in edito singularis, quem Syracusas et technophyon vocabat: huc transibat aut in alicuius libertorum suburbanum*). The connections made by Coarelli can at most characterise Hadrian's arrangement as a place for repose, like those which the Romans called by the Greek term *diaeta*; we are familiar with many of them in the history of the Roman villa, like the famous *Amalthea* installed first by Atticus at Buthrote in Epirus and then by Cicero in Tusculum.[30] The comparison with the room of Dionysius, however, does not fully explain

---

[28] Ueblacker 1985.   [29] Ibid., 52–53.   [30] See Sauron 2007b: 41–46.

the peculiarity of Hadrian's villa's structure, its circular plan and the leitmotif of curvilinear architecture.

Mathias Ueblacker and Catia Caprino had reason to call this construction Inselvilla, 'insular villa', and Ueblacker observed that, if we transpose the plan of the structure, replacing all curvilinear architectures by rectilinear ones, we get a plan of a villa with atrium/peristyle (the central plan recalls both, and the authors of the publication do not adjudicate between the two designations), *cubicula, balneum* and living rooms.[31] According to Ueblacker, the leitmotif of curvilinear architectures used here is only the expression of a particular aesthetic of the emperor, and he writes that the plan adopted for the Maritime Theatre presents '*als neues Element hadrianischer Architektur, vor allem kurvig bewegte Grundrißformen*'; he mentions the Piazza d'Oro, the Academy's belvedere in Hadrian's villa, and the gardens of Leonidaion of Olympia as others expressions of this particular aesthetic.

But I wonder if we should see something more in this unusual structure. This small insular villa, already extraordinary, is constructed entirely of curvilinear lines. My impression is that Hadrian may have wanted to evoke the 'heavenly home' reserved for his soul, according to Plato's expression (*Ti.* 44b: τὴν τοῦ συννόμου . . . οἴκησιν ἄστρου), revived by Cicero in the first book of his *Tusculan Disputations* (1.24, 51, 58 and 118) precisely because the sky is an area of circularity, sphericity and concavity. It seems that the only parts of the decoration we know of the Inselvilla, namely the Ionic friezes, would be in line with this interpretation. The marbles have been studied by Catia Caprino, in an appendix to the monograph of Ueblacker. There was, on one hand, the so-called marine *thiasos*, representing a variety of sea animals and monsters (Scylla, dolphins, griffins, horses, cats, goats, rams, dogs, deer, dragons, etc.), and these friezes decorated the peripheral part of the Inselvilla, which was adjacent to the circular basin. Caprino notes that in the friezes of the marine *thiasos* we can detect the important presence of Eros, who appears at least nine times. The other preserved friezes, which decorate the central part of the Inselvilla, designated by Ueblacker and Caprino as either the atrium or the peristyle, represent chariot races, with Eros as charioteer, and drawn by various animals.

That the race is located in a Roman circus is indicated by the presence of the carceres. It is striking to find in the Teatro Marittimo of Hadrian two themes, the marine *thiasos* and the chariot race, which belong to the

[31] Ueblacker 1985: 56ff.

repertoire of Roman funerary art, and in particular on sarcophagi. Actually, the marine *thiasos* had long been present in tombs, e.g. the mausoleum of the Julii at Glanum/Saint-Rémy-de-Provence.[32] The marine theme was long ago explained as the evocation of the ocean that must be crossed in order to reach the Blessed Isles, or even as an evocation of the celestial ocean – that is to say the moist, obscure, and dangerous area that stands between Earth and the moon, and that the soul must pass through during its heavenly *anodos*.[33] As regards the theme of the chariot helmed by Eros, we know that Franz Cumont had related it to a famous passage from Plato's *Phaedrus* (248a), describing 'winged souls animated by an ardent emulation, trying to push their chariots to the top of heaven, where they follow the circular path of the stars'.[34] According to Cumont, 'the allegory was even more transparent than any symbolism in the eyes of a Roman; reported by several writers, it made of the circus, devoted to the Sun, an image of the universe and explained its different parts as representing zodiacal signs, the planets, the ocean, the earth'.[35] What seems remarkable here is the omnipresence of Eros on the two friezes. If we sometimes find Eros among the representations of the marine *thiasos*, that's because the erotic scene requires his presence, as on the reliefs of the Altar of Domitius Ahenobarbus preserved in Munich, which focus on the evocation of the marriage between Poseidon and Amphitrite.

It seems to me that the decor of the Teatro Marittimo could evoke the peregrination of the soul returning to the sky, through the atmosphere, to its eternal rotation on some celestial circle, and that Eros was the central figure of Plato's allegory, the great daimon celebrated by all the protagonists of the *Symposium* of Plato, whom Diotima of Mantinea, mentioned by Socrates, renders the desire for celestial realities, the engine of deification of souls. One might wonder if there could be any relationship between the Teatro Marittimo and the circular mausoleum constructed by Hadrian on the right bank of the Tiber, which was connected with the Campus Martius by a bridge expressly built; and possibly we could be encouraged to extend the analogy to a portion of the sculptural decoration of the mausoleum; but we have no firm information about this. We can certainly object to this interpretation with the famous poem which is supposed to have been written by the dying Emperor in the *Vita Hadriani* (Hist. Aug. XXV, 9: *Et moriens quidem hos versus fecisse dicitur: animula uagula blandula, / hospes comesque corporis, / quae nunc abibis in loca / pallidula rigida*

---

[32] See Rolland 1969. On the meaning of this theme, see Salviat 1989.
[33] Cumont 1942: 130, 157 and 188.   [34] Ibid., 348.   [35] Ibid., 349.

nudula / nec, ut soles, dabis iocos!). Nevertheless, Cassius Dio never refers to this literary creation in his story of the Emperor's death (Cass. Dio 69.22.4), and some good arguments, objecting to the authenticity of this poem, have been proposed by Timothy D. Barnes.[36] It is hard to imagine a dying person writing a poem or even thinking on it. I would like to add that the Egyptian structure of Hadrian's villa has been interpreted by Jean-Claude Grenier as a mise-en-scène *in priuato* of Antinous' apotheosis[37] and, in 2002, the archaeologists of the Soprintendenza per i Beni Archeologici del Lazio found a structure next to the entrance of the villa and interpreted it as a monumental tomb or temple dedicated to Antinous as a god.[38] It is strange to imagine that Hadrian, instead of choosing an apotheosis for himself in Tivoli's imperial villa, would offer it to his young partner. The Teatro Marittimo was one of the first structures built in Tivoli's imperial villa, constructed during the period following his initiation to the Eleusinian Mysteries.

11.7   Conclusion

In concluding our brief analyses of these architectural examples, I would like to underline first the omnipresence of the representations of the *kosmos* in the Roman private sphere. Second, that the representations of the private sphere are arranged for the particular point of view of the person who frequents the place. Inspiration for these decorations seems to have come from Greek philosophers, chiefly Plato, but also from the Greek astronomers, who fascinated the Roman elite, as demonstrated by the Latin translations of the *Phaenomena* of Aratus first by Cicero, and then by Germanicus. We spoke of the 'power of the images' in Rome, but it was not simply a form of political rhetoric. It was for the Romans a vital necessity to express the world-order in architectural terms, not only to secure their own power, but also to express their unique mode of existence.

[36] Barnes 1968.   [37] Grenier 1989.   [38] Mari 2012.

CHAPTER 12

"The Deep-Sticking Boundary Stone"
Cosmology, Sublimity, and Knowledge in Lucretius' *De Rerum Natura* and Seneca's *Naturales Quaestiones*

W. H. Shearin*

οὐκοῦν ἐπὶ γε τῶν ἐν λόγοις μεγαλοφυῶν, ἐφ᾽ ὧν οὐκέτ᾽ ἔξω τῆς χρείας καὶ ὠφελείας πίπτει τὸ μέγεθος, προσήκει συνθεωρεῖν αὐτόθεν, ὅτι τοῦ ἀναμαρτήτου πολὺ ἀφεστῶτες οἱ τηλικοῦτοι ὅμως παντός εἰσιν **ἐπάνω τοῦ θνητοῦ**· καὶ τὰ μὲν ἄλλα τοὺς χρωμένους ἀνθρώπους ἐλέγχει, **τὸ δ᾽ ὕψος ἐγγὺς αἴρει μεγαλοφροσύνης θεοῦ.**

Further, for those who are sublime in language and whose greatness does not yet fall beyond use and utility, it is appropriate to observe immediately that – although they stand far apart from perfection – such authors nonetheless are **beyond anything mortal.** Other things prove their users men; **sublimity[1] raises its partisans near to divine greatness of mind.**   ps-Longinus, *On the Sublime* 36[2]

omnis de universo quaestio in caelestia sublimia terrena **diuiditur.**

All investigation concerning the universe **is separated** into heavenly, meteorological [*sublimia*], and terrestrial matters.
                                                   Seneca, *Natural Questions* 2.1.1[3]

Hardly any thing can strike the mind with its greatness, which does not make some sort of approach toward infinity; **which nothing can**

---

* I wish to thank Phil Horky for his help and patience during the gestation of this chapter. He has been a model of critical intelligence and editorial tact throughout. I also wish to thank the Department of Classics and Ancient History at Durham, which hosted me when I gave a preliminary version of this paper in January 2013. Barbara Graziosi, Don Lavigne, and Phil Horky, in particular, asked important questions that I have tried to answer in my revisions.

[1] As is customary in modern translations and scholarship, I render τὸ ὕψος with "sublimity" or "the sublime"; but this equivalence is not itself ancient. That is, τὸ ὕψος is not rendered with Latin *sublime* in antiquity. Instead, Nicolas Boileau-Despréaux appears to have pioneered this rendering in his 1674 French translation, which deeply influenced future discussion of the sublime throughout Europe. See further Saint-Girons 2014: 1093.

[2] The text of Longinus generally follows Russell 1968 (OCT), but it also has been compared to the later Russell 1995 (Loeb).

[3] All citations of Seneca's *Natural Questions* follow Hine 1996.

do whilst we are able to perceive its bounds; but to see an object distinctly, and to perceive its bounds, is one and the same thing. A clear idea is therefore another name for a little idea.

Burke 1958: 63 (II, 4)[4]

12.1 Introduction: Cosmology, Limit, and Sublimity

Cosmology is a difficult science. It is not simply that it is difficult to perceive the structures, both physical and metaphysical, that govern the natural world. It is difficult even to know the contours of such investigation. How does one begin to study the *kosmos*? Which procedures, experimental or intellectual, allow us to approach it as a known (or knowable) object? What are the *limits* of such study? Various chapters in the present volume demonstrate abundantly that cosmological investigation informed a wide range of ancient practices, influencing everything from philosophy and religion to political theory and metatheatrical commentary.[5] Yet it may seem, not without reason, that there are few obviously fixed terms or parameters in ancient cosmology.[6] Plato's Socrates demands a completely different explanation for what he observes in the heavens than Epicurus or the Samian philosopher's most famous Roman disciple, Lucretius; and this very difference may cause us to wonder not only whose explanation is correct – Socrates' or Lucretius' – but also to query the nature of their investigations more generally.[7]

Such a preamble no doubt creates the unwanted expectation that the ensuing discussion will fully untangle the complexities of ancient cosmological science, laying bare the fixed core of its methodology – at least for certain, central ancient authors. Yet – while the present chapter certainly aims to illuminate the approaches of Lucretius and Seneca toward cosmology – it comes to that science in a manner that initially may seem oblique: I access cosmology through *the sublime*, a topic which is often held to belong first and foremost to philosophical

---

[4] On this remark, see Monk 1960: 94.

[5] See inter alia Germany (Chapter 10), who connects cosmology to metatheatre.

[6] It is no doubt for this reason that cosmology as a distinct, speculative science is sometimes taken to begin not in antiquity but rather with the eighteenth-century German philosopher Christian Wolff (1679–1754), who penned *Cosmologia generalis* (1731). We may perhaps suggest (as Porter 2012: 52 does in reference to the sublime) that cosmology in antiquity has a "contaminated history," involving philosophical, scientific, literary, and cultural components.

[7] For Socrates' remarks on natural science (framed as a critique of Anaxagoras), see most famously Plato *Phaedo* 96a–99b, with Sedley 2007: 86–89. Lucretius is discussed in some detail in this chapter, but one passage that gives a sense of the Epicurean view of cosmic speculation is Lucr. 5.1204–10.

aesthetics, or aesthetic judgment. One implicit contention of the present chapter, however, is that the sublime, at least in the texts I consider, is not merely (or perhaps even primarily) aesthetic, in the modern sense of that term.[8] Indeed, the models of the sublime considered here in studying Lucretius and Seneca are, if anything, as epistemological and didactic as they are aesthetic.[9] The sublime, in other words, is deeply imbricated in both what we know (or can know) about the *kosmos* as well as in how we come to that knowledge.

The present discussion approaches and analyzes cosmology indirectly, highlighting the complexity of ancient cosmological investigation and, in particular, the difficulty of demarcating its limits, but it does so to a clear purpose: as we shall see, the texts I interrogate here – chiefly Lucretius' *On the Nature of Things* and Seneca's *Natural Questions* – themselves discuss and even take as a central theme the idea of "limit," a concept fundamental to all cosmological theories.[10] A key issue in these Epicurean and Stoic authors is precisely how and where to draw boundaries and limits in the natural world. As Seneca proclaims in the second epigraph at the beginning of the chapter, all investigation into the universe, the sum of extant things, may be separated (*dividitur*) into the heavenly, the terrestrial, and what falls in between – the meteorological (*sublimia*); yet who

---

[8] See the telling remarks of James I. Porter: "Suppose that the sublime has a contaminated history that involves not only literary and extra-literary contexts that we would want to call aesthetic today . . ., but also contexts that do not obviously involve either domain at all, such as cosmology or religion" (Porter 2012: 52). Or, as Porter observes elsewhere: "The sublime is broader than an aesthetic category" (Porter 2012: 5). Over many years, Porter has been revising the history of aesthetics (including the sublime) in antiquity, above all in Porter 2016, but also in Porter 2010 and elsewhere. Numerous other studies (e.g., Sluiter and Rosen 2012; Konstan 2015) are also contributing to this revival and revaluation of aesthetics in antiquity, which aims, in part, to show that field of aesthetics is not (at least in antiquity) simply about the abstract, disinterested contemplation of art. Porter (2012: 63, referring to Porter 2010), in particular, asserts that "all aesthetic experiences . . . involve a confrontation with sensuous matter." It is worth noting, too, that, at least on an etymological level, ancient terms for the *kosmos* are always in part about order and beauty; that is, even as the sublime is not purely aesthetic and is never absent from other discourses like the cosmological, so too the cosmological seems to have always been in part aesthetic. See Puhvel 1976, who traces κόσμος to a root meaning "to comb" and *mundus* to a root meaning "to cleanse."

[9] Compare the remarks of Gian Biagio Conte, who in discussing the Lucretian sublime asserts that it "operates within the text as a form of perception and knowledge even before it functions as a stylistic form . . . ; Epicurus' hard and difficult doctrine can only act by educating a reader disposed toward the sublime" (1994: 23).

[10] It is also the case that much of what appears in Seneca's *Natural Questions* (as well as some of what appears in Epicurus and Lucretius) falls under the ancient category of meteorology rather than cosmology. On this facet of Seneca's text, see, e.g., Inwood 2005: 163. On Epicurus' meteorology, see Taub 2009 as well as Caygill 2006, who looks at Epicurus' meteorology through Nietzsche's eyes.

makes these divisions and with what aim?[11] Where do the heavens yield to the *sublimia* and why should such a division matter?[12] Both implicitly and explicitly, such questions of limit will inform the ensuing discussion.

Finally – to detail still more the trajectory of the present chapter – the limits that are most significant in the following pages are, for both Lucretius and Seneca, the limits of the human mind. While at first brush it may seem that the boundaries of the mind and the limits of human intellectual capacity are only incidentally connected with actual limits in the physical world, as I hope to show, ancient philosophy – perhaps most especially the famously interior-looking world of Hellenistic and Roman philosophy – was often eager to make this connection. Indeed, in a famous passage Lucretius once employs the fortuitous phrase *templa mentis*, the "precincts of the mind," using the language of exterior, religious space to denote interior, mental regions, an example that shows that, at least at a linguistic level, transactions between the inside and outside of the mind, a sort of blurring of limits, did occur.[13] Seneca, too, when recounting the Pompeian earthquake of 62 CE at the beginning of his sixth book of *Natural Questions*, speaks not simply of the destruction of external, physical nature but also of mental disturbances, with the external movement of the earth inciting the internal movement of the mind (*QNat.* 6.1.3: *motae ... mentis*).[14] As we read through several key passages of Lucretius and Seneca in the ensuing pages, then, it will be my contention that these two authors both probe the limits of the mind in its encounter with the natural world and that they do so in a broadly similar fashion; yet they nonetheless also articulate divergent forms of sublimity – divergent sublimes rooted above all in

---

[11] Also see Chapter 11 by Sauron for a discussion of the supra- and sublunary worlds in the Roman imagination.

[12] I render *sublimia* here with "meteorological" (*OLD* s.v. 4), but I leave the original Latin to emphasize possible resonances with the sublime. Sublimity is often precisely about blurring boundaries, perhaps none more so than those delimiting the heavens.

[13] For the phrase *templa mentis*, see Lucr. 5.103. Consult, too, the discussion of augural ritual, *templa*, and *contemplatio* in Germany (Chapter 10).

[14] See, too, Seneca's elaborate preface to the first book of *Natural Questions*, where he proclaims a clear connection between our minds and the divine mind of the *kosmos* (*QNat.* 1 praef. 13–14): *quid est deus? mens universi ... quid ergo interest inter naturam dei et nostram? nostri melior pars animus est, in illo nulla pars extra animum est* ("What is god? The mind of the *kosmos* ... What then is the difference between the nature of god and our own? For us, the mind is the better part; in him, no part is outside the mind").

philosophically distinct approaches to natural science (knowledge) and cosmology.

12.2   Sublimes, Lucretian, Longinian, and Senecan

Epicurean cosmology is almost sublime by its very nature.[15] If, as Burke suggests in the third epigraph I quoted, greatness (i.e., sublimity) is always imbricated together with "some sort of approach towards infinity," then this observation is hardly surprising, for Epicurean cosmology is almost entirely concerned with the infinite. As Epicurus writes in his *Letter to Herodotus*:

> the all (τὸ πᾶν) is unlimited. For, what is delimited has an end, and the end is observed by comparison with something else. Thus, since the universe has no end, it has no limit; and if it should have no limit, it would be limitless and unbounded.[16]

By contrast with other contemporary philosophical schools such as the Stoics, Epicurus and his followers argued for an infinite universe, one comprising both infinite matter (atoms) and infinite void.[17] This infinite number of atoms knocking about in infinite space could produce an infinite number of possible worlds, including (given world enough and time) virtual copies of our own.[18] These notions are perhaps sublime enough in themselves, but it is Lucretius – as we shall soon see – who gives them their most sublime expression and puts the sublime to didactic use in ways it is worth taking care to examine. Indeed, while throughout this section cosmological principles and examples will continue to lurk in important ways, I would now like to shift the leading thread of discussion to a more detailed exposition of the sublime, its history, and its role in *On the Nature of Things*. Doing so will help us gain a fuller sense of what precisely it means to refer to the sublimity of Epicurean cosmology.[19]

---

[15] Compare Porter (2016: 461): "We have seen hints that Epicurus may have found sublimity . . . in the cosmos"). Useful accounts of Epicurean cosmology are Furley 1999: 418–32 and Taub 2009.

[16] Epicur. *Ep. Hdt.* 41 (L&S 10A, part).

[17] See, e.g., Epicur. *Ep. Hdt.* 42. For accounts of early Stoic cosmology, see Hahm 1977 and Furley 1999: 432–51. Among other things, early Stoics denied the existence of void within the *kosmos*.

[18] For scholarly discussion of Epicurean infinity, see Sedley 2007: 155–66. See, too, Segal 1990: 74–93 (Chapter 4, "Nothingness and Eternity"). For the idea that our world is not unique, see Lucr. 2.1044–57.

[19] I drafted this section before the appearance of Porter 2016, which offers a much more thorough and detailed treatment of the sublime in antiquity (as well as an extensive discussion of many modern theorists of the sublime). In my brief narrative, I hope to have avoided some of the Whiggishness (Porter 2016: 11) of many modern accounts of the sublime, which see ps-Longinus as appearing *ex nihilo* and which undersell the deep imbrication of rhetoric and sublime (psychic or spiritual) effect.

The sublime, it hardly needs to be said, has an extensive history.[20] For students of antiquity, the term is apt to conjure up first and foremost the ΠΕΡΙ ΥΨΟΥΣ of ps-Longinus; yet as a concept in modern philosophical aesthetics it was incubated most extensively in the eighteenth-century laboratories of Edmund Burke and Immanuel Kant. Of course, the writings of Burke and Kant were themselves nourished by the French translation of ps-Longinus produced by Nicolas Boileau-Despréaux as well as by a deep reading of Latin poetry and Roman philosophy, including of Lucretius' *On the Nature of Things*.[21] Thus, eighteenth-century discourse on the sublime, while hardly itself ancient, takes up many of the terms of Lucretius and Longinus. But in more recent times, the so-called postmodern sublime, which is closely associated with the names of Jacques Derrida and Jean-François Lyotard, has formulated itself first and foremost as an answer to the eighteenth century, consisting chiefly in a set of responses to Kant.[22] Hence, while it is clear that the eighteenth century is pivotal for modern discussions of the sublime, for those wishing to explore the sublime in ancient writing, the situation remains more complex: on the one hand, antiquity has in ps-Longinus (and the tradition he represents)[23] its own theorist of the sublime; on the other, even direct reading and interpretation of ps-Longinus is conditioned in various ways by more recent philosophical and critical work.[24]

In presenting this cursory history of the sublime, I wish to emphasize precisely its complexity and diversity: while there is no need to deny a certain unity to the Western tradition of reading and reinterpreting the sublime, the diverse responses to ps-Longinus, Burke, and Kant, among others, suggest that at least at times we are dealing with a variety of sublime

---

[20] For book-length accounts of the history of the sublime, see Monk 1960 (in detail on the eighteenth century) and Shaw 2006 (from Longinus to the postmodern sublime and beyond). Saint-Girons 2014 and Sertoli 2005 provide, in only a few pages each, access to several of the most important critical and philosophical issues.

[21] Burke quotes *inter alios* Lucretius and Cicero in his *Enquiry* (Burke 1958), while Lucretius was apparently, at least in his youth, Kant's favorite poet. See Ludwich (1899: 2), discussing Kant's youthful study of Latin: "Mit welchem Ernst und Erfolg diese Jugendübungen stattfanden, geht daraus hervor, dass gerade Lucrez Kant's Lieblingsdichter wurde, dessen schwieriges Lehrgedicht *de rerum natura* er noch im hohen Alter aus dem Gedächtniss theilweise wörtlich vorzutragen vermochte." See, too, Porter (2007: 178): "Kant knew both Burke and Lucretius well."

[22] For Derrida's reading of Kant, see Derrida 1987; for Lyotard's, see Lyotard 1994.

[23] Porter 2012: 52 asserts a belief that "Longinus' work is something of a collecting point for earlier traditions of the sublime in antiquity." See, too, Porter 2016: 11.

[24] Indeed, as I indicate later in connection with Conte 1994, it is clear how much his essay has been influenced by Kant and Schiller, even as he uses ps-Longinus to access the sublime in antiquity.

phenomena – that is, with sublimes – rather than with a single, uniform concept that travels under an easy definition.[25] Of course, there certainly are definitions of the sublime: *The Oxford English Dictionary*, for example, offers the broad yet concise assertion that sublime literature, language, or style "express[es] noble ideas in a grand and elevated manner" (*OED* s.v. 2). But the point is that – even in those instances where such a literary conception of the sublime applies (or appears to apply) – the ways in which given works express such "noble ideas" or the manners in which they are "elevated" may be distinct enough to speak of something besides a simple, monolithic sublime. Moreover, as I have already suggested, the importance of the sublime – in particular, its importance for ancient philosophical texts – may not lie so much in a style of expression as in the aims and effects of such style: the sublime names, at least in some instances, not only a dynamic blurring of boundaries in the natural world (or literary descriptions of such blurring) but also a dynamic force at work within the reader of a sublime text.

To clarify this point, it may be helpful to turn to recent remarks by Glenn Most, who engages in precisely the project I have been describing – that of distinguishing sublimes. Confronted by the twentieth-century resurgence of the sublime not only in theorists such as Lyotard but also in painters such as Barnett Newman and Mark Rothko, Most argues that the best way to comprehend this unexpected revival is to accept that the history of the sublime is not a series of footnotes to ps-Longinus (or, for that matter, to Kant) but rather that there is an important, if under-recognized, strain of the sublime that does not depend, as ps-Longinus' sublime clearly does, upon the active participation of the divine in the world.[26] Instead, there is, on the one hand, a "Longinian sublime" rooted in a divine, teleological worldview and, on the other, a rather atheistic "Lucretian sublime":

> Lucretius does not express anywhere an explicit theory of the sublime, but instead merely deploys the language and rhetoric of the sublime ... And yet it is not at all difficult to identify a characteristically Lucretian sublime and to distinguish it from the more familiar Longinian sublime. Whereas the Longinian sublime is fundamentally a form of theodicy, justifying human suffering by appeal to the superior logic of divine wisdom, the Lucretian

---

[25] I am thus in broad agreement with Porter 2016: 621: "there is no one canonical form of sublimity."

[26] One of the best passages for naming the Longinian sublime a "theodicy" rooted in a teleological worldview (as Most does) is *On the Sublime* 35.2–3, where the text suggests that man was made to pursue whatever is more divine than himself.

sublime venerates a form of human heroism possible within a universe that
has been left by the gods to its own devices. The Longinian sublime
presupposes the gods' benevolence within an ultimate teleological framework for human existence and provides a compensatory meaning for
suffering and loss in the form of the understanding of divine providence;
the Lucretian sublime posits the irrelevance of the gods and the fundamental
randomness and meaninglessness of the universe and identifies the sublime
as a gesture of courageous defiance in which humans compensate for the
absence of divine providence by giving themselves some form of meaning
nonetheless.[27]

As I have already indicated, Most's target in articulating this distinction
is largely modern rather than ancient; he aims first and foremost at
resolving a problem in twentieth-century aesthetics rather than at clarify-
ing problems in ancient aesthetics or poetics per se.[28] On the other hand,
his broad approach, it seems to me, holds promise for understanding the
dynamics of the ancient sublime, at least in certain contexts. In other
words, we can identify an ancient "Lucretian sublime" that differs in
important and striking ways from a more traditional ancient sublime
often associated with the name of ps-Longinus – or to put this claim
more directly in the terms of my larger argument in this chapter, we can
identify a "Lucretian sublime" that differs in ever so subtle ways from the
Stoicizing sublime articulated in the sixth book of Seneca's *Natural
Questions*.[29]

In recent scholarly literature, there has been extensive discussion of the
sublime in antiquity; and in particular, there has been extensive discussion
of the sublime in Lucretius.[30] James I. Porter, for example, has

[27] Most 2012: 249–50. Most is not the only scholar to distinguish sublimes: see, too, Porter 2012, who
speaks of "material" (pp. 57–59) and "immaterial" (pp. 59–60) sublimes. Porter's diagrams (pp. 63
and 66) dramatize the ways in which he sees these two sublimes functioning and interacting. They
are, in some ways, reminiscent of Neil Hertz's diagrams of the sublime (Hertz 2009: 252 and 266,
discussing Wordsworth).

[28] In characterizing Rothko with an atheistic sublime, Most in fact follows the lead of Rothko himself.
See Rothko 1947–48: 84: "Without monsters and gods, art cannot enact our dramas: art's most
profound moments express this frustration. When they were abandoned as untenable superstitions,
art sank into melancholy. It became fond of the dark, and enveloped its objects in the nostalgic
intimations of a half-lit world. For me the great achievements of the centuries in which the artist
accepted the probable and familiar as his subjects were the pictures of the single human figure –
alone in a moment of utter immobility."

[29] The discussion in Porter 2016 of the "material sublime" (his fifth chapter) over against the
"immaterial sublime" (his sixth chapter) in many ways parallels the division between Lucretius
and Seneca pursued here.

[30] In addition to the works discussed in the main text, see Segal 1990: 74–80 on sublimity in Lucretius.
For other recent discussions of the sublime in Roman antiquity, see Schrijvers 2006 (on Silius
Italicus), Day 2013 (on Lucan), and (on Seneca) Gunderson 2015 (esp. pp. 111–12).

demonstrated that Lucretius' arrangement of certain sublime material bears an uncanny resemblance to that of ps-Longinus.[31] Philip Hardie has studied a tradition of sublime personification that – while centered on Virgil's *Fama* – prominently includes Lucretius' *Religio*.[32] But it is Gian Biagio Conte's slightly older discussions (themselves based – at least in part – in Kant and Friedrich Schiller[33]) of the sublime in Lucretius that provide the chief basis for the connection with Seneca that I wish to examine in this chapter.[34] What is especially useful about Conte's account of the Lucretian sublime is not simply that he exemplifies certain lofty modes of Lucetian discourse and imagery although he does do this to good effect – but rather that he recognizes the key role that sublimity plays in the larger didactic aims of the poem. Thus, for example, in one of the most striking – and most canonically sublime – moments in Lucretius' poem, the poet writes of the quasi-religious feeling that overcomes him upon grasping the Epicurean vision of the universe. The Epicurean account of nature, the "true account" or *uera ratio*, allows him, he suggests, to see "all the things, which are conducted throughout the void beneath his feet" (Lucr. 3.26–27); and this fact inspires a pouring forth of seemingly contra-dictory emotions:

> his ibi me rebus quaedam diuina uoluptas
> percipit atque horror, quod sic natura tua ui
> tam manifesta patens ex omni parte retecta est.

> Then, because of these things, a certain divine pleasure
> seizes me and awe, that thus by your might nature
> has been uncovered, lying open so clearly on all sides.
> (Lucretius, *On the Nature of Things* 3.28–30)[35]

Here imagining the void brings on something that can only be compared to divine revelation. Indeed, in his commentary on these lines, Richard

[31] See Porter 2007: 172 on Lucr. 6.608–737 and ps-Longinus 35.2–5. Cf. Williams 2012: 222–23.
[32] Hardie 2009b.
[33] Classicists reading and engaging with Conte tend not to highlight how much his analysis owes to the German tradition of the sublime. But this fact is hardly a secret: Chapter 1 of Conte 1994 begins with an epigraph from Schiller's essay "On the Sublime."
[34] Conte 1994.
[35] The text of Lucretius, here and elsewhere, generally follows Bailey 1947, apart from in minor matters of punctuation. Significant differences are noted. The text also has been compared with Munro 1864 and the Rouse-Smith Loeb (Smith 1992). On the cited passage in connection with the sublime, see Segal 1990: 79, who compares Longinus' discussion of τὸ φοβερόν or τὸ δεινόν, including the battle of the gods at *On the Sublime* 9.6. Edmund Burke, who was deeply influential for Kant, also includes this passage (erroneously omitting the final *est* of 3.30) in his own discussion of the role of power in the sublime. See Burke 1958: 69.

Heinze glosses *horror* with "reverent awe as in the presence of the divine" (ehrfurchtsvoller Schauder wie in Götternähe) – but, within an Epicurean framework, this "divine" can only be something of an *Ersatz*-divinity, where "true knowledge" stands in place of traditional Roman religion.[36] Epicureanism, like other ancient philosophical sects, regularly partakes of the language of divinity and professes a goal of "godlikeness" – at times even speaking of its founder as a god – but the sublime articulated here has its roots in atoms and void.[37] It is closely connected with the infinite and with an unlimited nature lying completely exposed (*patens ex omni parte*).[38]

Many readers have been struck – both in the above lines and elsewhere – by Lucretius' emotional fervor, which is clearly connected directly to Epicurean *physiologia*, that school's study of nature and the *kosmos*; yet it is Conte's signal contribution to the explication of the Lucretian sublime to have formulated a model for how this sublime fits together with the larger consolatory aims of *On the Nature of Things*. In discussing Lucretius' description of human wonder at the heavens – for Epicureans the root impulse that inspires cosmology – Conte explains how the sublime may work upon a hypothetical reader, turning him from a passive to an active participant in overcoming human mental limitations:

> *Venit in mentem*, says Lucretius about the feeling that takes hold of the spectator from within his soul when he abandons himself to great thoughts about the ordered cosmos:

> nam cum suspicimus magni caelestia mundi
> templa super stellisque micantibus aethera fixum,   1205
> et uenit in mentem solis lunaeque uiarum,
> tunc aliis oppressa malis in pectora cura
> illa quoque expergefactum caput erigere infit,
> nequae forte deum nobis immensa potestas
> sit, uario motu quae candida sidera uerset.   1210

> When we look up at the celestial regions of the great world
> and at the aether above, fixed with twinkling stars,
> and thought of the paths of the sun and the moon comes to mind,
> then in our chests already burdened with other cares

---

[36] Heinze 1897: 54.

[37] See, e.g., Epicurus' *Letter to Menoeceus* 135, where he proclaims that – as a result of Epicurean teachings – "you shall live as a god among men." See, too, Konstan 2008: 127–52, which expounds the "life worthy of the gods" in the context of a larger discussion of Epicurean epistemology, and Shearin 2015: 30–31, where language of divinity is explained through its connection with religious authority and performative language.

[38] See Porter 2016: 491, which emphasizes the sublime "bottomless heights" envisioned in this passage.

that anxiety, too, begins to raise up its head, awakened,
that the power of the gods over us, which whirls about
the shining stars in varied motion, perhaps may be boundless.
(Lucretius, *On the Nature of Things* 5.1204–10)

Confronting the sublime, says Lucretius, at first the mind is dismayed and it yields to error if it does not know how to respond; thereby it engenders the most intense ambivalences – terror and magnificent discomfort, anguish and fear on the one hand, fascinated exaltation on the other. Nature's majesty both attracts and repels; the sublime elevates the mind pedagogically above human mediocrity and develops within the observer a consciousness of a disproportion requiring adaptation. The sublime reader or spectator feels that he overcomes the limitations of his inert passive forces by overcoming the discomfort of inferiority, by trying to adapt his consciousness to a greatness that transcends passive experience.[39]

Elsewhere Conte elaborates more fully upon this model of how the sublime engages the reader:

First the sublime reader's mind loses itself, "takes fright" (in Leopardi's phrase); then, enlightened by Epicurean *physiologia*, it almost overcomes nature's boundless power by understanding its secret norms. In this way, in its exalting effects and its dialectical mechanism, the sublime anticipates (almost reproduces in itself) the process of intellectual conquest by which the Epicurean "disciple's" mind learns to understand the rules of the universe and of life according to nature.[40]

While there is no need to argue that the sublime is the only manner in which Lucretius engages his reader, Conte provides us with a compelling and useful model: he offers strongly didactic and indeed strongly Epicurean reasons for the centrality of the sublime in Lucretian discourse.[41] As Conte characterizes it, the Lucretian sublime is that which awakens psychic change in the reader. In a negative gesture, the sublime causes a feeling of inadequacy in the attentive student; and this negative gesture inspires, in turn, a corresponding positive one whereby the student actively makes himself adequate to the grandeur of the natural world, apprehending its previously hidden rules. And it is only by taking this final, active step that the reader or pupil has any hope of

[39] Conte 1994: 22–23.   [40] Ibid., 24.

[41] While it may seem, in some respects, that Conte is imposing a (Kantian and Schillerian) model of the sublime (with "negative" and "positive" aspects) upon Lucretius, in the end, this criticism fails. The sublime (an ancient category) is *there* in Lucretius, and (as I read him) Conte is explaining its presence as firmly rooted in the didactic aims of Lucretius' poem. While one may dispute Conte's individual interpretation of Lucretian passages, his basic model seems to me not only steeped in the history of the sublime but also deeply rooted in close acquaintance with Lucretius and Epicureanism.

attaining the ultimate Epicurean goal of *ataraxia*, or freedom from disturbance.

Having sketched, albeit briefly and hastily, Conte's model of the Lucretian sublime, with both its negative and its positive gestures, I now wish to follow in the footsteps of Gareth Williams and use this model to look not merely at Lucretius but also at the sixth book of Seneca's *Natural Questions*.[42] What Williams has demonstrated with great success is that Lucretius lurks, perhaps not always so subtly, in the background of that book and that its consolatory strategies mimic in many ways the Lucretian sublime, as Conte describes it.[43] While I ultimately feel that Seneca leaves his Lucretian model behind – that is, as I have already suggested, I see here sublimes rather than a unitary sublime – there is little doubt that Seneca's examination of earthquakes draws extensively upon Lucretius and the consolatory traditions that he represents.

The sixth book of *Natural Questions*, which is chiefly devoted to expounding in almost encyclopedic fashion the various ancient scientific theories explaining earthquakes – the natural occurrence that rocks the entire *kosmos* at its roots – nonetheless begins and ends with what is a very Lucretian topic: the fear of death and more specifically, the fear of death at the hands of earthquakes. Seneca begins his exposition by recounting the details of the recent Pompeian earthquake in 62 CE, but he quickly turns to his consolatory theme. The study of nature, he suggests, will bring about solace, comfort in the face of inevitable tremors of the earth:

> quorum ut causas excutiamus, et propositi operis contextus exigit et ipse in hoc tempus congruens casus. quaerenda sunt trepidis solacia, et demendus ingens timor.

> Both the plan of the proposed work and this recent disaster itself demand that we discuss the causes of earthquakes. Comfort must be sought for the fearful, and their great terror needs to be eradicated. (Seneca, *Natural Questions* 6.1.3–4)

It seems clear enough that Seneca's second statement here explains his first: comfort must be sought, and it will be sought through examining

---

[42] Williams' reading of Seneca's adaptation of the Lucretian sublime is found in the sixth chapter of Williams 2012: 213–57.

[43] Williams' reading strategy represents general acceptance not only of Conte's reading of the Lucretian sublime but also of Margaret Graver's contention that by Seneca's day, "meteorology had acquired a distinctly Epicurean flavor" (2000: 51). Graver's statements are formulated as a critique of Chapter 6 of Inwood 2005, which was originally published (in shorter form) as Inwood 2000.

the causes of earthquakes. This very idea of seeking solace through *physiologia* in the face of death-dealing natural disaster may seem Lucretian enough, but there is another turn that makes Seneca's discussion still more reminiscent of the Lucretian sublime: in attempting to provide solace, it offers what Conte identifies as a negative gesture, that gesture in which the reader's mind "takes fright." In other words, rather than minimizing the dangers offered by earthquakes, Seneca in fact seems to magnify them:

> quid enim cuiquam satis tutum uideri potest, si mundus ipse concutitur et partes eius solidissimae labant, si quod unum inmobile est in illo fixumque ut cuncta in se intenta sustineat, fluctuatur, si quod proprium habet terra perdidit, stare? ubi tandem resident metus nostri?

> What indeed can seem adequately safe to anyone, if the world itself is shaken and its most solid parts slip; if the one thing in it that is immovable and fixed, so that it supports everything that converges on it, begins to wobble; if earth has lost what is proper to itself – the fact of standing still? Where, finally, will our fears rest? (Seneca, *Natural Questions* 6.1.4)

These lines argue quite forcefully for Williams' suggestion that Seneca's text inherits the Lucretian sublime. Outside of such a sublime context, one in which the reader feels ever smaller in the face of natural wonder as a prelude to active engagement with the deeper laws of nature, these words must strike us as quite strange, for in no obvious manner do they appear to comfort the frightened.[44] One might expect at this point that Seneca would turn to more direct instruction in the laws of nature, but in fact, his magnification of nature's destructive forces continues and becomes, at least in some ways, even more Epicurean:

> nullum maius solacium est mortis quam ipsa mortalitas, nullum autem omnium istorum quae extrinsecus terrent quam **quod innumerabilia pericula in ipso sinu sunt.** quid enim dementius quam ad tonitrua succidere et sub terram correpere fulminum metu? quid stultius quam timere <terrae> nutationem aut subitos montium lapsus et inruptiones maris extra litus eiecti, **cum mors ubique praesto sit et undique occurrat**, nihilque sit tam exiguum quod non in perniciem generis humani satis ualeat?

---

[44] It is worth noting, however, that there is at least one Stoic (rather than Epicurean) antecedent for a frightening god (who is, in Stoic thought, identical with the world). See Cic. *Nat.D.* 2.14, where in listing Cleanthes' four reasons why men have ideas (*notiones*) of gods, Balbus includes the suggestion that men have supposed there are gods because of lightning (*fulminibus*), storms (*tempestatibus*), and other characteristically sublime natural phenomena. See, too, the discussion of Long and Sedley on L&S 54C (vol. 2, p. 323).

There is no greater palliative for death than mortality itself, no greater comfort in the face of all these external things that terrify us than that **there are countless dangers in our very laps**. Indeed, what is madder than fainting at the sound of thunder and crawling beneath the earth out of fear of lightning? What is more thick-headed than fearing the rocking <of the earth> or the sudden collapse of mountains and floods from the sea cast out over the shore, **since death is present everywhere and attacks from all sides**, and nothing is so tiny that it does not suffice for destroying the human race? (Seneca, *Natural Questions* 6.2.6)

πρὸς μὲν τἄλλα δυνατὸν ἀσφάλειαν πορίσασθαι, **χάριν δὲ θανάτου πάντες ἄνθρωποι πόλιν ἀτείχιστον οἰκοῦμεν.**

While it is possible to obtain security towards all else, nevertheless **because of death we all, as humans, dwell in a city without walls**. (Epicurus, *Vatican Sentences* 31)

While there is no reason to oversell the similarities here, this continuation of the negative aspect of the sublime, the sense that nature, and the vast power of the ordered universe, *overwhelms* individual mortals, clearly resonates with Epicurean antecedents. In particular, Seneca's image of the dangers in our very laps seems quite close in spirit to Epicurus' (or perhaps Metrodorus') famous *dictum* that we inhabit a city without walls.[45] Given the overall Lucretian and Epicurean context to this point, we may take this Senecan passage as still further evidence broadly in support of Williams' thesis asserting the influence of the Lucretian, or Epicurean, sublime.

As the Senecan sublime turns from its negative to its positive aspect, however – that is, as it turns toward engaging the reader's active participation in apprehending the laws of nature – I suggest that a gap begins to open between the Lucretian and the Senecan sublimes. Gareth Williams contends that, for Seneca, this positive aspect consists largely in his demonstrating confident control over nature. Thus, on Williams' view, in the central sections of the sixth book of the *Natural Questions* (6.4–26), where Seneca examines the various different theories that have been proposed to explain and the various different elements (earth, air, fire, and water) that have been proposed to cause earthquakes, "the rightness or wrongness of any or all of the theories reviewed … matters less than the broader attitude to nature that Seneca asserts by activating an empowered mind-set throughout this section – a Senecan or Stoic variation on nature's subjugation to

---

[45] For an extended analysis of this maxim, see Gigandet 2012: 306–10.

'superior' Lucretian *ratio*."[46] Williams then demonstrates how Seneca's mastery over nature requires a variety of techniques, including taking stock of previous writers on earthquakes, writers from Thales onward, whom the Stoic scrutinizes in extensive detail. And it is precisely here that Seneca seems to me to depart from Lucretius. While Williams may be correct that what matters above all for the student of the sublime is Seneca's *attitude*, I suggest that Seneca and Lucretius demonstrate fundamentally different valuations of knowledge and further that these differing valuations are essential for understanding their individual sublimes.

Seneca, on the one hand, clearly values even the most basic knowledge about nature.[47] Before he begins to review the various different proposals for the causes of earthquakes, he makes this fact particularly clear:

> "Quod" inquis "erit pretium operae?" **quo nullum maius est, nosse naturam**. neque enim quicquam habet in se huius materiae tractatio pulchrius, cum multa habeat futura usui, quam quod hominem magnificentia sui detinet, nec mercede sed miraculo colitur. inspiciamus ergo quid sit propter quod haec accidant: quorum mihi adeo est dulcis inspectio ut, quamuis aliquando de motu terrarum uolumen iuuenis ediderim, tamen temptare me uoluerim et experiri <an> aetas aliquid nobis aut ad scientiam aut certe ad diligentiam adiecerit.

> "What" you say "will be the worth of this undertaking?" **A worth than which none is greater: knowing nature**, for consideration of this material – although it holds many things that are going to be of use – does not possess anything in itself more beautiful than that its magnificence engages mankind; and it is cultivated not for money but for its marvelousness. Therefore, let us investigate what is the reason why these things occur: for me, their investigation is so sweet that – although at some point as a youth I published a volume on earthquakes – I have desired to test myself and examine whether age has added something to our knowledge or at least to our attentiveness. (Seneca, *Natural Questions* 6.4.2)

While Seneca here mentions factors other than pure knowledge – he comments, for example, on how sweet, *dulcis*, scientific investigation is for him – the value placed on knowledge itself is nevertheless quite high. Indeed, if Williams is correct that a key component of the positive aspect of the sublime for Seneca lies in his demonstration of mastery over nature and further that

---

[46] Williams 2012: 230. The words "Senecan or Stoic variation" indicate that Williams allows for difference between the Senecan and Lucretian sublimes.

[47] This is not to say, however, that Seneca values knowledge per se, a point that I discuss further in the conclusion to this chapter.

one of the key means for demonstrating this mastery lies in the knowledge of earlier philosophical theory, then knowledge itself plays an important, if no doubt still instrumental, role in the articulation of the Senecan sublime.[48]

For Lucretius, by contrast, while *some* knowledge – specifically knowledge of the Epicurean *uera ratio* – plays a key role in the articulation of his sublime (something that we have already seen in Conte's discussion), the knowledge of the greatest consequence is in fact quite limited and circumscribed.[49] When Lucretius introduces the meteorological and other natural scientific investigations that occupy his analysis of the *mundus* in the sixth book, for example, he remarks as follows:

> et quoniam docui mundi mortalia templa
> esse <et> natiuo consistere corpore caelum,
> et quaecumque in eo fiunt fierique necessest,   45
> pleraque dissolui, quae restant percipe porro;
> quandoquidem semel insignem conscendere currum[50]
> ******
>
> uentorum existant, placentur, <ut> omnia rursum
> quae fuerint[51] sint placato conuersa furore,
> cetera quae fieri in terris caeloque tuentur   50
> mortales, pauidis cum pendent mentibu' saepe,
> et faciunt animos humilis formidine diuom
> depressosque premunt ad terram propterea quod
> ignorantia causarum conferre deorum
> cogit ad imperium res et concedere regnum.   55
> [quorum operum causas nulla ratione uidere
> possunt ac fieri diuino numine rentur.][52]
> nam bene qui didicere deos securum agere aeuum,
> si tamen interea mirantur qua ratione
> quaeque geri possint, praesertim rebus in illis   60
> quae supera caput aetheriis cernuntur in oris,

---

[48] Margaret Graver (2000: 45, responding to Inwood 2000) has suggested that ancient meteorology quite generally (including, then, Seneca's *Natural Questions*) "was in fact driven, all along, by concerns about the *limits of our knowledge* and about our relation to the divine" (my emphasis). This claim, which seems generally valid, still permits differing valuations of knowledge within the cosmological and meteorological traditions, which is what I observe in Lucretius and Seneca.

[49] A reader suggests that the level of knowledge attained here is, in fact, "an epic achievement of cosmic understanding" (and thus perhaps not so limited). The point, though, as I try to clarify in what follows, is that Epicurean scientific knowledge may be seen as both limited and epic; it is, in a sense, its very limitation that makes it epic or sublime.

[50] Jacob Bernays first posited the lacuna accepted here.

[51] Here I retain the manuscript reading *fuerint* (*OQ*) instead of Bailey's *fuerent*.

[52] These lines were first deleted by Richard Bentley. They also occur at Lucr. 1.153–54 and 6.90–91.

rursus in antiquas referuntur religiones
et dominos acris adsciscunt, omnia posse
quos miseri credunt, ignari **quid queat esse,**
quid nequeat, finita potestas denique cuique 65
quanam sit ratione atque alte terminus haerens;
quo magis errantes caeca ratione feruntur.

And since I have shown that the spaces of the world are mortal
and the sky is made from created body,
and of the things that are made in it and must be made,
I have discussed many. Learn, then, the rest,
since once to ascend an illustrious chariot

. . .

of winds arise, and how they are calmed, so that all things again
have been turned back to what they were, with their fury calmed;
and [learn?] the remaining things, which mortals observe on earth and in
   the heavens,
when they often hang upon their fearful thoughts
and make their spirits lowly from fear of the gods,
pressing them, crushed, to the earth because
ignorance of causes compels connecting
and conceding things to the rule and authority of the gods.
[Of which works they cannot see the causes
and they think that they arise by divine will.]
For those who have learned well that the gods lead a secure life,
if nevertheless they wonder in the meantime by which principle
each thing can be conducted, especially with regard to those things
which are observed above our heads on celestial shores,
they are carried back into the religions of old,
and they adopt bitter masters, whom they believe
can do all things, since they, the wretches, are ignorant of **what can be,**
of what cannot, how power is fixed for each
and the deep-sticking boundary stone;
by which all the more they are carried off course by blind reason.

(Lucretius, *On the Nature of Things* 6.43–67)

These lines, which closely resemble those noted earlier and discussed by
Conte in Lucretius' fifth book, provide a telling glimpse into the
precise amount and kind of knowledge that the Lucretian sublime
(and Epicurean cosmology more generally) demands: unlike the technical mastery demonstrated in Seneca's lengthy review of other philosophical opinions – which Williams suggests is key to the positive
aspect of his sublime – the Lucretian sublime is grounded firmly in
the knowledge of only a few rules and principles. As one might expect

in an Epicurean context, the key piece of knowledge is negative –
knowledge that the divine does not intervene in human affairs – but
it is part and parcel of a larger knowledge of power or possibility, of
what can be and what cannot.[53]

In fact, Epicurus himself confirms the circumscribed role of knowledge in Epicurean *physiologia*, presenting at least a mild contrast with
the position of Seneca. Scientific enquiry is not undertaken, as we saw
earlier, in order to "know nature" but rather for entirely ethical
reasons:

> πρῶτον μὲν οὖν μὴ ἄλλο τι τέλος ἐκ τῆς περὶ μετεώρων γνώσεως εἴτε κατὰ
> συναφὴν λεγομένων εἴτε αὐτοτελῶς νομίζειν <δεῖ> εἶναι ἤπερ ἀταραξίαν καὶ
> πίστιν βέβαιον, καθάπερ καὶ ἐπὶ τῶν λοιπῶν.

> First, <we should> not believe that there is any other goal in meteorological
> investigation – whether in connection with matters being discussed or
> arbitrarily – than *ataraxia* ("freedom from disturbance") and secure trust,
> just as also is the case in other matters. (Epicurus, *Epistle to Pythocles* 85)

Epicurus here could hardly be more adamant that scientific investigation is
not about knowledge per se.[54]

With this evidence, I hope now at least to have raised the suspicion that,
as I remarked at the outset, in their cosmological visions, the Senecan
sublime – however much it may owe to the Lucretian sublime – is also
identifiably distinct from it. Yet it may seem that this distinction is of
somewhat limited importance. If both sublimes follow a broad pattern in
which the reader-pupil is at first negatively diminished in the face of
nature's grandeur and then actively and positively built up through an
engagement with *physiologia*, how significant is the distinction I have
proposed, whereby Seneca values knowledge highly (at least at certain
times and in certain contexts) and Lucretius and Epicurean texts grant it
a much more circumscribed role?

In brief, I wish to suggest that this differing valuation of knowledge is
part and parcel of a more fundamental gulf between the Lucretian and
Senecan sublimes. If we were to sort Lucretius and Seneca into the

---

[53] See Shearin 2015: 51–57 (which – within a larger discussion of performative language in *On the Nature of Things* – highlights the importance of the language of power and potentiality for Lucretius) and 152–63 (which examines the metaphor of *terminus haerens* and its political significance).

[54] On this passage of Epicurus in conjunction with Seneca, see Williams 2012: 7. Williams (following Graver 2000) suggests that Seneca, too, does not necessarily value scientific knowledge per se. In some sense (as Inwood 2000, 2005 emphasize), Senecan cosmological and meteorological investigation is ultimately about ethical consolation and coming to know god (i.e., the world or *kosmos*), but my point is that pure scientific knowledge is accorded a higher role in Senecan cosmology.

categories proposed by Glenn Most at the outset of my discussion, Lucretius would of course exhibit the Lucretian sublime, but Seneca, in many respects, comes closer to the Longinian. Indeed, Gareth Williams, for all the similarities he sees between Lucretius and Seneca, also offers one important clue for their divergence:

> Given Lucretius' widespread presence elsewhere in Book 6, this sublimity of response to the Campanian earthquake may be markedly Lucretian in color; but Seneca elsewhere delineates a like mind-set without obvious connection to Lucretius. So in *Letters* 41, for example, on the effect of "the god within us" (cf. *prope est a te deus, tecum est, intus est,* 41.1), that divine presence inspires a sublime-like transcendence:[55]

> si hominem uideris interritum periculis, intactum cupiditatibus, inter aduersa felicem, in mediis tempestatibus placidum, ex superiore loco homines uidentem, ex aequo deos, non subibit te ueneratio eius? non dices, "ista res maior est altiorque quam ut credi similis huic in quo est corpusculo possit"? uis isto diuina descendit; animum excellentem, moderatum, omnia tamquam minora transeuntem, quidquid timemus optamusque ridentem, caelestis potentia agitat.

> If you see a man – one not frightened by dangers nor touched by desires, one happy in adverse circumstances and serene in the thick of tempests – who looks upon men from on high, upon gods from equal footing, will worship of him not overtake you? Surely you will say "this quality is greater and higher than that it can be believed of a kind with this little body in which it dwells." A divine force has descended upon this man; celestial power drives his soul, which is excellent, balanced, which endures all things as if they are of little account and laughs at our hopes and fears. (Seneca, *Moral Epistles* 41.4–5)

While Lucretius (and Epicureanism in general) is quite unafraid to use the language of the divine – at *On the Nature of Things* 5.8, for example, he famously calls Epicurus a god – Williams is undeniably right to underline a distinction between Seneca's and Lucretius' notions of divinity.[56] The Senecan divine – and therefore the Senecan sublime – tends toward omnipotence and, as we saw with regard to knowledge, encyclopedic omniscience.[57] By contrast, Epicurus, Lucretius's *Ersazt*-god, remains

---

[55] Williams 2012: 255–56.
[56] Lucr. 5.7–12: *nam si, ut ipsa petit maiestas cognita rerum, / dicendum est,* **deus ille fuit, deus**, *inclute Memmi, / qui princeps uitae rationem inuenit eam quae / nunc appellatur sapientia, quique per artem / fluctibus e tantis uitam tantisque tenebris / in tam tranquillo et tam clara luce locauit.*
[57] It is important to be clear that – even as Stoicism speaks of the divine within humans – such language likely does not attribute complete omniscience to humans, even to the "wise man" (*sapiens*) who serves as a model for so much human behavior.

forever in possession of only partial knowledge, a fact that Seneca himself demonstrates quite well.

When, for example, Seneca recounts Epicurus' position on the various causes of earthquakes, it is unmistakable how qualified the whole explanation turns out to be:

> omnes istas **posse** causas esse Epicurus ait, pluresque alias temptat, et illos qui aliquid unum ex istis esse adfirmauerunt corripit, cum sit arduum de his quae coniectura sequenda sunt aliquid certi promittere. "ergo" ut ait "**potest** terram mouere aqua si partes aliquas eluit et adrosit, quibus desiit **posse** extenuatis sustineri quod integris ferebatur. **potest** terram mouere impressio spiritus: **fortasse** enim aër et extrinsecus alio intrante aëre agitatur, **fortasse** aliqua parte subito decidente percutitur, et inde motum capit. **fortasse** aliqua pars terrae uelut columnia quibusdam ac pilis sustinetur, quibus uitiatis ac recedentibus tremit pondus impositum. **fortasse** calida uis spiritus in ignem uersa et fulmini similis cum magna strage obstantium fertur. **fortasse** palustres et iacentes aquas aliquis flatus impellit, et inde aut ictus terram quatit aut spiritus agitatio ipso motu crescens et se incitans ab imo in summa usque perfertur." nullam tamen illi placet causam motus esse maiorem quam spiritum.

> Epicurus says that all of these are **possible** explanations – and he tries many others, too. He also attacks those who have asserted that some one of them is correct, since it is difficult to promise some certain knowledge (*aliquid certi*) from these options that ought to be pursued by conjecture. "Therefore," as he says, "water **can** move the earth if it has washed over some parts and eaten them away. With these parts weakened, what was borne while they were whole ceased **to be able** to be supported. Air pressure **can** move the earth, for **perhaps** air is disturbed by still other air entering from outside, **perhaps** when part of the earth suddenly collapses, it causes a shock that sets the air in motion. **Perhaps** part of the earth is supported by some columns and piers, as it were, and when they are weakened and worn away, the weight placed on them shakes. **Perhaps** some hot breath that has turned to fire, like a lightning-bolt, moves forward, causing serious damage to anything in its path. **Perhaps** some breeze sets marshy, stagnant water moving, and then either the impact shakes the earth, or the agitation of the breath grows with its own movement, spurs itself on, and travels from the depths right up to the surface." But he thinks that no cause of motion is more important than breath. (Seneca, *Natural Questions* 6.20.5–7)

While the Epicureans are in some contexts famous for their use of the *pleonachos tropos*, or multiple explanations, this example verges on the extreme.[58] It is not merely that each given explanation of earthquakes is

---

[58] For a philosophical examination of the *pleonachos tropos* in Epicureanism, see Hankinson 2013. See, too, Shearin 2014: 185–86.

qualified with a "possibly" or a "perhaps" – a phenomenon that may be paralleled in other ancient contexts – but rather that Epicurus is explicitly portrayed as refusing to extract any *certain* knowledge from the investigation of earthquakes. Indeed, if it were at all in doubt, this passage confirms what we have already seen – that the form of knowledge assigned to Epicurean science (and which undergirds the Lucretian sublime) is precisely the knowledge of power and possibility, the knowledge of generative rules rather than of facts.

12.3 Conclusion: Cosmology, Limit, and Sublime Feelings

Let us return now to our point of departure – to cosmology and questions of limit. In ways that I have been unpacking throughout the present chapter, both Lucretius and Seneca engage in study of the *kosmos* – yet never, it appears, do they do so out of a pure thirst for scientific knowledge. As our look at the sublime and the consolatory strategy imbricated together with it in both authors has shown, cosmology is largely instrumental in the ethical project of each thinker. Lucretius and Seneca both urge their readers to turn to rational explanation of the heavens as part and parcel of a larger attempt to allay fears. In Seneca's case, this is above all fear of death; for Lucretius, it is fear of the divine and an inability to explain the workings of the world without recourse to the concept of a vengeful divinity. Of course, these two fears can be closely related, and for Lucretius allaying fear of death is also a central concern, especially in his much admired third book. But for Seneca these two fears are not so obviously linked – and this observation is of some significance.

Elsewhere in his *Natural Questions*, in the preface to his chapter "On <celestial> fires," a hypothetical interlocutor (no doubt intended to figure Lucilius, to whom the book is addressed) challenges Seneca to explain the value of his natural scientific (and cosmological) investigations. The philosopher mounts the following reply:

> "quid tibi" inquis "ista proderunt?" si nihil aliud, hoc certe: sciam omnia angusta esse mensus deum.

> "How will these things benefit you?" you ask. If nothing else, surely in this way: I shall know that everything is small after measuring god. (Seneca, *Natural Questions* 1 praef. 17)

This sublime response no doubt takes on greater meaning if we note that "god" in Stoic parlance could be identified with the world itself.[59] Measuring

---

[59] See, e.g., Cic. *Nat.D.* 1.39: *ipsumque mundum deum dicit* [*sc. Chrysippus*] *esse.*

the world, the *kosmos*, is meaningful because it is synonymous with measuring the divine. And the divine is not simply absent and uninvolved in human affairs, as is the case in Epicurean theology: the divine, as we have already noted, is part of us. Indeed, the divine, as Seneca remarks earlier in the same preface, in effect models for us our own minds: "What then is the difference between the nature of god and our own? For us, the mind is the better part; in him, no part is outside the mind" (*QNat.* 1 praef. 14).

The fact that the divine is within helps explain, I suggest, the differing valuations of knowledge we observed in the Senecan and Lucretian sublimes. For Seneca, even as scientific knowledge, knowledge of the *kosmos*, is only instrumental in allaying fear, the mind that pursues scientific knowledge learns about its better self, about what is divine within. And perhaps that is why the ideal of omniscience, even if it is humanly impossible, cannot entirely be set aside.[60] As Seneca's remark about "having measured the divine" suggests, god – and his omniscient mind that knows fate and providence – is the awesome goal of his science. And this ideal, as we have explored, helps create the dynamic of the sublime and – in the words of Longinus in my first epigraph – raises the yearning student "beyond anything mortal." We sublimely transcend our human limits in reaching for the divine.

For Lucretius, by contrast, the sensation of the sublime is, at least in key moments, quite different. In one of the most memorable moments of his poem, Lucretius describes, as he often does, how the mind seeks out natural scientific explanations. Yet here the problem confronting the mind is not learning of the divine within; it is nothing less than the problem of comprehending infinity:

> quaerit enim rationem animus, cum summa loci sit
> infinita foris haec extra moenia mundi,
> quid sit ibi porro quo prospicere usque uelit mens
> atque animi iactus liber quo peruolet ipse.
> principio nobis in cunctas undique partis
> et latere ex utroque <supra> subterque per omne
> nulla est finis; uti docui, res ipsaque per se
> uociferatur, et elucet natura profundi.
> nullo iam pacto **ueri simile** esse putandumst,
> undique cum uersum spatium uacet infinitum
> seminaque innumero numero summaque profunda
> multimodis uolitent aeterno percita motu,

---

[60] On the possible omniscience of the Stoic wise man (who, in some sense, models ethical human behavior), see Inwood and Donini 1999: 720, who are skeptical. For more positive evidence, see Cic. *Tusc.* 4.37.

hunc unum terrarum orbem caelumque creatum,
nil agere illa foris tot corpora materiai.

Indeed, the mind seeks an account – since the totality
of space is infinite outside, beyond these walls of the world –
of what is there, where the mind continually desires to look,
and where the very projection of the mind flies when free.
First off, in every direction, all around us,
and from each side, above and below, through everything,
there is no limit; as I have shown, the truth itself, by itself,
cries out, and the nature of the deep shines forth.
Now it ought to be thought in no way **probable**,
since infinite space lies open from all directions,
and since countless seeds flit about variously,
goaded onwards in eternal movement,
that this world and created heavens are unique,
that so many bodies of matter outside do nothing.

(Lucretius, *On the Nature of Things* 2.1044–57)

This moment, which is arguably the most sublime in the entire *De rerum natura*, is followed closely by the poet's account of the infinity of possible worlds (2.1067–89). Comprehending the infinite, in the Lucretian and Epicurean frame, is, on the one hand, a matter of combinatorial *possibility*; that is, the engine that drives the sublimity of Lucretius' poem is in one sense derived from a few basic principles and indeed from limited knowledge. The sublime is not *knowing* all the possible combinations but rather being able to imagine them, based on a few simple rules and principles. Moreover, cosmological contemplation is not about drawing closer to god: the Lucretian figure is stark and alone, projecting his mind where his physical and mental limits will not allow him to go. Lucretius' is thus a sublime that seems strongly rooted in human limitation – and in the desire to constantly challenge that limitation. While Seneca may have learned much of his sublimity and broad-scale consolatory strategy from Lucretius, as I hope to have demonstrated, he does not follow him in all respects – and in particular he fails to thematize the limits of human knowledge in the same way that Lucretius does. Our human limitations may consistently frustrate all of us; but in Lucretius' hands, they are, I suggest, a precondition for greatness.

CHAPTER 13

Cosmic Spiritualism among the Pythagoreans, Stoics, Jews and Early Christians

Phillip Sidney Horky

13.1 Introduction

It is a curious feature of human reasoning that it enjoys the use of analogies in order to explain the inexplicable: in Ancient Greece, from Homer onward we are constantly confronted with, for example, gods in human form, with human attributes that are often pushed to extremes.[1] Something striking, however, happened in the late sixth century BCE: Greek intellectuals began to criticise this representation of the gods and, by extension, the parts of the *kosmos* that the gods either were thought to embody[2] or to which they were thought to be assigned governance.[3] Instead, a new sort of 'god' arrived on the scene, one differentiated by its lack of human features, while at the same time being marked by its perfection and comprehension. Xenophanes of Colophon called this god 'Intellect' or 'Mind' (Nous), retaining the most positive attribute of the most authoritative gods in the Greek (Zeus) and Indo-Iranian (Ahura Mazda) pantheons.[4] This move would be decisive historically: for centuries – well into the second century CE – philosophers like Anaxagoras, Diogenes of Apollonia, Plato, the Early Platonists, and the Stoics would follow Xenophanes in positing an intelligent god, and extend his creative activities beyond himself in the act of cosmogony.[5] The first material object constructed by this intelligent god was the *kosmos*, the all-encompassing

---

[1] The classic work on analogy in ancient Greece remains Lloyd 1966, especially pp. 192–209.
[2] As in the case of Mesopotamian and Orphic cosmogonies. For an excellent general discussion, see Burkert 2008.
[3] As in the case of Homeric and Hesiodic theogonies.
[4] Xenophanes DK 21 B 10–26. Generally, on the distinctiveness of Xenophanes' *Nous*, see Benzi 2016. On the usually unremarked interrelationships between Greek philosophy and Zoroastrian theology, see Horky 2009.
[5] Anaxagoras DK 59 B 13; Diogenes of Apollonia DK 64 B 4–5; Pl. *Phlb.* 30d and *Ti.* 39d; for the Early Platonists, see Speusippus Frs. 89–91 IP; Xenocrates Fr. 133 IP²; for the Stoics, see L&S 46 A–B.

universe that was, one way or another, ordered and differentiated.[6] Similarly, in Hebrew traditions that are roughly contemporary, accounts of the generation of the universe and all its parts arise, and in the text of Genesis we see Yahweh as a primal cultivator, differentiating the parts of the *kosmos*, fashioning the manifold creatures to inhabit it, and assigning the human being the task of terrestrial oversight.[7] The adaptation of Hebrew traditions in the writings of early Christianity, starting from the latter part of the first century CE, sees the birth of a new spiritual cosmology, a celebration of the 'last' Adam and son of God who is to inherit the kingdom of heaven in the promise of apocalyptic fulfilment suggested by some of the more prophetic works of the Hebrew Bible.

It is agreed that πνεῦμα, which normally translates as 'breath' but eventually comes to mean 'spirit' in a marked sense, plays a fundamental role in the latter tradition, marking the filial inheritance of early Christianity from Judaism and setting out a new path of spiritual cosmology – a return of Man to the paternal source that had originally bestowed upon him life.[8] What is not often noted, however, is that much of the pneumatic theology that is found in the New Testament, which would come to exercise a tremendous effect on the world after Christianity's triumph in the Late Roman Empire, shows remarkable inheritances also from the secularising, scientific tradition of the Greek philosophical cosmology. For, as I will argue in this chapter, it is with Paul that we see not only the bridging of the Hebrew and Indo-European traditions of cosmogonic and anthropogonic pneumatics – that had already been anticipated by his predecessor Philo of Alexandria, a Hellenic Jew who was additionally a Platonist/Stoic philosopher – but also a subsuming of the scientific tradition under a notion of divine pneumatics that has an active role in religious teaching, understanding and even prophetics. Analogies with earlier pagan usages will be retained, but they will also be adapted to new and emergent spiritual concerns that eventually brought the Christian community together – the natural and logical extension of what the Stoics had thought was the primary ontological and natural function of 'breath'. Hence, I will approach the topic of cosmic spiritualism by tracing the history of the pneumatic cosmogony/anthropogony analogy, from its earliest expression in the lost works of the Pythagoreans, through the Stoics who adapted and modified it, including the deeply influential Posidonius

[6] See e.g. Anaxagoras DK 59 B 12–13; Diogenes of Apollonia DK 64 B 2–3; Pl. *Ti.* 31c–32a.
[7] Genesis 1:1–31.
[8] It is important to note from the beginning that the word for 'breath' and 'spirit' is the same in Greek: πνεῦμα. 'Breath' originates in Old English as *bræð*, and 'spirit' is an Anglicisation of Latin *spiritus*.

of Apamea and the remarkable and understudied Jewish philosopher Philo of Alexandria, to the texts of the New Testament, especially the creative re-imaginings of Paul.[9]

13.2 Origins of Cosmic Breathing: The Pythagoreans

Perhaps the very earliest evidence in the Western world of 'breath/spirit' (Greek πνεῦμα) occupying a formative place in both cosmic and human generation is associated with the enigmatic philosopher Pythagoras of Samos, who died in the first few decades of the fifth century BCE.[10] The evidence is, as is often the case with ancient philosophers who left no writings, late and subject to bias, but it nevertheless gives us a good starting point for our analysis of breath in the Hellenistic and Post-Hellenistic worlds, and beyond. Our materials come from Aristotle's lost text *On the Philosophy of Pythagoras*, probably written in the mid fourth century BCE, and it is as potent as it is enigmatic (a common problem for evidence regarding early Pythagoreanism). But it is confirmed and expanded by two other pieces of evidence, the first from Aristotle's *Physics* itself, and the second given by Simplicius in his much later commentary on that text:

> A. In the first book of *On the Philosophy of Pythagoras*, he [Aristotle] writes that heaven is one, and that time and breath, i.e. void, which differentiates the spaces of each thing in each case, was drawn in from the infinite; for there is a fiery place on the inside.

> ἐν δὲ τῷ Περὶ τῆς Πυθαγόρου φιλοσοφίας πρώτῳ γράφει τὸν μὲν οὐρανὸν εἶναι ἕνα, ἐπεισάγεσθαι δ' ἐκ τοῦ ἀπείρου χρόνον τε καὶ πνοὴν καὶ τὸ κενόν, ὃ διορίζει ἑκάστων τὰς χώρας ἀεί· ἔνδοθεν γὰρ εἶναι τόπον πύρινον.[11] (Stobaeus, *Eclogues* 1.18.1 c = Aristotle, Fr. 201 Rose³ = DK 58 B 30; tr. after Bernabé and Mendoza)

> B. The Pythagoreans, too, held that void exists and that it enters the heaven from the infinite breath, the *kosmos* inhaling also the void which distinguishes the natures of things as if it were what separates and distinguishes the terms of a series.

> εἶναι δ' ἔφασαν καὶ οἱ Πυθαγόρειοι κενόν, καὶ ἐπεισιέναι αὐτὸ τῷ οὐρανῷ ἐκ τοῦ ἀπείρου πνεύματος ὡς ἀναπνέοντι καὶ τὸ κενόν, ὃ διορίζει τὰς φύσεις,

---

[9] For a useful general study of Paul's relationship to Jewish and Hellenistic (including Stoic and Platonist) wisdom, see especially Alexander 2001.
[10] The most informative paper I have read on this subject remains Malcolm Schofield's 'Pythagoras the Plagiarist' (n.d.).
[11] Text from Primavesi 2018.

ὡς ὄντος τοῦ κενοῦ χωρισμοῦ τινὸς τῶν ἐφεξῆς καὶ [τῆς] διορίσεως.
(Aristotle, *Physics* 4.6.213b22–6; tr. after Hardie and Gaye)

C. They [the Pythagoreans] used to say that the void penetrates the *kosmos*, as if the latter inhaled it or exhaled it like a breath of what is diffused around it from the outside.

ἔλεγον γὰρ ἐκεῖνοι τὸ κενὸν ἐπεισιέναι τῷ κόσμῳ οἷον ἀναπνέοντι ἤτοι εἰσπνέοντι αὐτῷ ὥσπερ πνεῦμα ἀπὸ τοῦ ἔξωθεν περικεχυμένου·
(Simplicius, *Commentary on Aristotle's* Physics p. 651.39–41 Diels; tr. after Bernabé and Mendoza)

Hence, we see the ultimate beginnings of a mode that employs biological analogy to the purpose of explaining nothing less than the constitution of the entire well-ordered universe. This theory could be thought to set in motion what would, inevitably and after much mathematical speculation, lead to the modern concept of the oscillating expansion and retraction of the universe, often associated with the oscillating universe version of the 'big bang'. For the early Pythagoreans, the universe is understood to function, to *live*, as an animal – once it has been constituted and its parts set into motion, it inhales and exhales 'breath' from the infinity that surrounds it (perhaps explaining, by analogy, the expansion and contraction of the ordered universe), and from which it differentiates itself and its individual natures.[12] The vehicle for this differentiation is void, or the space that is occupied by matter, and that is like 'breath'.[13] The push and pull that demonstrates the universe's capacity for breathing in the void which (now) articulated matter occupies as the universe takes form.[14] The sign that the universe and its constituents are properly differentiated from what is chaotic and disorderly is the persistent motion indicated by regular respiration.

It had been common to anthropomorphise the gods among the Greeks, assuming that Zeus and Hera, Apollo and Athena, were sort of 'super-

[12] Aristotle probably means 'natures' here in the sense of 'substances'.
[13] Even if the concept of the void was an invention of the Eleatics, as Schofield (n.d.) hypothesises, the evidence could certainly be taken to refer to early Pythagorean philosophy in the wake of challenges brought by Parmenides' and Zeno's philosophy. For a similar approach to Pythagoreanism in the two generations after Pythagoras' death, see Horky 2013: 131–49.
[14] Beyond this very general description (which no doubt some will find anachronistic), it is unfortunately impossible from this information to deduce exactly what sort of 'void' is implied here. Did the Pythagoreans conceive of this void as absolute space, or as relative spaces between parts of the *kosmos*? Or is it possible that the Pythagoreans conceived of void as *both* absolute space (within which matter as a whole is situated) and the relative spaces between the parts of the *kosmos* after cosmogony? I am inclined towards the latter view, but this could be impossible to adjudicate, given the challenges with establishing the Aristotelian source text. For further thoughts, see Primavesi 2018: 122–25.

humans' who, while they did not of course die, nevertheless had the physical and especially emotional attributes of human beings, usually to extreme levels. Hence, we see that the Homeric gods *breathe*: in particular, they 'breathe into' humans certain insights – their breathing is a kind of divine gift or guidance, not at all indicative of their mortality, but rather the mark of their immortality.[15] This is of course not unlike what we see in the Hebrew Scriptures, especially the famous creation of the first human in Genesis 2.7, or its expansion in the Gospels in the New Testament, both of which we will discuss later on. But with the advent of Pythagorean philosophy in Greece[16] something had changed: the *kosmos* itself, understood in speculatively biomorphic terms, was now being associated with a unified, living being, whose self-constitution was regulated through its primal activity of breathing. The effect was immediate. Charles Kahn has argued that Xenophanes, whom we mentioned earlier, went so far as to reject a Pythagorean notion of cosmic respiration in his description of the god Mind.[17] Not much later, Empedocles, who was associated with the Pythagoreans by Hellenistic historiographers,[18] speculated about the workings of animal respiration, comparing it with the motion of clepsydra; this is not necessarily the same thing as cosmic breathing – the Pythagorean analogy is biomorphic, and the Empedoclean mechanical – but the analogy is nonetheless said to apply to all things in Empedocles' universe.[19] Indeed, the growth and expansion of the *kosmos* is analogous to what happens in animal birth about a generation later, in the writings of the mathematical Pythagorean Philolaus of Croton (fl. 420s–10s BCE), who, according to Aristotle's student Meno, observed:

> Immediately after birth, the animal breathes in the external air, which is cold. Then it sends it out again like a debt. Indeed, it is for this reason that there is desire for external air, so that our bodies, which were too hot before, by the drawing in of breath from the outside, are cooled thereby.

---

[15] E.g. Hom. *Od.* 19.138.

[16] Bernabé and Mendoza (2013) demonstrate the close connections between this Pythagorean account of the cosmogony and that of the *Rig Veda*.

[17] Kahn 2001: 36, by reference to DK 21 A1.19 = D.L. 9.19.

[18] Empedocles' relationship with Pythagoreanism remains difficult to pin down, although he was associated with the Pythagorean pretenders by Neanthes of Cyzicus (FGrHist 84 F 26 = D.L. 8.55) and Timaeus of Tauromenium (FGrHist 566 F 14 = D.L. 8.54). For Empedocles as 'democratising' Pythagorean, see Horky 2013: 116–19 and especially 2016.

[19] The fragment literally claims that 'all things' (πάντα) respire the way Empedocles describes (DK 31 B 100), but it is Aëtius (DK 31 A 74) who interprets this as referring to the first animal. Generally, on this material, see Lloyd 1966: 328–33.

με[τὰ γὰρ] τὴν ἔκτεξιν εὐθέως[το]τὸ ζῷον ἐπιστᾶται τὸ ἐκτὸς πνεῦμα ψυχρὸν ὄν· εἶτα πάλιν καθαπερεὶ χρέος ἐκπέμπει αὐτό. διὰ τοῦτο δὴ καὶ ὄρεξις τοῦ ἐκτὸς πνεύματος, ἵνα τῇ[ι] ἐπ<ε>ισάκτῳ τοῦ πνεύματος ὁλκῇ θερμ[ό]τερα ὑπάρχοντα τὰ ἡμέτερα σώματα πρὸς αὐτοῦ καταψύχηται. (Philolaus of Croton DK 44 A 27; tr. by Huffman)

That animal breathing expressed the intelligence, and the intelligibility, of the universe was suggested by Diogenes of Apollonia, who found in breathing (ἀναπνέοντα) the 'significant evidence' (μεγάλα σημεῖα) that both humans and other animals possessed intelligence (νόησις).[20] Such an analogy would take hold in remarkable ways throughout antiquity, informing many accounts that sought to combine the scientific with the ethical, the philosophical with the spiritual.

13.3 Breath as Sustaining Power: The Stoics and Posidonius of Apamea

The Pythagoreans' pneumatic cosmogony was generally ignored by fourth-century BCE philosophers, perhaps due to the authoritative cosmogonic visions that were presented by Plato and Aristotle.[21] There is some indication that Aristotle's student, Theophrastus, identified God with both the heavens and breath, but it is unclear how this association is supposed to be understood.[22] Moreover, due to scarcity of evidence, it is difficult to know whether the Pythagorean model offered traction to the early Stoics of the late fourth and third centuries BCE, but there are some suggestions that it did. It was adopted by the remarkable second-century BCE philosopher Posidonius of Apamea, whose investigations into nature reflected a particular declension of Stoicism:[23]

> The *kosmos*, they[24] say, is one and this is limited, having a spherical shape; for a shape of this sort is most suitable for motion, according to Posidonius in the fifth book of his *Natural Reason* and the followers of Antipater in their

[20] DK 64 B 4.
[21] Plato expressly rejected the notion that the World-Soul breathed or practised physical activities analogous to human life (*Ti.* 33c1–34a7), on which see Broadie 2012: 92–94. For further discussion of Plato and Aristotle, see the contributions by Brisson, Johnson, Gagné, and Boys-Stones (Chapters 6, 4, 9 and 5, respectively).
[22] Clem. *Protr.* 5.66.5 = Theophrastus F 252B FHS&G: 'And that man from Eresus, Theophrastus, the associate of Aristotle, supposes in one place that God is heaven (οὐρανόν), and in another that He is breath (πνεῦμα)'.
[23] The quotation also mentions the 'followers of Antipater', but Posidonius' fifth book of his *Natural Reason* is expressly cited.
[24] The Stoics are intended here.

works *On the Kosmos*. Outside this [sc. the *kosmos*] is diffused the unlimited void, which is incorporeal. By 'incorporeal' they mean that which, although it is capable of being occupied by corporeal things, is not occupied by them. There is no void in the *kosmos*, but it is wholly unified. For this [sc. unification] necessarily results from reciprocal breathing and tension of the heavenly things towards the terrestrial things [τοῦτο γὰρ ἀναγκάζειν τὴν τῶν οὐρανίων πρὸς τὰ ἐπίγεια σύμπνοιαν καὶ συντονίαν]. (Posidonius of Apamea Fr. 8 Kidd = Diogenes Laertius 7.140)

Posidonius adapts the Pythagorean cosmogony to a Stoic framework, elaborating a more complex theory of corporeals (i.e. bodies, or three-dimensional material objects) and incorporeals (i.e. empty space) according to the principle of potentiality: void is incorporeal, i.e. a space that *could* be occupied by corporeals, but currently is not. Void as such does not exist *in* the *kosmos*, but rather the persistent 'reciprocal breathing' (σύμπνοια) and 'tension' (συντονία) of the heavenly towards the earthly things indicates that all space within the ordered universe is, at all times, occupied by corporeal matter. Importantly, for Posidonius, as for earlier Stoics, the soul is defined as a 'hot breath' (πνεῦμα ἔνθερμον) and is matter, and it is soul that is said to 'hold together' bodies, 'just as glue controls both itself and what is outside' (ὥσπερ καὶ ἡ κόλλα καὶ ἑαυτὴν καὶ τὰ ἐκτὸς κρατεῖ).[25] In this way, soul, as hot breath, manifests a sort of 'tension' between things that brings coherence and cohesion between what is internal and what is external:[26] in this cosmic situation, the external is what is on the heavenly 'outside' or the edge of the ordered universe, and the internal is what is circumscribed under it. It is doubtful, however, that Posidonius understood the 'outside' to be in the infinite void beyond the heavenly outer rim of the universe, as the Pythagoreans did.[27] Perhaps at this point it is worth pointing out that, for Posidonius, the *kosmos* was defined as the 'systematic compound composed out of heaven, earth, and the natural constituents in them' (σύστημα ἐξ οὐρανοῦ καὶ γῆς καὶ τῶν ἐν τούτοις φύσεων).[28] Posidonius's strict commitment to materialism within the ordered universe reveals itself in the claim that soul, as *hot* breath, is

---

[25] Fr. 149 Kidd. For an excellent general discussion of Stoic *pneuma* and its antecedents in Hellenistic medicine, see Hankinson 2002: 298–301.

[26] For the Stoics, heat and cold are 'active' powers, whereas earth and water are 'passive' elements (cf. Nemesius p. 164.15–18 Matthaei = L&S 47 D).

[27] Here Posidonius follows Plato, who, contrary to the Pythagoreans, claims that the *kosmos*, as a perfect sphere, did not breathe in the outside air (*Ti.* 33c).

[28] Fr. 14 Kidd. Note that a second definition is also added that explains the first: 'a systematic compound composed out of gods, men, and what has come into being for their sake'. Compare these definitions with that of ps-Aristotle, *On the Kosmos* 391b9–12, and Chrysippus (*SVF* 2.527.1–3 = Arius Didymus Fr. 31), both discussed by Johnson in Chapter 4.

qualified <u>matter</u>, unlike the breath of the Pythagorean cosmogony, which was immaterial and described even as the void.[29] Indeed, someone might object that it would be absurd if 'void', i.e. the dimensions of external 'space', were to 'insert itself' into or 'penetrate' matter, as the Pythagoreans held in their biomorphic model of cosmology.[30]

Posidonius' account of breath as 'tension' taps firmly into Stoic orthodoxy. For 'breath', as we saw, is the rarified matter or stuff that, when qualified as 'hot',[31] actively *constitutes* soul, which itself makes sure that bodies remain unified as such (and identifiable as what-they-are). Or, another way to put it, 'breath' *sustains* animate corporeal objects-as-such.[32] What, then, does Posidonius mean by the rarified stuff or matter that is 'breath'? Here we see a fascinating, if challenging, pair of Stoic notions come into play: breath as the 'tension' (συντονία) *among* corporeal objects, or as the 'tenor' (τόνος or ἕξις) *within* them.[33] 'Tension' could be understood as the means by which diverse objects are able to interact successfully. It is fundamental, as we saw earlier with Posidonius, for the sustenance of the universe as an orderly composition of divine and mortal elements that belong in it. The metaphor employed by the Stoics for this aspect of 'breath' is both musical and biological: in Aristotle, it refers to the kinds of harmonic concords that are high-pitched,[34] but it is not a simple metaphor for psychic or political 'harmony'.[35] Of more relevance to our study of the Stoics, in the case of biology, Aristotle uses 'tension' (συντονία) to describe the quality of the sinews that connect the parts of animal bodies. In animals at their prime, the joints and sinews are more tense, whereas both prior and posterior to that age, they are more slack.[36]

---

[29] As Long helpfully puts it (1996: 227), 'The Stoics had reasons ... for insisting that the soul is corporeal; but those reasons fall within a general conceptual framework which denies that anything can exist which is not a body or a state of a body'.

[30] Compare again Plato's rejection of the presence of void inside the animate being in his discussion of breathing (*Ti.* 79b–c).

[31] Galen testifies that the breath which constitutes the soul's commanding faculty possesses two elements/qualities, which are 'air and fire'/'cold and hot' (L&S 47 H).

[32] See e.g. Galen's description of the physics involved (L&S 47 F): 'The chief proponents of the sustaining power [συνεκτικὴ δύναμιν], such as the Stoics, make what sustains one thing, and what is sustained different: the breathy substance is what sustains [πνευματικὴ οὐσία τὸ συνέχον], and the material substance what is sustained [ὑλικὴ τὸ συνεχόμενον]. And they say that air and fire sustain, and earth and water are sustained.'

[33] The terminology is inconsistent and depends on whether the evidence base is original to a Stoic or a critic. For example, Chrysippus himself probably used ἕξις, whereas the same concept appears to have been reinterpreted by later authors as τόνος.

[34] Arist. *Pol.* 8.7.1341b36–41.

[35] On the political deployment of κόσμος, see Atack's contribution to this volume (Chapter 8).

[36] Arist. *GA* 5.7.787b6–19.

Hence, so Aristotle argues, animals in their prime, when their sinews and joints are most 'tense', are strongest, and he gives as evidence for this mature bulls, who, according to him, have particularly sinewy hearts, which, thanks to the high tension in their flesh, produce the tense breathing that one observes when a bull breathes.[37] 'Tension' thus understood appears to be a force that marks the optimal physical conditions for system-wide performance, and hence it is no surprise that Posidonius, as a committed teleologist, adapted Aristotle's biological usage to his pneumatic cosmology.

The evidence for Stoic breath as internal 'tenor' (τόνος or ἕξις) is more substantial, but also more variegated and complex. First, we should consider the relationship between 'tension' and 'tenor', before going on to describe how 'tenor' was thought by the Stoics to be a species of the genus 'breath'. Now the best evidence for the relationship between external 'tension' and internal 'tenor' comes from the Christian bishop and philosopher Nemesius of Emesa, who flourished in the fourth century CE:

> Now if the soul is a body of any kind at all, even if it is of the rarest consistency, what is it that sustains it [sc. the soul]? For it has been proved that every body needs something to sustain it, which is an endless regress until we reach something incorporeal. If they should say, as the Stoics do, that there exists in bodies a kind of tensile movement [τονικὴ κίνησις] which moves simultaneously inwards and outwards, the outward movement producing quantities and qualities, and the inward one unity and substance, we must ask them (since every movement issues from some power), what this power is and in what substance it consists. (Nemesius, *On Human Nature* pp. 70.6–71.4 Matthaei = Long & Sedley 47 J; tr. by Long and Sedley)

As Long and Sedley note in their commentary on this passage, 'this is the most precise surviving testimony concerning the internal effects of πνεῦμα within a compound body'.[38] We should add that it is also the most precise surviving testimony on the relationship between 'tension' and 'tenor'. As we saw earlier, 'tension' occurs between bodies within a complex 'system', whereas 'tenor' is within an individual body as such. How do these relate? We can only conjecture, but Nemesius's passage gives us some grounds to do so. 'Tensile movement' goes both outwards and inwards: the outwards breathing of, say, an animal is the power that produces – or more literally 'brings to completion' (ἀποτελεστική) – qualities and quantities, which we can perceive in one another: hence, we might say that Aristotle's bull is 'swollen with anger' when we

---

[37] Ibid.   [38] L&S vol. II, p. 282.

perceive the bull's exhalation.[39] Contrariwise, the inwards breathing of an animal is what guarantees its unity, its identifiability as an individual substantial body – *this* animal;[40] in the absence of breath, the individual substance no longer exists, and this is the animal's 'death'.[41] After the matador has delivered the final blow, the bull, who cannot inhale breath because he has respired, ceases to be Aristotle's bull as such: he is no longer, from a metaphysical and epistemological point of view, identifiable as *this* individual bull, and the failure to inhale indicates the beginning of the partition of the bull's physical body into (what will eventually become) an infinite number of material parts or pieces. The same could be said, we would imagine, of all individual compound animate substances, whether they are animals of lower epistemic and aretaic capacities such as Aristotle's bull, or sages who possess full rational capacities, like Socrates.

What about individual simple substances within the broader physical world, such as 'this rock' or 'this piece of iron'? While they are, from our perspective, 'inanimate', i.e. they lack soul, the Stoics were so deeply committed to their comprehensive pneumatic cosmology that they believed objects such as 'this rock' and 'this piece of iron' to – in some qualified sense – 'breathe'. This makes some sense, at least in accordance with the Stoics' unique conceptualisation of internal breathing as 'tenor', i.e. the breathing that guarantees an individual corporeal object's existence as such. On the subject of their 'innate breath', Galen provides us with further evidence of division of the genus 'breath' into several species: 'physical' or 'natural' (τὸ φυσιχόν) breath, 'animate' (τὸ ψυχικόν) breath, and 'tensile' (τὸ ἑκτικόν) breath, which corresponds to the 'tenor' (ἕξις or τόνος) we just discussed:

> There are two kinds of innate breath, the physical kind [τὸ φυσικόν] and the animate kind [τὸ ψυχικόν]. Some people [sc. the Stoics] also posit a third, the tenor kind [τὸ ἑκτικόν]. The breath which sustains stones is of the tenor kind, the one which nurtures animals and plants the physical, and the animate breath is that which, in animate beings, makes animals capable of

---

[39] If this is indeed how to read the reference to 'quality and quantity', the former of which is literally 'magnitude' (μεγεθός). Plutarch apparently quotes Chrysippus (*De Rep. Stoic.* 1053f = L&S 47 M) as claiming that tenors are 'currents of air' which sustain bodies, and that specific essential qualities in simple bodies are owed to the power of the sustaining currents of air, e.g. hardness in iron, density in stone and whiteness in silver. What Chrysippus would have said about complex or compound bodies like animals is unclear and must remain conjectural. See Long 1996: 230.

[40] Or so I understand the appeal to οὐσία, in an Aristotelian sense of an 'individual' or a τόδε τι.

[41] Again, a reformulation of ideas already present in Plato's *Timaeus* (78e).

sensation and of moving in every way. (Galen, *Medical Introduction* 14, p. 726.7–11 Kühn = Long & Sedley 47 N; tr. after Long & Sedley)

As is common in their natural philosophy, the Stoics differentiate species of internal 'breath' as peculiar to objects within nature according to a hierarchy: all objects share of, or participate in, the cosmic kind of internal 'breath', i.e. the 'tenor' that not only unifies the entire *kosmos* and all the parts that belong to it, but also the 'tenor' that individualises complex and simple bodies, such as wise animals like Socrates of Athens or the *Kosmos*; animals that cannot achieve virtue and wisdom such as Aristotle's bull; plants such as *this* rose; and metals and stones like *this* piece of iron. At a higher level, the species of 'breath' that provides nutrition for growth is reserved from wise animals, unwise animals and plants, is 'physical' or 'natural'; stones and metals do not possess it. One step up is the kind of breath that animate objects, wise or unwise, possess: Galen calls it 'animate', or related to 'soul' traditionally understood as life-force that is manifest through sense perception. Galen does not explain here what sort of 'breath' is unique to wise animals such as Socrates and the *Kosmos*,[42] although the passage implies that there is more to the story than what he is telling.

In order to pursue this line of thought, we now need to turn to another philosopher with strong Platonist and Stoic commitments, in concert with a remarkably deep commitment to his Jewish faith: Philo of Alexandria, a philosopher who was probably writing about 125 years after the other Stoic we have been discussing so far, Posidonius. We are now firmly in what is often called the Post-Hellenistic intellectual world, where the destruction of the philosophical schools in Athens in the 80s BCE (the Academy and the Lyceum) was offset by the increased production of philosophical texts circulating throughout the Mediterranean. The effect of these changes was a brilliant and enigmatic kind of eclecticism. In the Post-Hellenistic world, pagan philosophy and Semitic religions coexist and inform one another without any obvious contradiction. As we will see in the case of Philo, pagan philosophy provides the explanatory models for biblical exegesis: rather than appeal to other Jewish exegetical texts in order to compose his own analysis of the book of Genesis, Philo looks to Plato, Aristotle, the Stoics and the Pythagoreans for guidance on how to interpret the infallible words of Yahweh.

---

[42] The notion that the *kosmos* was 'living' is implicit in Aristotle's account of Pythagorean cosmology (see earlier), but it was made explicit in Plato's *Timaeus* (see esp. *Ti.* 30b–d), although Plato did not commit to anthropological analogising of the World-Soul.

13.4 Philo of Alexandria and the Pneumatic Consubstantiation

Philo of Alexandria helps us to understand better how wise animals, such as Socrates and the *Kosmos,* can be thought to possess a pneumatic capacity beyond that of other individual substances in nature. Our first piece of evidence helps to understand, in particular, how 'tenor' is thought to work, but also mentions the highest species of breath, what binds bodies together 'by rational soul':

> He [God] bound some bodies by tenor [ἕξει], others by physique [φύσει], others by soul [ψυχῇ], and others by rational soul [λογικῇ ψυχῇ]. In stones, and logs which have been severed from their physical connection [sc. to the tree], he created tenor which is the strongest bond. This is breath which turns back towards itself [ἡ δὲ ἐστι πνεῦμα ἀναστρέφον ἐφ᾽ ἑαυτό]. It begins to extend itself from the centre to the extremities, and having made contact with the outer surfaces it bends back again until it returns to the same place from which it first set out. (Philo of Alexandria, *God's Immutability* 35–6 = Long & Sedley 47 Q; tr. by Long & Sedley)

'Tenor' so constructed is a kind of back-turning force that bonds material parts together into a compound, something like a magnetic polarity. It functions as a sort of circulatory system, moving around the object's interior and hence uniting it like a sort of 'glue'.[43] According to Philo, 'tenor' extends to all objects, living or lifeless, including not only stones and logs, mentioned here, but also bones, 'which resemble stones', as he says in *Allegories of the Laws* (2.22–3 = L&S 47 P).[44] Hence, objects like logs that have been separated from their natural origin for growth still possess the lowest form of breath – the same, we might wonder, could extend to, for example, severed limbs – at least until they begin to decay. Indeed, in the *Questions and Answers on Genesis* (2.4 = L&S 47 R), which survives only in a medieval Armenian translation from Greek, Philo explains that God is said to have commanded Noah to tar the ark both on the outside and the inside (Genesis 6:14), because all things derive their natural unity from the external and internal types of 'tenor'; the former is the corporeal type of tenor, which fixes the external boundaries of an individual human being; the latter is said to be his soul, which also circulates from the centre to the periphery rotationally. Hence, Philo appears to believe that humans – and Noah's Ark – possess two types of 'tenor', external and internal,

---

[43] The circulation metaphor is implied by the use of the term ἀναστρέφον, which is employed by Plato to refer to the circulation of blood within the veins (*Ti.* 85c).
[44] According to Diogenes Laertius (7.138–39 = L&S 47 O), breath pervades the body of an animal as 'tenor' at the point of its bones and sinews.

corresponding to the body and the soul.[45] About the highest 'rational' type of 'breath' in Philo's view, we will have to embark on an analysis of his exegetical works on Genesis, which requires us to go on a brief digression about the rise of 'exegetical' texts in the Post-Hellenistic world.

One major difference between Hellenistic and Post-Hellenistic intellectual cultures and philosophy is the formal emergence of an exegetical habit.[46] Prior to the dissolution of the philosophical schools in Athens in the 80s BCE, we have little direct evidence of dedicated exegetical practice with regard to what we might consider 'wisdom-texts', ranging from Homer and the Hebrew Bible to Plato's dialogues. Within the Platonist and Stoic schools, however, works that seek to explain what meanings, concepts, themes, and systems of ethics underlie wisdom-texts become codified into recognisable genres, and thus is born what is often generally understood to be the 'commentary tradition'. This represents an expansion of a genre of scientific literature that is often considered to have originated with the writings of Aristotle on Homer, and one might refer to this sort of scientific literature as 'zetetic', after the title of a lost work that comes down to us (the *Homeric Zetemata*, or, more colloquially, the *Homeric Questions*).[47] It is under the 'zetetic' genre of scientific literature that we should classify the work of Philo's that gives us his own unique point of view on 'breath' and its importance for the microcosm of the human being and the macrocosm of the ordered universe. As we saw earlier, this 'zetetic' genre tended to produce, for analysis, a single lemma of a wisdom-text and attempt to 'explain' it by appeal to lexical, philosophical, or ethical principles:[48] Philo quotes Genesis 6:14 ('Make yourself an ark of cypress' wood; make rooms in the ark, and cover it inside and out with pitch') and proceeds to use philosophical axioms to 'explain' what it was that God, whose word is of course perfect, said to Noah.[49] This genre presupposes a surplus of meaning in the wisdom-text that goes beyond mere literal interpretation, and it exhibits a deeply embedded commitment to

---

[45] This could create taxonomic confusions, but it may be that the text as translated from Aucher's Latin (printed in *SVF*) by Long and Sedley, and informed by the recent translations from the Armenian by Marcus and Mercier, is unclear.

[46] On exegetical approaches in Post-Hellenistic philosophy, see Boys-Stones 2001: Chapters 3 and 6. On Philo specifically, see Boys-Stones 2001: 90–95.

[47] A good recent discussion of this genre, and Aristotle's use of it, is Mayhew 2015. Of course, the posing of questions about Homer's words is anticipated by earlier intellectuals, but I am not aware that this activity constituted a genre as such.

[48] Here one might point to comparanda in Porphyry's *Homeric Questions on the* Iliad (see the recent edition of Macphail 2011) and Plutarch's *Homeric Studies* (Fragments 122–27 Sandbach).

[49] For a fuller assessment of Philo's Platonism/Stoicism and its relationship to exegesis of the Hebrew Bible, see Engberg-Pederson 2010: 22–26.

teleology and epistemological positivism: because God's word, transmitted through his medium Moses, *is* perfect, it is the exegete's responsibility to employ his capacities to unpack what it was that God *meant*, i.e. *why* he said it.[50] Implicit is the assumption that human beings are capable of obtaining knowledge (or at least justified true belief) about what God said or the prophets wrote. In this way, we now begin to see how it would be possible for Christianity, which arose in the second half of the first century CE (just after what is thought to be the date of Philo's death in 50 CE), to obtain its own unique character both (1) in the relief of pagan philosophy, which was well established, and (2) in response to philosophical-exegetical traditions already in place in Hellenic Jewish communities, such as Alexandria.

The imprimatur for approaching the formation of the macrocosm (i.e. the universe) and the microcosm (i.e. the human being) for Jewish and Christian authors was the first chapter of Genesis, which expressly presented a pneumatic cosmogony:

> In the beginning, God created the heaven and the earth. And the earth was formless and lacked arrangement [ἀόρατος καὶ ἀκατασκεύαστος], and a darkness lay upon the deep, and a breath of God was borne over the water [πνεῦμα θεοῦ ἐπεφέρετο ἐπάνω τοῦ ὕδατος]. And God said, 'let there be light'. And there was light. (Genesis 1:1–3, translated from the Greek version of the Septuagint)[51]

The pneumatic cosmogony of Genesis is remarkable for its divergence from the Pythagorean tradition discussed earlier: for the Pythagoreans, it is the *kosmos* itself that first breathes in, whereas Genesis has God acting as a sort of *prime breather* in the process of differentiating the parts of the *kosmos*.[52] A parallel passage of Genesis that Philo and the writers of the New Testament devoted a significant amount of effort to explaining and expanding is Chapter 2, verse 7: 'And God formed the man by taking clay from the earth, and breathed into his face a breath of life (ἐνεφύσησεν εἰς τὸ πρόσωπον αὐτοῦ πνοὴν ζωῆς), and the man became a living soul'.[53] In his *Allegorical Interpretation of Genesis 2 and 3*, Philo devotes a long

---

[50] Cf. Barclay 1996: 169.

[51] For texts of the Hebrew Bible, I work from the Greek translation of the Septuagint, because it is almost certainly the text known to and used by Philo and the writers of the New Testament.

[52] As contrasted with an Aristotelian notion of a *prime mover*. In Mesopotamian cosmology, the *Enuma Elish* similarly features wind as a cosmogonic force that Marduk employs in conquering Tiamat and shaping the parts of the universe (Tablets IV–V).

[53] It is remarkable that Augustine sought to prove that Plato's views about the separation of the elements in *Timaeus* were substantially related to the pneumatic cosmogony of *Genesis* (*De civ. D.* 8.11).

stretch of text (1.31–42) to a multifaceted explanation of this potent statement, which links the construction of the primal human being (Adam) to
God's cultivation of humankind and the activity of intellective
'inspiration'.[54] A sufficient analysis of Philo's exegesis would occupy far
more space than I am allotted, so I will focus on the aspects of his account
that help to fill out the conceptualisation of 'breath' as an intelligent
sustaining force.

Philo breaks down the passage with a lexical and philological analysis,
and he focuses on the meanings of key individual terms that require further
explanation. One of these terms is the 'in-breathing' (ἐνεφῦσησεν) mentioned by Moses:

> 'Breathed into' [ἐνεφῦσησεν], we note, is equivalent to 'inspired' or 'be-souled'
> the soulless [τῷ ἐνέπνευσεν ἢ ἐψύχωσε τὰ ἄψυχα]; for God forbid that we
> should be infected with such monstrous folly as to think that God employs for
> in-breathing organs such as mouth or nostrils; for God is not only not in the
> form of man, but belongs to no class or kind. Yet the expression clearly brings
> out something that accords with nature. For it implies of necessity three
> things: that which in-breathes, that which receives, that which is in-
> breathed: that which in-breathes is God [τὸ ἐμπνέον ἐστὶν ὁ θεός], that
> which receives is the intellect [τὸ δεχόμενον ὁ νοῦς], that which is in-
> breathed is breath [τὸ ἐμπνεόμενον τὸ πνεῦμα]. What, then, do we infer
> from these premises? A union [ἕνωσις] of the three comes about, as God
> extends the power [τείναντος ... τὴν δύναμιν] that proceeds from Himself
> through the mediant breath till it reaches the subject. And for what purpose
> save that we may obtain a conception [ἔννοια] of Him? For how could the soul
> have conceived of God had He not breathed into it and mightily laid hold of
> it? For the human intellect [ὁ ἀνθρώπινος νοῦς] would never have ventured to
> soar so high as to grasp the nature of God, had not God Himself drawn it up
> to Himself, so far as it was possible that the human intellect should be drawn
> up, and stamped it with the impress of the powers that are within the scope of
> its understanding. (Philo of Alexandria, *Allegorical Interpretation of Genesis 2
> and 3*, 1.36–38; tr. after Colson and Whittaker)

In this remarkable passage, we see the expansion of an idea of 'breath' that
is already present in the Stoic constructions mentioned earlier: the idea that
there is an 'active' and 'passive' element. For Philo, however, there is
a tripartition – indeed, a trinity produced anthropogonically: the 'active'
element is God (here functioning as something like efficient cause); the
'passive' element is the human mind (notably, not the body or the lower

---

[54] He also commits extensive analysis of this lemma in his *On the Creation* (46.143–40), where he
explains why human beings are superior to other animals. On God as cultivator, see *Questions and
Answers on Genesis* 1.50.

parts of the soul); and the medium of transferal of divine power is the breath itself. Interestingly, Philo follows the other Stoics in seeing breath as what constitutes a 'unity' (ἕνωσις) or synthesis of corporeal objects relative to one another, and that this unity signifies the conferral of the divine power that 'extends' (τείναντος) from God to Adam, the 'earthly man'.[55] The language used suggests that he is referring to the breath as 'tension' (συντονία) between objects in the *kosmos*.[56] But Philo goes further, explaining that God breathed into Adam not simply for the sake of bringing him to life, like other creatures, but specifically so as to make it possible for Adam, and by extension all of his progeny, to *know* God; for, without the unity that is achieved through 'in-breathing', it is implied, Man would never be able to conceptualise (sc. ἔννοια) God. It is implied that since Moses does not mention God 'in-breathing' into other animals, they in fact lack higher intellectual capacities and cannot know God.[57]

Finally, once the human 'intellect' has received the divine breath of God, how does it relate to the other parts of the soul and body? Philo explains (1.39–40) that God is not said by Moses to breathe into other parts, 'whether senses or organs of utterance and of reproduction; for these are secondary in capacity'. Hence, so Philo asks, by what were the organs of sensation, speech, and reproduction 'in-breathed' (ἐνεπνεύσθη)? The answer is that the intellect breathes into them:

> For the intellect [νοῦς] imparts the portion of the soul that is devoid of reason a share of that which it received from God, so that the intellect was be-souled by God, but the unreasoning part by the intellect. For the intellect is, so to speak, 'God' of the unreasoning part. In like manner he does not hesitate to speak of Moses as 'a God to Pharoah' [Exod. 7.1]. For, of the things which come into being, some come into being both by God's power and through God's agency, while others come into being by God's power by not by His agency. The most excellent things were made both by God and by God's agency ... to these the intellect belongs; but the part devoid of

---

[55] Philo has already (1.31–32) confusedly established that the human being who was created in this act was in fact not the 'heavenly Man' who is described as 'being made after the image of God' and 'altogether without part or lot in corruptible and terrestrial substance', but instead the 'terrestrial man' who is said to be 'compacted out of the matter scattered here and there'. One could speculate that the former exists only in the mind of God. We will later on see that Paul alters this story of two 'Adams' to make the first Adam, created by God, the 'terrestrial' Adam, and Jesus into the 'heavenly' one.

[56] As Engberg-Pederson writes (2010: 20), 'what distinguishes *nous* and *psyche* – and, indeed, *physis* and *hexis* – from one another as so many forms of the material *pneuma* is the degree of tension (*tonos*) to be found in either. In *nous* the tension of the *pneuma* is so strong that it may cover the whole world and reach the stars.'

[57] Cf. Philo, *On the Creation* 65–70.

reason was made by God's power but not by God's agency, but by [the agency] of the reasonable part [τὸ λογικόν] which rules and holds dominion in the soul. (Philo of Alexandria, *Allegorical Interpretation of Genesis 2 and 3*, 1.40–41; tr. after Colson and Whittaker)

Philo sets up a strict hierarchy of 'in-breathing', related to the animation of the many parts that make up the first human being: God breathes into the intellective part of the soul the activity of reasoning, whereas the intellective part of the soul passes on what it has of the divine pneumatic power to the lower, irrational part of the soul. The analogy is drawn: just as God is to reason, so reason is to unreason. Hence, God's capacity[58] imparts breath to both the human's intellect and to the irrational part of his soul, but his agency – his direct engagement as efficient cause, so to say – only happens with the intellect. The agent or efficient cause of the lower part of the soul's animation is the rational part of the soul, the intellect who is placed over and above it as its ruler.

Hence, the major contribution to the history of cosmogonic and anthropogonic breath made by Philo is the adaptation of the Stoic metaphysics into a unique epistemological and ethical system: in his exegesis of the anthropogony in Genesis, Philo finds the grounds for differentiation of human and other animal intellective capacities, rooted in a notion of the divine gift of breath. It is a further expression of God's cosmogonic will, as paradigmatically testified by His first act as efficient cause of the universe, when His breath was borne upon the waters of the void (Gen. 1:1). And, as is often the case in the ancient world, the so-called Praise of Man and his superior intellectual capacities brings in tow ethical and moral implications that reach far beyond the parameters of bare scientific explanation, such as we have seen in the cosmogony and anthropogony of the Pythagoreans. It only remains, now, to see how ancient notions of 'breath' arrive at their most powerful and influential formulation, in the writings of the New Testament.

13.5   Consubstantiation Expanded: The New Testament and the Christian Community

With the writings of the New Testament, we see emerge a somewhat haphazard, but nevertheless deeply informed, cosmic theology of 'breath/spirit' (πνεῦμα): it shares much in common with Philo's exegesis of divine

---

[58] If indeed this is what is meant by the phrase ὑπὸ θεοῦ, as contrasted with δι' αὐτοῦ, which must mean 'through Him', i.e. 'by God's agency'.

'breath' across the works we have surveyed in brief, including, as we will see, a similar ideation of what I am calling 'consubstantiation', and it also demonstrates a kind of parallelism with the Stoic cosmological pneumatics described by Posidonius. It is worth checking to see whether this is the case across all the texts of the New Testament, or if it only applies in some instances. One representative version of the divine conception via a special kind of 'breath', the Holy Spirit (τὸ ἅγιον πνεῦμα),[59] appears in the Gospel of Matthew:

> Now the birth of Jesus the Messiah took place in this way. When his mother Mary had been engaged to Joseph, but before they lived together, she was found to be with child from the Holy Spirit [ἐν γαστρὶ ἔχουσα ἐκ πνεύματος ἁγίου]. Her husband Joseph, being a righteous man and unwilling to expose her to public disgrace, planned to dismiss her quietly. But just when he resolved to do this, an angel of the Lord appeared to him in a dream and said, 'Joseph, son of David, do not be afraid to take Mary as your wife, for the child conceived in her is from the Holy Spirit [τὸ γὰρ ἐν αὐτῇ γεννηθὲν ἐκ πνεύματός ἐστιν ἁγίου]. She will bear a son, and you are to name him Jesus, for he will save his people from their sins'. (Gospel of Matthew 1:18–21; translation in NRSV)[60]

In the context of the philosophical treatment of breath that we have seen earlier, this seemingly familiar passage becomes defamiliarised: the repetition of the phrase 'from the Holy Spirit' (ἐκ πνεύματος ἁγίου) with regard to Mary's pregnancy and Jesus' conception indicates its importance, and we are invited to wonder about the precise inflection of 'out of' or 'from' (ἐκ). It is initially unclear whether the author of the Gospel of Matthew is ascribing any agency to the Holy Spirit: it may seem that the Holy Spirit is the *stuff* or *material* out of which the impregnation and conception occurs, or that the Holy Spirit is the instrument that makes it possible for impregnation and conception. And these would be reasonable interpretations that would follow from Philo's discussion of 'breath'. But a non-philosophical alternative, perfectly acceptable in Greek, is a usage of ἐκ + genitive that refers to parentage, and we would translate it agentially with the phrase 'by X'.[61] Hence, a non-philosophical translation that

---

[59] I translate 'Holy Spirit' according to convention, but it should be noted that 'spirit' and 'breath' are the same word in Greek (πνεῦμα), and the term ἅγιον πνεῦμα translates literally to 'holy breath'. The Gospel of Matthew has various terms that are traditionally assimilated to the Holy Spirit, including 'spirit of God' (πνεῦμα θεοῦ, 12:28) and 'spirit of the father' (τὸ πνεῦμα τοῦ πατρὸς, 10:20).

[60] Throughout this section, I modify the NRSV only when I believe that the terms used have specific philosophical antecedents that are of relevance to this discussion (such as in the writings of Paul).

[61] See Smyth 1920: 1688.

retains Greek colloquy would rather be 'found to be pregnant by the Holy Spirit' or 'conceived in her by the Holy Spirit', and given the context here of Jesus' potentially dubious parentage, I would suggest this colloquial, non-philosophical usage is the best for this passage.

It is perhaps not so surprising, given the pneumatic cosmogony and anthropogony in Genesis, that the birth of Jesus would involve a similar transmission of divine breath. But, as is well known, the 'Holy Spirit' features in a variety of places in the Gospels and receives a multifaceted treatment throughout those works, sometimes in reference to certain parts of the Hebrew Bible.[62] For the purpose of my argument here, I start with the Gospels before turning to Paul's writings. In the account of the Gospel of Luke 1:35, an angel explains to Mary that 'the Holy Spirit will come upon' her (πνεῦμα ἅγιον ἐπελεύσεται ἐπὶ σέ), and 'the power of the Highest will overshadow' her (δύναμις ὑψίστου ἐπισκιάσει σοι). The semantics here make it sound like the impregnation is a kind of physical invasion, a sort of 'climbing upon' Mary, perhaps recalling God's breath being borne upon the water (πνεῦμα θεοῦ ἐπεφέρετο ἐπάνω τοῦ ὕδατος) in the primal cosmogonic act of Genesis.[63] Moreover, the Holy Spirit also appears to be responsible for impregnating Elisabeth with John the Baptist, if this is what is meant by referring to her as 'filled up' (ἐπλήσθη πνεύματος ἁγίου) with it (Luke 1:41–43). By communicating divine information from heaven in the 'corporeal form' (σωματικῷ εἴδει) of the dove, it motivates the second, higher kind of baptism (Luke 3:15–21, 4:1; cf. the simpler version of Mark 1:10–13).[64] It also motivates prophesy and inspires teaching (Luke 1:67; Luke 4:14). It itself acts as a teacher and, even, an advocate for Jesus after his death, transmitting his words posthumously (John 14:15–26 and 16:13–15).[65] Finally, when Jesus dies (Luke 23:46), after darkness has fallen upon the land, Jesus calls out to His Father and screams 'into your hands I commend my spirit' (εἰς χεῖράς σου παρατίθεμαι τὸ πνεῦμά μου), after which, so Luke states brutally, 'he breathed his last' (ἐξέπνευσεν).[66] Thus, in Luke's colourful and sensitive narrative, Jesus' birth and death

---

[62] See e.g. the citation/translation of Isaiah 61:1 at Luke 4:18.

[63] Gen. 1:3, employing the Septuagint's translation.

[64] Not only does it inform Jesus that he is the son of God; it also leads Jesus into the wilderness to be tempted. The inclusion of the qualifying marker 'in corporeal shape' here indicates that the breath itself is incorporeal, contrary to Stoic assumptions. It should be remarked that Luke, also likely a Hellenic Jew from Antioch, was said by Paul to have been a physician (Col. 4:14).

[65] In the Gospel of Mark, it will act on behalf of his disciples when they are arraigned, even speaking *for them* on trial (Mark 13:11).

[66] Luke places a certain emphasis on 'breath' through Jesus' quotation of Psalm 31:5, which is wholly absent from the accounts of Mark (15:33–37) and Matthew (27:49–50).

occur in parallel circumstances, with the transaction of breath between God and Man, and the settling down of shadows.

Other works of the New Testament, including the Acts of the Apostles (which presents itself as a sequel to the Gospel of Luke)[67] and the writings of the Apostle Paul (especially Romans and 1 Corinthians), feature more elaborate pneumatic systems for early Christianity. There, we see a simple cosmological spiritualism contrasted against one more groundbreaking and radical. Speaking in Acts (17:24–25) of the '*kosmos* and everything in it' (ὁ κόσμος καὶ πάντα τὰ ἐν αὐτῷ) that God created, Paul asserts that God has no need of human works because it is He himself who has given to humans 'life, and breath, and all things' (αὐτὸς διδοὺς πᾶσι ζωὴν καὶ πνοὴν καὶ τὰ πάντα). One suspects that 'breath' (πνοή) in this circumstance is not the same thing as the Holy Spirit, but simply the breath *of life*. Indeed, there are indications in Letter to the Ephesians that when he speaks of the κόσμος, Paul refers to the world that is subject to birth and destruction, and not to the heavenly realm that is pervaded with the Holy Spirit.[68] Elsewhere in Acts, the Holy Spirit becomes the primary medium for the transmission of Jesus' teachings, and even the catalyst for speaking prophesy among the disciples themselves. Importantly, there is the idea that the Holy Spirit, like Philo's divine breath, possesses its own inherent power but transmits its information through intermediary vessels, in this case the Apostles. The martyr Stephen receives the wisdom of the Holy Spirit only to have his audiences reject his word and brand him a heretic (Acts 6:3–5, 6:8–15, 6:55–56); and as they stone him to death in the presence of Saul (7:58–59), he imitates Jesus when he too breathes out his final words: 'Lord Jesus, receive my breath' (Κύριε Ἰησοῦ, δέξαι τὸ πνεῦμά μου). The transition from Jesus to Stephen as 'recipient' serves to highlight the transitional power of the divine breath: just as Jesus receives the Holy Spirit from God the Father, so too Stephen receives it from Jesus the Son. And on and on. There is a relatively consistent pattern here: a chain of disciples is established, and the passing of divine breath on from disciple to disciple, in the form of the Holy Spirit, reveals itself as the perpetual re-enactment of the original divine activities of in-breathing of both Adam and Jesus. The Holy Spirit becomes the vehicle for the transmission of God's power from generation to generation, thus constituting and sustaining the Christian community over time. It becomes the vehicle for the Christian *body* of

---

[67] The narrator 'Luke' begins the Acts 1:1–2 by saying, 'In the first book, Theophilius, I wrote about all that Jesus did and taught from the beginning until the day when he was taken up into heaven, after giving instructions through the Holy Spirit to the apostles whom he had chosen'.

[68] Eph. 1:3 and 2:2. Also see Col. 2:4 and 2:20.

adherents – a cosmopolitan expression of Stoic pneumatology, with the shift of focus from the universe to the human individual.

When we turn to the writings of Paul, the pneumatology starts to dovetail more strictly with its expression in the writings of Philo, the Stoics and the Pythagoreans. As Troels Engberg-Pederson has noted extensively, the work of Paul that most effectively situates his thought in a broader philosophical present is 1 Corinthians.[69] The Holy Spirit there takes on certain powers that reflect what appears to be philosophical training, or at least familiarity, on Paul's part. For example, in 1 Corinthians 12, a short digression entitled 'On the Spiritual [Gifts]' (Περὶ τῶν πνευματικῶν),[70] Paul develops an elaborate description of how the Holy Spirit unifies the community under Christ:

> Now there are divisions [διαιρέσεις] of gifts, but the same Spirit [τὸ αὐτὸ πνεῦμα]; and there are divisions of services, but the same Lord [ὁ αὐτὸς κύριος]; and there are divisions of activities, but it is the same God who activates all of them in everyone [ὁ ἐνεργῶν τὰ πάντα ἐν πᾶσιν]. To each is given the manifestation of the Spirit [φανέρωσις τοῦ πνεύματος] for the common good. To one is given through the Spirit the utterance of wisdom [λόγος σοφίας], and to another the utterance of knowledge according to the same Spirit [λόγος γνώσεως κατὰ τὸ αὐτὸ πνεῦμα], to another gifts of healing by the one Spirit, to another the working of miracles, to another prophecy, to another the discernment of spirits [διακρίσεις πνευμάτων], to another various kinds of tongues, to another the interpretation of tongues [ἑρμηνεία γλωσσῶν]. All these are activated by the one and the same Spirit [ἐνεργεῖ τὸ ἓν καὶ τὸ αὐτὸ πνεῦμα], who allots to each individually just as the Spirit chooses. For just as the body is one and has many members, and all the members of the body, though many, are one body, so it is with Christ. For in the one Spirit we were all baptized into one body – Jews or Greeks, slaves or free – and we were all made to drink of one Spirit. (1 Corinthians 12:4–13, translation after NRSV)

As the passage demonstrates, Paul marshals a range of concepts familiar from Hellenistic and Post-Hellenistic philosophy ('the same breath', or alternatively 'the breath itself' (τὸ αὐτὸ πνεῦμα); 'activates/activity' (ἐνεργῶν; ἐνεργεῖ); 'differentiation/discernment' (διαιρέσεις; διακρίσεις); 'the speech/reasoning of wisdom' (λόγος σοφίας); 'the speech/reasoning of knowledge' (λόγος γνώσεως); 'the one and the breath itself' (τὸ ἓν καὶ τὸ αὐτὸ πνεῦμα)) to make the case that the community of followers of Christ

---

[69] Generally, see Engberg-Pederson 2010.
[70] The passage begins with these words, setting the theme. But titles of Greek philosophical and theological works have the same format: 'On X'. The digression lasts until Chapter 15.

is like the body that has many (corporeal) members, all brought into unity by the 'one breath' that is the Holy Spirit. Hence, for Paul, the Holy Spirit not only unites all the parts of the 'body of Christ'; it also differentiates what sorts of activities each person is best suited to do, according to the will of the Holy Spirit. What, however, is the ontological status of the 'breath' that unites the Christian body, assigns each part of it its proper function, and renders the whole compound wise and capable of understanding God and his wisdom, which is otherwise 'secret and hidden'?[71] In order to gain ground on this issue, we need to consider Paul's rereading of the primordial anthropogony in Genesis 2:7, which I mentioned earlier:

> If there is an animate body [σῶμα ψυχικόν], then there is a spiritual body too [καὶ πνευματικόν]. Thus it is written: 'The first man, Adam, became a living being'; the last Adam became a life-giving Spirit [ὁ ἔσχατος Ἀδὰμ εἰς πνεῦμα ζῳοποιοῦν]. But it is not the spiritual that is first, but the animate, and then the spiritual. The first man was from the earth, a man of dust; the second man is from heaven. As was the man of dust, so are those who are of the dust; and as is the man of heaven, so are those who are of heaven. Just as we have borne the image of the man of dust, we will also bear the image of the man of heaven [φορέσομεν καὶ τὴν εἰκόνα τοῦ ἐπουρανίου].
> (1 Corinthians 15.44–49; translation after NRSV)

Just as we saw with Philo above, Paul differentiates two sorts of 'Adams', by reference to his exegesis of Genesis 2:7. For Philo (*Allegorical Interpretation of Genesis 2 and 3*, 1.31–32), there is a heavenly or cosmic Adam who was 'made after the image of God' and 'altogether without part or lot in corruptible and terrestrial substance', as contrasted with the 'terrestrial Adam' who is said to be 'compacted out of the matter scattered here and there'; for Paul, the 'last' or heavenly Adam is Christ, the 'life-giving Spirit' (πνεῦμα ζῳοποιοῦν) that constitutes the spiritual body of the community of Christians, whereas the terrestrial Adam is the figure whom God created on the sixth day, the 'man of dust'. It is true, as Engberg-Pederson has argued impressively by reference to this passage, that Paul is employing Stoic terms and concepts, reflecting his intellectual environs and reacting to Philonic exegesis.[72] But that is not everything. Through the act of differentiating the 'animate' from the 'pneumatic' Christian bodies, Paul effectively appropriates the kinds of theological speculation found in the writings of Philo (and no doubt other philosophical Hellenic Jews whose works we have lost) to *reject* their accounts, and to highlight the status of the human being with reference to divine breath as incomplete in the

---

[71] See 1 Cor. 2:6–13.   [72] Engberg-Pederson 2010: 26–31.

account of Moses.[73] In doing so, he establishes the theological foundations of Christianity with characteristic aplomb, reconstructing it out of the scattered and even perhaps eclectic material that constituted Hellenic Jews' unique blend of Platonist metaphysics, Stoic physics and Jewish biblical exegesis. Consubstantiation within the Christian community now goes beyond Philo's Stoic trinity of 'God, Adam, Breath', or the Gospels' 'Father, Son, Holy Spirit': it reaches across the entire *body* of Christ's followers, from the death and rebirth of the 'last Adam' until the final return after the Judgement.

13.6 Conclusions

In tracing a particular genealogy of spiritual cosmologies from the early Pythagoreans of the fifth century BCE to the writers of the New Testament in the mid to late first century CE, we have examined how various notions of 'breath' (πνεῦμα) have informed the description of the ordered world (κόσμος). Most notably, we have seen a shift away from employing 'breath' as a biomorphic instrument for explanation of how individuals obtain proper order and differentiation in the thought of the Pythagoreans and Stoics to a prime candidate for supplementing incomplete understandings of human creation and salvation in the writings of Philo and the authors of the New Testament. While conceptualisations of the *kosmos* have remained static, for the most part, the notion of 'breath' has expanded and become more comprehensive as we have proceeded through the Hellenistic to the Post-Hellenistic world. Despite these important connections, no revolution in spiritual cosmology in the Greco-Roman world can be said to be greater than what occurred among the Early Christians. Speaking to the apostle Philip in the Gospel of John, Jesus promises to intercede on behalf of his followers and request from His Father an intercessor, to act on their behalf:

> If you love me, you will keep my commandments. And I will ask the Father, and He will give you another advocate, in order that I might be with you for all of eternity [εἰς τὸν αἰῶνα], the Spirit of Truth [τὸ πνεῦμα τῆς ἀληθείας], *which the kosmos does not have the capacity to grasp* [ὃ ὁ κόσμος οὐ δύναται λαβεῖν], *because it does not contemplate it and it does not know it* [ὅτι οὐ θεωρεῖ αὐτὸ οὐδὲ γινώσκει]; *you know it,* because it abides by you, and it

---

[73] Cf. Boys-Stones 2001: 165–67. For Paul's account of the restoration of the *kosmos* through Christ as 'life-giving Spirit' (πνεῦμα ζῳοποιοῦν), see White 2008: 103–4.

will be in you [ὑμεῖς γινώσκετε αὐτό, ὅτι παρ' ὑμῖν μένει καὶ ἐν ὑμῖν ἔσται].[74] (Gospel of John 14:15–17)

Here we see the most compelling evidence of the Christian rejection of the spiritual *kosmos* of ancient Greek philosophy for an alternative spiritualism. Whereas the Pythagorean *kosmos* obtained its birth from an act of breathing in the external void, and the Stoic *kosmos* persisted uniquely through the reciprocal activities of respiration, the *kosmos* as described by John is blind and deaf to the Spirit of Truth, neither recognising it nor contemplating it. This is neither the biomorphic *kosmos* of the Pythagoreans, nor the intelligent *kosmos* of the Stoics: this *kosmos* is wholly bereft of the Spirit of Truth, which functions here as the eternal guarantor of co-presence with Jesus. Cosmic and human pneumatic analogies have been rejected and replaced with a new sense of the Spirit of Truth (τὸ πνεῦμα τῆς ἀληθείας), which the *kosmos* is unable to admit due to its insufficiency. Hence, in the Gospel of John, we witness the ultimate rejection of the pagan spiritual cosmologies – with all their metaphysical and physical entailments – of the Pythagoreans, Stoics, and Hellenic Jews, and their replacement with the eternal community of Christian believers, unified through the Holy Spirit, and not limited by this *kosmos*.

To be sure, this rejection of pagan spiritual cosmologies is not a total abandonment of the principle of *kosmos*. As Engberg-Pederson has argued in speaking about Paul's spiritualism, '*pneuma* ... is an entity that is primarily connected with being in the group. It highlights a certain stable state of the believer.'[75] As far as Paul's ethics of belief go, we should note that, for Engberg-Pederson, πνεῦμα 'is stated to be responsible for certain states of mind, namely mental attitudes, in fact for nothing other than the virtues in the Greek philosophical tradition'.[76] This represents a notable shift away from what we saw in the Stoics and Philo, who attributed to 'breath' notions of intelligence and discriminatory capacity, but did not take the further step of advancing upon moral psychology. Moreover, because of its importance for community-building among the Christians, the Holy Spirit, or the Spirit of Truth, possesses eschatological significance: after all, it is the guarantee of (among other things) a post-Apocalyptic community of believers that makes Christianity attractive within the competitive intellectual and religious economy of the early Roman

---

[74] Translation mine; italics mine, for emphasis.   [75] Engberg-Pederson 2000: 158.
[76] Ibid., 160, by reference to the virtues of love, joy, peacefulness, magnanimity, kindness, goodness, loyalty, mildness and self-control (Galatians 5: 22–23).

Empire.[77] In this light, consider the prophetic vision offered to John of Patmos – effected by the Holy Spirit (Revelation 1:10, 21:10) – of the promised invitation to the city of New Jerusalem:

> The Spirit and the bride say, 'Come'.
> And let everyone who hears say, 'Come'.

We are meant to understand that the Holy Spirit, wed to its 'bride', the city of New Jerusalem (Revelation 21:2, 21:9), calls those who have heeded the words of John's book. All this is an expression of the heaven and earth that are revealed after the final Judgement, New Heaven and New Earth (Revelation 21:1), where there will be no more darkness of night, banished by the light that is God diffused throughout New Jerusalem (Revelation 22:5) – a second banishment of the darkness of the void from *Genesis*. This place is what John of Patmos calls the 'holy city' (ἡ πόλις ἀγίη): it is constituted through the binding of the Holy Spirit to the bride and presented as a place of unity for those who have heeded the words of prophesy. In the end, it is the Christian *kosmopolis*, heralded by the Holy Spirit, that manifests a new vision of the *kosmos* of Greek philosophy.

---

[77] For the usefulness of 'wisdom' as a point of comparison among Hellenistic, Jewish and Christian intellectual communities, see Alexander 2001: 122–26.

Afterword

Victoria Wohl

The most beautiful *kosmos* is like the sweeping at random of things scattered.

Heraclitus DK 22 B 124

The Greek word *kosmos* is at once familiar to us and, as this volume so beautifully illustrates, quite unfamiliar. It denotes "the cosmos," in our modern sense of the whole universe, but also beauty, ornamentation, and order. The shifting relation among these different definitions of the word, the evolution of its meaning and its transformation across different discursive registers (philosophy, art, politics), cultures (Greek, Latin), and mentalités (aristocratic and democratic, pagan and monotheistic), constitute a vital chapter in the history of Western thought. *Cosmos in the Ancient World* traces that history, from the origin of the concept in archaic Greece (Horky, Chapter 1) to its absorption into Christian theology in the early centuries after Christ (Horky, Chapter 13). The trajectory from beginning to end was not itself linear or orderly, however. Schofield (Chapter 3), Johnson (Chapter 4), and Shearin (Chapter 12) demonstrate that *kosmos* and related terms were a persistent flash point for debate between different philosophical schools and their different visions of the universe. Furthermore, the term's meaning alters subtly but significantly with its translation into Latin, where the different spheres metaphorically linked in the Greek *kosmos* are linguistically superimposed in the Latin *mundus*, which denotes at once heavens and earth (Germany, Chapter 10). The balance between celestial and terrestrial shifts again with the transition to a monotheistic world-order. Across this variegated history, *kosmos* adorns physics and metaphysics; politics and psychology; ethics, aesthetics, and theology.[1]

---

[1] It also has particular resonance for that modern *kosmopolis*, the university. If, as Horky proposes (Introduction), the word became popularized in English due to translations of Alexander von Humboldt's exhaustive 1845 compendium of natural science, *Cosmos: A Sketch of a Physical Description of the Universe*, then *kosmos* was swept into modern thought on the same wave of scientific universalism as the university.

The beauty of the term, as this volume shows, is the way it traverses these different realms of thought and facilitates analogies among them.[2] With a tendency toward meta-systematicity that we will return to later, *kosmos* functions as a general signifier of order at both the macro- and microcosmic levels. It names, and indeed enacts, the fundamental organization of human reality that Jacques Rancière terms *le partage du sensible*: "the system of *a priori* forms determining what presents itself to sense experience ... a delimitation of spaces and times, of the visible and the invisible, of speech and noise, that simultaneously determines the place and stakes of politics as a form of experience."[3] *Kosmein* (and the cognate *diakosmein*) signified the act of creating order through separation or division, the distribution of each thing to its proper place.[4] Its distributive function links *kosmos* not only to social propriety and social order but to the social as such: a common sense of the beautiful and orderly defines "the common," be it the temporary collective of an army or chorus, the citizen body of a polis, or a congregation of Christian believers. It divides those who have a share in the community from those who do not. It also distributes shares differentially within that community and is thus, as Rancière insists and many of the essays in this volume bear out, inherently and inevitably political.

The "'aesthetics' at the core of politics" (Rancière 2004: 13), *kosmos* roots both aesthetics and politics in a fundamental perception of reality. Germany (Chapter 10) details the way reflection on the cosmos (*contemplatio mundi*) worked to organize not only Roman society but "the sensible" in Rancière's sense. *Contemplatio* (from the root *tem-*, "to cut") originates in a division of physical space (in the first instance, the sky as zone of divinatory signification) that shapes the embodied experience of individuals and their relations to one another; it marks a cut between the visible and the invisible – between the mortal realm and the divine, the present and the future – even as it crosses the divide between the fictional world of the theatre and the Roman spectators' reality. Germany suggests that these divisions are not secondary cuts in a preexisting reality but instead provide the cognitive structure that allowed the Romans to

---

[2] It is not the only term to do so. One might consider, for example, *kairos* (appropriateness, the opportune moment), *aitia* (cause, explanation, origin), or *eikos* (the probable, likely, or reasonable); on the last, see Wohl 2014.

[3] Rancière 2004: 13.

[4] *Kosmos* is thus connected to *nomos* (law/custom), which also derives from a verb for distribution (*nemein*); see, e.g., Pl. *Prot.* 320d3–e1, where Prometheus distributes powers and attributes to earthly creatures (*kosmêsai te kai neimai*). Brisson (Chapter 6) discusses the connection of *kosmos* and *nomos*.

comprehend reality in the first place and to navigate it in their daily activities, both practical and theoretical. Germany's point is confirmed by Sauron's analysis (in Chapter 11) of the Romans' built environment: the architectural organization of private space could prompt philosophical reflection on man's place in the world, turning a quotidian practice like eating dinner into an embodied *contemplatio mundi*. *Kosmos* emerges in the essays of this volume as the object of philosophical theorization but also as part of the subconscious pattern of daily life: in proprioception and perception (Germany, Sauron); in metaphor and movement (Gagné); in deliberation and action (Boys-Stones, Remes); in the simple act of breathing (Horky, Chapter 13). *Kosmos* thus denotes not just the order we perceive in the world but the order that allows us to perceive the world and to exist within it, an order that is reproduced, imperceptibly, in and as that existence.

To gloss *kosmos* as "the order we perceive in the world" raises an important question: are the structures we perceive inherent to reality, independent of and prior to our perception of it, or are they in fact structures of this perception itself? This question, as Malcolm Schofield shows (Chapter 3), was a matter of debate among the earliest cosmological thinkers, with Heraclitus presenting the *kosmos* as an eternal and preexistent reality ("neither any man nor god created it, but it always was and is and will be," DK 22 B 30) against Parmenides' depiction of reality as a human construction. Macé elaborates on the latter position in Chapter 2. "We forget that calling the universe a '*kosmos*' was once a metaphorical act," he notes at the beginning of his chapter. But Parmenides reminds us and forces us to attend to the phenomenological consequences: his goddess's beautiful but deceptive *kosmos epeôn* calls into question the relation between order and ornament and between linguistic order and the order of truth. Are the cosmic verities we strive to comprehend in fact just the product of our own verbal constructions? Is the divine demiurge just a human poet in disguise (cf. Schofield, Chapter 3)? This possibility, damaging though it might be for our epistemological pretensions, might well have appealed to the poets discussed by Gagné in Chapter 9. In his chapter, *kosmos*, as enacted in the trope of the astral chorus, appears not only as a metaphor for poetic ordering but as itself productive of poetic order. Contemplating the inevitable gap between "absolute model and imperfect reflection," the poet confronts the limitations of poetic representation. But this limitation in turn provides the impetus for ornate metapoetic self-reflection and, hence, for more poetic order. The idea that the cosmic order is a projection of human ordering might not have worried poets who sought to capture "mimesis in action" and to build worlds of words that, in their intricacy and dynamism, rivaled the dance of the stars.

The proximity between cosmic original and human copy is not just an aesthetic issue but also an ethical and political one. Part of the utility of the term *kosmos* for ancient thinkers was its mediation between the macro-level and micro-level, between the universe and the polis (Brisson, Atack) or the soul (Remes, Boys-Stones), or both (as, most famously, in Plato's *Timaeus-Critias*). These analogies functioned heuristically: they worked as philosophical metaphors, with one term deployed to explain the other. But the analogy is also always implicitly or explicitly prescriptive, as Horky notes (Chapter 1): the universe offers a model of beautiful wholeness and perfect order that we humans must try to reproduce in our lives and laws. For the individual, the beauty of the universe provides a paradigm for the inner beauty of the soul – virtue – but the relation between macrocosm and microcosm is dynamic and reciprocal, as Boys-Stones (Chapter 5) and Remes (Chapter 7) demonstrate, and its ethical imperative far from straightforward. Boys-Stones disputes the usual assumption that Plato localizes moral beauty within the individual soul, stressing its inwardness through contrast with the superficial beauty (or, in Socrates' case, ugliness) of the body. Instead, for Plato, Boys-Stones argues, inner moral beauty is manifested in bodily action and appreciated only in the context of the beauty of the whole, which is both its point of reference and its ultimate goal. Far from solipsistic, then, eudaimonism (the individual's pursuit of happiness through virtue) becomes a cosmic endeavor: "To be virtuous is to promote its [the *kosmos*'] orderliness and beauty – and it is in doing so ... that one becomes beautiful and orderly." Part and whole are also reciprocally intermeshed in Remes' reading of Plotinus' ethics. But whereas Plato stressed (and Boys-Stones underlines) the continuities between the universe and the soul, Plotinus emphasizes the discontinuities. Perfect, complete and self-sufficient, the divine *kosmos* provides "a regulative ideal of selfhood and moral agency," but one that human beings can never achieve, for as parts of that perfect whole we are in ourselves necessarily partial, incomplete, and imperfect. We cannot replicate the order of the *kosmos* but instead must strive to understand and fulfill our particular role within its providential distribution. Thus these two chapters demonstrate that, despite their different views of the relation between microcosm and macrocosm, for both Plotinus and Plato, that relation is mutually sustaining: the individual's psychic beauty is neither divorced from the beauty of the universe nor merely its degraded copy; instead her virtuous soul actively contributes to the cosmic order and derives its meaning and value from that contribution.

A similar reciprocity characterizes the analogy between *kosmos* and polis, as Luc Brisson shows in his study of Plato's *Laws* (Chapter 6). The rational order of the divine *kosmos* provides a model for the laws that create order in the city and in the souls of its citizens. The ideal legislator follows this model with mathematical precision: under the aegis of this "political demiurge," polis, psyche, and *kosmos* are mutually reinforcing, and all three work to reinforce the authority of the legislator himself and the city's political elite. The members of the ruling Nocturnal Council ensure *kosmos* within the polis thanks to their knowledge of its heavenly form: "their knowledge of reality" authorizes them to impose social reality. The holism of Plato's *politeia* lends a new urgency to the questions Parmenides asked about the social construction of divine *kosmos*, as a specific image of the universe provides a veridical – and therefore incontestable – foundation for both the political and psychic order, and vice versa. Here we might recall the military origins of the word *kosmos*: Magnesia's enlightened legislator is the direct descendent of the Homeric *basileis* who, in imitation of the divine *basileus* Zeus, first imposed *kosmos* on their troops. Indeed, as Atack argues (Chapter 8), the word never lost that martial or authoritarian undertone, and the political structure it describes (and prescribes) retained a strong center of power in the individual legislator, magistrate, or monarch who (as in Plato's *Laws*) knows the cosmic order and imposes it on the city and its citizens.

This suggests that *kosmos* functions as a normative ideal not only in a specific and substantive sense (i.e. a particular vision of cosmic order legitimates a particular vision of political order) but, more generally, in its basic assumption that beauty, virtue, propriety, the collective and individual good all consist in order or orderliness. *Kosmos* sustains a political ontology of the whole, an aesthetics of politics that privileges unity, coherence, stability, and centripedality; like the heavenly spheres it imitates, it orbits around a strong center. This may explain the apparent wariness of fifth-century Athenians toward the political metaphor of *kosmos*. Atack's reading of Aristophanes' *Wasps* suggests that the Athenians had difficulty in thinking about collective action in terms of *kosmos*: in the comic poet's "democratic re-imagining of the political and cosmic order," the individual citizen becomes a mundane Zeus, but the result is not political order but instead the violent civic disorder with which the play ends. The traditional *kosmos*–polis analogy seems to falter at the door of the Greek polis par excellence. But this is explicable if, as Sheldon

Wolin has proposed, Athens' radical democracy was premised on a different aesthetics from that of *kosmos*, an aesthetics of disorder and disruption, unpredictability and impermanence, that to its enemies looked very much like chaos.[5]

The very concept of *kosmos*, then, apart from any specific content it may have been given in particular political contexts, militates for a certain vision of the political and precludes others.[6] It precludes, for instance, a vision of politics as rhizomatic and nomadic, or a definition of beauty that privileges dissonance, impermanence, randomness – what Deleuze terms (after Joyce) "chaosmos."[7] That the Greeks could imagine such a chaotic *kosmos* is suggested by the fragment of Heraclitus that serves as an epigram to this chapter: "The most beautiful *kosmos* is like the sweeping at random of things scattered" (ὥσπερ σάρμα εἰκῆ κεχυμένων ὁ κάλλιστος [ὁ] κόσμος, DK 22 B 124). The fragment implies that there are different forms or definitions of *kosmos*, among which – indeed, the best or "most beautiful" of which – is an order created out of multiplicity and dispersion. But the ambiguous placement of the adverb *eikê* (at random) renders the whole (the "sweeping") as random as its parts (the "scattered things").[8] This formless and provisional heap suggests a very different concept of *kosmos* from the stable, integrated, and unified world-order of Plato's *Timaeus*, something perhaps closer to the multiple and ever-changing *diakosmêsis* of the Atomists (cf. Schofield's and Johnson's chapters). Another example of this sort of disorderly order might be seen in the "exuberant disruption of Dionysiac chorality" in Nonnus' *Dionysiaca*, discussed by Gagné (Chapter 9): breaching its narrative boundaries, Dionysus' chorus

---

[5] Wolin 1994. He differentiates the "rational disorganization" of fifth-century Athens from the orderly constitutionalism of the fourth-century democracy; the aesthetic shift he identifies seems to track with Atack's observation about the resurgence of the *kosmos*–polis analogy in fourth-century Athenian political discourse. Cf. Nelson's critique of the politics of wholeness in American representative democracy; she proposes a counteraesthetics, "ugly democracy," which "affirms not wholeness and symbolic consensus but the inevitable incompleteness of always dissensual community" (2002: 220).

[6] Indeed, if "politics exists simply because no social order is based on nature" (Rancière 1999: 16), then *kosmos* would be not just antidemocratic (at least in the terms of fifth-century Athens's radical democracy) but antipolitical. Cf. Rancière 1999: 19 (in reference to Athenian democracy): politics is the introduction of an incommensurability that "ruins in advance the project of the city ordered according to the proportion of the cosmos and based on the *arkhê* of the community."

[7] For Deleuze's chaosmos, see Deleuze 1990: 172–76, 260–66; 2004: 65–9, 81–83, 150–51, 249, 271–72, 372; Deleuze and Guattari 1994: 201–18.

[8] The rare noun *sarma* is obscure but is presumed to be from *sairô* (to sweep). Another possible meaning of *sarma* is "chasm in the earth" (*Etym. Magn.* 709, from *sairô*, "to grin"), which finds an interesting echo in the subterranean vault of the mundus, discussed by Germany in Chapter 10.

threatens the stability not only of the Olympian order but of the very poem, as Gagné argues: the chorus, a metaphor for *kosmos*, is itself *akosmos*.

Indeed, these essays suggest that there is a certain *akosmia* inherent within the very notion of *kosmos*. *Kosmos* is, virtually by definition, complete and perfect, whole and self-sufficient (see esp. Remes). And yet its analogic tendency (universe = city = soul = . . .) means that *kosmos* is constantly self-supplementing. "World" becomes "worlds," as in the multiple *mundi* studied by Germany or the aleatory microcosms of the Atomists. The whole is always multiplying, generating doubles of itself, always breaching its boundaries through its metaphorical extension, and in the process exposing its own insufficiency: the whole is not whole. Likewise, if *kosmos* is sublime (as Shearin argues persuasively in Chapter 12) it is also self-sublimating: always rising above itself in a push toward ever higher orders of order. Itself a meta-system (Horky), *kosmos* is continually spawning further meta-systems, higher or prior levels of organization, as *explicans* becomes *explicandum*.[9] *Kosmos*'s theoretical universe is always expanding. But, again, there is something oddly improper and disorderly about this expansion: *kosmos* cannot serve as its own first principle or self-sufficient cause; it cannot maintain its own limits. Perhaps this is why, as Johnson shows in Chapter 4, Aristotle avoided the term and preferred other expressions for wholeness (*ho ouranos, to holon, to pan*). Johnson notes Aristotle's rejection of cosmogony and the idea of a universe generated by an external cause, and his scorn for the theory of multiple worlds expounded by some of his predecessors. *Kosmos*, for him, is too plural and partial: it opens the door to contradiction, causal regression, logical impropriety. It requires supplementing, and Aristotle obliges, turning to *physis* for a singular, whole, and self-sufficient meta-concept. Aristotle was not one for random sweepings.

And yet perhaps it is just this tendency toward self-sublimation and self-supplementation that makes *kosmos* sublime: always expanding, it always exceeds our attempts to know or describe it. If that is true, the insufficiency is not in the *kosmos* but in our comprehension of it. Shearin opens Chapter 12 by asking, "How does one begin to study the *kosmos*? Which procedures, experimental or intellectual, allow us to approach it as a known (or knowable) object? What are the limits of such study?" The sublimity of

---

[9] The word *diakosmos*, as a second-order ordering of *kosmos*'s order, illustrates this point. What is the force of *dia-* in this compound? If it is just a doubling down on *kosmos*'s sense of distribution or an intensification of its sense of extensiveness, why did ancient philosophers feel the need for the supplementary coinage? On *diakosmos* and *diakosmêsis*, see the contributions of Schofield and Johnson (Chapters 3 and 4, respectively).

the *kosmos*, Shearin argues, exposes the limits of human understanding and challenges philosophers either to overleap those limits and reach for omniscience (as Seneca does) or (like Lucretius) to embrace them as the grounds for an ethics of *ataraxia*. Lucretius' sense of awe and inadequacy in the face of the sublime void highlights a theme that recurs throughout the essays: the possibility that there exists a fundamental and unbridgeable schism between the structures of the physical world and the structures of the human mind. Ancient thinkers attempted to deny that schism through analogy and its assumption (or assertion) that *kosmos*, polis, and psyche share the same essential makeup. This assumption, as we have seen, accounts for much of the appeal and utility of *kosmos* as a concept, and its reassuring consonance of mind and matter has echoed persistently through the history of Western thought from Plato on. But what if this assumption is false? What if the order of the *kosmos* is fundamentally different from the order of human thought, and the barriers to our under-standing of reality are not merely epistemological but in fact ontological? This possibility was recognized by Epicurus and Lucretius: owning up to its consequences was for them the height of intellectual courage (Shearin). It was acknowledged, too, by Plotinus, for whom the human soul and the world soul are as different as part and whole (Remes), and by Parmenides, for whom our linguistic construction of reality leaves the truth of the latter a divine mystery (Macé). It was intuited by the poets and priests when they contemplated the alien movements of the stars (Gagné) or of prophetic birds in the "temple of the sky" (Germany).

   This confrontation with the radical alterity of the universe posed intel-lectual and ethical challenges, as these chapters have shown. Perhaps the greatest challenge was to resist the urge to reduce this alterity through homology – assimilating the mysterious to the familiar – and instead to accept that the structure of the *kosmos* may be irreducibly alien to the structure of our minds and that reality may thus always exceed the order we attribute to it.[10] Kant (in an aphorism quoted by both Brisson and Germany) remarked that "two things fill the mind with ever new and waxing wonder and awe, the more often and steadily they are considered: the starry heavens above me and the moral law within me."[11] For Kant, philosophical awe arises from the mysterious affinity between macrocosm

---

[10]   This is to say that *kosmos* names not reality but the Real, which is inaccessible to human thought but shapes our lives and perceptions precisely by its absence. Rancière's "distribution of the sensible," as a means of coping with ontological lack and disorder, might be considered a translation into the symbolic of our nonrelation to the Real.

[11] A.A. V. 161. Following Germany's translation.

and microcosm, the heavens and the human heart. But the preceding essays have shown that by accepting the discontinuity between the two – by embracing the schism between our minds and the world, between the *kosmos* we perceive (or impose) and the *kosmos* always beyond our perception – we might gain greater insight into the beautiful order of each, and that this, too, is awesome.

Bibliography

Accorinti, D. 1995. 'Hermes e Cristo in Nonno', *Prometheus* 21: 24–32.
(ed.) 2016. *Brill's Companion to Nonnus of Panopolis*. Leiden: Brill.
Accorinti, D., and Chuvin, P. (eds.) 2003. *Des géants à Dionysos. Mélanges de mythologie et de poésie grecques offerts à Francis Vian*. Alessandria, Italy: Edizioni dell'Orso.
Acosta-Hughes, B. 2016. 'Composing the Masters: an Essay on Nonnus and Hellenistic Poetry', in Accorinti, D. (ed.), pp. 507–28.
Adamson, P. 2014. 'Freedom, Providence and Fate', in Remes, P. and Slaveva-Griffin, S. (eds.), pp. 437–52.
Agnosini, M. 2010. 'Lo scudo di Dioniso (*Dionysiaca* XXV 380–572)', *Maia* 62: 334–52.
Agócs, P., Carey, C., and Rawles, R. (eds.) 2012. *Receiving the Komos: Ancient and Modern Receptions of the Victory Ode*. London: Institute of Classical Studies.
Agosti, G. 2004. *Nonno di Panopoli: Le Dionisiache (Canti XXV–XXXIX)*. Milan: BUR.
  2006. 'Immagini e Poesia nella Tarda Antichità. Per Uno Studio dell'Estetica Visuale della Poesia Greca fra III e IV sec. d.C', in Cristiani, L. (ed.), pp. 351–74.
  2014. 'Contextualizing Nonnus' Visual World', in Spanoudakis, K. (ed.), pp. 141–74.
Aktüre, Z. 2007. 'Typological Studies of Ancient Theatre Architecture: the Tree vs. the Rhizome Model', in Fenwick, C., Wiggins, M. and Wythe, D. (eds.), pp. 89–107.
Alexander, L. 2001. 'IPSE DIXIT: Citation of Authority in Paul and in the Jewish and Hellenistic Schools', in Engberg-Pederson, T. (ed.), pp. 103–28.
Alföldi, A. 1975. 'Redeunt Saturnia Regna IV: Apollo und die Sibylle in der Epoche der Bürgerkriege', *Chiron* 5: 165–92.
Algeo, J. 1998. 'Vocabulary,' in Hogg, R. M., Blake, N. F., Romaine, S., Lass, R. and Burchfield R. W. (eds.), pp. 57–91.
Algra, K., Barnes, J., Mansfeld, J. and Schofield, M. (eds.) 1999. *The Cambridge History of Hellenistic Philosophy*. Cambridge: Cambridge University Press.
Algra, K., and Ierodiakonou, K. (eds.) 2015. *Sextus Empiricus and Ancient Physics*. Cambridge: Cambridge University Press.

Allen, P., and Jeffreys, E. (eds.) 1996. *The Sixth Century: End or Beginning?* Brisbane: Australian Association of Byzantine Studies.

Andreae, B. 1994. *Praetorium Speluncae: Tiberius und Ovid in Sperlonga, unter philolog. Beratung durch Ulrich Schmitzer, Abhandlungen der Geistes und Sozialwissenschaftlichen Klasse.* Akademie der Wissenschaften und der Literatur Mainz 12. Mainz-Stuttgart.

Andrews, N. E. 2004. 'Tragic Re-Presentation and the Semantics of Space in Plautus' *Casina*', *Mnemosyne* 57: 445–64.

Anscombe, E. 1957. *Intention.* Cambridge, MA: Harvard University Press.

Arcellaschi, A. 1990. *Médée dans le théâtre latin d'Ennius à Sénèque.* Rome: École Française.

Arieti, J. A. 1995. *Discourses on the First Book of Herodotus.* Lanham, MD: Littlefield Adams Books.

Aringer, N. 2012. 'Kadmos und Typhon als vorausdeutende Figuren in den *Dionysiaka*. Bemerkungen zur Kompositionskunst des Nonnos von Panopolis', *WS* 125: 85–105.

Armstrong, A. H. 1976. 'The Apprehension of Divinity in the Self and Cosmos in Plotinus', in Harris, R. B. (ed.), pp. 187–98.

Asheri, D. 2007. 'Book I', in Asheri, D., Lloyd, A. B. and Corcella, A. (eds.), pp. 57–218.

Asheri, D., Lloyd, A. B. and Corcella, A. (eds.) 2007. *A Commentary on Herodotus Books I–IV.* Oxford: Oxford University Press.

Athanassaki, L. and Bowie, E. (eds.) 2011. *Archaic and Classical Choral Song: Performance, Politics and Dissemination.* Berlin: Walter De Gruyter.

Aubenque, P. (ed.) 1987. *Études sur Parménide. Tome II, Problèmes d'interprétation, Bibliothèque d'histoire de la philosophie.* Paris: J. Vrin.

Augoustakis, A. 2008. 'Castrate the He-Goat! Overpowering the Pater Familias in Plautus' *Mercator*', *Scholia* 17: 37–48.

Baertschi, A. 2010. 'Drama and Epic Narrative: The Test Case of Messenger Speech in Seneca's *Agamemnon*', in Gildenhard, I. and Revermann, M. (eds.), pp. 243–63.

Balland, A. 1967. 'Une transposition de la grotte de Tibère à Sperlonga, le ninfeo Bergantino de Castelgandolfo', *Mélanges d'Archéologie et d'Histoire de l'École française de Rome* 79: 421–502.

Bailey, C. (ed.) 1947. *Titi Lucreti Cari De Rerum Natura Libri Sex.* 3 vols. Oxford: Oxford University Press.

Bakola, E. 2010. *Cratinus and the Art of Comedy.* Oxford: Oxford University Press.

Baltes, M. 1976. *Die Weltentstehung des Platonischen Timaios nach den antiken Interpreten.* Leiden: Brill.

Bannert, H. and Kröll, N. 2016. 'Nonnus and the Homeric Poems', in D. Accorinti (ed.), pp. 479–506.

(eds.) 2017. *Nonnus of Panopolis in Context II. Poetry, Religion, and Society.* Leiden: Brill.

Barclay, J. M. G. 1996. *Jews in the Mediterranean Diaspora from Alexander to Trajan (323 BCE–117 CE).* Edinburgh: T&T Clark.

Barnes, J. (ed.) 1984. *The Complete Works of Aristotle: The Revised Oxford Translation*. 2 vols. Princeton, NJ: Princeton University Press.

Barnes, T. D. 1968. 'Hadrian's Farewell to Life', *CQ* 18: 384–86.

Barney, R., Brennan, T. and Brittain, C. (eds.) 2012. *Plato and the Divided Self*. Cambridge: Cambridge University Press.

Bartsch, S. and Elsner, J. (eds.) 2007. 'Special Issue on Ekphrasis'. *CP* 102.

Basta Donzelli, G. 1995. *Euripides: Electra*. Stuttgart: Teubner.

Baumbach, M. 2007. 'Die Poetik der Schilde. Form und Funktion von Ekphraseis in den Posthomerica des Quintus Smyrnaeus', in Baumbach, M. and Bär, S. (eds.), pp. 107–42.

Baumbach, M. and Bär, S. (eds.) 2007. *Quintus Smyrnaeus. Transforming Homer in Second Sophistic Epic*. Berlin: Walter De Gruyter.

Beard, M., North, J. and Price, S. 1998. *Religions of Rome: Vol. 1, A History*. Cambridge: Cambridge University Press.

Becker, A. S. 1995. *The Shield of Achilles and the Poetics of Ekphrasis*. Lanham, MD: Rowman & Littlefield.

Belloni, L. 2006. 'Deioce, o "della regalità": (Erodoto 1.95–101)', *Prometheus* 32: 208–16.

Bénatouïl, T. and Bonazzi, M. (eds.) 2012. *Theoria, Praxis, and the Contemplative Life after Plato and Aristotle*. Leiden: Brill.

Benzi, N. 2016. '*Noos* and Mortal Enquiry in the Poetry of Xenophanes and Parmenides', *Methodos* 16: 2–17.

Bernabé, A. and Mendoza, J. 2013. 'Pythagorean Cosmogony and Vedic Cosmogony (*RV* 10.129): Analogies and Differences', *Phronesis* 58.1: 32–51.

Betegh, G. 2016. 'Archelaus on Cosmogony and the Origins of Social Institutions', *Oxford Studies in Ancient Philosophy* 51: 1–40.

Bett, R. 2010. 'Beauty and Its Relation to Goodness in Stoicism', in Nightingale, A. and Sedley, D. (eds.), pp. 130–52.

Bettini, M. and Short, W. M. (eds.) 2014. *Con i romani. Un' antropologia della cultura antica*. Bologna: Il Mulino.

Beyen, H. G. 1957. 'The Wall-Decoration of the Cubiculum of the Villa of P. Fannius Synistor near Boscoreale in its Relation to Ancient Stage-Painting', *Mnemosyne* 10: 147–53.

Bien, G. 1982. 'Himmelsbetrachter und Glücksforscher: Zwei Ausprägungen des antiken Philosophiebegriffs', *Archiv für Begriffsgeschichte* 26: 171–78.

Bill, C. P. 1901. 'Notes on the Greek θεωρός and θεωρία', *TAPA* 32: 196–204.

Billings, J., Budelmann, F. and MacIntosh, F. (eds.) 2013. *Choruses, Ancient and Modern*. Oxford: Oxford University Press.

Bobonich, C. 2002. *Plato's Utopia Recast*. Oxford: Oxford University Press.

Boeckh, A. 1819. *Philolaos des Pythagoreers Lehren nebst den Bruchstücken seines Werkes*. Berlin: In der Vossischen Buchhandlung.

Boehm, G. and Pfotenhauer, H. (eds.) 1995. *Beschreibungskunst-Kunstbeschreibung: Ekphrasis von der Antike bis zur Gegenwart*. Munich: Wilhelm Fink.

Bogner, H. 1934. 'Die Religion des Nonnos von Panopolis', *Philologus* 89: 320–33.

Bollack, J. 1990. 'La cosmologie parménidéenne de Parménide', in Brague, R. and Courtine, J.-F. (eds.), pp. 17–53.

2006. *Parménide: de l'étant au monde.* Verdier poche. Verdier: Lagrasse.

Bonazzi, M. and Schorn, S. (eds.) 2016. *Bios Philosophos: Philosophy in Ancient Greek Biography.* Turnhout: Brepols.

Bonazzi, M., Lévy, C. and Steel, C. (eds.) 2007. *A Platonic Pythagoras: Platonism and Pythagoreanism in the Imperial Age.* Turnhout: Brepols.

Borecký, B. 1965. Survivals of Some Tribal Ideas in Classical Greek: the Use and the Meaning of lagchanō, dateomai, and the Origin of ison echein, ison nemein, and Related Idioms. Acta Universitatis Carolinae. Philosophica et historica. Prague: Univerzita Karlova.

Borg, B. E. (ed.) 2004. *Paideia: The World of the Second Sophistic.* Berlin: Walter De Gruyter.

Bourcier, P. 1989. *Danser devant les dieux. La notion de divin dans l'orchestique.* Paris: Chiron.

Bowra, C. M. 1937. 'The Proem of Parmenides', *CP* 32: 97–112.

Boyancé, P. 1940. 'Aedes Catuli', *Mélanges d'Archéologie et d'Histoire de l'École française de Rome* 57: 64–71.

Boyle, A. J. 1983. 'The Tragic Worlds of Seneca's *Agamemnon* and *Thyestes*', in Boyle, A. J. (ed.), pp. 199–228.

(ed.) 1983. *Seneca Tragicus: Ramus Essays on Senecan Drama.* Berwick, VC: Aureal.

Boys-Stones, G. 2001. *Post-Hellenistic Philosophy: A Study of Its Development from the Stoics to Origen.* Oxford: Oxford University Press.

(ed.) 2003. *Metaphor, Allegory and the Classical Tradition.* Oxford: Oxford University Press.

Braden, G. 1974. 'Nonnus' Typhon: *Dionysiaca* Books I and II', *Texas Studies in Literature and Language* 15: 851–79.

Brague, R. and Courtine, J.-F. (eds.) 1990. *Herméneutique et ontologie: mélanges en hommage à Pierre Aubenque.* Paris: Presses universitaires de France.

Bram, S. 2006. 'Ekphrasis as a Shield: Ekphrasis and the Mimetic Tradition', *Word & Image* 22: 372–78.

Bremer, D., Flashar, H. and Rechenauer, G. (eds.) 2013. *Die Philosophie der Antike.* Grundriss der Geschichte der Philosophie. Vol. 1. Basel: Schwabe.

Bremer, J. M., Radt, S. L. and Ruijgh, C. J. (eds.) 1976. *Miscellanea tragica in honorem J. C. Kamerbeek.* Amsterdam: Hakkert.

Brendel, O. 1977. *Symbolism of the Sphere: A Contribution to the History of Earlier Greek Philosophy.* Leiden: Brill.

Brennan, T. 2015. 'Number: *M.* 10.248-309', in Algra, K. and Ierodiakonou, K. (eds.), pp. 324–64.

Brisson, L. 2000. 'Le Collège de veille (nukterinòs súllogos)', in Lisi, F. (ed.), pp. 161–77.

2003. 'Le corps des dieux', in Laurent, J. (ed.), pp. 11–23.

2005. 'Ethics and Politics in Plato's *Laws*', *Oxford Studies in Ancient Philosophy* 28: 93–121.

Brisson, L. and Pradeau, J.-F. (eds.) 2006. *Platon: Les Lois*. Paris: Flammarion.

Broadie, S. 2012. *Nature and Divinity in Plato's 'Timaeus'*. Cambridge: Cambridge University Press.

Bryan, J. 2012. *Likeness and Likelihood in the Presocratics and Plato*. Cambridge: Cambridge University Press.

Bulwer, J. 1653. *Anthropometamorphosis: Man Transform'd; or the Artificiall Changeling*. 2nd edn. London: William Hunt.

Bulloch, A. 2006. 'Jason's Cloak', *Hermes* 134: 44–68.

Burke, E. 1958. *A Philosophical Enquiry into the Origin of Our Ideas of the Sublime and Beautiful*. 2nd edn. Edited by J. T. Boulton. London: Routledge and Kegan. (Originally published in 1759)

Burkert, W. 1972. *Lore and Science in Ancient Pythagoreanism*. Translation into English by E. L. Minar. Cambridge, MA: Harvard University Press.

    2008. 'Prehistory of Presocratic Philosophy in an Orientalizing Context,' in Curd, P. and Graham, D. (eds.), pp. 55–85.

Bury, R. G. (ed.) 1926. *Plato: The Laws*. London: G. P. Putnam.

Butler, S. and Purves, A. (eds.) 2013. *Synaesthesia and the Ancient Senses*. London: Routledge.

Calame, C. 2004. 'Deictic Ambiguity and Auto-referentiality: Some Examples from Greek Poetics', *Arethusa* 37: 415–43.

    2011. 'Review of Ferrari 2008', *Mnemosyne* 64: 661–64.

Caluori, D. 2015. *Plotinus on the Soul*. Cambridge: Cambridge University Press.

Calvo, T. 2000. 'El orden de la virtudes y las Leyes de Platón', in Lisi, F. (ed.), pp. 51–63.

Calvo, T. and Brisson, L. (eds.) 1997. *Interpreting the Timaeus-Critias: Proceedings of the IV Symposium Platonicum: Selected Papers*. Sankt Augustin: Academia Verlag.

Capra, F. and Luisi, P. L. 2014. *A Systems View of Life: A Unifying Vision*. Cambridge: Cambridge University Press.

Carlier, P. 1984. *La royauté en Grèce avant Alexandre*. Strasbourg: AECR.

Carone, G. R. 1994–95. 'Teleology and Evil in *Laws* 10', *Review of Metaphysics* 48: 275–98.

    1997. 'The Ethical Function of Astronomy in Plato's *Timaeus*', in Calvo, T. and Brisson, L. (eds.), pp. 341–49.

    2005. *Plato's Cosmology and Its Ethical Dimensions*. Cambridge: Cambridge University Press.

Carrière, J.-C. 1979. *Le carnaval et la politique. Une introduction à la comédie grecque*. Paris: Les Belles Lettres.

    2004. 'Politique, éducation et pulsions "naturelles" dans les "Guêpes": de la comédie sociale "réaliste" à la subversion comique "carnavalesque" et au triomphe de Dionysos', *Dioniso* 3: 66–89.

Carruesco, J. 2012. 'Helen's Voice and Choral Mimesis from Homer to Stesichorus', in Riu, X. and Pòrtulas, J. (eds.), pp. 149–72.

2016. 'Choral Performance and Geometric Patterns in Epic Poetry and Iconographic Representations', in Cazzato, V. and Lardinois, A. P. M. H. (eds.), pp. 69–107.

Carter, J. B. and Morris, S. P. (eds.) 1995. *The Ages of Homer: A Tribute to Emily Townsend Vermeule.* Austin: University of Texas Press.

Cartledge, P. 1998. 'Introduction: Defining a Kosmos', in Cartledge, P., Millett, P. and von Reden, S. (eds.), pp. 1–12.

2001. *Spartan Reflections.* London: Duckworth.

2009. *Ancient Greek Political Thought in Practice.* Cambridge: Cambridge University Press.

Cartledge, P., Millett, P. and von Reden, S. (eds.) 1998. *Kosmos: Essays in Order, Conflict and Community in Classical Athens.* Cambridge: Cambridge University Press.

Cassin, B. (ed.) 2014. *Dictionary of Untranslatables: A Philosophical Lexicon.* Princeton, NJ: Princeton University Press.

Castelnérac, B. 2014. 'Le Parménide de Platon et le Parménide de l'histoire', *Dialogue: Canadian Philosophical Review/Revue canadienne de philosophie* 53: 435–64.

Caston, V. and Graham, D. W. (eds.) 2002. *Presocratic Philosophy: Essays in Honour of Alexander Mourelatos.* Aldershot: Ashgate.

Castronovo, R. and Nelson, D. D. (eds.) 2002. *Materializing Democracy: Toward a Revitalized Cultural Politics.* Durham, NC: Duke University Press.

Catalano, P. 1960. *Contributi allo studio del diritto augurale.* Torino: G. Giappichelli.

Caygill, H. 2006. 'Under the Epicurean Skies', *Angelaki* 2.3: 107–15.

Cazzato, V. and Lardinois, A. P. M. H. (eds.) 2016. *The Look of Lyric: Greek Song and the Visual.* Leiden: Brill.

Ceccarelli, P. 2013. 'Cyclic Choroi and the Dithyramb in the Classical and Hellenistic Period: a Problem of Definition', in Kowalzig, B. and Wilson, P. (eds.), pp. 153–70.

Chapouthier F. 1935. *Les Dioscures au service d'une déesse. Étude d'iconographie religieuse.* Paris: Boccard.

Chaniotis, A. (ed.) 2018. *Unveiling Emotions: Sources and Methods for the Study of Emotions in the Greek World.* Vol. 3. Stuttgart: Franz Steiner.

Chantraine, P. (ed.) 1968–80. *Dictionnaire étymologique de la langue grecque. Histoire des mots.* Paris: Klincksieck.

Chantraine, P., Taillardat, J., Masson, O., Perpillou, J. L., Blanc, A. and Lamberterie C. D. 2009. *Dictionnaire étymologique de la langue grecque: histoire des mots.* Paris: Klincksieck.

Cherniss, H. 1954. 'The Sources of Evil According to Plato', *Proceedings of the American Philosophical Society* 98.1: 23–30.

Cherubin, R. 2005. 'Light, Night, and the Opinions of Mortals: Parmenides B 8.51–61 and B 9', *Ancient Philosophy* 25: 1–23.

Chroust, A. H. 1973. *Aristotle: New Light on His Life and on Some of His Lost Works.* 2 vols. London: Routledge.

Chuvin, P. 1986. 'Nonnos de Panopolis entre paganisme et christianisme', *BAGB* 45: 387–96.

1991. *Mythologie et géographie dionysiaques: Recherches sur l'oeuvre de Nonnos de Panopolis*. Clermont-Ferrand: Éditions Adosa.

2003. *Nonnos de Panopolis: 'Les Dionysiaques t. III': Chants VI–VIII*. Paris: Les Belles Lettres.

Clay, J. S. 1983. 'What the Muses Sang: *Theogony* 1–115', *GRBS* 25: 27–38.

Cleary, J. (ed.) 1999. *Traditions of Platonism: Essays in Honour of John Dillon*. Ashgate: Aldershot.

Cleary, J. and Gurtler, G. M. (eds.) 2000. *Proceedings of the Boston Area Colloquium in Ancient Philosophy*. Vol. 15. Leiden: Brill.

Clements, A. 2014. *Aristophanes' Thesmophoriazusae: Philosophizing Theatre and the Politics of Perception in Late Fifth-Century Athens*. Cambridge: Cambridge University Press.

Codoñer (Merino), C. (ed.) 1979. *L. Annaei Senecae Naturales Quaestiones*. 2 vols. Madrid: Consejo Superior de Investigaciones Científicas.

Collatz, C. F., Dummer, J., Kollesch, J. and Werlitz, M.-L. (eds.) 1998. *Dissertatiunculae criticae: Festschrift für Günther Christian Hansen*. Würzburg: Königshausen & Neumann.

Conte, G. B. 1994. 'Instructions for a Sublime Reader: Form of the Text and Form of the Addressee in Lucretius's *De rerum natura*', in Conte, G. B. (ed.), pp. 1–34.

(ed.) 1994. *Genres and Readers: Lucretius, Love Elegy, Pliny's Encyclopedia*. Baltimore: Johns Hopkins University Press.

Cooper, J. 2003. 'Plato and Aristotle on "Finality" and "(Self-)Sufficiency"', in Heinaman, R. (ed.), pp. 117–47.

Cousland, J. R. C. and Hume, J. R. (eds.) 2009. *The Play of Text and Fragments: Essays in Honour of Martin Cropp*. Leiden: Brill.

Coxon, A. H. (ed.) 2009. *The Fragments of Parmenides*. Rev. and Exp. edn. Las Vegas, NV: Parmenides.

Cristiani, L. (ed.) 2006. *Incontri Triestini di Filologia Classica*. Vol. 4. Trieste: Edizioni Università di Trieste.

Cropp, M. J. (ed.) 1988. *Euripides: Electra*. Warminster: Aris & Phillips.

Csapo, E. 1999–2000. 'Later Euripidean Music', *ICS* 24–25: 399–436.

2004. 'The Politics of the New Music', in Murray, P. and Wilson, P. J. (eds.), pp. 207–48.

2008. 'Star Choruses: Eleusis, Orphism and New Musical Imagery and Dance', in Revermann, M. and Wilson, P. J. (eds.), pp. 262–90.

2009. 'New Music's Gallery of Images: The "Dithyrambic" First Stasimon of Euripides' *Electra*', in Cousland. J. R. C. and Hume, J. R. (eds.), pp. 95–109.

Cumont, F. 1942. *Recherches sur le symbolisme funéraire des Romains*. Paris: Geuthner.

Curd, P. and Graham, D. (eds.) 2008. *The Oxford Handbook of Presocratic Philosophy*. Oxford: Oxford University Press.

D'Acunto, M. and Palmisciano, R. (eds.) 2009. *Lo scudo di Achilles nell' Iliade: esperienze ermeneutische a confronto.* Pisa: Fabrizio Serra Editore.

D'Alfonso, F. 1993. 'La χορεία astrale in un passo del *Fedro* platonico (246e–247a)', *Helikon* 23: 453–57.

D'Angour, A. 1997. 'How the Dithyramb Got Its Shape', *CQ* 47: 331–51.

Davidson, J. F. 1986. 'The Circle and the Tragic Chorus', *G&R* 33: 38–46.

Davie, J. N. 1979. 'Herodotus and Aristophanes on Monarchy', *G&R* 26: 160–68.

Day, H. J. M. 1981. *Lucan and the Sublime: Power, Representation and Aesthetic Experience.* Cambridge: Cambridge University Press.

De Finis, L. (ed.) 1989. *Scena e spettacolo nell'antichità.* Florence: Leo S. Olschki.

Deleuze, G. 1990. *The Logic of Sense.* Trans. M. Lester, Ed. C. V. Boundas. New York: Columbia University Press.

2004. *Difference and Repetition.* Trans. P. Patton. London: Bloomsbury.

Deleuze, G. and Guattari, F. 1994. *What Is Philosophy?* Trans. H. Tomlinson and G. Burchell. New York: Columbia University Press.

Demont, P. 1978. 'Remarques sur le sens de τρέφω', *Rev. Études Grecques* 91: 358–84.

Denniston, J. 1939. *Euripides: Electra.* Oxford: Oxford University Press.

Deroux, C. (ed.) 2006. *Studies in Latin Literature and Roman History XIII. Collection Latomus 301.* Brussels: Latomus.

Derrida, J. 1987. *The Truth in Painting.* Trans. G. Bennington and I. McLeod. Chicago: University of Chicago Press.

Derron, P. (ed.) 2015. *Cosmologies et cosmogonies dans la littérature antique: huit exposés suivis de discussions et d'un epilogue.* Entretiens sur l'Antiquité classique 61. Vandœuvres: Fondation Hardt pour l'étude de l'Antiquité classique.

Deschamps, L. 1987. 'La salle à manger de Varron à Casinum ou "Dis-moi où tu manges, je te dirai qui tu es."' *Bulletin de la Société toulousaine d'Études classiques* 191–92: 63–93.

Desclos, M.-L. and Fronterotta, F. (eds.) 2013. *La Sagesse Présocratique: Communication des Savoirs en Grèce Archaïque: des Lieux et des Hommes.* Paris: Armand Colin.

Destrée, P. and Giannopoulou, Z. (eds.) 2017, *Plato's Symposium: A Critical Guide.* Cambridge: Cambridge University Press.

De Vries, J. G. 1976. 'Dancing Stars (Sophocles, *Antigone* 1146)', in Bremer, J. M., Radt, S. L. and Ruijgh, C. J. (eds.), pp. 471–74.

Diels, H. and Kranz, W. (eds.) 1951. *Die Fragmente der Vorsokratiker: griechisch und deutsch.* Berlin: Weidmann.

Dijkstra, J. H. F. 2016. 'The Religious Background of Nonnus', in D. Accorinti (ed.), pp. 75–88.

Diller, H. 1956. 'Der vorphilosophische Gebrauch von κόσμος und κοσμεῖν', in *Festschrift Bruno Snell zum 60. Geburtstag am 18. Juni 1956 von Freunden und Schülern überreicht.* Munich: C. H. Beck, pp. 47–60.

Dillon, J. 1993. *Alcinous: The Handbook of Platonism.* Oxford: Oxford University Press.

2014. 'Pythagoreanism in the Academic tradition: the Early Academy to Numenius', in Huffman, C. A. (ed.), pp. 250–73.

Dodds, E. R. 1959. *Plato: Gorgias. A Revised Text, with Introduction and Commentary.* Oxford: Clarendon.

Dover, K. J. 1972. *Aristophanic Comedy.* London: Batsford.

Drabkin, N. 1937. *The Medea Exul of Ennius.* Geneva, NY: W. F. Humphrey.

Dunsch, B. 2005. 'Sat habeo, si cras fero: Zur dramatischen Funktion der temporalen Deixis bei Plautus, Terenz und Menander', *Würzburger Jahrbücher für die Altertumswissenschaft N. F.* 29: 123–50.

du Sablon, V. 2014. *Le système conceptuel de l'ordre du monde dans la pensée grecque à l'époque archaïque: timè, moira, kosmos, themis et dikè chez Homère et Hésiode.* Leuven: Peeters.

Ebert, T. 1989. 'Wo beginnt der Weg der Doxa? Eine Textumstellung im Fragment 8 des Parmenides', *Phronesis* 34: 121–38.

Ebrey, D. (ed.) 2015. *Theory and Practice in Aristotle's Natural Science.* Cambridge: Cambridge University Press.

Eckerman, C. 2010. 'The *ΚΩΜΟΣ* of Pindar and Bacchylides and the Semantics of Celebration', *CQ* 60: 302–12.

Edmonds, J. M. (trans.) 1931. *Elegy and Iambus: Being the Remains of all the Greek Elegiac and Iambic Poets from Callinus to Crates, excepting the Choliambic Writers.* London: W. Heinemann.

Edwards, M. J. 1991. 'Middle Platonism on the Beautiful and the Good', *Mnemosyne* 44: 161–67.

Effe, B. 1970. *Studien zur Kosmologie und Theologie der Aristotelischen Schrift 'Über die Philosophie.'* Munich: Beck.

Ehlers, W.-W. 1998. 'Zum Prologschluß der Casina', in Collatz, C. F., Dummer, J., Kollesch, J. and Werlitz, M.-L. (eds.), pp. 183–92.

Éliade, M. 1964. *Traité d'histoire des religions.* Paris: Payot.

Elmer, D. F., 2010. '*Kita* and *Kosmos*: The Poetics of Ornamentation in Bosniac and Homeric Epic', *Journal of American Folklore* 123: 276–303.

2013. *The Poetics of Consent: Collective Decision Making & the Iliad.* Baltimore: Johns Hopkins University Press.

Elsner, J. 2002. 'The Genres of Ekphrasis', *Ramus* 31: 1–18.

Emilsson, E. K. 2007. *Plotinus on Intellect.* Oxford: Oxford University Press.

2012. 'Plato and Plotinus on Soul and Action', in Barney, R., Brennan, T. and Brittain, C. (eds.), pp. 350–67.

2017. *Plotinus.* Abingdon: Routledge.

Engberg-Pederson, T. 2000. *Paul and the Stoics.* London: T&T Clark.

2010. *Cosmology and the Self in the Apostle Paul: The Material Spirit.* Oxford: Oxford University Press.

(ed.) 2001. *Paul Beyond the Judaism/Hellenism Divide.* Louisville, KY: Westminster John Knox Press.

England, E. B. (ed.) 1921. *Plato: The Laws.* Manchester: University Press.

Enno, R. (ed.) 1995. *Polis und Kosmos: Naturphilosophie und politische Philosophie bei Platon.* Darmstadt: Wissenschaftliche Buchgesellschaft.

Euben, J. P., Wallach, J. R. and Ober, J. (eds.) 1994. *Athenian Political Thought and the Reconstruction of American Democracy*. Ithaca, NY: Cornell University Press.

Evans, J. 1998. *The History & Practice of Ancient Astronomy*. Oxford: Oxford University Press.

Faber, R. 2016. 'Nonnus and the Poetry of Ekphrasis in the *Dionysiaka*', in D. Accorinti (ed.), pp. 443–59.

Fantuzzi, M. 2018. 'Describing Images/Connoting Feelings: Choral Ekphrasis in Euripides', in Chaniotis, A. (ed.), pp. 21–49.

Färber, H. 1936. *Die Lyrik in der Kunsttheorie der Antike*. Munich: Neuer Filser.

Farrar, C. 1988. *The Origins of Democratic Thinking: The Invention of Politics in Classical Athens*. Cambridge: Cambridge University Press.

Fauth, W. 1981. *Eidos Poikilon. Zur Thematik der Metamorphose und zum Prinzip der Wandlung aus dem Gegensatz in den Dionysiaka des Nonnos von Panopolis*. Göttingen: Vandenhoeck & Ruprecht.

Fayant, M.-Ch. 1998. 'Hermes dans les *Dionysiaques*', *REG* III: 145–59.

Fenwick, C., Wiggins, M. and Wythe, D. (eds.) 2017. *TRAC 2007: Proceedings of the Seventeenth Annual Theoretical Roman Archaeology Conference*. London: TRAC Proceedings.

Ferrari, G. 2008. *Alcman and the Cosmos of Sparta*. Chicago: University of Chicago Press.

Ferri, S. 1932–33. 'Coro melico e coro tragico', *Dionyso* 3: 336–45.

Festugière, A. J. 1956. 'Un fragment nouveau du "Protreptique" d'Aristote', *Revue philosophique de la France et l'Étranger* 146: 117–27.

Fincher, J. 2017. 'The Tablets of Harmonia and the Role of Poet and Reader in the *Dionysiaca*', in Bannert, H. and Kröll, N. (eds.), pp. 120–37.

Fine, G. 1993. *On Ideas: Aristotle's Criticism of Plato's Theory of the Forms*. Oxford: Oxford University Press.

Finkelberg, A. 1998. 'On the History of the Greek ΚΟΣΜΟΣ', *HSCP* 98: 103–36.

Finley, M. I. 1954. *The World of Odysseus*. New York: Viking Press.

Forceville, C. and Urios-Aparisi, E. (ed.) 2009. *Multimodal Metaphor*. Berlin: Mouton De Gruyter.

Fowler, W. W. 1912. 'Mundus Patet. 24th August, 5th October, 8th November', *JRS* 2: 25–33.

Francis, J. A. 2009. 'Metal Maidens, Achilles' Shield and Pandora: The Beginnings of "Ekphrasis"', *AJP* 130: 1–23.

2012. 'The Value of Chorality in Ancient Greece', in Papadopoulos, J. and Urton, G. (eds.), pp. 218–35.

Frangoulis, H. 2003. 'Les pierres magiques dans les *Dionysiaques* de Nonnos de Panopolis', in Accorinti, D. and Chuvin, P. (eds.), pp. 433–45.

Fränkel, H., 1962. *Dichtung und Philosophie des frühen Griechentums: eine Geschichte der griechischen Epik, Lyrik und Prosa bis zur Mitte des fünften Jahrhunderts*. Munich: C. H. Beck.

Franklin, J. C. 2006. 'The Wisdom of the Lyre: Soundings in Ancient Greece, Cyprus and the Near East', in Hickmann, E. and Eichmann, R. (eds.), pp. 379–97.

2013. '"Songbenders of Circular Choruses": Dithyramb and the "Demise of Music"', in Kowalzig, B. and Wilson, P. (eds.), pp. 213–36.

Frère, J., 1987. 'Parménide et l'ordre du monde: fr. VIII, 50–61', in Aubenque, P. (ed.), pp. 192–212.

Furley, D. J. 1987. *The Greek Cosmologists*. Cambridge: Cambridge University Press.

1989. *Cosmic Problems: Essays on Greek and Roman Philosophy of Nature*. Cambridge: Cambridge University Press.

1999. 'Cosmology', in Algra, K., Barnes, J., Mansfeld, J. and Schofield, M. (eds.), pp. 412–51.

Gagarin, M. 1986. *Early Greek Law*. Berkeley: University of California Press.

Gagarin, M. and Perlman, P. J. 2016. *The Laws of Ancient Crete c.650–400 BCE*. Oxford: Oxford University Press.

Gagné, R. and Hopman, M. 2013a. 'The Chorus in the Middle', in Gagné, R. and Hopman, M. (eds.), pp. 1–35.

(eds.) 2013b. *Choral Mediations in Greek Tragedy*. Cambridge: Cambridge University Press.

Gagné, R. and Höschele, R. 2009. 'Works and Nights (Marcus Argentarius, *AP* 9.161)', *CCJ* 55: 59–72.

Gartziou-Tatti, A. 2004. 'Η ΑΣΠΙΔΑ ΚΑΙ ΤΑ ΟΠΛΑ ΤΟΥ ΑΧΙΛΛΕΑ. ΕΥΡΙΠΙΔΗ, Ἠλέκτρα στ. 455-475', *Métis* 2: 71–102.

Germany, R. 2014. 'The Unity of Time in Menander', in Sommerstein, A. H. (ed.), pp. 90–105.

Gernet, L. 1947. 'Jeux et Droit (remarques sur le XXIIIᵉ chant de l'*Iliade*)', *Comptes rendus des séances de l'Académie des Inscriptions et Belles-Lettres* 91: 572–74.

Gibbon, W. B. 1972. 'Asiatic Parallels in North American Star Lore: Milky Way, Pleiades, Orion', *Journal of American Folklore* 85: 236–47.

Gibbs, R. W. (ed.) 2008. *The Cambridge Handbook of Metaphor and Thought*. Cambridge: Cambridge University Press.

Gigandet, A. 2012. 'Epicurean Presences in Foucault's *The Hermeneutics of the Subject*', in Holmes, B. and Shearin, W. H. (eds.), pp. 303–15.

Gigli Piccardi, D. 1985. *Metafora e poetica in Nonno di Panopoli*. Florence: Università degli studi di Firenze.

Gildenhard, I. and Revermann, M. (eds.) 2010. *Beyond the Fifth Century: Interactions with Greek Tragedy from the Fourth Century BCE to the Middle Ages*. Berlin: Walter De Gruyter.

Gill, C. 2000. 'The Body's Fault? Plato's *Timaeus* on Psychic Illness', in Wright, M. R. (ed.), pp. 59–84.

Gill, C. and McCabe, M. M. (eds.) 1996. *Form and Argument in Late Plato*. Oxford: Oxford University Press.

Gillespie, S. and Hardie, P. (eds.) 2007. *The Cambridge Companion to Lucretius*. Cambridge: Cambridge University Press.

Goff, B. 1988. 'The Shields of *Phoenissae*', *GRBS* 29: 135–52.

Gold, B. 1998. '"Vested Interests" in Plautus' *Casina*: Cross-Dressing in Roman Comedy', *Helios* 25: 17–29.

Goldberg, S. 1998. 'Plautus on the Palatine', *JRS* 88: 1–20.

Goldhill, S. 1999. 'Programme Notes', in Goldhill, S. and Osborne, R. (eds.), pp. 1–29.

Goldhill, S. and Osborne, R. (eds.) 1994. *Art and Text in Ancient Greek Culture.* Cambridge: Cambridge University Press.

(eds.) 1999. *Performance Culture and Athenian Democracy.* Cambridge: Cambridge University Press.

Goslin, O. 2010. 'Hesiod's Typhonomachy and the Ordering of Sound', *TAPA* 140: 351–73.

Gotthelf, A. (ed.) 1985. *Aristotle on Nature and Living Things. Philosophical and Historical Studies Presented to D.M. Balme on His Seventieth Birthday.* Pittsburgh, PA: Mathesis.

Gow, A. S. F. and Page, D. (eds.) 1968. *The Greek Anthology: The Garland of Philip.* 2 vols. Cambridge: Cambridge University Press.

Graf, F. 1995. 'Ekphrasis: Die Entstehung der Gattung in der Antike', in Boehm, G. and Pfotenhauer, H. (eds.), pp. 143–55.

Graham, D. W. 2005. 'The Topology and Dynamics of Empedocles' Cycle', in Pierris, A. L. (ed.), pp. 225–44.

2006. *Explaining the Cosmos: The Ionian Tradition of Scientific Philosophy.* Princeton, NJ: Princeton University Press.

2013. *Science before Socrates: Parmenides, Anaxagoras, and the New Astronomy.* Oxford: Oxford University Press.

Graindor, P. 1915. 'Les cosmètes du Musée d'Athènes', *Bulletin de correspondance hellénique* 39: 241–401.

Graßhoff, G., Heinzelmann, M. and Wäfler, M. (eds.) 2009. *The Pantheon in Rome: Contributions to the Conference, Bern, November 9–12, 2006.* Bern Studies.

Graver, M. 2000. 'Commentary on Inwood', in Cleary, J. J. and Gurtler, G. M. (eds.), pp. 44–51.

Gregory, A. 2007. *Ancient Greek Cosmogony.* London: Duckworth.

2014. 'Parmenides, Cosmology and Sufficient Reason', *Apeiron* 47: 16–47.

Grenier, J.-Cl. 1989. 'La décoration statuaire du "Serapeum" du "Canope" de la Villa Adriana. Essai de reconstition et d'interprétation', *MEFRA* 101: 925–1019.

Griffith, T. 1986. *Symposium of Plato.* Marlborough: Libanus Press.

Guéroult, M. 1924. 'Le Xe livre des *Lois* et la dernière forme de la physique platonicienne', *Revue des Études Grecques* 37: 27–78.

Gulick, C. B. 1896. 'Omens and Augury in Plautus', *HSCP* 7: 235–47.

Gundel, H. G. 1972. *Zodiakos. Der Tierkreis in der antiken Literatur und Kunst, mit einem Beitrag über den Tierkreis im Alten Orient von Robert Böker.* Munich: Alfred Druckenmüller.

Gunderson, E. 2015. *The Sublime Seneca: Ethics, Literature, Metaphysics.* Cambridge: Cambridge University Press.

Hadjittofi, F. 2010. 'Nonnus' Unclassical Epic: Imaginary Geography in the *Dionysiaca*', in Kelly, C., Flower, R. and Stewart, M. (eds.), pp. 29–42.

2016. 'Major Themes and Motifs in the *Dionysiaca*', in Accorinti, D. (ed.), pp. 125–51.

Hahm, D. E. 1977. *The Origins of Stoic Cosmology*. Columbus: Ohio State University Press.

Hankinson, R. J. 2002. 'Stoicism and Medicine', in Inwood, B. (ed.), pp. 295–308.

(trans.) 2004. *Simplicius: On Aristotle's On the Heavens 1.1–4*. Ithaca, NY: Cornell University Press.

2013. 'Lucretius, Epicurus, and the Logic of Multiple Explanations', in Lehoux, D., Morrison, A. D. and Sharrock, A. (eds.), pp. 69–97.

Hansen, M. H. and Nielsen, T. H. (eds.) 2004. *An Inventory of Archaic and Classical Poleis*. Oxford: Oxford University Press.

Hanson, J. A. 1959. *Roman Theater Temples*. Princeton, NJ: Princeton University Press.

Hardie, P. 1985. 'Imago Mundi: Cosmological and Ideological Aspects of the Shield of Achilles', *JHS* 105: 11–31.

2009a. 'Virgil's Fama and the Sublime', in Hardie, P. (ed.), pp. 67–135.

(ed.) 2009b. *Lucretian Receptions*. Cambridge: Cambridge University Press.

Harris, R. B. (ed.) 1976. *The Significance of Neoplatonism: From Theory to Method and Back Again*. Norfolk: Old Dominion University Research Foundation.

Harte, V. 2002. *Plato on Parts and Wholes*. Oxford: Oxford University Press.

Hartkamp, R. and Hurka, F. (eds.) 2004. *Studien zu Plautus' Cistellaria*. Tübingen: Gunter Narr.

Heath, M. 1988. 'Receiving the *Kōmos*: The Context and Performance of Epinician', *AJP* 109: 180–95.

Heinaman, R. (ed.) 2003. *Plato and Aristotle's Ethics*. London: Ashgate.

Heinze, R. (ed.) 1897. *T. Lucretius Carus De Rerum Natura Buch III*. Leipzig: Teubner.

Helleman-Elgersma, W. 1980. *Soul-Sisters: A Commentary on 'Enneads' IV 3 (27), 1–8 of Plotinus*. Amsterdam: Rodopi.

Helm, P. R. 1981. 'Herodotus' "Mêdikos Logos" and Median History', *Iran* 19: 85–90.

Hendry, M. 1991. 'A Hermetic Pun in Marcus Argentarius XII GP (*A.P.* 5.127)', *Hermes* 119: 497.

1992. 'Frigidus Lusus: Marcus Argentarius XXXIV Gow–Page (*Anth. Pal.* 11.320)', *GRBS* 32: 197–201.

1997. 'An Abysmal Pun: Marcus Argentarius VI GP (*A.P.* 5.104)', *Mnemosyne* 50: 325–28.

Henrichs, A. 1994–95. '"Why Should I Dance?" Choral Self-Referentiality in Greek Tragedy', *Arion* 3: 56–111.

Hertz, N. 2009. *The End of the Line*. Rev. edn. Aurora, CO: Davies Group.

Hetland, L. 2009. 'Zur Datierung des Pantheon', in Graßhoff, G., Heinzelmann, M. and Wäfler, M. (eds.), pp. 107–16.

Hickmann, E. and Eichmann, R. (eds.) 2006. *Studies in Music Archaeology V*. Rahden: Leidorf.

Himmelmann, N. 1995. *Sperlonga: die homerischen Gruppen und ihre Bildquellen*, Vorträge / Nordrhein-Westfälische Akademie der Wissenschaften (Düsseldorf): Geisteswissenschaften G 340. Opladen: Westdeutscher.

Hine, H. M. (ed.) 1981. *An Edition with Commentary of Seneca, Natural Questions, Book 2*. New York: Arno Press.

(ed.) 1996. *L. Annaei Senecae Naturalium Quaestionum Libri*. Stuttgart: Teubner.

Hogg, R. M., Blake, N. F., Romaine, S., Lass, R. and Burchfield R. W. (eds.) 1998. *The Cambridge History of the English Language*. Vol. 4. Cambridge: Cambridge University Press.

Holmes, B. and Shearin, W. H. (eds.) 2012. *Dynamic Reading: Studies in the Reception of Epicureanism*. Oxford: Oxford University Press.

Holt, R. (ed.) 1878. *The Ormulum, with the Notes and Glossary of R. M. White*. 2 vols. Oxford: Clarendon Press.

Hopkinson, N. 1994. *Studies in the Dionysiaca of Nonnus*. Cambridge: Cambridge University Press.

Horky, P. S. 2006. 'The Imprint of the Soul: Psychosomatic Affection in Plato, Gorgias, and the "Orphic" Gold Tablets', *Mouseion* 3.6: 383–98.

2009. 'Persian Cosmos and Greek Philosophy: Plato's Associates and the Zoroastrian Magoi,' *Oxford Studies in Ancient Philosophy* 37 (Winter): 47–103.

2013. *Plato and Pythagoreanism*. Oxford: Oxford University Press.

2016. 'Empedocles Democraticus: Hellenistic Biography at the Intersection of Philosophy and Politics', in Bonazzi, M. and Schorn, S. (eds.), pp. 37–71.

Hornung, E. and Schweizer, A. (eds.) 2011. *Jenseitsreisen: Eranos 2009 und 2010*. Basel: Schwabe.

Höschele, R. and Konstan, D. (n.d.) 'The Erotic World of Marcus Argentarius'.

Hose, M. 1991. *Studien zum Chor bei Euripides*. Vol. 2. Stuttgart: Teubner.

Howatson, M. C. (trans.) and Sheffield, F. C. C. (ed.) 2008. *Plato: The Symposium*. Cambridge: Cambridge University Press.

Huffman, C. A. 1993. *Philolaus of Croton: Pythagorean and Presocratic*. Cambridge: Cambridge University Press.

2002. 'Archytas and the Sophists', in Caston, V. and Graham, D. (eds.), pp. 251–70.

2005. *Archytas of Tarentum: Pythagorean, Philosopher, and Mathematician King*. Cambridge: Cambridge University Press.

2008. 'Heraclitus' Critique of Pythagoras' Enquiry in Fragment 129', *Oxford Studies in Ancient Philosophy* 35: 19–47.

(ed.) 2014. *A History of Pythagoreanism*. Cambridge: Cambridge University Press.

Hülsz, E. 2012. 'Heraclitus on the Sun', in Patterson, R., Karasmanis, V. and Hermann, A. (eds.), pp. 3–24.

von Humboldt, A. 1845. *Cosmos: A Survey of the General History of the Universe*. Trans. A. Prichard. London: Hippolyte Baillière.

1845. *Kosmos: Entwurf einer physischen Weltbeschreibung.* Vol. 1. Stuttgart: J. G. Cotta.

1849. *Cosmos: A Sketch of a Physical Description of the Universe.* Trans. E. C. Otté. London: Henry G. Bohn.

Humm, M. 2004. 'Le *mundus* et le Comitium: représentations symboliques de l'espace de la cité', *Histoire urbaine* 10: 43–61.

Hussey, E. 1995. 'Ionian Inquiries: On Understanding the Presocratic Beginnings of Science', in Powell, A. (ed.), pp. 530–49.

Hutchinson, D. S. and Johnson, M. R. 2005. 'Authenticating Aristotle's *Protrepticus*', *Oxford Studies in Ancient Philosophy* 29: 193–294.

Hutchinson, G. O. 2011. 'House Politics and City Politics in Aristophanes', *CQ* 61: 48–70.

Huxley, G. 1971. 'Crete in Aristotle's *Politics*', *GRBS* 12: 505–15.

Immerwahr, H. R. 1966. *Form and Thought in Herodotus.* Cleveland, OH: Western Reserve University Press.

Inwood, B. 2000. 'The Will in Seneca the Younger'. *Classical Philology* 95: 44–60.

2002a. *The Poem of Empedocles.* 2nd edn. Toronto: University of Toronto Press.

(ed.) 2002b. *The Cambridge Companion to Stoicism.* Cambridge: Cambridge University Press.

2005. *Reading Seneca: Stoic Philosophy at Rome.* Oxford: Oxford University Press.

Inwood, B. and Donini, P. 1999. 'Stoic Ethics', in Algra, K., Barnes, J., Mansfeld, J. and Schofield, M. (eds.), pp. 675–738.

Ioppolo, A. 1993, 'The Academic Position of Favorinus of Arelate', *Phronesis* 38.2: 183–213.

Irwin, E. 2005. *Solon and Early Greek Poetry: The Politics of Exhortation.* Cambridge: Cambridge University Press.

Jaeger, W. 1961. *Aristotle: Fundamentals of the History of His Development.* Trans. R. Robinson. 2nd edn. Oxford: Oxford University Press. (Originall published in German as *Aristoteles: Grundlegung einer Geschichte seiner Entwicklung*, 1st edn., Berlin, 1923; 2nd edn., Berlin, 1955)

1966a. 'Solon's Eunomia', in W. Jaeger (ed.), pp. 101–43.

(ed.) 1966b. *Five Essays.* Montreal: Casalini.

Jocelyn, H. D. 1967. *The Tragedies of Ennius.* Cambridge: Cambridge University Press.

Johansen, T. 1998. 'Truth, Lies and History in Plato's *Timaeus-Critias*', *Histos* 2: 192–215.

2004. *Plato's Natural Philosophy: A Study of the Timaeus-Critias.* Oxford: Oxford University Press.

Johnson, M. R. 2005. *Aristotle on Teleology.* Oxford: Oxford University Press.

2009. 'Spontaneity, Democritean Causality, and Freedom', *Elenchos* 30: 5–52.

2015. 'Aristotle's Architectonic Sciences', in Ebrey, D. (ed.), 163–86.

2017. 'Aristotelian Mechanistic Explanation', in Rocca, J. (ed.), pp. 107–24.

Jordan, J. S. (ed.) 1998. *Systems Theories and A Priori Aspects of Perception.* Amsterdam: Elsevier Science.

Jowett, B. (trans.) 1892. *The Dialogues of Plato*.5 vols. Oxford: Oxford University Press.

(trans.) 1935. *Plato's Symposium, or The Drinking Party*. London: Everyman.

Ju, A. E. 2013. 'Posidonius as Historian of Philosophy: an Interpretation of Plutarch, de *Animae Procreatione in Timaeo* 22, 1023b–c', in Schofield, M. (ed.), pp. 95–117.

Kahn, C. H. 1960. *Anaximander and the Origins of Greek Cosmology*. New York: Columbia University Press.

1979. *The Art and Thought of Heraclitus*. Cambridge: Cambridge University Press.

2001. *Pythagoras and the Pythagoreans: A Brief History*. Indianapolis, IN: Hackett.

2009. 'The Myth of the *Statesman*', in Partenie, C. (ed.), pp. 148–66.

2010. 'The Place of Cosmology in Plato's Later Dialogues', in Mohr, R. D. and Sattler, B. M. (eds.), pp. 69–77.

Kamtekar, R. 2010. 'Ethics and Politics in Socrates' Defense of Justice', in McPherran, M. L. (ed.), pp. 65–82.

Karsten, F. J. 1964. *Studier over Platons Parmenides i dens forhold til tidligere platoniske dialoger* (Thèse). København, Danemark: Munksgaard.

Karenga, M. 2004. *Maat: The Moral Ideal in Ancient Egypt*. London: Routledge.

Kelly, C., Flower, R. and Stewart, M. (eds.) 2010. *Unclassical Traditions: Vol. 2, Perspectives from East and West in Late Antiquity*. Cambridge: Cambridge University Press.

Ker, J. 2000. 'Solon's *Theôria* and the End of the City', *CA* 19: 304–29.

Kerferd, G. B. 1964. 'Order in the Universe. Jula Kerschensteiner: *Kosmos: quellenkritische Untersuchungen zu den Vorsokratikern*. (Zetemata, Heft 30.) Pp. xi+245. Munich: Beck, 1964', *Classical Review* 14.2: 182–84.

Kerschensteiner, J. 1962. *Kosmos: quellenkritische Untersuchungen zu den Vorsokratikern*. Munich: Beck.

Keydell, R. 1931. 'Die griechische Poesie der Kaiserzeit (bis 1929)', *JAW* 230: 41–161.

Kindl, A. 1991. '*A.P.* 5.104 (Markus Argentarius)', *Hermes* 119: 495–96.

King, K. C. 1980. 'The Force of Tradition: The Achilles Ode in Euripides' *Electra*', *TAPA* 110: 195–212.

Kirk, G. S. 1954. *Heraclitus: The Cosmic Fragments*. Cambridge: Cambridge University Press.

1962. *Heraclitus: The Cosmic Fragments*. Reprinted with corrections. Cambridge: Cambridge University Press.

Kirk, G. S., Raven, J. and Schofield, M. 1983. *The Presocratic Philosophers: A Critical History with a Selection of Texts*. Cambridge: Cambridge University Press.

Kohn, T. D. 2013. *The Dramaturgy of Senecan Tragedy*. Ann Arbor: University of Michigan Press.

Konstan, D. 1985. 'The Politics of Aristophanes' *Wasps*', *TAPA* 115: 27–46.

2008. *A Life Worthy of the Gods: The Materialist Psychology of Epicurus*. Las Vegas, NV: Parmenides.

2015. *Beauty: The Fortunes of an Ancient Greek Idea*. Oxford: Oxford University Press.

Kövecses, Z. 2005. *Metaphor in Culture: Universality and Variation*. Cambridge: Cambridge University Press.

Kowalzig, B. and Wilson, P. (eds.) 2013. *Dithyramb in Context*. Oxford: Oxford University Press.

Kranz, W. 1938. *Stasimon*. Berlin: Weidmann.

1938. 'Kosmos als philosophischer Begriff frühgriechischer Zeit', *Philologus* 93: 430–48.

1955. 'Kosmos, Volume 1'. *Archiv für Begriffsgeschichte* 2.1: 1–113.

1958. *Kosmos, Archiv für Begriffsgeschichte*. Bausteine zu einem historischen Wörterbuch der Philosophie. Bonn: H. Bouvier.

Kraus, C., Foley, H. P. and Elsner, J. (eds.) 2007. *Visualizing the Tragic*. Oxford: Oxford University Press.

Kröll, N. 2013. 'Ekphrasis im spätantiken Epos. Die *Dionysiaka* des Nonnos von Panopolis', *Graeco-Latina Brunensia* 18: 117–30.

Kuhlmann, P. 1999. 'Zeus in den *Dionysiaka* des Nonnos: die Demontage einer epischen Götterfigur', *RhM* 142: 392–417.

Kukkonen, T. 2014. 'On Aristotle's World', *Oxford Studies in Ancient Philosophy* 46: 311–52.

Kunze, C. 1996. 'Zur Datierung des Laokoon und der Skyllagruppe aus Sperlonga,' *Jahrbuch des deutschen archäologischen Instituts* 111: 139–223.

Küppers, J. 1996. '"Kosmosschau" und *virtus* in den Philosophica Senecas', *AA* 42: 57–75.

Kurke, L. 1995. 'Herodotus and the Language of Metals', *Helios* 22: 36–64.

Ladewig, H. G. T. 1848. *Analecta scenica*. Neustrelitz: Barnewitz.

Lakoff, G. and Johnson, M. 1980. *Metaphors We Live By*. Chicago: University of Chicago Press.

Lakoff, G. and Turner, M. 1989. *More Than Cool Reason: A Field Guide to Poetic Metaphor*. Chicago: University of Chicago Press.

Laks, A. 1990. 'Legislation and Demiurgy: On the Relationship between Plato's *Republic* and *Laws*', *CA* 9: 209–29.

2005. *Médiation et coercition. Pour une lecture des* Lois *de Platon*. Lille: Septentrion.

Lampert, L. and Planeaux, C. 1998. 'Who's Who in Plato's *Timaeus-Critias* and Why', *Review of Metaphysics* 52: 87–125.

Lane, M. 2007. 'Virtue as the Love of Knowledge in Plato's *Symposium* and *Republic*', in Scott, D. (ed.), pp. 44–67.

Lasek, A. M. 2016. 'Nonnus and the Play of Genres', in Accorinti, D. (ed.), pp. 402–21.

Laszlo, A. and Krippner, S. 1998. 'Systems Theories: Their Origins, Foundation, and Development', in Jordan, J. S. (ed.), pp. 47–74.

Laszlo, E. 1972. *Introduction to Systems Philosophy*. New York: Gordon and Breach.

Latacz, J. 1991a. 'Die Erforschung der Ilias-Struktur', in Latacz, J. (ed.), pp. 381–414.

(ed.) 1991b. *Zweihundert Jahre Homer-Forschung: Rückblick und Ausblick.* Stuttgart: B. G. Teubner.

Laurent, J. (ed.) 2003. *Les dieux de Platon. Actes du Colloque international organisé à l'Université de Caen Basse-Normandie, les 24, 25 et 26 janvier 2002: textes réunis et présentés par Jérôme Laurent.* Caen: Presses universitaires de Caen.

Lauritzen, D. and Tardieu, M. (eds.) 2013. *Le Voyage des Legends. Hommages à Pierre Chuvin.* Paris: CNRS Editions.

Lavagne, H. 1988. *Operosa antra. Recherches sur la grotte à Rome de Sylla à Hadrien (BEFAR, 272).* Rome: École Française.

Lawler, L. B. 1960. 'Cosmic Dance and Dithyramb', in Lawler, L. B., Robathan, D. M. and Korfmacher, W. C. (eds.), pp. 12–16.

Lawler, L. B., Robathan, D. M. and Korfmacher, W. C. (eds.) 1960. *Studies in Honor of B. L. Ullman.* St Louis, MI: University Classical Bulletin.

Lear, G. 2006. 'Plato on Learning to Love Beauty', in Santas, G. (ed.), pp. 104–24.

Lech, M. L. 2009. 'Choral Performance in Athens', *GRBS* 49: 343–61.

Lecoq, A.-M. 2010. *Le bouclier d'Achille: un tableau qui bouge.* Paris: Gallimard.

Lehoux, D., Morrison, A. D. and Sharrock, A. (eds.) 2013. *Lucretius: Poetry, Philosophy, Science.* Oxford: Oxford University Press.

Leigh, M. 2010. 'Forms of exile in the *Rudens* of Plautus', *CQ* 60: 110–17.

Lévêque, P. and Vidal-Naquet, P. 1964. *Clisthène l'Athénien.* Paris: Annales litteraires de l'Université de Besançon.

Lévy, E. (ed.) 1987. *Le système palatial en Orient, en Grèce et à Rome.* Leiden: Brill.

Lewis, J. 2006. *Solon the Thinker: Political Thought in Archaic Athens.* London: Duckworth.

Liebeschuetz, W. 1996. 'The Use of Pagan Mythology in the Christian Empire with Particular Reference to the *Dionysiaca* of Nonnus', in Allen, P. and Jeffreys, E. (eds.), pp. 75–91.

Linderski, J. 1986. 'The Augural Law', *ANRW* II 16.3: 2146–312.

Lisi, F. (ed.) 2000. *Plato's Laws and Its Historical Significance. Selected Papers of the 1st International Congress on Ancient Thought, Salamanca, 1998.* Sankt Augustin: Academia.

Livrea, E. 1987. 'Il poeta e il vescovo: la questione nonniana e la storia', *Prometheus* 13: 97–123.

1989. *Nonno di Panopoli. Parafrasi del vangelo di S. Giovanni. Canto XVIII.* Naples: D'Auria.

2003. 'The Nonnus Question Revisited', in Accorinti, D. and Chuvin, P. (eds.), pp. 447–55.

Long, A. A. 1996. *Stoic Studies.* Cambridge: Cambridge University Press.

2013. 'The Eclectic Pythagoreanism of Alexander Polyhistor', in Schofield, M. (ed.), pp. 139–59.

Long, A. A. and Sedley, D. N. 1987. *The Hellenistic Philosophers.* 2 vols. Cambridge: Cambridge University Press.

Lloyd, G. E. R. 1966. *Polarity and Analogy: Two Types of Argumentation in Early Greek Thought*. Cambridge: Cambridge University Press.

2003. 'The Problem of Metaphor: Chinese Reflections', in Boys-Stones, G. (ed.), pp. 101–14.

Lonsdale, S. H. 1994–95. '*Homeric Hymn to Apollo*: Prototype and Paradigm of Choral Performance', *Arion* 3: 25–40.

1995. 'A Dancing Floor for Ariadne (*Iliad* 18.590–592): Aspects of Ritual Movement in Homer and Minoan Religion', in Carter, J. B. and Morris, S. P. (eds.), pp. 273–84.

Lovatt, H. 2013. *The Epic Gaze: Vision, Gender and Narrative in Ancient Epic*. Cambridge: Cambridge University Press.

Lowenstam, S. 1993. 'The Arming of Achilleus on Early Greek Vases', *CA* 12: 199–218.

Ludwich, A. 1899. *Kant's Stellung zum Griechenthum*. Königsberg: Hartungsche Buchdruckerei.

Lyotard, J.-F. 1994. *Lessons on the Analytic of the Sublime*. Trans. E. Rottenberg. Stanford, CA: Stanford University Press.

Macé, A. 2006. *Platon, Philosophie de l'agir at du pâtir*. Sankt Augustin: Akademia.

2008. 'Plato's Doctrine of Order and Harmony in Bodies, Souls, Cities, and the Universe', *Journal of Graeco-Roman Studies* 34 (Winter): 37–50.

2014. 'Two Forms of the Common in Ancient Greece.' *Annales. Histoire, Sciences Sociales* 69.3: 441–69.

Macé, A. and Therme, A.-L. 2013. 'Anaxagore et Homère: trier les moutons, trier les hommes, trier l'univers', in Desclos, M.-L. and Fronterotta, F. (eds.), pp. 235–61.

MacDowell, D. M. 1971. *Aristophanes: Wasps*. Oxford: Clarendon Press.

MacIver, C. A. 2016. 'Nonnus and Imperial Greek Poetry', in Accorinti, D. (ed.), pp. 529–48.

Macphail, J. 2011. *Porphyry's Homeric Questions on the Iliad: Text, Translation, Commentary*. Berlin: Walter De Gruyter.

de Mahieu, W. 1963–64. 'La doctrine des athées au Xe livre des *Lois* de Platon', *Revue Belge de Philologie et d' Histoire* 41: 5–34 and 42: 16–47.

Mansfeld, J. 1964. *Die Offenbarung des Parmenides und die menschliche Welt* (Thèse). Assen: Van Gorcum.

1971. *The Pseudo-Hippocratic Tract ΠΕΡΙ ʽΕΒΔΟΜΑΔΩΝ Ch. 1–11 and Greek Philosophy*. Assen: Van Gorcum.

1990. *Studies in the Historiography of Greek Philosophy*. Assen: Van Gorcum.

1992. 'ΠΕΡΙ ΚΟΣΜΟΥ: A Note on the History of a Title'. *Vigiliae Christianae* 46: 391–411.

Mansfeld, J. and Runia, D. T. 1997–2010. *Aëtiana: The Method and Intellectual Context of a Doxographer*. 3 vols. Leiden: Brill.

Manuwald, G. 2004. 'Das verlorene Kästchen – Die gefährdete Anagnorisis in Plautus' *Cistellaria*', in Hartkamp, R. and Hurka, F. (eds.), pp. 137–48.

Mari, Z. 2012. 'Antinoo a Villa Adriana', in Sappelli Ragni, M. (ed.), pp. 78–91.

Marmodoro, A. and Viltanioti, E. (eds.) 2017. *Divine Powers in Late Antiquity*. Oxford: Oxford University Press.

Marshall, C. W. 1980. 'Theatrical Reference in Euripides' *Electra*', *ICS* 25: 325–41.

2006. *The Stagecraft and Performance of Roman Comedy*. Cambridge: Cambridge University Press.

2010. 'Living Next Door to a Roman Comedy: Structure in Plautus' *Mercator*', *NECJ* 37: 65–78.

Martin, R. 2007. 'Outer Limits, Choral Space', in Kraus, C., Foley, H. P. and Elsner, J. (eds.), pp. 35–62.

Mason, H. C. 2016. 'Jason's Cloak and the *Shield of Herakles*', *Mnemosyne* 69: 183–201.

Massa, F. 2014. *Tra la vigna e la croce. Dioniso nei discorsi letterari e figurativi cristiani*. Stuttgart: Franz Steiner.

Matzner, S. 2016. *Rethinking Metonymy: Literary Theory and Poetic Practice from Pindar to Jakobson*. Oxford: Oxford University Press.

Mayhew, R. 2015. 'Aristotle's Biology and His Lost *Homeric Puzzles*'. *Classical Quarterly* 65.1: 109–33.

McGlew, J. F. 1993. *Tyranny and Political Culture in Ancient Greece*. Ithaca, NY: Cornell University Press.

McNeill, W. 1999. *The Glance of the Eye: Heidegger, Aristotle, and the Ends of Theory*. Albany: SUNY Press.

McPherran, M. L. (ed.) 2010. *Plato's Republic: A Critical Guide*. Cambridge: Cambridge University Press.

Meier, M., Patzek, B., Walter, U. and Wiesehöfer, J. (eds.) 2004. *Deiokes, König der Meder: eine Herodot-Episode in ihren Kontexten*. Oriens et Occidens 7. Stuttgart: Franz Steiner.

Merlan, P. 1953. *From Platonism to Neoplatonism*. The Hague: Martinus Nijhoff.

1960. *From Platonism to Neoplatonism*. 2nd edn. The Hague: Martinus Nijhoff.

1967. 'Aristoteles' und Epikurs müssige Götter', *Zeitschrift für philosophische Forschung* 21: 485–98.

Miguélez-Cavero, L. 2008. *Poems in Context: Greek Poetry in the Egyptian Thebaid 200–600 AD*. Berlin: Walter De Gruyter.

2009. 'The Appearance of the Gods in the *Dionysiaca* of Nonnus', *GRBS* 49: 557–83.

2013. 'Cosmic and Terrestrial Personifications in Nonnus' *Dionysiaca*', *GRBS* 53: 350–78.

Miller, J. 1986. *Measures of Wisdom: The Cosmic Dance in Classical and Christian Antiquity*. Toronto: University of Toronto Press.

Mohr, R. D. and Sattler, B. M. (eds.) 2010. *One Book, the Whole Universe: Plato's Timaeus Today*. Las Vegas, NV: Parmenides.

Monk, S. H. 1960. *The Sublime: A Study of Critical Theories in XVIII-Century England*. Ann Arbor: University of Michigan Press.

Monoson, S. S. 2000. *Plato's Democratic Entanglements: Athenian Politics and the Practice of Philosophy*. Princeton, NJ: Princeton University Press.

Montanari, F. 1989. 'Evoluzioni del coro e movimenti celesti', in De Finis, L. (ed), pp. 149–63.

Moraux, P. 1951. *Les listes anciennes des ouvrages d'Aristote*. Louvain: Éditions universitaires.

Morin, B. 2004. 'Les monstres des armes d'Achille dans l'*Électre* d'Euripide (v. 452–477): une mise en abîme de l'action?', *RPhA* 22: 101–25.

Morwood, J. H. W. 1981. 'The Pattern of Euripides' *Electra*', *AJP* 102: 362–70.

Moss, J. 2005. 'Shame, Pleasure and the Divided Soul', *Oxford Studies in Ancient Philosophy* 29: 137–70.

Most, G. W. 2012. 'The Sublime, Today?', in Holmes, B. and Shearin, W. H. (eds.), pp. 239–66.

Mourelatos, A. P. 2008. *The Route of Parmenides*. Rev. and Exp. edn. Las Vegas, NV: Parmenides.

Mullen, W. 1982. *Choreia: Pindar and Dance*. Princeton, NJ: Princeton University Press.

Mulryne, J. R. 1977. 'Poetic Structures in the *Electra* of Euripides', *LCM* 2: 31–8 and 41–50.

Murray, P. and Wilson, P. J. (eds.) 2004. *Music and the Muses: The Politics of 'Mousike' in the Classical Athenian City*. Oxford: Oxford University Press.

Naddaf, G. 1992. *L'origine et l'évolution du concept grec de phúsis d'après le livre X des Lois de Platon*. Lewiston: Edwin Mellen.

   1996. 'Plato's Theologia Revisited', *Méthexis* 9: 5–18.

Naerebout, F. G. 1997. *Attractive Performances. Ancient Greek Dance: Three Preliminary Studies*. Amsterdam: Gieben.

Nagy, G. 2002. *Plato's Rhapsody and Homer's Music: The Poetics of the Panathenaic Festival in Classical Athens*. Washington, DC: Center for Hellenic Studies.

Nauta, R. R., Van Dam, H.-J. and Smolenaars J. L. L. (eds.) 2006. *Flavian Poetry*. Leiden: Brill.

Nehamas, A. 2007. 'Beauty of Body, Nobility of Soul: The Pursuit of Love in Plato's *Symposium*', in Scott, D. (ed.), pp. 97–135.

Nehamas, A. and Woodruff, P. (trans.) 1989. *Plato: Symposium*. With introduction and notes. Indianapolis, IN: Hackett.

Nelsestuen, G. 2017. '*Oikonomia* as a Theory of Empire in the Political Thought of Xenophon and Aristotle', *GRBS* 57.1: 74–104.

Nelson, D. D. 2002. 'Representative/Democracy: The Political Work of Countersymbolic Representation', in Castronovo, R. and Nelson, D. D. (eds.), pp. 218–47.

Nightingale, A. W. 1993. 'The Folly of Praise: Plato's Critique of Encomiastic Discourse in the *Lysis* and *Symposium*', *CQ* 43:112–30.

   2004. *Spectacles of Truth in Classical Greek Philosophy: Theoria in Its Cultural Context*. Cambridge: Cambridge University Press.

   2010. *Once Out of Nature: Augustine on Time and the Body*. Chicago: University of Chicago Press.

Nightingale, A. W. and Sedley, D. (eds.) 2010. *Ancient Models of Mind*. Cambridge: Cambridge University Press.

Noussia-Fantuzzi, M. 2010. *Solon the Athenian, the Poetic Fragments*. Leiden: Brill.

O'Brien, M. J. 1964. 'Orestes and the Gorgon: Euripides' *Elektra*', *AJP* 85: 13–39.

O'Bryhim, S. 1989. 'The Originality of Plautus' *Casina*', *AJP* 110: 81–103.

O'Connor, T. and Sandis, C. (eds.) 2010. *A Companion to the Philosophy of Action*. Malden, MA: Wiley-Blackwell.

Olson, S. D. 1996. 'Politics and Poetry in Aristophanes' *Wasps*', *TAPA* 126: 129–50.

O'Meara, D. 2003. *Platonopolis*. Oxford: Oxford University Press.

Osborne, C. 1996. 'Space, Time, Shape and Direction: Creative Discourse in the *Timaeus*', in Gill, C. and McCabe, M. M. (eds.), pp. 179–211.

Ostwald, M. 1969. *Nomos and the Beginnings of the Athenian Democracy*. Oxford: Clarendon.

Palmer, J. A. 2009. *Parmenides and Presocratic Philosophy*. Oxford: Oxford University Press.

2014. 'The Pythagoreans and Plato', in Huffman, C. A. (ed.), pp. 204–26.

Panagl, O. 1971. *Die dithyrambischen Stasima des Euripides: Untersuchungen zur Komposition und Erzähltechnik*. Vienna: Notring.

Papadopoulos, J. and Urton, G. (eds.) 2012. *The Construction of Value in the Ancient World*. Los Angeles, CA: Cotsen Institute of Archaeology Press.

Parker, R. 1989. 'Spartan Religion', in Powell, A. and Cartledge, P. (eds.), pp. 142–72.

Partenie, C. (ed.) 2009. *Plato's Myths*. Cambridge: Cambridge University Press.

Pascal, C. 1899. 'Quaestionum Ennianarum: Particula IV', *RFIC* 27: 1–10.

Patterson, R., Karasmanis, V. and Hermann, A. (eds.) 2012. *Presocratics and Plato: Festschrift at Delphi in Honor of Charles Kahn*. Las Vegas, NV: Parmenides.

Patzer, H. 1952. 'ΡΑΨΩΙΔΟΣ', *Hermes* 80, 314–25.

Peek, W. 1968–75. *Lexikon zu den Dionysiaka des Nonnos*. 4 vols. Berlin: Olms.

Pennington, J. T. and McDonough, S. M. (eds.) 2008. *Cosmology and New Testament Theology*. London: T&T Clark.

Peponi, A.-E. 2009. '*Choreia* and Aesthetics in the *Homeric Hymn to Apollo*: the Performance of the Delian Maidens (lines 156–64)', *CA* 28: 39–70.

2013. 'Theorizing the Chorus in Greece', in Billings, J., Budelmann, F. and MacIntosh, F. (eds.), pp. 15–34.

Perlman, P. 1992. 'One Hundred-Citied Crete and the "Cretan Politeia"', *CP* 87: 193–205.

Perrin, Y. 1982. 'Nicolas Ponce et la Domus aurea de Néron: une documentation inédite', *Mélanges de l'Ecole française de Rome. Antiquité* 94: 843–91.

1987. 'La Domus Aurea et l'idéologie néronienne', in Lévy, E. (ed.), pp. 359–91.

Pettersson, O. 2013. *A Multiform Desire: A Study of Appetite in Plato's Timaeus, Republic* and *Phaedrus* (Dissertation). Uppsala: Department of Philosophy, Uppsala University.

Piérart, M. 2008. *Platon et la cité grecque*. Paris: Les Belles Lettres.

Pierris, A. L. (ed.) 2005. *The Empedoclean Κόσμος: Structure, Process and the Question of Cyclicity*. Patras: Institute for Philosophical Research.

Pilkington, A. 2000. *Poetic Effects: A Relevance Theory Perspective*. Amsterdam: J. Benjamins.

Plank, H. L. 1807. *Q. Ennii Medea*. Göttingen.

Pohlenz, M. 1932. 'τὸ πρέπον. Ein Beitrag zur Geschichte des griechischen Geistes', *Nachrichten von der Gesellschaft der Wissenschaften zu Göttingen* (Philologisch-Historische Klasse) I.1.16: 53–92.

Porat, R. and Shen, Y. 2015. 'Imposed Metaphoricity', *Metaphor and Symbol* 30: 77–94.

Porter, J. I. 2007. 'Lucretius and the Sublime', in Gillespie, S. and Hardie, P. (eds.), pp. 167–84.

   2010. *The Origins of Aesthetic Thought in Ancient Greece: Matter, Sensation, and Experience*. Cambridge: Cambridge University Press.

   2012. 'Is the Sublime an Aesthetic Value?', in Sluiter, I. and Rosen, R. M. (eds.), pp. 47–70.

   2013. 'Why Are There Nine Muses?', in Butler, S. and Purves, A. (eds.), pp. 9–26.

   2016. *The Sublime in Antiquity*. Cambridge: Cambridge University Press.

Powell, A. (ed.) 1995. *The Greek World*. London: Routledge.

Powell, A. and Cartledge, P. (eds.) 1989. *Classical Sparta. Techniques Behind her Success*. London: Routledge.

Pradeau, J.-F. 2002. *Plato and the City*. Trans. J. Lloyd. Exeter: University of Exeter Press.

Primavesi, O. 2018. 'Pythagorean Cosmology in Aëtius: An Aristotelian Fragment and the Doxographical Tradition', in Mansfeld, J. and Runia, D. T. (eds.), pp. 103–29.

Puhvel, J. 1976. 'The Origins of Greek *Kosmos* and Latin *Mundus*', *AJP* 97: 154–67.

Raaflaub, K. A. 2000. 'Poets, Lawgivers and the Beginnings of Political Reflection in Archaic Greece', in Rowe, C. J. and Schofield, M. (eds.), pp. 23–59.

Rancière, J. 1999. *Disagreement: Politics and Philosophy*. Trans. J. Rose. Minneapolis: University of Minnesota Press.

   2004. *The Politics of Aesthetics: The Distribution of the Sensible*. Trans. G. Rockhill. London: Continuum.

Reale, G. 1990. *A History of Ancient Philosophy IV: The Schools of the Imperial Age*. Trans. J. R. Catan. Albany: SUNY Press.

Remes, P. 2006. 'Plotinus' Ethics of Disinterested Interest', *Journal of the History of Philosophy* 44: 1–23.

   2017. 'Human Action and Divine Power in Plotinus', in Marmodoro, A. and Viltanioti, E. (eds.), pp. 38–60.

Remes, P. and Slaveva-Griffin, S. (eds.) 2014. *The Routledge Handbook of Neoplatonism*. London: Routledge.

Revermann, M. and Wilson, P. J. (eds.) 2008. *Performance, Iconography, Reception*. Oxford: Oxford University Press.

Reydams-Schils, G. (1999) *Demiurge and Providence: Stoic and Platonist Readings of Plato's Timaeus*. Turnhout: Brepols.

Rhodes, P. J. 1993. *A Commentary on the Aristotelian Athenaion Politeia*. Oxford: Clarendon Press.

Rhodes, P. J. and Osborne, R. 2003. *Greek Historical Inscriptions: 404–323 BC*. Oxford: Oxford University Press.

Richards, I. A. 1936. *The Philosophy of Rhetoric*. Oxford: Oxford University Press.

Riedweg, C. 2005. *Pythagoras: His Life, Teaching, and Influence*. Trans. S. Rendall. Ithaca, NY: Cornell University Press.

Riemer, P. 1997. 'Zur dramaturgischen Konzeption von Senecas *Agamemnon*', in Zimmermann, B. (ed.), pp. 135–51.

Riu, X. and Pòrtulas, J. (eds.) 2012. *Approaches to Archaic Greek Poetry*. Messina: Dipartimento di scienze dell'antichità.

Rocca, J. (ed.) 2017. *Teleology and the Ancient World*. Cambridge: Cambridge University Press.

Rolland, H. 1969. *Le Mausolée de Glanum (Saint-Rémyde-Provence)*. *Gallia Suppl.* 21. Paris: Centre National de la Recherche Scientifique.

Rosen, R. 1991. *Life Itself: A Comprehensive Inquiry into the Nature, Origin, and Fabrication of Life*. New York: Columbia University Press.

Ross, W. D. 1924. *Aristotle's Metaphysics*. 2 vols. Oxford: Oxford University Press.

(trans.) 1952. *Select Fragments*. Oxford: Oxford University Press.

(ed.) 1955. *Aristotelis fragmenta selecta*. Oxford: Oxford University Press.

(trans.) 1984. 'Aristotle: *Metaphysics*', in Barnes, J. (ed.), vol. 2, pp. 1552–728.

Rothko, M. 1947–48. 'The Romantics Were Prompted', *Possibilities* 1.1: 84.

Rowe, C. J. and Schofield, M. (eds.) 2000. *The Cambridge History of Greek and Roman Political Thought*. Cambridge: Cambridge University Press.

Runia, D. 1999. 'A Brief History of the Term *Kosmos Noetos*', in Cleary, J. (ed.), pp. 151–71.

Russell, D. A. (ed.) 1968. *Longinus Libellus de Sublimitate*. Oxford: Oxford University Press.

(ed.) 1995. *Longinus: On the Sublime*. Trans. W. H. Fyfe. 2nd edn. Cambridge, MA: Harvard University Press.

Rutherford, I. 1998. 'Theoria as Theatre: The Pilgrimage Theme in Greek Drama', *Papers of the Leeds International Latin Seminar* 10: 131–56.

Sachs, C. 1937. *World History of the Dance*, New York: W. W. Norton.

1963. 'A Fallacy in Plato's *Republic*', *Philosophical Review* 72: 141–58. (Reprinted in G. Vlastos (ed.), *Plato: A Collection of Critical Essays*, vol. 2, Garden City, NY: Anchor Books, 1971, pp. 35–51)

Saint-Girons, B. 2014. 'Sublime', in Cassin, B. (ed.), pp. 1091–6.

Salviat, F. 1989. 'Symbolisme cosmique et funéraire au mausolée de Glanum.' *Les dossiers d'archéologie* 140: 46–51.

Santas, G. (ed.) 2006. *The Blackwell Guide to Plato's Republic*. Oxford: Blackwell.

Sappelli Ragni, M. (ed.) 2012. *Antinoo. Il fascino della bellezza*. Milan: Mondadori Electa.

Saunders, T. J. (1962) 'The Structure of the Soul and the State in Plato's *Laws*', *Eranos* 60: 37–65.

Sauron, G. 1991. 'De Buthrote à Sperlonga: à propos d'une étude récente sur le thème de la grotte dans les décors romains', *RA* 1: 3–42.

2007a. 'Un *Amaltheum* dans la villa d'Oplontis/Torre Annunziata?', in *Rivista di Studi Pompeiani* XVIII: 41–46.

2007b. *La peinture allégorique à Pompéi. Le regard de Cicéron*. Paris: Picard.

2009. *Dans l'intimité des maîtres du monde. Les décors privés des Romains.* Paris: Picard.

Scully, S. 2003. 'Reading the Shield of Achilles: Terror, Anger, Delight', *HSCP* 101: 29–47.

Seaford, R. 2012. *Cosmology and the Polis: The Social Construction of Space and Time in the Tragedies of Aeschylus.* Cambridge: Cambridge University Press.

Schofield, M. 1986. 'Euboulia in the *Iliad*', *CQ* 36: 6–31.

(ed.) 2013. *Aristotle, Plato and Pythagoreanism in the First Century BC.* Cambridge: Cambridge University Press,

n.d. 'Pythagoras the Plagiarist'. Unpublished paper.

Schmalzriedt, E. (1970) *ΠΕΡΙ ΦΥΣΕΩΣ: zur Frühgeschichte der Buchtitel.* Munich: W. Fink.

Schorn, S. 2014. 'Pythagoras in the Historical Tradition: From Herodotus to Diodorus Siculus', in Huffman, C. A. (ed.), pp. 296–314.

Schrijvers, P. H. 2006. 'Silius Italicus and the Roman Sublime', in Nauta, R. R., Van Dam, H.-J. and Smolenaars, J. L. L. (eds.), pp. 97–111.

Schweizer-Füllers, R. 2011. '"Siehst du nicht, in welchen Tempel du gekommen bist?": Der grosse Traum des Scipio – eine Himmelsreise im alten Rom', in Hornung, E. and Schweizer, A. (eds.), pp. 57–91.

Schwindt, J. P. 1994. *Das Motiv der Tagesspanne: Ein Beitrag zur Ästhetik der Zeitgestaltung im griechisch-römischen Drama.* Paderborn: F. Schöningh.

Scott, D. (ed.) 2007. *Maieusis.* Oxford: Oxford University Press.

Sedley, D. N. 1991. 'Is Aristotle's Teleology Anthropocentric?', *Phronesis* 36: 179–96.

2003. *Plato's Cratylus.* Cambridge: Cambridge University Press.

2007. *Creationism and Its Critics in Antiquity.* Berkeley: University of California Press.

2017. 'Divinisation', in Destrée, P. and Giannopoulou, Z. (eds.), pp. 88–107.

Segal, C. 1990. *Lucretius on Death and Anxiety.* Princeton, NJ: Princeton University Press.

Sertoli, G. 2005. 'Burke, Edmund', in Groden, M., Kreiswirth, M. and Szeman, I. (eds.) 2005. *The Johns Hopkins Guide to Literary Theory & Criticism.* 2nd edn., online. Baltimore: Johns Hopkins University Press.

Seure, G. and des Anges, C. 1932. 'La volière de Varron', *Revue de Philologie* 58: 217–90.

Sharples, R. and Sheppard, A. (eds.) 2003. *Ancient Approaches to Plato's Timaeus.* BICS Supplement 78. London: Institute of Classical Studies.

Sharrock, A. 2009. *Reading Roman Comedy: Poetics and Playfulness in Plautus and Terence.* Cambridge: Cambridge University Press.

Shaw, P. 2006. *The Sublime.* London: Routledge.

Shearin, W. H. 2014. 'Concealed Pleasure: Lucretius, *De rerum natura* 3.237-42', *CQ* 64.1: 183–96.

2015. *The Language of Atoms: Performativity and Politics in Lucretius' De Rerum Natura.* Oxford: Oxford University Press.

Sheffield, F. 'The *Symposium* and Platonic Ethics: Plato, Vlastos, and a Misguided Debate', *Phronesis* 57: 117–41.

Shen, Y. 2008. 'Metaphor and Poetic Figures', in Gibbs, R. W. (ed.), pp. 295–307.

Shorrock, R. 2001. *The Challenge of Epic: Allusive Engagement in the Dionysiaca of Nonnus*. Leiden: Brill.

2011. *Myth of Paganism: Nonnus, Dionysus and the World of Late Antiquity*. Bristol: Bristol University Press.

Short, W. M. 2014. 'Metafora', in Bettini, M. and Short, W. M. (eds.), pp. 329–52.

Silk, M. 2003. 'Metaphor and Metonymy: Aristotle, Jakobson, Ricoeur, and Others', in Boys-Stones, G. (ed.), pp. 115–47.

Skemp, J. B. 1967. *The Theory of Motion in Plato's Later Dialogues*. Amsterdam: Hakkert.

1985. 'The Disorderly Motions Again', in Gotthelf, A. (ed.), pp. 289–99.

Sluiter, I. and Rosen, R. M. (eds.) 2012. *Aesthetic Value in Classical Antiquity*. Leiden: Brill.

Small, S. G. P. 1951. *Marcus Argentarius: A Poet of the Greek Anthology*. New Haven, CT: Yale University Press.

Smith, M. F. (ed.) 1992. *Lucretius, De Rerum Natura*. Originally trans. W. H. D. Rouse. Cambridge, MA: Harvard University Press.

Smyth, H. W. 1920. *Greek Grammar*. Rev. G. M. Messing. Cambridge, MA: Harvard University Press.

Snell, B. 1924. *Die Ausdrücke für den Begriff des Wissens in der vorplatonischen Philosophie: sophia, gnōmē, synesis, historia, mathēma, epistēmē*. Philologische Untersuchungen. Berlin: Weidmann.

Solmsen, F. 1958. 'Aristotle and Presocratic Cosmogony.' *HSCP* 63: 265–82.

Sommerstein, A. H. (ed.) 2014. *Menander in Contexts*. London: Routledge.

Sorabji, R. 2004. *The Philosophy of the Commentators 200–600 AD, A Sourcebook. Vol. 2: Physics*. London: Duckworth.

Spanoudakis, K. 2013. 'The Resurrections of Tylus and Lazarus in Nonnus of Panopolis (Dion. XXV 451–552 and Par. Λ)', in Lauritzen, D. and Tardieu, M. (eds.), pp. 191–208.

2014a. 'The Shield of Salvation: Dionysus' Shield in Nonnus' *Dionysiaca* 25.380-572', in Spanoudakis, K. (ed.), pp. 333–71.

(ed.) 2014b. *Nonnus of Panopolis in Context: Poetry and Cultural Milieu in Late Antiquity*. Berlin: Walter De Gruyter.

Spyridakis, S. 1969. 'Aristotle on the Election of *kosmoi*', *La Parola del Passato* 24: 265–68.

1970. *Ptolemaic Itanos and Hellenistic Crete*. Berkeley: University of California Press.

Squire, M. 2013. 'Ekphrasis at the Forge and the Forging of Ekphrasis: The "Shield of Achilles" in Graeco-Roman Word and Image', *Word & Image* 29.2: 157–91.

Stegemann, V. 1930. *Astrologie und Universalgeschichte. Studien und Interpretationen zu den Dionysiaka des Nonnos von Panopolis*. Leipzig: B. G. Teubner.

Steiner, D. 2011. 'Dancing with the Stars: *Choreia* in the Third Stasimon of Euripides' *Helen*', *CP* 106: 299–323.

Stevens, J. A. 2006. 'The Imagery of Cicero's Somnium Scipionis', in Deroux, C. (ed.), pp. 155–65.

Stocks, J. L. (trans.) 1984. 'Aristotle: *On the Heavens*', in Barnes, J. (ed.), vol. 1, pp. 447–511.

Sutton, D. 1986. *Seneca on the Stage*. Leiden: Brill.

Szlezák, T. 1996. 'Psyche – Polis – Kosmos', in Enno, R. (ed.), pp. 26–42.

Tarrant, R. J. 1976. *Seneca: Agamemnon*. Cambridge: Cambridge University Press.

Taub, L. 2003. *Ancient Meteorology*. London: Routledge.

    2009. 'Cosmology and Meteorology', in Warren, J. (ed.), pp. 105–24.

Taylor, R. 2000. 'Watching the Skies: Janus, Auspication, and the Shrine in the Roman Forum', *MAAR* 45: 1–40.

Thom, J. C. 2014. *Cosmic Order and Divine Power: Pseudo-Aristotle, On the Cosmos*. SAPERE 23. Tübingen: Mohr Siebeck.

Thomas, C. J. 2010. 'Plato', in O'Connor, T. and Sandis, C. (eds.), pp. 429–48.

Torrance, I. 2013. *Metapoetry in Euripides*. Oxford: Oxford University Press.

Torelli, M. 1995a. 'A Templum Augurale of the Republican Period at Bantia', in Torelli, M. (ed.), pp. 97–129.

    (ed.) 1995b. *Studies in the Romanization of Italy*. Ed. and trans. H. Fracchia and M. Gualtieri. Edmonton: University of Alberta Press.

Ueblacker, M. 1985. *Das Teatro Marittimo in der Villa Hadriana*. DAI Rom Sonderschriften 5. Mit einem Beitrag von Catia Caprino. Mainz-am-Rhein: Philipp von Zabern.

Vahlen, J. 1903. *Ennianae poesis reliquiae*. Leipzig: Teubner.

Vernant, J.-P. 1982. *The Origins of Greek Thought*. Ithaca, NY: Cornell University Press.

    1983. *Myth and Thought among the Greeks*. London: Routledge & Kegan Paul.

Vian, F. 1990. *Nonnos de Panopolis. 'Les Dionysiaques t. IX'*: Chants XXV–XXIX. Paris: Les Belles Lettres.

    1993. 'Préludes cosmiques dans les *Dionysiaques* de Nonnos de Panopolis', *Prometheus* 19: 39–52.

    1994. 'Théogamies et sotériologies dans les *Dionysiaques* de Nonnos', *Journal des Savants* 1994: 197–233.

Vlastos, G. 1946. 'Solonian Justice', *CP* 41: 65–83.

    1947. 'Equality and Justice in Early Greek Cosmologies', *CP* 42: 156–78.

    1991. *Socrates: Ironist and Moral Philosopher*. Cambridge: Cambridge University Press.

    2008. '"Names" of Being in Parmenides', in Mourelatos, A. P., pp. 367–86.

von Bertalanffy, L. 1968. *General System Theory: Foundations, Development, Applications*. Rev. edn. New York: George Braziller.

von Freeden, J. 1983. *OIKIA KYPPHΣTOY. Studien zum sogenannten Turm der Winde in Athen*. Rome: Bretschneider.

Walbank, F. W. 1957–79. *A Historical Commentary on Polybius*. 3 vols. Oxford: Clarendon Press.

Walsh, G. B. 1977. 'The First Stasimon of Euripides' *Electra*', *YClS* 25: 277–89.

Walter, U. 2004. '"Da sah er das Volk ganz in seiner Hand" – Deiokes und die Entstehung monarchischer Herrschaft im Geschichtswerk Herodots', in Meier, M., Patzek, B., Walter, U. and Wiesehöfer, J. (eds.), pp. 75–95.

Ward, A. 2008. *Herodotus and the Philosophy of Empire*. Waco, TX: Baylor University Press.

Warren, J. (ed.) 2009. *The Cambridge Companion to Epicureanism*. Cambridge: Cambridge University Press.

Webb, R. 1999. 'Ekphrasis Ancient and Modern: The Invention of a Genre', *Word & Image* 15: 7–18.

2008. *Demons and Dancers: Performance in Late Antiquity*. Cambridge, MA: Harvard University Press.

2009. *Ekphrasis, Imagination and Persuasion in Ancient Rhetorical Theory and Practice*. Farnham: Ashgate.

Weinstock, S. 1932. 'Templum', *Mitteilungen des Deutschen Archäologischen Instituts, Römische Abteilung* 47: 95–121.

West, M. L. 1967. 'Alcman and Pythagoras', *CQ* 17: 1–15.

(ed.) 1972. *Iambi e elegi graeci ante Alexandrum cantati*. Oxford: Clarendon Press.

2010. *The Hymns of Zoroaster: A New Translation of the Most Ancient Sacred Texts of Iran*. London: I. B. Tauris.

White, J. 2008. 'Paul's Cosmology: The Witness of Romans, 1 and 2 Corinthians, and Galatians', in Pennington, J. T. and McDonough, S. M. (eds.), pp. 90–106.

Whitman, C. H. 1964. *Aristophanes and the Comic Hero*. Cambridge, MA: Harvard University Press.

Whitmarsh, T. 2004. 'The Cretan Lyre Paradox: Mesomedes, Hadrian and the Poetics of Patronage', in Borg, B. E. (ed.), pp. 377–402.

Wiesehöfer, J. 2004. 'Daiukku, Deiokes und die medische Reichsbildung', in Meier, M., Patzek, B., Walter, U. and Wiesehöfer, J. (eds.), pp. 15–26.

Wilberding, J. 2006. *Plotinus' Cosmology: A Study of Ennead II.1 (40): Text, Translation, and Commentary*. Oxford: Oxford University Press.

2008. 'Automatic Action in Plotinus', *Oxford Studies in Ancient Philosophy* 34: 373–407.

Willetts, R. F. 1955. *Aristocratic Society in Ancient Crete*. London: Routledge and Kegan Paul.

1967. *The Law Code of Gortyn*. Berlin: Walter De Gruyter.

Williams, G. D. 2012. *The Cosmic Viewpoint: A Study of Seneca's Natural Questions*. Oxford: Oxford University Press.

Wohl, V. 2010. *Law's Cosmos: Juridical Discourse in Athenian Forensic Oratory*. Cambridge: Cambridge University Press.

(ed.) 2014. *Probabilities, Hypotheticals, and Counterfactuals in Ancient Greek Thought*. Cambridge: Cambridge University Press.

Wolin, S. 1994. 'Norm and Form: The Constitutionalizing of Democracy', in Euben, J. P., Wallach, J. R. and Ober, J. (eds.), pp. 29–58.

Woodruff, P. 1982. *Plato, Hippias Major*. Oxford: Blackwell.

Wright, M. R. 1995. *Cosmology in Antiquity*. London: Routledge.

(ed.) 2000. *Reason and Necessity. Essays on Plato's Timaeus*. London: Duckworth/Classical Press of Wales.

2008. 'Presocratic Cosmologies', in Curd, P. and Graham, D. W. (eds.), pp. 413–33.

Yourcenar, M. 1979. *La Couronne et la Lyre. Poèmes*. Paris: Gallimard.

Zanini, A. 2012. "Horizonterweiterung durch Perspektivenwechsel: das *Somnium Scipionis*," *AU* 55: 40–44.

Zeitlin, F. I. 1982. *Under the Sign of the Shield: Semiotics and Aeschylus' Seven against Thebes*. Lanham, MD: Lexington Books.

1994. 'The Artful Eye: Vision, Ecphrasis and Spectacle in Euripidean Theatre', in Goldhill, S. and Osborne, R. (eds.), pp. 138–96.

2013. 'Figure: Ekphrasis', *Greece & Rome* 60: 17–31.

Zetzel, J. (ed. and trans.) 1999. *Cicero: On the Commonwealth and On the Laws*. Cambridge: Cambridge University Press.

Zhmud, L. 2006. *The Origin of the History of Science in Classical Antiquity*. Trans. A. Chernoglazov. Berlin: Walter De Gruyter.

2012. *Pythagoras and the Early Pythagoreans*. Trans. K. Windle and R. Ireland. Oxford: Oxford University Press.

2013. 'Die doxographische Tradition', in Bremer, D., Flashar, H. and Rechenauer, G. (eds.), pp. 150–74.

Zimmermann, B. (ed.) 1995. *Griechisch-römische Komödie und Tragödie II*. Stuttgart: Franz Steiner.

Index Locorum

General Index

Academy, Platonic, 6, 26, 27, 29, 32, 40, 80, 244, 280
Achilles, 26, 58, 157, 198, 202, 205, 206, 209, 210
Ahura Mazda, 174, 270
Alcibiades of Athens, 14, 111, 112, 113, 114, 117, 118, 121
Alexander of Aphrodisias, 92, 99, 152
Ampelius, L., vi, 4
analogy, xvi, 5, 16, 52, 57, 61, 109, 133, 162, 164, 165, 166, 167, 169, 170, 171, 172, 173, 174, 175, 176, 179, 180, 181, 184, 187, 189, 228, 231, 245, 270, 271, 273, 274, 275, 286, 298, 299, 300, 302
Anaxagoras of Clazomenae, 28, 37, 61, 62, 63, 64, 65, 66, 67, 68, 71, 72, 73, 75, 82, 83, 90, 91, 101, 248, 270, 271
Anaximander of Miletus, 10, 22, 23, 25, 70, 71, 79, 103, 104, 105, 165
Anaximenes of Miletus, 28, 42, 62
anthropogony, 20, 21, 271, 286, 288, 291
Archytas of Tarentum, 31, 32, 34, 35, 40
Argentarius, M., 17, 190, 191, 192, 195, 211
Aristophanes of Athens, 17, 165, 174, 175, 176, 177, 178, 179, 187, 191, 299
Aristotle, ix, x, xvii, 6, 7, 8, 9, 12, 13, 14, 16, 19, 20, 23, 25, 26, 27, 30, 32, 36, 37, 40, 42, 54, 62, 63, 66, 73, 74, 75, 76, 77, 78, 79, 80, 81, 82, 83, 84, 85, 86, 88, 89, 90, 91, 92, 93, 94, 95, 96, 97, 98, 99, 100, 101, 102, 103, 104, 105, 106, 107, 145, 154, 180, 182, 185, 186, 228, 231, 272, 273, 274, 275, 276, 278, 279, 280, 282, 301
on breath, 279
on Crete, 182
on democracy, 135
on Epizephyrian Locri, 183
on Gortyn, 182
on heaven, 77, 78, 79, 84, 86, 89, 92, 93, 94, 98, 272
on *kosmos*, 14, 27, 74, 76, 77, 78, 79, 83, 85, 87, 88, 89, 90, 91, 92, 93, 94, 97, 99, 102, 103, 106, 280

on mathematics, 24, 33, 80, 97
on nature (*physis*), 75, 81, 89, 91, 94, 100, 101, 102, 107
on self-sufficiency, 145
on the soul (*psyche*), 33, 35
on Sparta, 180
on tension, 277, 278
protreptics, 80
Aristoxenus of Tarentum, 23, 26, 31, 34, 40
arithmetic, 26, 31, 97, 130, 139
astronomy, 27, 28, 41, 58, 97, 137, 138, 139, 140
Athens, xi, xii, 3, 6, 17, 111, 130, 135, 165, 166, 168, 169, 170, 171, 172, 174, 181, 182, 184, 185, 186, 187, 213, 218, 223, 226, 230, 233, 280, 282, 300
Atomists, 13, 19, 63, 67, 73, 79, 85, 89, 90, 101, 178, 300, 301
atoms, 19, 40, 63, 66, 67, 90, 251, 256
Augustus, 241, 243

Babylonians, 10
Beauty, vi, vii, xvi, 7, 14, 15, 84, 108, 109, 111, 112, 114, 115, 116, 117, 118, 119, 120, 121, 122, 123, 134, 140, 145, 146, 151, 152, 153, 154, 155, 157, 249, 295, 296, 298, 299, 300
big bang, 98, 106, 273
body, xv, 4, 5, 7, 15, 20, 30, 33, 44, 52, 53, 67, 73, 78, 79, 86, 87, 89, 91, 92, 93, 94, 95, 97, 99, 103, 105, 111, 112, 113, 114, 115, 116, 117, 118, 123, 124, 125, 126, 128, 134, 137, 140, 143, 145, 147, 149, 150, 158, 159, 160, 162, 193, 204, 227, 236, 263, 265, 276, 277, 278, 279, 281, 282, 284, 285, 288, 289, 290, 291, 296, 298
breath, xiii, 20, 36, 39, 136, 221, 266, 271, 272, 273, 274, 275, 276, 277, 278, 279, 280, 281, 282, 283, 284, 285, 286, 287, 288, 289, 290, 291, 292, 293
as Holy Spirit, 20, 21, 287, 288, 289, 290, 291, 292, 293, 294
as *spiritus*/spirit, 152, 212, 225, 260, 266, 271, 272, 286, 287, 288

343